Foreign Trade and Investment

Foreign Trade and Investment
*Economic Development
in the Newly Industrializing
Asian Countries*

Edited by
Walter Galenson

The University of Wisconsin Press

Published 1985

The University of Wisconsin Press
114 North Murray Street
Madison, Wisconsin 53715

The University of Wisconsin Press, Ltd.
1 Gower Street
London WC1E 6HA, England

Copyright © 1985
The Board of Regents of the University of Wisconsin System
All rights reserved

First printing

Printed in the United States of America

For LC CIP information see the colophon

This volume is the result of a project sponsored by the Joint Committee on American-Chinese (Taiwan) Cooperation in the Humanities and Social Sciences, of the American Council of Learned Societies and the Social Science Research Council.

ISBN 0-299-10100-2

Dedicated to
Simon Kuznets
friend and teacher

Contents

Contributors ix

Preface xi

Introduction 3
    Lawrence B. Krause

I   **The Republic of China**

    1 Causes and Roles of Export Expansion in the Republic of China 45
       Shirley W. Y. Kuo and John C. H. Fei
    2 Direct Foreign Investment in Taiwan's Development 85
       Gustav Ranis and Chi Schive

II   **The Republic of Korea**

    3 The Role of Foreign Trade in the Economic Development of Korea 141
       Bela Balassa
    4 The Role of Direct Foreign Investment in Korea's Recent Economic Growth 176
       Bohn Young Koo

III Hong Kong

5 Trade, Foreign Investment, and Development in Hong Kong 219
Tzong-biau Lin and Victor Mok

IV Singapore

6 The Role of Foreign Trade and Investment in the Development of Singapore 259
Chia Siow Yue

V Comparative Aspects of Development in the Four Nations

7 Foreign Trade and Investment as Boosters for Take-off: The Experiences of the Four Asian Newly Industrializing Countries 301
S. C. Tsiang and Rong-I Wu

8 Industrialization and Employment in Hong Kong, Korea, Singapore, and Taiwan 333
Gary S. Fields

Index 379

Contributors

Bela Balassa, *The World Bank*

Chia Siow Yue, *National University of Singapore*

John C. H. Fei, *Yale University*

Gary S. Fields, *Cornell University*

Bohn Young Koo, *Korea Development Institute*

Walter Galenson, *Cornell University*

Lawrence B. Krause, *The Brookings Institute*

Shirley W. Y. Kuo, *The Central Bank of China*

Tzong-biau Lin, *The Chinese University of Hong Kong*

Victor Mok, *The Chinese University of Hong Kong*

Gustav Ranis, *Yale University*

Chi Shive, *National Taiwan University*

S. C. Tsiang, *Cornell University*

Rong-I Wu, *National Chung Hsing University*

Preface

This volume is the result of cooperative endeavors by scholars in four East Asian countries and the United States. Based upon the experiences of Hong Kong, the Republic of Korea, the Republic of China, and Singapore, its purpose is to assess the importance of foreign trade and investment in stimulating economic growth. It is scarcely necessary to add that these countries are among the nations of the world that have had the most favorable rates of economic development during the past three decades. The mechanisms through which this has been achieved should be of great interest to those concerned with current development problems.

Among those who made the greatest contribution to the project that led to this book are Dr. K. T. Li and Mr. Chi-wu Wang, respectively chairman and executive secretary of the Republic of China Committee for Scientific and Scholarly Cooperation with the United States, and Dr. Shirley W. Y. Kuo, deputy governor of the Central Bank of China. The American Council of Learned Societies provided an efficient organizational base for the project.

This volume is dedicated to Professor Simon Kuznets, who has long had a scholarly interest in East Asian economic studies, and whose pioneering work on economic development has been a major determinant of the way in which all of us analyze the growth process.

Walter Galenson

Foreign Trade and Investment

Introduction
Lawrence B. Krause

There would clearly be much less interest in the four Asian Newly Industrializing Countries (NICs) if they had not been so remarkably successful in achieving rapid economic growth. They have led the world and in recent years they have grown twice as fast as Japan, the most successful industrial country in the postwar era. The natural question to ask is, "Can the miracle continue?" Some believe that it cannot.[1] The skeptics point to the recent decline in world trade that will particularly inhibit these export-led economies. It is also noted that labor costs have risen in each of them and are now above those prevailing in neighboring countries with whom they must compete for world markets in labor-intensive products. Moreover, automation (robotics) in advanced countries is reducing the need for labor-intensive assembly operations that many firms had previously transferred to these countries. Moving up the technological ladder will be very difficult for the NICs because, it is said, different skills are required and large expenditures will be needed for research and development, training skilled labor, and long-range industrial planning. Finally they will be in competition with one another and that will limit success.

Some equally impressive reasons can be marshalled to suggest that the miracle has not reached its end. First and most important, the NICs have not yet reached the technological level in industry that prevails in advanced countries. As long as a technological backlog exists, the catch-up process can continue. These countries have already started the climb up the technology ladder and there is no evidence that the next rung is any harder to achieve than the previous ones. To be sure, some policy adjustments may be necessary, but this was also true in the past. Moreover these

---

The views are those of the author and should not be attributed to other staff members, officers, or trustees of the Brookings Institution.

1. See *Business Week* (March 28, 1983), "The Four Dragons Lose Their Fire."

countries, especially Singapore and Hong Kong, are heavily committed to producing and exporting services, which is the trend of the future even in older industrial countries. Finally, unlike some developing countries in Latin America and elsewhere, the NICs are not burdened with excessive foreign bank debt that could cause problems.

Importance of the External Environment

A constant refrain that appears in all the chapters in this volume (including this one) is the correlation of success with an outward orientation. This would seemingly make the NICs very sensitive to their external environment, particularly in the advanced countries. In one sense this is true. The two decades from 1960 to 1980 were characterized by a permissive world environment engineered by the advanced countries in which expansion of international trade was possible, including heroic growth of manufactured goods exports by the NICs. The story might well have been different if the advanced countries had been trying to frustrate the growth of the NICs rather than to encourage it. In another sense, however, the NICs were not particularly upset by the major economic disturbances of the seventies, although they were affected by them. Rather than there being a magnification of world economic fluctuations as one might have expected, there was a dampening. The sharp world recessions in 1974-75, and again after 1979, were reflected in the economy of the Asian NICs, but only by a comparatively modest decline in growth. The sharp correction that did occur in Korea in 1980 was the result of domestic factors, not the world economy. Unlike advanced countries where the recovery following the 1974-75 recession was decidedly less vigorous than in the sixties and early seventies, growth rates in the Asian NICs were sustained and may have even accelerated. How could such trade-dependent countries perform so well?

The answer appears to lie in several variables that characterize these countries. First, they export manufactured products rather than primary commodities. In a cyclical downturn, the prices as well as the volume of primary commodities decline in international trade and developing countries heavily dependent upon them for exports suffer a magnified contraction.[2] The reverse occurs in a cyclical recovery. Manufactured goods are much less cyclically sensitive, and since the NICs specialize in manufactures and are not dominant in any world market (in terms of supplying a large share of world consumption), they were able to substitute new manufactures for others for which demand was weakening.

2. This may not happen if a country is broadly diversified in the production and export of both minerals and agricultural commodities, since each commodity has its own cycle. However, producers in the country must be very adept at responding to market signals.

Introduction 5

Second, the Asian NICs have been successful in diversifying their markets, which has also reduced their cyclical sensitivity. While they all export intensively to the United States, they have developed important markets in Europe and even in Japan. Furthermore, they export many manufactures to other developing countries, and in fact have a brisk trade among themselves. Thus, if there is anything less than full economic synchronization in the world, they will find some market that is expanding to offset the ones that are contracting.

What seems to be found in abundance in each of these countries, but in short supply elsewhere, is an ability to adjust to changing circumstances. An example of this is seen in Korea, where large firms developed overseas construction companies to do contract work in the Middle East following the oil price shock. If that is where the money is and construction is what is wanted, Korean companies prepared themselves to respond. Now that the bloom is off the OPEC rose, Korean companies are likely to look elsewhere to sell these services or to reorient themselves to opportunities for construction work in Korea. The theme of adjustability appears frequently in the chapters that follow, and is traced to both government policy and reactions of private economic actors.

Another sign that the Asian NICs have sustained their own economic direction rather than merely reflecting developments in the world economy can be seen in their inflation experience. Several of them, especially Taiwan and Singapore, developed a strong antipathy to inflation. Through exercise of monetary policy (including exchange rate adjustments) they were able to contain inflation quite successfully. Thus, while it is obviously true that they are dependent on the world economy, and to a greater extent than the world economy is dependent on them, it is not true that the Asian NICs have lost their ability to direct their economies as they see fit, albeit within limits.

Protectionism

The sensitivity of the Asian NICs to trade protectionism cannot be exaggerated. To repeat, the permissive world economic environment was instrumental in their growth. Expressions of concern over competition from the NICs, frequently sounded in Europe and occasionally in the United States and Japan, raise fear of protectionism. Protectionism, however, has always existed and some of it was aimed at the NICs even during the 1960–80 period. What the earlier experience demonstrated was that while protectionism is never welcomed, a moderate amount may not be critical. The Asian NICs have been able to upgrade products and use other devices so that increased revenue was earned on a stagnant or declining volume of trade (Yoffie and Keohane 1981).

This experience should not lead to complacency over protectionism. The renewal of the Multi-Fiber Arrangement in 1982 did reduce the trading opportunities of the Asian NICs in the United States and especially in the European Community. Moreover, a serious outbreak of protectionism could stymie the growth of all market economies, including the NICs and the United States as well. This suggests that all countries have a responsibility to keep it from happening. Liberalization of imports in Korea and Taiwan does not go unnoticed—Singapore and Hong Kong already have free trade. The domestic content rules of several developing countries were cited in the U.S. Congress in the unsuccessful effort in 1982 to limit automobile imports into the United States. The advanced countries, particularly the United States and Japan, have special responsibilities in this regard, but Korea and Taiwan are also important. What follows is an examination of the trade regimes of the Asian NICs and the consequences they have had.

Nature of the Foreign Trade and Payments Regime

The Republic of China (Taiwan)

The trade and payments regime of the Republic of China (Taiwan) has gone through several changes in the postwar period. In 1949, a monetary reform was effected and attention was directed to trade policy in the early fifties. In 1952 a program of import substitution was initiated. In chapter 1 Kuo and Fei identify five factors that could have conditioned this decision. First, the major export product of Taiwan had been rice and with the inflow of significant numbers of people from the mainland, more rice was being consumed locally and thus less was available for export. Second, both of Taiwan's traditional markets for exports, Japan and the mainland of China, were closed to it. These two factors made exporting seem unattractive and reinforced an inward focus. Third, Taiwan was experiencing a significant imbalance in its trade as imports were almost twice the value of exports. Although the trade deficit was being financed by U.S. aid, the imbalance was of concern, and reducing imports was seen as a policy imperative. Another significant factor was the inexperience of the local entrepreneurs who had taken over management of firms after the Japanese departure. It was believed that they required time to become efficient and that protection from competitive imports was necessary. Finally, Japanese consumer products were well known in Taiwan and were thought to be too competitive for local manufactures.

What is of interest here is that these factors were based on existing conditions and circumstances rather than ideology. Distrust of the market mechanism and the supposed inevitable deterioration in the terms of trade of developing countries, which played such a central role in Latin American thinking and which promoted import substitution there were not mentioned. By implication, if the conditions and circumstances were to change, then less intellectual opposition to a change in policy could be expected.

Circumstances did change in the latter half of the fifties when Taiwan completed the relatively easy task of replacing imports of nondurable consumer goods with domestic production. Then it was faced with a problem that is now well recognized as inherent in an import-substitution strategy. Growth of manufacturing output began to slow as the limited domestic market for consumer nondurables became saturated, capacity utilization in several manufacturing industries dropped, prices for several manufactured products declined sharply, and hard-pressed domestic producers attempted to form domestic cartels to control the market and sought government help to stave off bankruptcy. Policy could respond to these circumstances either by broadening and deepening import substitution to include consumer durables and some capital equipment, or by reversing its thrust and beginning to promote exports. Taiwan chose a strategy of export substitution, sometimes called export promotion.

In an earlier work, Ranis (1979) identified three factors of importance in choosing export substitution. Of greatest importance was the relatively small size of the domestic market which would continue to condemn any strategy of import substitution to low-volume, high-cost output. Next, Taiwan faced continuing pressure of surplus labor, which could be absorbed through expansion of production of labor-intensive consumer goods, and which appeared to work to Taiwan's comparative advantage in exporting. Finally, a strategy of broadening and deepening import substitution would have required production of capital- and skill-intensive products which would have involved steeply rising costs for Taiwan.

The transition from import substitution to export substitution was rather smooth. Between 1954 and 1958 there were signs that a new strategy was evolving, although much hesitancy remained. Kuo and Fei note that in 1954, tax rebates were begun on the import content of exports, and in 1956, import quotas were awarded to enterprises in response to their success in exporting—this is the same export-link system used successfully in Japan. The export-substitution strategy became more clearly dominant in 1960–61 as part of the third Four Year Plan, which contained both financial reform and some liberalization of trade controls. Another step toward an export-oriented development strategy was taken in 1965, when export-processing zones (EPZs) were authorized and one was established in Kaohsiung. This outward-oriented strategy has been sustained to the present.

The Republic of Korea

South Korea emerged from World War II with a distorted and underdeveloped economy. As the colonial power, Japan had allocated all heavy industry to the northern part of the Korean peninsula and had encouraged the south only in raw material production, especially agriculture. In his chapter, Balassa notes that Japan reserved for itself the production of consumer goods for the Korean market and only some small-scale light industry developed in the south. The severing of the colonial link to Japan, the division of the Korean peninsula into two antagonistic entities, and the Korean War itself all contributed heavily to economic dislocation in the south. Thus the modernizing of Korea did not begin until 1953.

After 1953, South Korea started to industrialize on the basis of a strategy of import substitution. There is no evidence that an alternative was considered and import substitution was obviously in vogue with economists at that time. The program was originally directed toward encouraging production of nondurable consumer goods. The devices used to promote domestic production were quotas and licensing of imports; indeed, imports of competitive products were simply not permitted. Some growth in industrial production did occur between 1953 and 1960, but the general disorganization of the economy prevented rapid progress. Government policy was directed more toward reconstruction and price stabilization than toward growth during the fifties (Mason et al. 1980).

Proper management of the exchange rate was very difficult for the Koreans, as Balassa emphasizes. After being devalued in 1953, the won was pegged rigidly to the U.S. dollar throughout the fifties despite adverse inflation differentials. The result was significant overvaluation of the won, which seriously constrained exports. The balance of payments developed a gigantic deficit made possible by massive inflows of aid from the United States. Some concern over exports did surface and a system that linked import-licensing to exports did provide some stimulus to exports, but this was not enough to overcome the major disincentive provided by the overvalued currency. Various other export stimulants were discussed and partially implemented, but not with great effect. Industrial production did increase at an annual rate of about 20 percent between 1953–56, but subsequently the growth rate was cut in half as the first stage of import replacement became exhausted and domestic production came to account for 90 percent of consumption of nondurable consumer goods. Stagnation of the economy may have contributed to the political unrest which resulted in the student revolution and the fall of President Syngman Rhee in April 1960.

Scholars differ as to the timing of a second or transitional phase of Korean policy. Balassa terminates the transition in 1964, but Mason et al. (1980)

Introduction

extend it through 1965. The whole period was one of policy experimentation, and probably is best considered as a continuum, although the policy initiatives in 1964–65 were significantly more effective.

The 1964–65 policy changes included expanded preferences to exporters in granting import licenses, duty-free imports when used for exporting, large wastage allowances, while the number and types of preferential loans were increased and an export-promotion agency (KOTRA) was established. The won was devalued from 130 to 257 per U.S. dollar, exchange rates were unified, and imports were liberalized. An additional group of policies was directed to the macro workings of the domestic economy. Private savings were promoted through higher interest rates on deposits. Efforts were made to reduce the government's fiscal deficit (increase its savings) through improved tax collection, and expenditures were held down. As a result, inflation declined and a real rate of return could be earned on bank deposits.

The 1964–65 program of Korea was one of outward orientation, but like that of Taiwan it was not a truly liberal program, since government policy did take a very active role in its implementation. Overt subsidies were used to promote exports through preferential rates for electricity and transportation. These applied to all export products with the exception of ginseng and seaweed. Targets were set for individual exporters by the government, though no instruments were designed to enable the targets to be reached. To be sure, it is likely that unspecified benefits were given to successful exporters. Balassa describes a psychological impact from government interest in exporting that may have been important in Korean society. Thus export substitution replaced import substitution in this period.

Export substitution remained the dominant policy of Korea during the 10 years from 1965 to 1975. A significant step was taken to liberalize imports in 1967 when a selective list of items that were permitted to be imported was replaced by a more limited list of items still requiring specific authorization to import. Balassa reports on some research relating to the period of the late sixties in which six semi-industrial countries were compared with respect to the degree to which they favored manufacturing over primary production and domestic over foreign markets. The results suggest that Korea gave somewhat greater effective protection to manufacturing than to primary activities, but the effective subsidy rates had a reverse bias so that little net bias existed. This stands in contrast to countries such as Colombia and Argentina which strongly favored manufacturing. Moreover, Korea gave relatively small net incentives to sell primary products in the home market and manufactured goods in foreign markets, as compared with other semi-industrial countries.

Since 1975, Korea has been buffeted by external economic shocks and an internal political upheaval. Nevertheless, it has maintained its outward orientation and has gradually become more liberal. The several shocks have had a negative impact on the performance of the economy, but Korea has proven resilient in response.

Hong Kong

The situation of Hong Kong is unique, but analysis of its industrial development may well be of great interest because there are lessons there for other countries. Historically, Hong Kong evolved economically as an entrepôt for South China and politically as a colony of Great Britain. The entrepôt function was interrupted during World War II, when Hong Kong endured great suffering and witnessed a considerable decline of its population. It was interrupted again in 1950 as a result of the U.N. embargo on trade with the mainland of China because of the participation of the People's Republic of China in the Korean War. During this period, however, the population of Hong Kong was expanding massively due to the inflow of refugees from the mainland. The situation was desperate. Foreign aid could not provide a solution because it would be seen, quite rightly, as leading to an even larger inflow of refugees. The only alternative was for Hong Kong to become a producer of industrial goods rather than just a trader of such products. Given the size of Hong Kong and the limitations of its scarce agricultural lands, observers there recognized that they must import raw materials and export to pay for them, that is, import substitution was not an option open to them. An outward-oriented growth strategy grew out of necessity.

The question still remained as to what sort of policy would best support an outward-oriented strategy. Under colonial rule and as entrepôt, Hong Kong had developed a well-established tradition of free trade, as Lin and Mok emphasize in chapter 5. Given the uncertainties of the fifties, free trade embedded in a more general laissez-faire regime became the obvious choice because no one knew what else to do. Industrialization in Hong Kong was created not by design, but by the dictates of the market and social necessity.

Hong Kong turned to manufacturing products oriented to export markets. Free trade permitted the buying of inputs, including raw material and capital equipment, in the cheapest markets, which was a great advantage. Furthermore, Hong Kong benefited from the skills of the refugees, including factory workers and particularly the entrepreneurs from Shanghai who had managed to bring some capital with them. From its previous experience, Hong Kong already had banking, communication, and transport facilities and important trade connections. Hong Kong also benefited from being small and being the first developing country to attempt this path; it had little initial competition. It became a very successful producer and exporter of labor-intensive products which were sold mainly in the markets of developed countries, but also in some less developed countries (LDCs) as well. Employment in manufacturing rose from 3.7 percent of the labor force in 1950 to 7 percent of a much larger number of employees in 1960. By 1980, 37 percent of the work force was employed in manufacturing. While much has changed during the last three decades, Hong Kong has steadfastly retained its free trade and a laissez-faire policy from which it has gained greatly.

Singapore

Singapore's development began in the early nineteenth century under British rule. It served as the premier port for Southeast Asia and subsequently as a naval base. Singapore was valued by the British because of its natural harbor and also because of its strategic geographical location at the entrance to the Strait of Malacca that links the Indian and Pacific oceans. The city-state thus evolved as an entrepôt and service center, and these functions have remained important to the present day. As part of its original economic base, Singapore developed an efficient network of commercial, financial, and transportation services and institutions, a capability that has promoted and shaped its subsequent industrialization. The early development occurred under private enterprise with a minimum of government interference.

Singapore experienced difficulties immediately after World War II. Its political situation had changed greatly and its future was uncertain, its population expanded dramatically, and industrial unrest became endemic. The economic basis for its entrepôt business was receding due to the economic nationalism of the countries in the region. When Singapore became independent in 1960, its unemployment rate was about 10 percent. Because of the turmoil, the People's Action Party (PAP) came into power under Lee Kwan Yue and has remained the governing force ever since. Singapore's administration believed that industrialization was necessary and that it would not be possible without strong government direction. In fact, as reported by Chia Siow Yue in chapter 6, Singapore developed a governmental style that was both authoritarian and effective, the reverse of Hong Kong's laissez-faire doctrine. The rationale for taking strong government action to foster industrialization rested on three factors: the lack of natural resources, the small size of the domestic market, and the legacy of high wages that remained from the entrepôt business. While this rationale can be debated, these characteristics did shape Singapore's industrialization. Singapore seems to have gone through the same stages as most other advanced developing countries, but it seems to have done so at a much faster rate.

The first stage began in 1960 when Singapore adopted a moderate import-substitution strategy for the dual purpose of promoting domestic manufacturing and undertaking to harmonize its trade barriers with those of Peninsular Malaysia, to which it was joined at that time in the Federation of Malaysia. Tariffs were raised and quotas introduced, with the intention of developing sufficient capacity to serve the entire Malaysian market. Development began, but proceeded rather slowly because of political uncertainty and the remnants of industrial unrest. Moreover, Indonesia mounted an economic confrontation with Singapore in 1964–65 which disrupted trade between those traditional partners. The import-substitution stage ended abruptly in 1965 when, with little preparation, Singapore was separated politically from Malaysia.

A transition period from 1965 to 1968 and 1969 followed. Part of the reaction to the separation from Malaysia was an increase in import-substitution protection on the ground that excess capacity was likely to be created by the change. In addition, the withdrawal of British military forces became another source of disruption, since it led to a reduction in service earnings and placed a new defense burden on Singapore. These circumstances reinforced the inward reaction. As a result, tariffs were raised in 1965 and again in 1968, although quotas were seldom used after 1966. The other part of Singapore's reaction to these twin challenges was to look beyond Malaysia for markets and to stimulate exports. Duties on imported inputs into production were exempted to help achieve export competitiveness and an export-promotion center was started. Double-expensing of export-promotion expenses for income tax purposes was initiated. Accelerated depreciation and a limited income tax holiday were initiated. The government also recognized the importance of foreign entrepreneurs for private-sector investments and new incentives were given to export-oriented direct foreign investment. New labor market measures were introduced to provide wage stability and industrial peace in order to improve export prospects. The educational system was restructured to prepare workers better for jobs in export-oriented industries.

A new phase began in 1968–69 when Singapore realized that import substitution was unnecessary and was responsible for raising costs and prices. It moved rapidly to free trade. Import restrictions were reduced and exchange controls eliminated. Indeed, there was an overall decline of economic nationalism. In 1973 all quotas were removed and tariffs were further reduced. Two years later all import licensing was discontinued. In 1974 a small preference for export credit was introduced and discounting facilities for export credit were expanded in 1976. In 1977 the double-expensing provisions for exports were extended to traders and bankers.

The last phase began in 1979 with policies for economic restructuring. By then Singapore had reached full employment and was experiencing social problems as a result of large numbers of foreign guest workers. It was feeling the competition from other developing countries for labor-intensive products as well as encountering rising trade barriers for such products in developed countries. Thus a conscious effort was started to upgrade labor skills for input into the production of goods and services. Wages were forced up and restraints were placed on the entrance of foreign workers. A Central Provident Fund was set up, to which compulsory personal savings were committed in order to provide financial resources necessary for the restructuring. A Skills Development Fund with joint contributions by business and government was established to make provision for direct labor training, subsidies for labor training within private industry, subsidies for machinery investment, and subsidies for the use of consultants' services to upgrade industrial activity. These and other measures are designed to increase Singapore's competitiveness in the exporting of high-skill, high-technology goods and services.

Specifics of Trade Performance

The Republic of China

The quantitative importance of international trade to Taiwan, shown in table 1, is substantial and has been growing. In 1952 exports of merchandise were equal to 8.6 percent of GNP and by 1961 had risen to 11.2 percent. Following the adoption of the export-substitution strategy, however, exports grew much more rapidly in relation to GNP, reaching

Table 1. Exports and Imports of Merchandise as a Ratio to Gross National Product in Current Prices (%)

	Exports			Imports		
Country	1960	1970	1980	1960	1970	1980
Republic of China (Taiwan)	11.3	29.7	53.7	18.9	29.7	55.1
Republic of Korea	0.9	9.5	28.1	9.0	22.6	35.8
Hong Kong (including entrepôt)	64.5	79.3	91.2	96.1	91.6	103.7
Singapore (including entrepôt)	161.7	81.9	176.3	190.0	129.8	218.4

Sources: Council for Economic Planning and Development (1983); International Monetary Fund (1982); United Nations Secretariat Statistical Office (1983).

48.7 percent in 1981. Similarly, imports of merchandise were equal to 14.8 percent of GNP in 1952, and despite a decade of successful import substitution, had risen to 18.5 percent in 1961. These figures reflect both the relatively small size of Taiwan and the need for imports to accommodate domestic growth, including production of exported products. Under the more liberal export-substitution regime, imports grew more rapidly, reaching 45.7 percent in 1981. Thus while exports and imports both grew faster than GNP, exports were the most rapid growers, and turned a large trade deficit in 1952 into a surplus in 1981.

The structural transformation of the Taiwanese economy is reflected in the structure of its exports. Agricultural products made up 92 percent of total exports in 1952, but only 8 percent in 1981, while industrial products were just the reverse. In 1952, rice and sugar exports alone were 74 percent of the total, but dwindled to 3 percent by 1970. The expansion of manufactured-goods exports first comprised processed foods, which accounted for 94 percent of manufactured exports in 1952, but their share in the total was later eclipsed by textiles, and subsequently even more so by electronics (including electrical machinery).

As the product structure of Taiwan's exports changed, so did its trading partners. The United States replaced Japan as Taiwan's largest market. Kuo and Fei conclude that the 33.1 percent annual growth rate of Taiwan's exports to the United States between 1954 and 1981 was the most important stimulus to the rapid growth of Taiwan during that period. Meanwhile, Japan was becoming a relatively smaller market, declining from 29.0 percent in 1961 to 11.0 percent in 1981. Europe and other countries became greater markets, particularly during the seventies. In the later seventies, Taiwan's exports of electrical machinery grew more rapidly for Hong Kong, Europe, and other countries than for the United States (its largest market for these products).

The pattern of Taiwan's imports by country differs from its export pattern, and therein may lie a potential problem. Of the US $19.7 billion of Taiwan imports in 1980, 27.1 percent were from Japan, its largest supplier, and only 23.7 percent from the United States, its largest market. Thus, while Taiwan's trade overall was only slightly in surplus in 1980, it ran a US $3.2 billion trade deficit with Japan and a US $2.1 billion surplus with the United States. In a well-working global system, bilateral balances can be ignored and only multilateral balances need be considered. Given the deficiencies of the global system, however, Taiwan could be caught by rising sensitivity in the United States to the bilateral deficit, even though Taiwan itself was not in surplus. It is for this reason that Taiwan has attempted to pressure Japan to reduce its surplus with Taiwan by admitting more of its imports.

Introduction 15

The Republic of Korea

As is shown in table 1, the rise in the share of international trade in the economy of Korea has been phenomenal. From only 3.6 percent of GNP in 1961, exports rose to 48.6 percent in 1981 (measured in constant 1975 prices). Imports rose similarly from 10.7 percent in 1961 to 53.7 percent in 1981. The large gap between the levels of imports and exports in 1961 reflects the availability of large amounts of U.S. aid in that year. Subsequently, the gap narrowed, but it was sustained through 1981, although the financing was done through commercial markets.

In the early sixties, primary products made up 86 percent of Korea's merchandise exports and manufactures only 14 percent. The transformation of the economy and the adoption of export substitution as a development strategy were reflected in a structural change in exports. By 1970, Balassa notes, manufactures constituted 76.7 percent of total exports, almost an exact reversal from 1960. Most of these manufactures were relatively simple items such as wigs, plywood and veneer, cotton yarn and fabrics, other textiles and apparel, electronic parts, and footwear. Subsequently, clothing became more important and was the largest export item in 1975. It was replaced, however, by machinery and transport equipment, which became the largest single category of exports in 1980. All these changes reflected continual growth and change in the Korean economy.

Hong Kong

Referring to table 1, it is seen that even in 1962, exports constituted more than 50 percent of GNP in Hong Kong, and that figure grew to 92 percent in 1980. Several observations need be made about these figures. Historically, a huge volume of exports had always entered world trade from Hong Kong, but previously they were of goods produced elsewhere and re-exported via Hong Kong. Much of the early phase of export growth was the substituting of Hong Kong–made goods for re-exports. Second, Hong Kong exports are believed to embody a large amount of imports. If one were able to calculate a net export figure for Hong Kong which excluded both direct and indirect imported inputs, then its relationship to GNP might be more like that of other countries. Nevertheless, the outward orientation of Hong Kong as suggested by these figures is remarkably large. What was said for exports applies also to imports. Hong Kong sustained a net deficit in the merchandise trade throughout the period.

While some modest changes have occurred in the structure of Hong Kong exports, as compared to other rapidly developing countries they have shown remarkable stability. Because of the absence of distortions from either import barriers or export subsidies, Hong Kong's industry developed on the basis of comparative advantage, which dictated that Hong Kong export labor-intensive goods. Thus clothing made up 35.4 percent of its exports in 1960 and still accounted for 34.4 percent in 1980. Similarly, miscellaneous manufactured goods (toys) were 13.8 percent of exports in 1960 and were up slightly, to 16.3 percent, in 1980. Textiles (spinning and weaving) and shoes, however, saw a steady and significant erosion of their share, while electrical machinery and instruments (watches and clocks) expanded.

The country distribution of Hong Kong's trade was also stable, although some changes did occur. Hong Kong has looked to developed countries for markets, especially the United States, the United Kingdom, and West Germany; while the U.K. share has declined, the German share has expanded. Indeed, the concentration of sales to developed countries has increased despite trade restraints in those countries, while exports to developing countries such as Thailand, Malaysia, and Indonesia have been reduced because of the import-replacing strategies of those countries. Singapore, however, continues to be an important market. On the import side, Japan, the People's Republic of China, the United States, and the United Kingdom are important, with Japan's share rising and the United Kingdom's falling. In fact, Taiwan and Singapore have surpassed the United Kingdom as suppliers to Hong Kong.

Singapore

As the largest seaport in the world, Singapore would be expected to have its economy heavily involved in international trade. Even so, the degree of involvement is surprising. Along with its own domestically generated commerce, Singapore remains an important entrepôt for surrounding countries. As seen in table 1, the ratio of exports and imports of merchandise to GNP for Singapore is a dimension larger than for even the other trade-dependent countries examined in this volume. The numbers are large even when entrepôt trade is excluded. Singapore's nonentrepôt exports were 10 percent of GNP in the early sixties (about the same as Taiwan's). By the early eighties the figure had reached 112 percent (more than twice that of Taiwan). According to the World Bank tables, Singapore and Hong Kong are first and second in the world in this respect. Obviously the import content of Singapore's exports is very high. Using a 1973 input-output table, Chia estimated that the import content of exports was 53.9 percent. It is also estimated that in value terms, exports of services are about 30 percent as large as exports of merchandise. Singapore's net output is tied to world demand to a truly remarkable extent, and it may still be growing.

Over time, certain characteristics of Singapore's merchandise exports have changed. In the early sixties, entrepôt exports were several times larger than exports of domestic products. By the early seventies there was rough equivalency between the two, but a decade later, export of domestic product was considerably larger. The entrepôt function in the early sixties also determined what kinds of products could be made in Singapore and exported. For example, locally refined bunkering fuel was sold in large amounts to foreign vessels, and locally processed food was important. On the other hand, the high wages paid to entrepôt employees prevented Singapore from developing an export based upon the textile and clothing industry. After the transition to free trade, Singapore's exports became increasingly labor-intensive on the one hand and related to petroleum refining on the other (both fuels and petrochemicals). Meanwhile, processed natural resources declined. Given the high level of unemployment in Singapore, the development was quite natural. The unemployed were rapidly absorbed, but the government's wage restraints kept the market from making an adjustment. Instead, foreign guest workers were attracted and, until a policy reversal in 1979, were permitted to enter to solve the labor shortage. Nevertheless, there was some upgrading of Singapore's exports as they became more skill- and technology-intensive. Machinery and transport equipment became much more important—second only to mineral fuels.

As for markets, they differed greatly according to the products involved. Japan, Hong Kong, and Malaysia were the largest markets for Singapore's exports of petroleum products. The United States and Europe were the largest markets for such manufactured products as electrical machinery, electronic valves, and telecommunication equipment.

Stages of Economic Development and Export Performance

International trade theory holds that the comparative advantage of a country is largely determined by the relative availabilities of factors of production in the country compared with other countries. Comparative advantage will change over time as relative factors of production change within the country, and in other countries, and as technology itself changes. In a country enjoying rapid economic growth, changes in its own relative factor availabilities are likely to be the most important variable. For countries with unexploited natural resources whose development is the driving force in its growth, rapid growth may not change comparative advantage very much, although shifts from one commodity to another in its export basket and increased processing of natural resources would still be possible. For countries with a relative shortage of natural resources and a relative abundance of human resources, significant changes in its comparative advantage are very likely, and are closely related to the stages of its own economic development. Such is the case of the four Asian NICs considered in this study.

In the early fifties Taiwan exported agriculturally based natural-resource-intensive goods, but that pattern was not sustainable. The net in-migration of mainlanders to the island added 25 percent to its population in the late forties and gave Taiwan one of the highest population densities in the world—greater than that of Korea or the Netherlands, and 50 percent higher than Japan, suggesting that there would be a reorientation toward labor-intensive production.[3] Thus the first phase of postwar development involved expanding industry, particularly replacing imported nondurable consumer products. At that time, Taiwan's most dynamic exports were of processed foods. Industrialization during the fifties under an import-substitution strategy restrained Taiwan's international trade to a lower share of output than was usual during its colonial period. The approaching end of this stage of development was signaled by the declining share of consumer products in imports; in 1958 imports of consumption goods were reduced to 6.4 percent of the total.

The next stage of development for Taiwan involved the expansion of production of labor-intensive manufactured goods, especially for export—referred to earlier as primary export substitution. Exports of industrial products expanded rapidly after 1959, reaching half of total exports by 1962. The basis for this growth was the easy availability of a literate and energetic labor force employable at low wages and the existence of domestic entrepreneurs who had by then had a decade of experience in the organization of industrial production. Not surprisingly, the production and export of textiles and apparel were particularly important in this period, since the factors of production needed for these goods were exactly those in abundance in Taiwan.

In the first half of the sixties, production of industrial goods grew rapidly but did not absorb any excess labor, although employment did increase by the number of new entrants into the labor force. The explanation lies in the rapid advance of productivity in those years as firms utilized excess capacity in response to the removal of the distortions coming from the previous import-substitution policies. Kuo and Fei found that the capital/labor ratio rose in the production of goods sold in domestic markets. Increasing the capital/labor ratio tends to raise the output/labor ratio. Since domestic sales still constituted two-thirds of manufacturing production, the effect was significant for the overall economy. The capital/labor ratio continued to rise

---

3. See Simon Kuznets, "Growth and Structural Shifts" in Galenson (1979); and Republic of China, Council for Economic Planning and Development, *Taiwan Statistical Data Book* (1981), p. 5.

Introduction

during the second half of the sixties, but increasingly output was going to export sales where the level of the capital/labor ratio was lower. Thus, excess labor was absorbed through the expansion of production of labor-intensive products for export. Exports to advanced countries were more labor-intensive than those sold to developing countries.

The next stage in Taiwan's development was signaled by the drying up of surplus labor, which Kuo and Fei date in 1971. From then on, real wages rose quite rapidly, changing the basis for Taiwan's comparative advantage. Taiwan entered a new stage described as secondary import and export substitution. The labor-skill intensity of manufactured goods produced to compete with imports increased throughout the period 1961–76, although the skill intensity in export products sold to developed countries did not increase until after 1971, when it rose sharply. Thus, after reaching full employment, producers in Taiwan could not count on cheap wages to remain competitive, but instead moved up the scale of technology, which required more skills in production.

Several studies which have analyzed the factor content of the shifting comparative advantage of Korea are cited by Balassa in chapter 3. In 1960, when Korean exports were largely primary products, exports required more capital per unit of labor than did domestic output or even imports. This could hardly be sustained in a country that was labor-rich and capital-poor. Even as early as 1960, the small portion of exports that were manufactured products did have the expected characteristic of being more labor-intensive than were imports of manufactured products. As the economy grew, the availability of low-cost labor became more dominant in determining exports. While domestic output in general became marginally more capital-intensive, production for exports became increasingly labor-intensive. By 1968, exports were more labor-intensive than imports, reflecting both shifts in production methods and the growing concentration of manufactures in Korea's export basket. Subsequent to 1968, when Korean development strategy began to emphasize heavy industry and the chemical industry, the capital intensity of export and probably of total production began to rise, and by 1975 it may have exceeded that of imports.

Lin and Mok in chapter 5 leave little doubt that Hong Kong's growth has been export-led and that trade has been the engine of growth. As an open economy, Hong Kong has had to adjust to foreign developments and has managed very well. Because of limitations on availability of data, Lin and Mok concentrated on only four industries—clothing, footwear, furniture, and precision instruments. They found that an insignificant portion of the growth of these industries could be attributed to import replacement; a small amount of growth did occur from domestic demand (especially for footwear and furniture); export growth provided most demand for all four industries. The importance of trade for growth can also be established through analysis demonstrating that exports were more labor-intensive and less capital-intensive than imports, and that there was little change in the capital/labor ratio in exports over time, but a decided rise of the ratio in imports. Hong Kong's trade, based on undistorted comparative advantage, made good use of its abundant factor—labor—and increasingly conserved its scarce factor—capital.

While Hong Kong's exports remained labor-intensive, a subtle change did take place as the economy developed. The labor force became fully utilized and wages began to rise rapidly. It is at this point in the development of Taiwan and Korea that exports became more capital-intensive. A different kind of adjustment was made in Hong Kong, however. Certain export industries, such as textiles and footwear, suffered a relative decline because Hong Kong without cheap labor could not sustain its comparative advantage in them. Other labor-intensive industries did expand, including clothing, toys and plastic goods, electrical goods, and horological instruments. In these industries it was possible to introduce higher technology without greater capital intensity and to substitute higher quality and more skilled labor, which were found in relatively greater abundance in Hong Kong, for unskilled labor. Furthermore, these industries have few economies of scale, thus permitting the highly skilled, small entrepreneurs who are abundant in Hong Kong to prosper.

A third stage may have been reached about 1975 when clothing, the most important export industry, finally peaked. It is conceivable that the possibilities of utilizing skilled labor to overcome wage increases may have finally been exhausted, or alternatively, trade restraints in importing countries (both developed and developing) became so burdensome as to prevent further rapid growth. In any event, the leadership of industrial expansion passed to other industries. It should also be noted that services were prospering, and re-exports from Mainland China grew rapidly during the late seventies.

The continued export orientation of Hong Kong's manufacturing is confirmed by the observation that as early as 1964, some 87 percent of employment in manufacturing was devoted to exports. It was estimated that two-thirds of total value added in the economy occurred in firms that exported over 50 percent of their output. Analysis of the factors responsible for Hong Kong's success in exporting suggested that 56 percent was due to the commodity composition of trade, that is, to the ability of Hong Kong's entrepreneurs to provide the products in great demand; 42 percent to the general expansion of world trade; and only 5 percent to increased competitiveness. There was a loss of 3 percent because of a tendency to export heavily to relatively slow-growing countries.

Chia Siow Yue in chapter 6 describes Singapore as a country remarkably dependent on the world economy for its economic stimulation. In the sixties about half of the growth of the economy was due to export demand, and that dependence—the sum of goods and services—rose to 70 percent in the seventies. There was great variance in the annual growth rate of trade, but the trend in real terms was very rapid. It is apparent that GNP fluctuations were highly correlated with trade fluctuations, especially entrepôt trade. In the seventies the export of services was growing particularly rapidly. Despite the high level of dependence, instability of export markets has not been a particularly serious problem for Singapore because of its wide diversification of both products and markets.

Singapore's development was impeded by the oil crisis of 1973–74 and the world recession that followed it. Domestic growth was reduced, but only temporarily. A similar phenomenon occurred with the second oil crisis, but its effects are also likely to be temporary.

Foreign Capital and Development

Foreign capital can play an important, some would say critical, role in the growth of developing countries, particularly in the earliest stages of economic development. Much will depend on its magnitude, its form (for instance, as between concessional aid, bank loans, or direct investment), and the policies and circumstances of the receiving country.

For Taiwan, aid from the United States was particularly important from 1951 through 1962, when it constituted over 90 percent of all foreign capital commitments and between 35 percent and 45 percent of gross domestic capital formation in each year (Ranis 1979). U.S. aid declined rapidly in the early sixties, and direct foreign investment then began to increase. Nevertheless, foreign capital was no longer a major share of domestic investment. Beginning in 1971, Taiwan became a net provider of capital to other countries rather than a recipient.

In chapter 2 Ranis and Schive conclude that direct foreign investment (DFI) has been of considerable quantitative importance to Taiwan, especially during the late sixties, and that it assumed growing quantitative importance in the years that followed. From 1951 to 1960, during the import-substitution phase of Taiwan's development, DFI represented only 1.8 percent of total investment and 3.9 percent of private investment. This investment was made primarily to serve the domestic market and in response to incentives to replace imports. During 1961–70, the primary export-substitution stage, DFI increased to 3.2 percent of total investment and 5.1 percent of private investment. It was during this period that the Kaohsiung and other export-processing zones (EPZs) were authorized and begun. DFI in this period was particularly important in providing information on international markets and bringing new technology to Taiwan. During the next stage of secondary import-substitution and export substitution, from 1971 to 1980, DFI increased in absolute amounts but declined to 2.0 percent of total investment and 3.8 percent of private investment. In this stage, which is still continuing, the motivations for DFI are the desire of investors to make the most of their particular proprietary interests and the need of the country for continuing technology transfer. While Ranis and Schive conclude that it is impossible to quantify the role of DFI in the development process, they cite a study of the Investment Commission in Taipei which estimated that foreign firms contributed between 6.4 percent and 8.3 percent to GNP during the years 1974–79.

A significant characteristic of DFI in Taiwan is that a substantial share comes from Overseas Chinese investors; about 30 percent of all DFI during the fifties and sixties was from Overseas Chinese, and some 37 percent in the seventies. Overseas Chinese investment was encouraged on a preferential basis as early as 1952 and some preferences still exist, as in banking. Firms owned by Overseas Chinese behave very much like Taiwanese-owned firms and seem to consider themselves domestic entities.

EPZs were initiated in the mid-sixties as a transitional device to create employment and promote exports. The device was particularly attractive to Japanese firms, who were enticed by cheap wages. Firms in the EPZs export most of their output, but they contributed less than 5 percent of total exports from Taiwan in the late sixties, and only about 8 percent during the seventies.

Government policy during the post-colonial period began by discouraging DFI in order to promote a new industrial entrepreneurial class in Taiwan. Subsequently, DFI opportunities were liberalized, along with the lessening of other restrictions, in the early sixties. The EPZ effort was a real departure in policy. Once full employment was reached, the *raison d'être* of the EPZs ended, and they became a relic of the past rather than a mechanism of the future. Recently, promotional efforts have been made to create a high-technology park not far from Taipei in order to bring together a critical mass of advanced technology companies, not restricted to foreign-owned enterprises.

Direct investment by foreign firms can have a significant impact on the exports of a developing country because of the marketing ability of the firms, which often sell goods to other affiliates of the same firm. Ranis and

Introduction

Schive confirm this effect of DFI in Taiwan. On average, DFI firms export about 46 percent of their sales, while domestic enterprises in manufacturing are less outside-oriented, exporting only 34 percent of sales. The existence of the EPZs biases the result, since those ventures were undertaken for the sole purpose of exporting; they also utilize a larger share of imported inputs than do domestic firms. The EPZs, however, only amounted to about one-third of total exports of DFI, so the bias does not undermine the observation that DFIs are more export-oriented than domestic firms.

A second modification to this proposition is that minority-share DFIs seem to be more export-oriented than wholly owned DFIs, so exporting does not seem so directly related to foreign control. This observation, however, may also be somewhat biased, since some domestic firms take on a minority foreign partner explicitly to help them export, and may set up separate legal entities to do so. When partnerships are involved, the DFI enterprises generally rely on foreign partners for market information. Nevertheless, when a correction is made for the share of foreign ownership, the DFI portion of Taiwan's exports drops from about 20 percent to 15 percent, and there is some evidence that this figure was declining in the late seventies.

Finally, with respect to exports, U.S.-owned DFI firms in Taiwan seem to be somewhat more export-oriented than those owned by Japanese. This observation runs counter to the theory of Kiyoshi Kojima who hypothesized that the reverse would be true (Kojima 1978).

A second noteworthy area of impact of DFI on receiving countries concerns the relative use of factors of production as this relates to the use of "appropriate" technology by DFIs and their impact on income distribution. DFIs have absorbed a great deal of labor in Taiwan, but this is due to the fact that they are heavy exporters and all firms operating in Taiwan use more labor for export than for domestic sales. This finding is confirmed by the observation that DFIs have higher capital/labor ratios if they sell domestically than if they export. A comparison of the capital intensity of DFIs and domestic-owned firms in the same industry indicates that DFIs are more capital-intensive; however, on average they tend to be larger than domestic firms, so the capital intensity may be related more to size than to foreign interest. Two other related findings are a bit sharper, but not startling. As expected, DFIs in the EPZs are more labor-intensive than DFIs outside the EPZs, since firms were attracted to the zones by cheap wages. Also, DFIs use more foreign technology than domestic firms; the higher the rate of foreign ownership, the higher the use of foreign technology. This is to be expected, since DFIs have more knowledge of and greater access to foreign technology. None of these observations, however, casts light on the more controversial assertions in the literature about multinational firms.

Another area of impact by DFIs on the economy can be by means of backward and forward linkages. Ranis and Schive cite a case study of the Singer Company in Taiwan, whose investment in sewing machines did lead to considerable backward and some forward linkage, with great benefit to many domestically owned firms and to exports. They also cite evidence to show that the longer the DFIs exist in Taiwan, the larger is their share of local procurement, a finding which is consistent with the belief that DFIs have important spread effects on the economy.

Ranis and Schive make a final observation that relates to the relative power of DFIs in Taiwan. They conclude that the DFIs "dance to the tune of the domestic economy" rather than transform it to suit themselves. This has obvious advantages in that no one need fear being controlled from abroad, but it also means that, just as with domestic firms, DFIs may set up and operate inefficient enterprises if they are heavily protected, as has happened in the case of automobile assemblies.

Foreign capital in all its forms has made an important contribution to the Korean economy, but the contribution of direct foreign investment alone has not been of great importance. In the years immediately following the Korean War, aid from the United States was massive and constituted all of the resources available for investment, since there were no domestic savings. U.S. aid permitted the society to hold together while recovering from the devastation of the war, but it also had negative effects. It permitted the government to sustain an overvalued currency, which discouraged exports; it led to the underpricing of agricultural commodities, which discouraged agricultural production; and it involved too many foreigners in the planning and execution of development projects.

As reported by Bohn Young Koo in chapter 4, in 1960 legal provision was made for direct foreign investment, which included equality of treatment and even some tax incentives, but no significant investment took place because of the disorganized state of the economy. The first Five Year Plan, begun in 1962, also indicated that direct foreign investment would be approved, but only if it would not hurt domestically owned firms. Still there was no great response, because of political and economic uncertainty. It was not until Korea's relations with Japan were normalized in 1965 that DFI began to mount.

The more rapid expansion of DFI led to a major policy change in 1970 and the adoption of general guidelines. The purpose was to encourage joint ventures rather than wholly foreign-owned firms. Specific projects not open to foreign investors were also indicated. In general, the regulations can be characterized as heavy-handed and sometimes conflicting. It was not until September 1980 that the guidelines were liberalized; subsequent measures have also moved in that direction. In sum, for almost all of the postwar period, Korean policy has been quite restrictive with respect to foreign investors.

Direct foreign investment in Korea was valued at only US $1 billion at the end of 1980. Japanese firms were dominant, supplying 57 percent of the value and 76 percent of the number of ventures. Three factors are identified by Koo as being of greatest importance in bringing about this result. First, the geographical proximity of Japan makes it a logical investor. Second, rapidly rising wages in Japan made the availability of cheap labor in Korea very attractive. Finally, some permanent Korean residents in Japan were given special treatment when investing in Korea, although their investments were still counted as foreign-owned. From about 1974 onward, U.S. and European investors became more important, as they seemed to be less deterred than the Japanese by rising labor costs in Korea, but total investment slackened.

As evidenced by special surveys conducted in 1976 and 1978, the distribution of direct foreign investment by industry seemed to reflect government policy; it was permitted if it was export-oriented, and promoted if it upgraded Korean technology, but it was not allowed to compete with domestic firms. For example, Japanese joint ventures in textiles were approved to enlarge Korean access to foreign markets. U.S. investment in chemicals and petroleum refining were encouraged because there were no Korean capabilities in these fields. Service investment, however, was severely restricted, although some U.S. investment in finance did go forward.

The precise consequences of this investment for the Korean economy are difficult to establish because of both the ambiguity of the question and the absence of data. Nevertheless, some links can be documented. DFI as a share of gross domestic capital formation never reached 3 percent in any year except 1973, when it was 4.7 percent. In most years it was 1 percent or less. DFI has been more important in manufacturing alone; and in 1973–75 its share exceeded 10 percent, though in most years its share in manufacturing has been 4 percent or less. Thus DFI has made at most a modest contribution to the Korean economy. This is also seen from the labor market, since only 2.3 percent of the labor force was employed in foreign firms in 1978. Since this exceeded the investment share by foreigners, it implies that foreign-owned firms are more labor-intensive than Korean-owned firms, either because they are concentrated in labor-intensive industries or because they use labor-intensive techniques. From examining various bits of data, Koo in chapter 4 concludes that DFI contributed about 1 percent per year to Korea's growth in the late seventies.

DFI can also have particularly strong effects on the balance of payments, and this seemed to be true in Korea, but it is still subject to the question whether DFI production that was sold in the domestic market was import-replacing. Foreign firms accounted for between 22 percent and 25 percent of Korean exports during the late seventies, which is higher than their share of output. They also imported a larger share of their sales value than Korean-owned firms. When the trade, service, and capital account items are all considered, it appears that DFI had a positive, but relatively minor, impact on Korea's balance of payments.

There may have been some indirect effects of DFI, but they are impossible to measure. Foreign firms did tend to introduce new technology, provide significant amount of worker training in some industries, and improve marketing, and they probably added to employment creation. In general, Koo concludes that DFI has made a positive contribution to the Korean economy because it responded to the direction and regulation of the Korean government.

Much about the role of foreign investment in Hong Kong is not known. Indeed, even the term "foreign" is ambiguous, given the role of British firms that have been resident in the colony for over a hundred years, and the existence of "Overseas Chinese" owners who have recently taken up residence in Hong Kong. Furthermore, in the reported data, which are incomplete, adequate distinction between portfolio and direct foreign investment is not made. Nevertheless, Lin and Mok have utilized what information is available and provide many important insights.

There was no ambiguity about Hong Kong's policy toward direct foreign investment—to permit it freely. Even business licensing does not exist except for public utilities and banking. All exchange controls were abolished when the Hong Kong dollar was floated in 1974 under the more flexible international arrangements following the collapse of the Bretton Woods system. Thus Hong Kong firms and foreign-owned firms operate side by side without discrimination or control.

In the fifties, when industrialization was beginning in Hong Kong, political uncertainty was so great as to discourage foreign investors. Some direct foreign investment did come in during the following decade, but it remained less than 1 percent of all enterprises. In the seventies (for which more data are available), DFI tripled. As in the sixties, export-oriented DFI was dominant in electronics and garments, although the foreign share declined in these industries. In some more capital-intensive, sophisticated industries, however, such as electrical products, chemicals, and printing, DFI expanded both absolutely and relatively. Much of the output of these enterprises was also exported, but even more was sold domestically.

The largest source of foreign investment was the United States, although its share declined relative to that of other countries over time. The Japanese share has been the next largest and has tended to be sustained. The U.K. share was smaller and has declined. Investors from Switzerland, the Netherlands, Thailand, the Philippines, and West Germany have accounted for a rising share of foreign investment.

Most of the DFI was in joint ventures, although American investment was more likely to be in wholly owned enterprises in which U.S. technology was particularly important. However, in certain industries, such as clothing, joint ventures predominated regardless of the nationality of the foreign partner.

As noted above, foreign firms never exceeded 1 percent of the total number of enterprises in Hong Kong, but the data for the 1970s indicate that they employed 10 percent of all employees and accounted for between 13 percent and 15 percent of value added in manufacturing. Thus foreign-owned enterprises tended on average to be larger and more capital-intensive than domestically owned firms. Significantly, however, both domestic investors and DFI firms tended to reduce the size of their factories over time. Domestic and DFI firms tended to export about the same share of their output.

Lin and Mok suggest that DFI has made a modest overall contribution to the industrialization of Hong Kong. Foreign firms saw Hong Kong as a profitable export platform and as a place to earn a return on their technology. No special incentives were required to attract them, just a favorable business environment. Conventional wisdom holds that governments of developing countries must regulate and control DFI in order to keep it from dominating the economy, to ensure that domestic firms are accepted as joint venture partners, to aid domestic firms to get a stake in industries in which DFI dominates, to force DFI to export, and to get DFI to transfer technology to the host country and have it spread to domestically owned firms. No regulations or controls exist in Hong Kong, and none of the bad and all of the good things happened there. It would be disingenuous to imply that all developing countries can industrialize as fast as Hong Kong by following a laissez-faire policy, for unique factors were at work there. Nevertheless, Hong Kong does demonstrate the force and value of such a policy.

Singapore has relied very little on foreign financial capital, but has been greatly reliant on foreign entrepreneurship. Foreign-owned firms have been the ones that created employment, introduced new technology, and exported to foreign markets. No other country has been as reliant on foreign entrepreneurs in this respect as Singapore.

Singapore's policy has consistently been to encourage direct foreign investment. There is an absence of restriction and discrimination—there is no specific foreign investment law. Tax holidays of five years were provided for investment, which seemed to fit the needs of foreign investors at least as well as or better than they do those of domestic entrepreneurs. Tax incentives have recently been added for research and development activities. Supporting facilities have been provided by the government through expenditures for social overhead capital and even for plant structures, which were then rented to foreign owners at reasonable costs.

There was very little DFI in Singapore before the sixties because of the general turmoil in those years. Early in the sixties, the Royal Dutch Shell Company invested in an oil refinery to serve the market for bunkering fuel, enticed by a liberal tax holiday. During the import-substitution period, very little DFI was attracted to manufacturing, although some small investments were made in textiles and garments by investors from Hong Kong and Taiwan as a means of circumventing the restrictive quotas of developed countries. The major influx of foreign investment came after 1968, particularly in electrical goods, electronics, and precision instruments. The new investors were from the United States, Europe, Japan, and Hong Kong. In 1963, about half of total output in manufacturing was by firms wholly locally owned; by 1980 the local share had been reduced to 15 percent. Wholly foreign-owned firms began to dominate manufacturing in the sixties and seventies, and by 1980, produced 59 percent of all manufactured goods. Joint ventures produced 23 percent of output in 1963 and 26 percent in 1980. Wholly foreign-owned firms and joint ventures employed 70 percent of all employees in manufacturing and made 93 percent of all export sales. Thus, foreign-owned firms were responsible for most of the success of Singapore's manufacturing. The incidence of bankruptcy was three times more common among wholly locally owned firms than among joint ventures (38 percent vs. 13 percent) and more than six times than among wholly foreign-owned firms (6 percent). Foreign firms were larger, had a higher level of productivity, and paid higher wages than locally owned firms. Thus the wage-correction policy of 1979–82 impinged more heavily on local than on foreign firms.

In her analysis, Chia Siow Yue concludes that the government should take a greater role in overcoming the weakness of local entrepreneurs in manufacturing. She points out that export is one area in which local entrepreneurs are particularly weak. Foreign firms are a much less potent

Introduction

force in service, where the ownership share is only 28 percent (33 percent in finance and insurance). Since Singapore is likely to become more service-oriented, the foreign share in the overall economy may decline.

Some observers have suggested that cultural factors, such as the Confucian ethic, are responsible for the success of the four Asian NICs. Emphasis is given in this volume to economic factors. It should be noted, however, that all four areas suffered societal shocks before rapid growth began. In Hong Kong it was the inflow of refugees from 1949 onward, combined with the U.N. embargo of trade with Mainland China during the Korean War. Taiwan had to accommodate to a massive inflow of mainlanders, and faced a severe security threat as well. The splitting of the Korean peninsula into two antagonistic entities, the return of thousands of Korean refugees from abroad and into South Korea from the north, and the Korean War itself, constituted an enormous challenge to that society. Singapore also had rapid growth of population, but the more traumatic shock was the sudden political separation from Malaysia and the abandonment of British military facilities. Given these disturbances and the responses to them in each country, some credence is provided for a Toynbee-type theory that great success only comes from a great challenge.

Foreign Trade and Investment in Self-Sustaining Growth

S. C. Tsiang and Rong-I Wu, in chapter 7, establish another broad area of similarities among the four Asian NICs. They all were enabled to attain rapid growth by following sensible policies based on sound classical economic principles. In the main, these were supply-side policies that emphasized the expansion of productive potential. The goal was to achieve self-sustaining growth of per capita income. The mechanism for bringing this about involved raising real productive capacity per capita by increasing capital in production and by improving productivity through better techniques.

The Tsiang and Wu analysis of the process of creating self-sustaining growth establishes several crucial relationships. First, the necessary increase in productive capital must be financed through savings. Second, foreign sources of savings can be helpful in creating the conditions permitting the rise of domestic savings and can have a continuing role in the development of a country, though self-sustaining growth requires sufficient domestic savings to maintain the process by itself if required to do so. Third, the rate of growth of technical progress is a significant variable both in theory and practice. Fourth, the necessary condition for self-sustaining growth can be formulated as follows: the average propensity to save in the economy as a whole should be greater than the average capital/output ratio times the rate of population growth. To achieve this, a developing country should reduce its growth of population, raise its savings ratio, and introduce improved technology.

Certain policy prescriptions follow directly from this analysis. Campaigns to reduce birth rates are desirable. Programs to raise the propensity to save, including monetary and tax policies that provide incentives to save and to invest in productive enterprises, are also desirable. Programs to introduce appropriate and improved technologies in all fields of production are also useful. Finally, government policy should assist in the allocation of available resources to optimum uses.

The role of foreign trade and investment in this process can be crucial, and certainly was in the history of these four countries. Expansion of international trade has the same effect as an enormous improvement in technology. The benefit can be obtained when trade is determined by comparative advantage, for then resources are guided into their best usage. Foreign investment, in addition to providing savings, can improve technology, management methods, and marketing skills, which may be most helpful in exporting.

An empirical examination of the macro-economic experience of the four countries revealed that they all "took-off" into self-sustaining growth within a five-year period: Hong Kong was first in 1961; Taiwan followed in 1963; Singapore was third in 1964; and Korea came along in 1966–67. It would be unrealistic to expect to find a uniform causation for such complex developments, and there are differences among the countries, but there are also similarities. They all experienced notable acceleration in the growth of their exports at the time of their take-off, which continued for the entire period of rapid growth.[4] This points up once again the importance of outward orientation for economic growth.

Taiwan took a significant step as early as 1950, when real interest rates were made positive, halting an inflationary spiral. This in turn led to an increase in domestic savings rates, which took a large upward jump in 1963 and marked the take-off point. Gross capital formation had risen gradually several years earlier, and when it began to increase at a faster rate, growth accelerated. Taiwan also devalued its currency in the late fifties and kept it at an equilibrium rate. Thus when trade policy was liberalized in the early sixties, both exports and imports could expand. The consequence can be seen in the sharp decline in the capital/output ratio from the early fifties to the mid-sixties. This was influenced by the shift into more efficient industrial investment which trade liberalization supported. Population growth

---

4. Singapore may seem like an exception, but if figures for nonentrepôt exports are used for the analysis rather than total exports including re-exports, the same phenomenon is seen.

slowed rather steadily in Taiwan, which eased the attainment of the take-off.

Korea also had an important monetary reform, but it did not come until 1966, which may in part explain the later take-off there. When real interest rates were made positive, domestic savings did increase. In preparation for the monetary reform, Korea devalued the currency (again) in 1964–65, finally correcting its overvaluation. The take-off point was marked by a large increase in gross fixed capital formation. While domestic savings growth was very important, almost half of the investment was financed from abroad at the time of the take-off. Trade liberalization also made a contribution, and the capital/output ratio declined, as in Taiwan.

The situation in Singapore was somewhat different. The take-off point in 1964 was helped by a rise in domestic savings, but much of the rise in gross investment was financed from abroad. In this case, direct foreign investment was very important. Trade protection was never strong, so its liberalization was not important; indeed, the capital/output ratio was always quite low, and it drifted lower. Singapore did make a successful effort to reduce the rate of population growth, which helped to bring about the take-off.

The case of Hong Kong is difficult to analyze because less is known about it. Since the colony always followed a laissez-faire policy, there was no need for a monetary reform or trade liberalization. The only factor that can be identified is that export growth accelerated at the point of take-off, possibly because of an acceleration of growth in the world economy, and thus the expansion was export-led.

Workers and Labor Markets

In chapter 8, on industrialization and employment, Gary Fields has identified a number of similarities among the Asian NICs. There is a complex interaction between industrial growth and developments in the labor market, with causation flowing in both directions. For example, Fields notes that economic growth raises family income, which improves worker well-being and especially increases longevity or life expectancy. Since workers anticipate that they will live a long time after retirement, however, they permit their sons to remain in school longer and they also increase household savings, both of which promote economic growth.

Six similar characteristics which Fields has noted in the four countries are:

> 1. There were large increases in employment, reductions in unemployment rates, and increases in participation rates.
> 2. There were shifts out of agricultural employment into manufacturing and other higher-paying activities.

3. There was an upgrading of employment composition according to activity status, occupation, and education.
4. There was an increase in real wages.
5. There was a decrease in inequality (with some differences among countries).
6. There was a decline in absolute poverty.

A question remains as to what caused these developments, or what drove the system. Fields has come to some analytical conclusions based on his empirical findings. First, from examining interindustry relationships, it was determined that rapid growth in employment occurred in industries in which output was growing rapidly, and output growth occurred in industries whose exports were rising particularly fast. Thus, the metal products industry was a very large and rapidly growing employer, the output of this industry was growing rapidly, and a large and increasing share of the output was being exported. A similar observation was made with respect to textiles and garments. For the food, beverage, and tobacco industries, export growth was small (or even became negative), output grew less than the average, and employment grew only slowly, that is, less than proportional to output. Thus he concluded that exports were the driving force in economic growth. This confirms the views of others who have emphasized the outward orientation of policy (or export substitution) as a major factor promoting growth. The observation that the exports that were most successful were the ones that were labor-intensive links growth in exports to particularly fast employment growth.

Second, it was also observed from interindustry analysis that the faster the growth in wages in an industry, the slower the growth in exports and, therefore, in output and employment. This strongly suggests that low wages relative to those of competitors were the bases for the comparative advantage of these countries, and that the market mechanism was the determinant of both wages and export growth.

Third, Fields concludes that more than average growth of wages causes low or even negative rates of growth of employment, output, and exports. For example, high wages in food, beverages, and tobacco led to the substitution of capital for labor—a rational economic response—but it substituted the scarce factor of production for the abundant factor and limited the development of comparative advantage in these industries. What differentiates these countries from other developing countries that have been less successful is that minimum wage laws have been avoided, labor unions have not existed or do not foster high wages, pay for government workers has not been excessive, and multinational firms have not been a force pushing up wages. Wage setting has occurred in a free-market context rather than being pushed up artificially by means of government or non-government institutions. This has permitted the development of comparative advantage in labor-intensive products, the rapid expansion of such exports, and ultimately, full use of the labor supply. Exports may have been driving the system, but the market-determined wage-setting process made it possible.

Government policy in the main has been addressed to maintaining stability.[5] Indeed the Singapore government erred in restricting the level of wages and created a labor shortage. The wage-adjustment program of 1979–82 in Singapore was necessary to correct that error. In general, wages went up in all four countries when and only when the labor market required and permitted it.

The benefits of greater exports and faster economic growth spread to the labor force through several mechanisms, and in the process raised real wages by a factor of four during the two decades from 1960 to 1980. One of the most striking consequences was the sharp rise in the number of people employed. Unemployment rates were reduced and participation rates increased, reflecting the phenomenon of the "encouraged worker effect"; that is, as jobs became available, more people, especially women, were induced to enter, return to, and stay in the labor force. Another consequence was a shift in the industrial structure of the labor force from lower- to higher-paying jobs. Workers were pulled rather than pushed out of agriculture into manufacturing. Manufacturing jobs were not particularly high-wage jobs in these countries, unlike the situation in other developing countries, and increasing numbers of workers were pulled into higher-paying jobs in services. Employment in manufacturing peaked in Hong Kong in 1976, and the other countries will follow this phenomenon in time. For Korea, which still has a large percentage of its work force in agriculture, the peak in manufacturing employment may be some years off. In Singapore and Hong Kong, a shift can be seen within services from low-paying traditional services to such modern services as commerce and finance.

Another consequence was the occupational shift of workers from self-employment, unpaid family work, and casual employment to higher-paying occupations. Just as in advanced countries, there is a hierarchy of remuneration, with administrative and managerial positions at the top, followed by professional and technical, clerical, sales and services, and production workers (operatives), with agricultural workers at the bottom. As both a consequence and a source of growth, there has been a steady increase in the educational level of the labor force, particularly of people completing secondary and higher levels of schooling. Literacy levels in

---

5. An exception occurred at the end of the regime of President Park in Korea, when the government attempted to push up wages beyond what the market indicated.

these countries have long surpassed those of other countries at the same level of income.

Finally, as a consequence of these developments, inequality has been reduced in all four countries, to different degrees and not monotonically. The four Asian NICs have a much more nearly equal distribution of income than do most other developing countries. This may seem surprising, since these NICs have few explicit policies to bring this about, in contrast to other LDCs. It appears that income equality arises from the reduction of unemployment and the transfer of workers into the modern sector from traditional pursuits. Absolute poverty has been sharply reduced because of these factors and because more family members were working. Population growth has also declined despite the lengthening of the lifespan, because of lower birth rates and reduced immigration. The process which has operated in these countries some would describe with prejudice as having a "trickle down" effect, but from their example one must conclude that the market can work very well. Rather than leading to a trickle, it results in a torrent.

Differences among the Four Asian NICs

No four countries can really be alike, so the tendency to group the four Asian NICs together as the "four dragons" runs the significant risk of paying too little attention to the differences among them. Their political histories were quite distinct, a fact which has had an impact on government policies and economic performance.

Size

Clearly the most striking difference is one of size. Two of the areas are city-states and two have substantial land masses. Before this pairing is accepted as the whole story, however, it should be noted that Hong Kong has more than twice the population of Singapore (5.5 million compared to 2.5 million), and has less than twice the area, even counting the leased New Territories. If one also excludes the areas in Hong Kong where the gradient is too steep for economic activity, then the difference is magnified. This is part of the reason that Hong Kong is more devoted to labor-intensive manufacturing and light industry than Singapore. Korea has more than twice the population of Taiwan (41.1 million compared to 18.5 million), but its area is almost two and three-quarters times as large, though a greater percentage is mountainous.

Korea and Taiwan have true rural areas, but Hong Kong and Singapore do not. In the development of Taiwan and Korea, accordingly, agricultural policy has played a role, and it remains a factor in their trade policies. Like Japan, Taiwan and Korea both had land reforms after World War II, which contributed to the rise of agricultural productivity and provided a base for industrial growth. The land reform also tended to even the distribution of wealth. The compensation to Taiwan landlords served as a stimulus to new entrepreneurial activity in industry. Taiwan and Korea may have been blessed with some natural resources, but not very many. Thus they have been forced to rely on the development of their human resources.

Having an agricultural sector may become a danger in the course of development if it leads to policies that distort prices and international trade, as in Japan. There is an understandable temptation to raise rural incomes in line with urban incomes through agricultural price supports because productivity growth per person in agriculture cannot keep pace with that in industry. The temptation may be particularly hard to resist if the ruling government gains much of its support from rural areas. Unless it is strongly resisted, however, the result will be not only unnecessarily high food prices for everyone, but increased land prices as well. A misallocation of land can become a serious barrier to growth, as is now becoming evident in Japan. Furthermore, high domestic price supports must be buttressed by controls on international trade, which can cause vigorous trade disputes with trading partners, as in the case of Japan and the United States. A better way to handle the rural income problem is through a strategy that relies in part on the dispersal of industry so that members of rural households can find industrial jobs nearby and in part on permitting and encouraging larger farms in which output per worker can rise significantly. In this respect Taiwan is on a better course than Korea.

The lack of rural areas may also be a significant barrier to the development of heavy industry and the chemical industry. This is most evident in Hong Kong, where the resource price of land does not permit it to be used for heavy industry, and where the topography prevents orderly dispersal of noxious fumes and other pollutants associated with chemical manufacturing. Petroleum refining has developed in Singapore because of the peculiar needs of an entrepôt, but may well be in a stage of decline because nearby crude oil producers are investing in more refining capacity themselves, and Singapore is unable to encourage the downstream extension of refining because of congestion problems.

Role of Government

Another striking difference among the four Asian NICs is the role that government has played in the development of the economy and society generally. If one were to array the four along a unidimensional scale, Singapore would have to be judged as having the most intrusive government, followed by Korea, Taiwan, and Hong Kong a distant last. No doubt the peculiar political history of each area explains the phenomenon, but what are its implications? When the government of Singapore gives explicit direction in navigating the economy through stages of economic growth, it takes on an awesome responsibility. Policy mistakes can be made, and apparently they were when wages were kept down too long and local entrepreneurs were not given sufficient encouragement. It also means that confidence in the government is a prerequisite to good performance of the economy. Singapore has been blessed with a stable and wise government, but will that always be the case? If it should be questioned, then the economy will suffer. Hong Kong is the opposite extreme. The Hong Kong administration is responsible for certain ground rules of enterprise and basic public services, but no more. The long-term political status of Hong Kong is uncertain, but Hong Kong entrepreneurs have been given appropriate training for living and prospering in that environment.

Korea and Taiwan stand between Singapore and Hong Kong, in the sense that government policy is very influential in the evolution of their economies, but market forces are given greatest weight in policy choices. Moreover, the economic policy makers in both countries tend to be technocratic in background, and are allowed some insulation from the larger political issues. A distinctive element in Korea is the degree to which government has interfered with direct foreign investment and kept it under constraint. While that may have been costless or even beneficial to Korea at earlier stages of growth, it is a burden now that higher levels of technology transfers are required, since it is hard to make the new liberalization policy credible to prospective foreign investors.

A distinctive characteristic of Taiwan is the surprising 20 percent share of government-owned enterprise in the economy. Its origin is understandable, since the government became the custodian of equity when the Japanese were driven out, but its continuance is curious, particularly since the share has been stable. Capital shortages and the unwillingness of private entrepreneurs to take risks for big projects is partially an answer, but it does not explain why government shares have not been sold once viability was established. The social risk in government ownership is seen in the difficulties of the government's petrochemical enterprise. It was able to pass along to others its own problems by forcing firms to buy from it at administered prices. Sometimes private firms are forced to undergo consequences of their mistakes, while government enterprises are not forced to do so, often to the detriment of the economy.

Conclusion

Examination of the four Asian NICs has much to offer with respect to the development process and the role played by foreign trade and finance. Almost every finding, however, gives rise to an intriguing question which has not been answered. Seven major findings are summarized below, along with the questions they raise.

Value of Outward Orientation

By far the most important conclusion we find in this study is that the adoption of outward-oriented policies has ushered in an era of faster growth. Both the expansion effect and the redirection of resources toward more efficient uses have been significant factors in increasing productivity in industry. An important element in this process was the efficient operation of the labor market. Because wages were not artificially inflated, comparative advantage was created and sustained in labor-intensive manufacturing until a state of full employment was achieved. Then and only then did real wages rise significantly. A more mixed judgment is required when we consider the role of direct foreign investment, although in each of the countries some form of inflow of foreign capital was important. In Singapore, direct foreign investment was critical at each of its stages, while it was considerably less so in the other three.

The question that arises from this finding is this: Was it necessary for the countries to have gone through a period of import substitution in order to get the subsequent benefits from outward orientation or export substitution? The experience of Hong Kong suggests that it was not, because it never adopted an import-substitution strategy, but there is so much peculiar to Hong Kong that a definitive judgment cannot be made based on its experience alone. Clearly an import-substitution strategy is very difficult to change once it is in place, and if the choice is between never having import substitution and always having it, the former option is preferable. However, a sequential strategy of import substitution first and then export substitution may be better than either strategy alone, and this is what is uncertain.

Pacific Basin Connection

There is a strong presumption, if not an established conclusion, that the fact that these countries are located in the Pacific Basin and reasonably close to one another had a positive impact on their development. A rationale for this finding is easy to establish. Japan has been the most successful postwar industrial country, and most of the positive spillover effects of Japanese growth occur in the Pacific area. Furthermore, having successful neighbors raises growth expectations of all participants in the economy and the goal becomes self-fulfilling. For example, government policies and programs biased against growth receive little support, an attitude which makes growth possible and likely. Moreover, Pacific Basin countries are oriented to sell exports of manufactures to the United States, which is the easiest market to penetrate. This Pacific Basin differential does not occur because the United States discriminates in favor of these countries, but rather because the long involvement of U.S. business firms in the area makes the United States a natural trading partner. This differs, for instance, from Africa, where European business firms have been dominant and U.S. firms comparatively inactive.

Given this regional orientation, however, it is still unclear whether there would be a significant positive pay-off from a conscious effort to promote Pacific Basin cooperation. Efforts have been made by various governments, academics, and business groups in the area to promote this idea, but progress has been slight because of doubt whether it would significantly improve economic welfare. These efforts are apt to continue, but a real breakthrough is unlikely unless the benefits become clearer.

Intra-NIC Trade and Cross-ownership Patterns

It is noteworthy that the trading partners of the four Asian NICs included one another in an important way. A conclusion we find in this work is that this trade had beneficial allocative effects for them, and that trade barriers of LDCs that restrict trade of other LDCs is a serious matter because they reduce trading opportunities. It is also observed that there was cross-investment within the group. These countries may have been in a particularly advantageous position to be successful in the foreign environment in which they invested because it was so similar to their accustomed environment. This helped diffuse the growth process and may explain why these NICs all achieved their take-off into self-sustained growth at about the same time.

The question that remains is: Can this experience be generalized or was it peculiar to these countries? Three of them can appropriately be described as Chinese, and Korea is not without its Chinese heritage. The entrepreneurial activities of Overseas Chinese are evident throughout East and Southeast Asia. It is also noticeable that Korea was much less involved in such activities, although that may be due to its more restrictive policy for both trade and investment. Is this, then, just a "Chinese" variable or a more general phenomenon?

The Value of Not Skipping a Stage of Development

All of these countries went through similar stages in their growth process, and it seems apparent that all of the stages were necessary, that none of them could be skipped for the purpose of accelerating the growth process. Each stage has a purpose. The early one is necessary to reach full employment, which yields social benefits in equalizing income distribution and reducing poverty. Later ones are necessary to prepare the labor force, to train domestic entrepreneurs, and to permit those entrepreneurs to amass private capital for larger-scale investment so they can avoid undue reliance upon the government.

This suggests an analytical question as to whether growth can ever be speeded up by sizable governmental intervention, or whether this must always retard growth. If government action is only a negative force, then it follows that what has been achieved by the Asian NICs should not be called a miracle but a natural state of affairs, and that governments elsewhere are development inhibitors.

Copying Success

It appears that these countries have benefited by applying classical economic policies learned from others. For several, this involved copying the so-called Japanese growth model. They learned to adopt the policy measures tried earlier by Japan, and like Japan, they adapted them to their own needs and circumstances. They also learned not to copy mindlessly. In particular, it was recognized that the distribution and agricultural policies of Japan were very deficient, and should not be emulated. Thus each country had to be selective in copying and had to develop its own model for growth.

The question is how choices are to be made. Overall economic success tends to enhance every policy choice made by the successful country. How are individual policies to be evaluated? This is a central problem of policy making even when successful models are available and the political will to follow them exists.

The Positive Value of Not Having Natural Resources

The four Asian NICs were not well endowed by nature. This so-called deprivation forced them to stress manufacturing as an engine of growth, especially before and immediately after their take-off. It has been observed that in countries where minimum income levels are determined by a well-endowed natural resource sector, real wages may be too high to begin industrialization at a low enough level, and that condition may retard the entire industrialization process. In such countries, resource rents must be captured and invested in productive enterprises without hurting incentives within or without the resource sector. This would be a formidable task in any country, and nearly impossible in an LDC, where governmental technical and administrative skills are underdeveloped. It is more likely that a combination of mistakes in allocating resources to excessively capital-intensive projects and of widespread corruption will undermine the economy and destroy the will for real development. Thus the four Asian NICs have prospered by being resource-poor.

This raises the difficult analytical question of what should be the development strategy for LDCs that are well endowed by nature. Should they slow natural resource development below what the market dictates for the doubtful advantage of holding down the real wage in manufacturing?

Stable Government and Economic Growth

It will be seen from the conclusions reached in these chapters that a stable governmental environment promotes economic growth. This finding is hardly surprising, since avoiding uncertainty is known to promote saving and encourage investment. During such events as those which occurred in Singapore in 1960 and in Korea before 1963 and again in 1980, when governments were not stable, economic growth suffered. A stable government environment implies that policy grows out of a consensus and that it reflects the popular will, or at least is not seriously inconsistent with it. It is expected that as incomes rise, greater diversity will occur in the population and forming a consensus will become more difficult. This implies that the richer the country, the more difficult it is to govern.

A question is raised by this finding. Is it necessary to achieve political development to sustain a process of economic development? Do stable government institutions replace the role played by a strong political leader in promoting growth? These cross-disciplinary questions are the most difficult to answer.

A Final Observation

As a final observation it may be noted that there is a mismatch in the domains where these countries are involved, namely, that they are more important as actors in the world economy than in the world polity. In a very prescient article written before the first oil crisis, Robert Keohane and Joseph Nye (1973) suggested that such mismatches, which they saw in the Arab Middle East, could not last. If this is so, how might this mismatch be adjusted?

One answer could be that no mismatch exists. After all, the sum of the populations of the four Asian NICs is only 72 percent of that of Bangladesh, which is not a very active member of the world community. These countries are not poor, however; they are the fastest-growing countries in the world and they seemingly have something to contribute to the world scene.

An answer that is both positive and possible is that these NICs are capable of providing technical assistance to other LDCs, and when they begin to do so, their political role will be enhanced. For example, they could provide economic advisers to a country such as Mexico that has not yet found a formula for solving its economic and social problems. Advice from these countries would carry authority, yet would not be suspect, as advice given by advisers from an advanced country or even an international institution might be. A combined effort of the four might be very powerful indeed.

References

Council for Economic Planning and Development, Executive Yuan. 1983. *Taiwan Statistical Data Book.* Taipei.

Galenson, Walter, ed. 1979. *Economic Growth and Structural Change in Taiwan.* Ithaca, N.Y.: Cornell University Press.

International Monetary Fund. 1982. *International Financial Statistics Yearbook.* Washington, D.C.

Keohane, Robert O., and Joseph S. Nye. 1973. "World Politics and the International Economic System." Chapter 5 in C. Fred Bergsten, *The Future of the International Economic Order: An Agenda for Research.* Lexington, Mass.: D.C. Heath & Co.

Kojima, Kiyoshi. 1978. *Direct Foreign Investment: A Japanese Model of Multinational Business Operations.* London: Croom Helm.

Mason, Edward S., Mahn Je Kim, Dwight H. Perkins, Kwang Suk Kim, and David C. Cole, with Leroy Jones, Il Sakong, Donald R. Snodgrass, and Noel F. McGinn. 1980. *The Economic and Social Modernization of the Republic of Korea.* Cambridge, Mass.: Harvard University Press.

Ranis, Gustav. 1979. "Industrial Development." Chapter 3 in Walter Galenson, ed., *Economic Growth and Structural Change in Taiwan.* Ithaca, N.Y.: Cornell University Press.

United Nations. Secretariat Statistical Office. 1983. *1981 Statistical Yearbook.* United Nations.

Yoffie, David, and Robert O. Keohane. 1981. "Responding to the 'New Protectionism': Strategies for the ADCs." In Wontack Hong and Lawrence B. Krause, eds., *Trade and Growth of the Advanced Developing Countries in the Pacific Basin,* 560–94. Seoul: Korea Development Institute.

I The Republic of China

1   Causes and Roles of Export Expansion in the Republic of China
Shirley W. Y. Kuo and John C. H. Fei

Introduction

The economy of Taiwan in the Republic of China developed rapidly over the last three decades, a phenomenon manifested in stable prices, successful labor absorption, and improved income distribution.

At the outset of the postwar period Taiwan was still a predominantly agricultural economy, with more than half of its labor force employed in agriculture. As a result of successful industrialization, however, this proportion declined dramatically over the following decades. By the end of the sixties unemployment was virtually eliminated. The rate of inflation slowed in the fifties and was very stable in the sixties. Although it accelerated during the oil crises of 1974 and 1979–80, inflation was brought under control immediately following each crisis. Taiwan's income distribution has become one of the most equitable in the developing world.

The expansion of foreign trade is considered decisive among the factors that contributed to Taiwan's economic growth. In 1981, with exports of US$22.6 billion and imports of US$21.2 billion, the Republic of China became the twentieth largest trading country in the world and the eighth largest trading partner of the United States. Taiwan's export content shifted from including little besides sugar and rice in the fifties to being made up of more than 90 percent industrial goods by the late sixties. With the transformation of the economic structure, not only has the composition of exports shown a marked change, but so has the selection of trading partners. Speedy export expansion has led in a direction consistent with Taiwan's comparative advantage. Foreign trade has contributed to high growth rates, rapid labor absorption, and more equitable income distribution.

The purpose of this study is to examine the causes and roles of export expansion in the Republic of China for the period 1952–81. Section I of this chapter investigates causes of trade expansion and structural change for the period 1952–70. Section II elaborates on trading partners, commodity contents, and comparative advantages during 1952–81. Section III gives a quantitative appraisal of the contribution of export expansion to economic growth and employment. Section IV highlights growth, inflation and trade balance after the oil shocks. Finally, Section V provides a summary and conclusions.

Causes of Trade Expansion and Structural Change, 1952–70

Between 1952 and 1970, the economy of Taiwan grew at an annual rate of 7.6 percent in 1952–60 and 9.9 percent in 1961–70, in real terms (table 1.1). Exports expanded at annual rates of 6.4 percent and 21.8 percent during the two subperiods, and imports increased at annual rates of 4.7 percent and 17.3 percent, both in real terms. As a result, the share of exports in the GNP expanded from 8.6 percent in 1952 to 9.6 percent in 1960 and to 26.3 percent in 1970. The share of imports in the GNP also increased, from 14.8 percent to 17.4 percent and 27.1 percent for the same years. The rapid increase in the degree of dependence on both exports and imports is an indication of Taiwan's limitations in natural resources, raw materials, and capital equipment for industrialization, and of the island's need for a broader market to expand its domestic production, as well as to acquire foreign exchange for further import. Thus, foreign trade played a decisive role in the development of the Taiwan economy.

The volume of exports also grew during this period as the economy moved away from exporting primary goods toward exporting manufactured

Table 1.1. Growth Rate and Share of Trade (in 1976 constant prices; %)

Period	Growth Rate of GNP	Growth Rate of Exports	Share of Exports in GNP	Growth Rate of Imports	Share of Imports in GNP
1952–60	7.6	6.4	8.6 (1952)	4.7	14.8 (1952)
1961–70	9.9	21.8	9.6 (1960)	17.3	17.4 (1960)
1971–81	8.8	13.5	26.3 (1970) 48.7 (1981)	11.6	27.1 (1970) 45.7 (1981)

Sources: Directorate-General of Budget, Accounting and Statistics, Executive Yuan (1981b); Ministry of Finance (1982a).

Note: Shares of exports and imports in GNP are measured in terms of current prices, while growth rates of GNP, exports, and imports are measured in terms of constant prices, deflated respectively by their corresponding deflators.

Table 1.2. Share of Exports of Sugar, Rice, and Industrial Products in Total Exports (%)

	Exports of Sugar and Rice			Exports of Industrial
Period	Subtotal	Sugar	Rice	Products
1952–54	72.6	61.4	11.2	9.0
1955–57	71.3	54.8	16.5	13.3
1958–60	57.1	45.5	11.6	23.3
1961–63	31.2	26.9	4.3	44.2
1964–66	23.9	17.5	6.4	47.9
1967–69	7.3	5.6	1.7	68.0
1970	3.2	3.1	0.1	78.6

Source: Council for Economic Planning and Development (1981).

goods (table 1.2). Heavy reliance upon only one or two primary exports is regarded as a sign of backwardness in developing economies. In Taiwan, until 1958, sugar and rice constituted more than two-thirds of the total exports. A rapid decrease in the export of these goods occurred after 1959, however, with their share dropping to 3.2 percent in 1970. In the same period, the share of industrial products, excluding processed agricultural products, increased from 8.1 percent in 1952 to 78.6 percent in 1970. Both agricultural and manufactured exports underwent a rapid diversification in the sixties, (Kuo 1970) reflecting a diversification of domestic output and a decline in the degree of dependence on one or two primary products.

Several essential factors contributed to this remarkable success. First. Changes in the institutional environment in the late fifties favored the full exercise of private entrepreneurial talent. The "internally oriented" import-substitution strategy of the fifties gave way to more liberalized "externally oriented" policies that allowed entrepreneurs to play a more active role in exploring the internal, and especially the foreign, market. Not to be minimized is the fact that the inflation of the fifties was brought under control so that the externally oriented growth occurred in an environment characterized by price stability conducive to rational entrepreneurial calculation and efficiency.

Taiwan's resources—both capital and labor—constituted a second factor that contributed to its rapid economic growth. In an open economy, investment can be financed by domestic and/or foreign savings. The latter corresponds to an import surplus which, when financed by foreign aid and/or capital inflow, can make up for both the trade gap (i.e., the import-export gap) and the savings-investment gap. The success of the Republic of China can be attributed, in part, to the availability of resources from abroad which augmented its import and investment capacity. Under an internally oriented import-substituting strategy, an underdeveloped economy finds it profitable to export only primary products (e.g., sugar and rice in the case of Taiwan). With a liberalized externally oriented policy in the sixties, however, Taiwan was rapidly able to expand manufactured exports based on its abundance of inexpensive and educated labor. These factors provided a very favorable environment for private entrepreneurs.

From Import Substitution to Export-Promotion Policies

The economic development of Taiwan over the last three decades represented a transition growth process that went through two phases: the import-substitution phase in the fifties and the externally oriented phase thereafter.

At the beginning of the fifties, the government faced a difficult choice between inward-looking and outward-looking policies. The domestic market was obviously too small to be depended upon as a source of sustained growth, but the ready markets of Japan and mainland China were no longer available. At the same time, the rapid influx of people from the mainland resulted in an abrupt population increase that substantially reduced surpluses of rice and other agricultural products.

Import Substitution Policies: The Fifties and the Early Sixties. Notwithstanding the obstacles to inward-looking measures, import controls had to be implemented for two reasons. By 1951, Taiwan was confronted with a sizable trade deficit, which was to continue throughout the 1950s. Numerous small enterprises had gone into business immediately after the war, partly by acquiring old Japanese facilities that produced simple manufactures of poor quality but at high cost. Many of these enterprises not only encountered difficulties in marketing abroad, but also had to compete with the superior Japanese products. In view of these conditions, import-substitution policies were adopted.

Many less developed countries started the transition growth process with an import-substitution policy similar to that of Taiwan. Moreover, Taiwan had begun a drive to modern economic growth through industrialization. Under then prevailing conditions, the import-substitution policy was the natural and perhaps most suitable path to take.

In 1949, when monetary reform was instituted, a functionally simple exchange rate was adopted. Domestic currency was exchanged for foreign currency partly in cash at a rate of NT$5 to US$1, and partly in exchange settlement certificates (ESCs) of equivalent value. These ESCs were freely negotiable on the market and could be sold to the Bank of Taiwan at the official rate. Under this system, the market rate was usually much higher than the official rate. For importers, foreign exchange was approved rather liberally, and the ESCs were sold by the monetary authority for importation of permissible items at the official rate. Due to the great trade deficit and continued inflation, however, applications for foreign exchange soon outgrew the available supply. The official supply price of ESCs was repeatedly devalued, but it never caught up to purchasing power parity. Hence, throughout the import-substitution phase the currency at the official exchange rate was overvalued.

In 1951, along with the currency devaluation, a multiple exchange rate was introduced as a policy instrument. A lower official rate was assigned to goods imported by the public sector, and to plant and important raw materials and intermediate inputs imported by the private sector; imports of other goods were given a higher, less favorable ESC rate. The export earnings of sugar, rice, and salt were assigned a lower ESC rate.

After several devaluations, the foreign exchange system was revised again in November 1958. This time, exchange settlement certificates were to be equally applied to all kinds of exports and imports, as the multiple exchange rate system gave way to a unified one. In addition, the price of ESCs was fixed at a price level close to the market rate. These developments paved the way for the liberalization movement as the import-substitution phase drew to an end.

The government permitted the Taiwan Sugar Corporation, which held a huge number of the ESCs, to sell them at a price very close to the market price, and then after July 1, 1960, allowed Taiwan Sugar to sell them at a fixed price below the market price (beginning in August 1960 the price of an ESC incorporated the official basic foreign exchange rate). This gradually stabilized the market exchange rate at NT$40 to US$1. The high international sugar price in 1963 permitted the company to earn a large amount of foreign exchange. Making use of this abundance of foreign exchange, the government finally abolished the system of ESCs and a direct exchange settlement system took its place. The economy was ready for an external drive as the foreign exchange instrument became rationalized.

In the beginning of the fifties, the price ratio of import substitutes to export goods went up appreciably. The relative prices of cotton textiles and rice rose dramatically from 2:1 in 1949–50 to 4–5:1 in 1951–52 (Lee 1971). This change was of particular significance. Rice was Taiwan's main agricultural product and an export product, while textiles were important imports at that time. Import substitution of textile goods, therefore, received full official support (Lin 1973), while the primary-product-exporting sector, which was discriminated against by official policy, bore the full burden of the import-substitution policy—as happened in all other developing countries during their import-substitution growth phase.

K. Y. Yin, then vice chairman of the Taiwan Production Board, emphasized "long-run" comparative advantage and organized a textile group to give full support to the expansion of cotton yarn fabric production by providing the necessary raw materials to manufacturing firms through allocation of imports and financing. Some export-promotion measures were enacted in the early fifties. In 1954, the government introduced a system of tax rebates that reimbursed import duties on raw materials. In 1956, it implemented a system that allowed a proportion of foreign exchange earnings to be used to import raw materials. Overvaluation of the local currency and the multiple exchange rate structure, however, still tended to favor import substitution.

Easy import substitution came to an end due to the limited domestic market and urgent need for foreign exchange earnings. By 1958, the investment climate was gloomy and more fundamental policy changes were needed. The strategy of development then turned toward export promotion.

Export Promotion Schemes: the Early Sixties

The policy was changed between 1956 and 1960. A growth target of 8 percent was set in the Third Four-Year Plan covering the period from 1961 to 1964, and the important "Nineteen-point Supporting Measures" were introduced. The essential elements of these measures were as follows:

1. A thorough review of earlier control measures, with a view to liberalization.
2. Preferential treatment for private business in the areas of taxes, foreign exchange, and financing.
3. Reform of the tax system and its administration to enhance capital formation.
4. Reform of the foreign exchange and trade systems in order to establish a unitary exchange rate, and liberalization of trade controls within the limits imposed by required payments.
5. Broadening of measures encouraging exports, improvement of procedures governing settlement of foreign exchange earned by exporters, and an increase in the number of contracts with foreign business organizations.

The Statute for Encouragement of Investment[1] also was enacted, mainly to facilitate the acquisition of plant sites and to provide tax exemptions and deductions. Its salient points were:

---

1. The Statute for Encouragement of Investment was amended 14 times: in 1965: January, June; 1967: June; 1970: June, August; 1973: March, December; 1974: December; 1977: December; 1978: December; 1979: January, July; 1980: August; 1982: August.

1. Income tax holiday: the strongest incentive was a five-year tax holiday set forth in Article 5, whereby a productive enterprise that conformed to the statute's criteria was exempted from income tax for a period of five consecutive years.
2. Business income tax: the maximum rate of income tax, including all forms of surtax payable by a productive enterprise, was limited to 18 percent of its total annual income, compared to 32.5 percent for ordinary profit-seeking enterprises.
3. Tax exemption for undistributed profit: the amount reinvested for productive purposes was deductible from taxable income.
4. Tax deduction for exports: within certain limits, the statute permitted a deduction from taxable income of 2 percent of annual export proceeds.
5. Stamp tax: this tax was either waived or reduced for a large number of enterprises.
6. Productive enterprises were allowed to set aside 7 percent of the unpaid balance of their foreign currency debts, calculated in local currency. This was regarded as profits before taxation and as a reserve against possible loss caused by exchange rate revisions.

The response of industry toward export expansion remained slow in the early sixties. In 1965, the situation changed drastically as, by then, the external drive went into full swing. The Kaohsiung Export Processing Zone was set up, within which no duties were imposed on imports. Development strategy at the time became entirely export-oriented as the import-substitution phase came to a definitive end.

The reduction of taxes as a result of the Statute for Encouragement of Investment and the tax and duty rebates for exportation amounted to a large proportion of the levies, as seen from table 1.3. In the externally oriented phase, the government recognized that private entrepreneurs had to play a much greater role than in the previous phase. The largest income tax reductions, in percentage terms, 25.2 percent and 23.4 percent, were realized in 1963 and 1967 respectively.

Similar in principle to the Kaohsiung Export Processing Zone was the tariff rebate system, through which producers of exported goods could acquire imported inputs at international prices; they were not saddled with import duties. This development represented still another step in linking the domestic market with the larger world market, helping Taiwan's natural-resources-deficient economy reap the full advantage of the international division of labor.

Table 1.3. Tax Reductions and Rebates (as percentage of the corresponding tax)

Fiscal Year[a]	Income Tax	Stamp Tax	Customs Duties	Commodity Tax	Total Rebate of the Four Taxes
1955			2.3	0.2	1.5
1956			4.2	0.3	2.6
1957			2.9	3.0	2.9
1958			6.6	2.8	5.1
1960			13.5	8.5	11.5
1961	2.4	25.3	14.5	12.5	11.9
1962	21.5	37.6	20.3	24.3	23.2
1963	25.2	16.5	21.6	13.0	19.0
1964	17.3	20.3	38.8	18.0	26.4
1965	17.2	20.3	31.0	21.2	24.5
1966	21.4	51.1	32.6	20.1	28.1
1967	23.4	49.7	40.5	22.0	32.2
1968	19.0	48.2	39.2	23.0	31.1
1969	14.6	45.4	36.4	18.7	26.6
1970	15.1	52.2	49.2	25.1	34.1

Source: Ministry of Finance (1982b), pp. 130–31, 134.
[a] Fiscal year 1958 runs July 1958–June 1959; fiscal year 1960 runs July 1959–June 1960, due to a change in the fiscal year system.

As the economy made the transition from import substitution to external orientation, it became more open and less isolated. Although the most important features of the tariff structure remained unchanged between 1961 and 1971, the nominal rate of protection changed appreciably. As can be seen in table 1.4, the nominal rate of protection for manufacturing, measured by a comparison of domestic prices for commodities with international prices (Kuo 1983), weighted by domestic sales, dropped from 0.535 in 1961 to 0.395 in 1966 and then to 0.300 in 1971, indicating a decisive tendency toward "openers."

The decrease between 1961 and 1966 was larger than that between 1966 and 1971. The nominal rates of protection weighted by exports were about the same by size. Weighted by imports, they were not only comparatively lower than those weighted by domestic sales or exports, but also illustrated a different tendency, decreasing more rapidly in the period from 1966 to 1971 than from 1961 to 1966. The high rate of protection in 1961 was mainly attributable to the high level of protection for food processing at that time.

Manufacturing products can be divided into four categories—export competing, export-import competing, import competing, and non-import

Table 1.4. Nominal Rate of Protection of Manufacturing (ratio of domestic prices to international prices−1)

Item	1961	1966	1971
Nominal rate of protection weighted by domestic sales			
Manufacturing (including food processing)	0.535	0.395	0.300
Manufacturing (excluding food processing)	0.384	0.309	0.285
Nominal rate of protection weighted by exports			
Manufacturing (including food processing)	0.563	0.391	0.360
Manufacturing (excluding food processing)	0.330	0.331	0.373
Nominal rate of protection weighted by imports			
Manufacturing (including food processing)	0.411	0.361	0.283
Manufacturing (excluding food processing)	0.416	0.368	0.288

Source: Kuo (1983).

competing.[2] The highest rate of protection was extended to export-competing industries, with export-import-competing industry ranked second, and non-import-competing industry third. The difference between the rate of protection for these four categories was large in 1961, but by 1971 it had been reduced considerably. The rate for export-competing industry was high in 1961 due to the high rates for monosodium glutamate and sugar, non-alcoholic beverages, and miscellaneous fabrics. Monosodium glutamate and sugar retained high rates throughout the period, although their shares in manufacturing decreased greatly. The rates of protection for nonalcoholic beverages and miscellaneous fabrics had decreased appreciably by 1971, causing a decrease in the average rate for this category. Thus, the changes in nominal rates of protection reflect the policy change from import substitution to export promotion in the sixties.

Financial Sources of Imports and Investment

During the period 1952–70, imports grew at an annual rate of 11.1 percent in real terms, with capital goods and raw materials constituting close to 90

2. The definitions of export competing, export-import competing, import competing, and nonimport competing are as follows: (1) export competing: the ratio of exports in domestic production is more than 10 percent, and the ratio of imports in domestic use is less than 10 percent; (2) export-import competing: the ratios of exports in domestic production and imports in domestic use are both more than 10 percent; (3) import competing: the ratio of exports in domestic production is less than 10 percent, and the ratio of imports in domestic use is more than 10 percent; (4) nonimport competing: the ratios of exports in domestic production and imports in domestic use are both less than 10 percent. All of these ratios are based on 1971 data.

percent of the total. Over the same period, investments grew at a 12.6 percent annual rate, raising the share of investments in the GNP from 15.4 percent in 1952 to 25.7 percent in 1970. This rapid growth of imports and investments, a necessary condition for speedy industrialization, was made possible by two basic factors—the availability of financing and the profitability of production.

As Paauw and Fei (1973) analyzed it, earnings from primary exports were an important financial source of imports. Exports of sugar and rice constituted more than two-thirds of total exports before 1958. Export earnings, however, were not able to generate all the funds needed for imports. As can be seen from table 1.5, the import share in the GNP far exceeded the export share in the fifties. There was a trade deficit every year before 1963. U.S. aid filled this gap, financing more than one-third of all imports in the fifties (see table 1.6).

Table 1.5. Shares of Exports, Imports and Trade Balance in Gross National Product (%)

Period	Exports	Imports	Trade Balance
1951–53	9.0	14.3	−5.3
1954–56	8.0	14.5	−6.5
1957–59	10.8	17.4	−6.6
1960–62	12.9	19.5	−6.6
1963–65	18.7	19.8	−1.1
1966–68	22.3	23.8	−1.5
1969–70	28.0	28.5	−0.5

Source: Directorate-General of Budget, Accounting and Statistics, Executive Yuan (1981b).

Table 1.6. Financial Sources of Imports (percentage distribution)

Period	Total	Exchange Settlement	U.S. Aid	Others
1952–54	100.0	54.2	43.4	2.4
1955–57	100.0	51.1	42.8	6.1
1958–60	100.0	57.7	33.8	8.5
1961–63	100.0	65.0	26.8	8.2
1964–66	100.0	82.4	9.1	8.5
1967–69	100.0	82.7	2.2	15.1
1970	100.0	92.4	0.0	7.6

Source: Council for Economic Planning and Development (1981).

Foreign capital flowed into Taiwan in the form of both direct foreign investment and foreign loans only after 1961. Its significance, however, was in the advancement of technology and expansion of foreign markets rather than as a financial source for imports, because the trade deficits were greatly reduced after 1964, due to a rapid increase in exports.

As a result of changes in the net terms of trade,[3] each year's (except for the base year) real national income was different from the net national product. The net terms of trade moved favorably in 1952–70, resulting in the economy earning more than its real exports. This can be seen from the gains due to changes in the terms of trade every year except 1959, 1960, and 1961 (see table 1.7). Gains or losses were closely linked to changes in the net terms of trade and the international sugar price, which fluctuated and was higher in 1957, 1963, and 1964. The unusually high price of sugar in 1964 made the net terms of trade most favorable, which gave the economy its greatest gain during the sixties. As the percentage of sugar exports decreased, however, going below 5 percent of exports in the later sixties, the effect of changes in the sugar price on the terms of trade declined. The gain in 1970 was due to a favorable change in manufactured exports, not in sugar prices.

From the fifties to the mid-sixties, a large part of the agricultural surplus accrued to the government in the form of a "hidden rice tax." The government instituted a rice-fertilizer barter system and a land tax payment in kind, paid at the government's purchasing price, which was far lower than the market price. The hidden rice tax exceeded the total income tax of the whole economy almost every year before 1963 (Kuo 1975a). This helped to make possible light taxation for the industrial sector, so as to generate high profits for entrepreneurs to use for further investment.

The domestic savings ratio began to exceed 10 percent of the GNP in the early sixties. Naturally, this higher savings rate constituted the main source of domestic investments in that decade. Thus, while export earnings and U.S. aid provided the majority of financing for imports and investments in the fifties domestic savings contributed a much larger portion in the sixties (see table 1.8).

---

3. Among many kinds of terms of trade, net terms of trade will be used here. Net terms of trade is expressed as the ratio of the unit value index of exports (p_x) to the unit value index of imports (p_m), i.e., p_x/p_m. An increase of the net barter terms of trade reflects a smaller increase in import prices than in export prices, which makes the volume of imports converted from an equivalent volume of exports larger than before. Because of the dominant share of sugar exports, the unit value index for exports was greatly affected by the change in the sugar price, and so were the net terms of trade, which moved closely with the index of sugar prices during 1951–66.

Table 1.7. Gain or Loss Due to Changes in the Terms of Trade (NT$ millions; %)

Year	Value of Exports X	Value of Imports M	Index of Export Sugar Price	Net Terms of Trade P_x/P_m	Gain or Loss due to Changes in the Terms of Trade $X\left(\dfrac{1}{P_m}-\dfrac{1}{P_x}\right)$ or $M\left(\dfrac{1}{P_m}-\dfrac{1}{P_x}\right)$ (in 1966 constant prices)
1951	1,170	1,696	n.a.	110.3	374
1952	1,345	2,278	228	110.2	427
1953	1,928	2,869	154	108.1	410
1954	1,587	3,263	161	104.6	172
1955	2,357	3,393	164	107.5	342
1956	2,886	4,901	161	107.1	345
1957	3,462	5,375	191	113.6	718
1958	4,549	7,633	154	101.7	107
1959	5,957	9,619	134	98.7	−92
1960	6,288	10,424	131	92.1	−620
1961	7,976	12,678	136	96.5	−308
1962	9,140	13,662	115	103.5	344
1963	13,870	14,418	245	117.3	2,196
1964	17,879	16,936	249	122.4	3,409
1965	18,401	22,115	117	101.0	195
1966	22,158	24,801	100	100.0	0
1967	27,445	30,993	107	103.4	896
1968	33,963	39,201	105	105.2	1,668
1969	44,043	47,518	136	106.3	2,537
1970	59,537	59,480	170	106.6	3,456

Source: Directorate-General of Budget, Accounting and Statistics, Executive Yuan (1981b); Taiwan Sugar Corporation (1981).

High Profitability of Production

High profitability in the period 1952–70 was an essential factor in inducing high rates of imports and investments. Although the real interest rate was high during this period, it was far exceeded by the rate of profits (table 1.9).

This high profitability was due to both demand and supply factors. From

Table 1.8. Domestic Savings, Investment, U.S. Aid, and Foreign Capital Inflow (%)

Period	Ratio of Net Domestic Savings to NNP	Ratio of Net Domestic Investment to NNP	Ratio of Domestic Savings to Domestic Investment	Ratio of Foreign Capital Inflow to Domestic Investment
1951–53	5.2	11.5	63.4	36.6
1954–56	4.3	12.3	57.5	42.5
1957–59	5.3	13.9	60.1	39.9
1960–62	7.7	16.1	65.2	34.8
1963–65	15.4	16.9	94.4	5.6
1966–68	19.6	21.8	93.1	6.9
1969–70	23.0	23.7	97.8	2.2

Source: Directorate-General of Budget, Accounting and Statistics, Executive Yuan (1981b).

Table 1.9. Rates of Profit in Manufacturing and Real Interest Rate (%)

Period	Rate of Profit	Real Interest Rate
1951–53	8.9	20.8
1954–56	16.2	11.3
1957–59	27.2	14.6
1960–62	27.9	11.5
1963–65	34.5	10.4
1966–68	32.5	8.0
1969–70	35.8	9.1

Source: Directorate-General of Budget, Accounting and Statistics, Executive Yuan (1981b); The Central Bank of China, Economic Research Department (December, 1956, 1961, 1966, and 1971); Directorate-General of Budget, Accounting and Statistics, Executive Yuan (1982a).

the demand side, it was attributable to worldwide prosperity in the fifties and particularly in the sixties. From the supply side, it was attributable to Taiwan's rapid transition from an agricultural to an industrial economy. In due course, the incentives offered by the government—tax holidays, tariff rebates—helped greatly to reduce production costs. Furthermore, labor utilization, technology, prices, and foreign exchange all developed in a direction encouraging increased competitiveness. Thus, the availability of funds together with high profitability spurred the rapid growth of imports and investments. This was a decisive factor in rapid industrialization.

Manpower Utilization

In the fifties and until 1964, Taiwan's unemployment rate was persistently above 6 percent. As a result, real wages did not rise significantly. The quality of labor was relatively high, since primary education was widespread and the workers were diligent. The pattern of decentralized industrialization made it possible to include in the labor force farmers who could work part time at other jobs and nonskilled workers who were able to commute from their homes. Particularly noteworthy was a substantial absorption of young female workers at very low opportunity costs. Thus, the availability of efficient labor at relatively low costs also contributed greatly to increased profitability in 1952–70.

Technical Progress

The rate of technical progress measures the rate of increase in output that is not caused by an increase in input, but by an advancement in the efficiency of production. Assessments by a Cobb-Douglas production function and CES production function both show that economic growth in Taiwan in the fifties was largely attributable to technical progress. According to the assessment by a Cobb-Douglas production function, technical progress explained approximately 50 percent of the growth of the nonagricultural sector in 1952–60 and 30 percent in 1961–70 (Kuo 1975b). An assessment by a CES production function also shows a large growth of labor productivity during 1952–70, although a much greater growth of labor productivity was observed in the fifties than in the 1960s (Kuo 1975b).

Thus, environmental, resource, and technological factors were essential to Taiwan's success. A change in economic policies provided an environment that was favorable to the full exercise of private entrepreneurial talent. The inflation of the fifties was brought under control.[4] The availability of funds and efficient labor was conducive to rational entrepreneurial calculation, resulting in high profits that induced further investment (see table 1.9).

---

4. The Taiwan economy suffered serious hyper-inflation right after World War II. Prices rose at an annual 5-fold rate in 1946–48 and then accelerated to about 30-fold in the first half of 1949. If inflation had continued to rise at the same rate, no industrialization or export expansion could have taken place. Inflation was successfully curbed in the fifties by the implementation of efficient anti-inflation policies, e.g., monetary reform and a high interest rate policy. The annual increase in prices dropped to 8.8 percent in 1952–60, and to 2.9 percent in the sixties.

Trading Partners, Commodity Content, and Comparative Advantage

Trading Partners

For historical and geographical reasons, Japan was the major trading partner at the start. In the early fifties, the shares of exports to and imports from Japan constituted respectively about one-half and one-third of total exports and imports. The share of exports to the United States in that period accounted for less than 10 percent of the total, while the share of imports from the United States reached close to 40 percent of the total in the fifties due to compulsory purchase in exchange for U.S. aid. As the economy grew, however, this trading pattern changed appreciably. The United States replaced Japan as the largest market after 1967. The share of exports to the United States gradually increased, to reach a peak of 41.7 percent in 1971. In response, the government policy in the seventies was to diversify markets.

The success of the diversification policy is shown by the reduction in average annual export growth rates to the United States, with a concomitant increase in growth rates of exports to Japan and to Europe and other destinations (table 1.10). This diversification of export markets transformed the export structure, as shown in table 1.11. Growth rates of imports, however, revealed a different pattern. Imports from the United States increased at an annual average rate of 12 percent in the sixties, and then climbed to 27.9 percent in the seventies. The growth rates of imports

Table 1.10. Growth Rate of Exports by Destination (in current prices; %)

Period	Total	U.S.A.	Japan	Europe	Others
1952–60	4.4	21.1	0.1	6.1	6.3
1961–70	25.3	33.2	16.0	28.5	23.9
1971–81	27.1	25.2	26.0	30.3	28.3
1961–81	26.8	30.0	20.8	29.8	26.7

Source: Ministry of Finance, Department of Statistics (August 1982a).

Table 1.11. Structure of Exports by Destination (%)

Year	U.S.A.	Japan	Europe	Others
1961	21.9	29.0	8.0	41.1
1971	41.7	11.9	9.9	36.5
1981	36.1	11.0	12.7	40.2

Source: See table 1.10.

Table 1.12. Growth Rate of Imports by Import Origin (in current prices; %)

Period	Total	U.S.A.	Japan	Europe	Others
1952–60	5.9	18.5	7.6	13.3	−7.8
1961–70	18.8	12.0	23.2	19.4	21.7
1971–81	27.7	27.9	21.8	25.9	35.4
1961–81	23.3	19.7	22.7	23.3	28.0

Source: See table 1.10.

from Japan decreased slightly and imports from Europe increased over the same period (table 1.12).

Commodity Content of Exports and Imports

The rapid growth of Taiwan's exports was led by manufacturing. Manufactured exports accounted for about 33 percent of total manufacturing production in 1980. Manufacturing development in Taiwan was characterized by product cycles in each of the leading industries, first food processing, then textiles, and then electrical machinery. As an extension of agriculture, the food processing industry was the most important manufacturing subindustry in the early period. In 1952, food processing constituted 44 percent of manufacturing production and 94 percent of manufacturing exports; however, in 1980 the share of production decreased to 12 percent, and the share of exports to 7 percent.

The textile industry expanded its share of exports from 1 percent to 25 percent over the same period. The most rapid expansion in both production and exports in the sixties, however, took place in electronics. Thus, in 1980 exports of textiles and electronics amounted to US$8.2 billion, constituting 50.4 percent of total exports.

The major markets for textiles and electrical machinery were the United States, Europe, Hong Kong, and Japan. Exports of textiles to these countries and areas constituted 63.7 percent of total textile exports in 1976 and 65.2 percent in 1980; and exports of electrical machinery to these four destinations constituted 78.8 percent of total electrical exports in 1976 and 67.5 percent in 1980. During this period, however, the U.S. market share was decreasing while Europe's share was increasing. The market shares of Hong Kong and Japan did not change significantly. For example, over the years 1976–80, the share of textile exports to the United States decreased from 33.3 percent to 31.5 percent, and exports of electrical machinery from 54.8 percent to 40.5 percent, while the share of textile exports to Europe increased from 10.9 percent to 12.4 percent, and of electrical machinery from 8.6 percent to 10.6 percent.

The expansion of the European market was the result of concerted efforts by the government and entrepreneurs to diversify markets, which was necessary for several reasons: a large trade surplus with the United States, too much concentration on the U.S. market, and more serious import restrictions than previously in the United States. For the expansion of trade to Europe, among other things, trade liaison offices were set up in several European countries where there had been none, and six European bank branches and two representative offices were established in Taipei between 1980 and 1982.

Taiwan mainly imported capital goods, particularly machinery and equipment, from Europe. The major imports from the United States were machinery and tools, chemicals and pharmaceuticals, transportation equipment, and agricultural products (soybeans, wheat, and raw cotton).

In the early period (1961–71) we can see a triangular trading structure in which Taiwan imported much of its needed producer goods from Japan while exporting its labor-intensive manufactures to the U.S. market. This triangle was modified in the period 1971–81, however; Taiwan's productive capacity advanced and made possible more exports to the European and Japanese markets, and the island also relied increasingly on the United States as a source of manufacturing and agricultural imports.

Import Content in Domestic Demand and Exports

Final demand (domestic final demand plus exports) incorporates two types of production input: domestic content and import content. The domestic content (i.e., the value added in the domestic economy) can be further divided into three components: labor earnings, capital earnings, and "indirect taxes"—assessable in the input-output approach.

Import content refers to the amount or proportion of imported intermediate goods that are required for the production of final demand for domestic use and export. Technically the "import content" coefficient is the portion of imported intermediate goods that is used in one dollar value of final demand. In an open economy like Taiwan's, with technological and natural resource deficiencies, it plays an instrumental role because imported materials and intermediate goods are important components in virtually all domestic production processes.

In this regard, we seek to study the magnitude and change over time of import content as classified separately for domestic final demand and exports, and as classified by industry. Conceptually, this calculation is based on the following equation system:

$$\left. \begin{array}{l} M^d = \hat{m}\,(I - A^d)^{-1}\,F^d \\ M^E = \hat{m}\,(I - A^d)^{-1}\,E \\ M^{E_k} = \hat{m}\,(I - A^d)^{-1}\,E_k \end{array} \right\} \quad (1.1)$$

where the symbols stand for:

M = the induced amount of import used for each source of final demand, column vector

m = the portion of imported intermediate goods used in one dollar value of production, i.e., the import coefficient, diagonal matrix

$(I - A^d)^{-1}$ = inverse matrix of domestic I-O coefficient

F^d = domestic final demand (including consumption and investment), column vector

d = domestic;   ^ = diagonal matrix

E = export

k = area or country of destination, e.g., US = United States

e = Europe

The results, shown in table 1.13, indicate that in 1961, 77 percent of imported intermediate goods were used in the production of domestic final demand, and only 23 percent were used for the production of exported goods and were thus re-exported. The latter figure increased steadily, however, to 22.9 percent (1961), 37.9 percent (1966), 47.4 percent (1971), and 63.0 percent (1976). Thus, as compared with the initial period (1961), the situation had changed drastically by 1976.

The share of import content in exports grew at a rapid rate primarily because of a high rate of export expansion. This rate of export expansion was possible only because of a swift increase in imported intermediate goods. Furthermore, with the new external orientation the economy came increasingly to rely on domestic labor to process imported intermediate goods for re-export. Here again we see the importance of imports. The opportunity to export was equally crucial because exports broadened the market to provide more productive opportunities, and at the same time earned the foreign exchange necessary for the import of materials and equipment needed for processing.

Comparative Advantage

In the early fifties, Taiwan had the characteristics of a typical labor-surplus economy as defined by Lewis (1954) and by Ranis and Fei (1961). It may, therefore, be safely assumed that Taiwan's comparative advantage, at least during those years, lay in labor-intensive rather than capital-intensive activities, although a country's comparative advantage is determined not only by factor endowment but also by many other conditions. If this assumption is correct, then the allocative efficiency of Taiwan's industrialization can be assessed, although only partially, in terms of the factor intensity of trade.

The factor intensity of imports and exports is calculated as follows:
For the estimation of factor intensity of exports, the formulas used are:

$$\left. \begin{array}{l} K = \hat{k}\,(I - A^d)^{-1}\,E \\ L = \hat{\ell}\,(I - A^d)^{-1}\,E \end{array} \right\} \qquad (1.2)$$

where k and ℓ are respectively capital coefficient and labor coefficient. A^d is the matrix of domestic input-output coefficients, and E, exports.

For the estimation of factor intensity of imports, the formulas used are:

$$\left. \begin{array}{l} K = \hat{k}\,(I - A^d - A^{cm})^{-1}\,M^{cm} \\ L = \hat{\ell}\,(I - A^d - A^{cm})^{-1}\,M^{cm} \end{array} \right\} \qquad (1.3)$$

where A^{cm} is the matrix of input-output coefficient of competitive imports,[5] and M^{cm} is the column vector of the amount of M_j^{cm} of competitive imports.

The total factor intensity in terms of K/L ratios shown in table 1.14 was obtained by dividing the corresponding K and L according to formulas (1.2) and (1.3).

As can be seen from table 1.14, the total capital intensity shows the following:

1. The total capital intensity of competitive imports was always higher than that of exports; Taiwan's exports required less capital per worker than did its import competing goods. This result supports the Heckscher-Ohlin theorem: a country exports goods that make intensive use of its relatively abundant factor of production. In the Republic of China, this was labor. The fact that Taiwan's exports were more labor-intensive than its import proved that development in Taiwan was in accord with its comparative advantage. Wontack Hong (1975) found a similar pattern in Korea.
2. Capital intensity of both exports and competitive imports increased during the period from 1961 to 1971. The rate of increase was higher in 1966–71 than in 1961–66.
3. It is interesting to note that the capital intensity of exports to developed countries was always lower than that to developing countries. In other words, more labor-intensive commodities were exported to the developed countries.

---

5. Competitive imports and noncompetitive imports are classified at commodity levels of four-digit I-O classification. If imports of a commodity exceeded 90 percent of the total domestic use in the past and will exceed 90 percent of total domestic use in a certain period of the future, they are classified as noncompetitive imports.

Table 1.13. Import Content in Domestic Final Demand and Exports (as percentage of total imports)

Year and Industry[a]	Import Content in Total Final Demand TF	Import Content in Domestic Final Demand F^d	Import Content in Total Exports E	Import Content in Exports to the U.S.A. E_{us}	Import Content in Exports to Japan E_j	Import Content in Exports to Other Asian Countries E_a	Import Content in Exports to Europe and Canada E_e	Import Content in Exports to Other Places E_o
1961								
A—sector	6.4	5.6	0.8	0.1	0.3	0.2	0.1	0.1
M—sector	83.1	62.8	20.3	4.5	1.6	10.9	2.1	1.2
S—sector	6.8	5.2	1.6	0.4	0.4	0.6	0.1	0.1
Others	3.7	3.5	0.2	0.03	0.1	0.1	0.01	0.01
All sectors	100.0	77.1	22.9	5.0	2.4	11.8	2.3	1.4

1966							
A—sector	3.0	2.5	0.5	0.1	0.2	0.1	0.1	0.03
M—sector	81.4	48.8	32.6	7.0	2.0	17.1	3.0	3.5
S—sector	12.9	8.4	4.5	1.0	1.0	1.6	0.5	0.4
Others	2.7	2.4	0.3	0.1	0.1	0.1	0.04	0.03
All sectors	100.0	62.1	37.9	8.2	3.3	18.9	3.6	4.0
1971								
A—sector	3.3	2.5	0.8	0.1	0.4	0.1	0.1	0.1
M—sector	87.7	43.6	44.1	18.9	3.5	11.7	5.7	4.3
S—sector	6.5	4.3	2.2	0.9	0.3	0.5	0.3	0.2
Others	2.5	2.2	0.3	0.1	0.04	0.1	0.1	0.03
All sectors	100.0	52.6	47.4	20.0	4.2	12.4	6.2	4.6
1976								
A—sector	2.1	1.5	0.6	0.1	0.3	0.1	0.1	0.01
M—sector	90.8	30.6	60.2	27.4	5.8	9.2	10.1	7.7
S—sector	4.8	3.0	1.8	0.7	0.3	0.3	0.3	0.2
Others	2.3	1.9	0.4	0.1	0.04	0.1	0.1	0.1
All sectors	100.0	37.0	63.0	28.3	6.4	9.7	10.6	8.0

Source: Calculation based on the Input/Output data consistently deflated to 1971 constant domestic prices.
[a] A, M, and S stand for agricultural, manufacturing, and services sectors of industry.

Table 1.14. Total Factor Intensity of Exports and Competitive Imports (Capital/Labor ratio including direct and indirect effects; NT$1,000/person)

Year	Total Factor Intensity (Capital/Labor Ratio)			
	Competitive Imports	Exports	Exports to Developed Countries	Exports to Developing Countries
1961	88.3	84.8	82.8	87.8
1966	98.9	88.5	80.2	100.7
1971	113.6	98.3	92.8	110.1

Source: See table 1.13.

Contribution of Export Expansion to Growth and Employment

What are the sources of growth that have propelled Taiwan's industrialization? How much have exports contributed to rapid growth? How many job opportunities have exports created? In order to deal with these questions, this section analyzes the sources of growth of value added and employment for the period 1956–76.[6]

Since value added (V) is the product of the value added ratio (v) and gross output (X) (i.e., since $V = vX$), we have:

$$\Delta V = v \cdot \Delta X + \Delta v \cdot X$$

Once the output increment (ΔX) is decomposed, the increment of value added (ΔV) can be decomposed as well. Since the level of employment (L) is the product of output (X) and the labor coefficient (ℓ) (i.e., since $L = \ell X$), we have:

$$\Delta L = \ell \cdot \Delta X + \Delta \ell \cdot X$$

Thus, the expansion of employment (ΔL) can be decomposed once ΔX is decomposed. The decomposition of ΔX is done in this study by a sources-of-demand expansion formula which is based on an input-output analysis (Kuo 1979a). Sources of output expansion are classified into four categories: domestic expansion, export expansion, import substitution, and those due to changes in input coefficients. Contributions of export expansion to economic growth in terms of expansions of output and employment will be reported in this section.

6. For this calculation, we use the input-output data deflated into consistent domestic constant prices. The measurements are done for 58 sectors, and observations are for the five years 1956, 1961, 1966, 1971, and 1976. Accordingly, the period of observation is 1956–76.

Economic Growth Due to Export Expansion

The Overall Economy. It is noteworthy that export expansion as a source of value-added expansion (ΔV) became increasingly important over the 20-year period under observation. In the early period, 1956–61, the contribution of export expansion to output expansion was 22.5 percent; it then rapidly increased to 35.0 percent in 1961–66, 45.9 percent in 1966–71, and 67.7 percent in 1971–76 (table 1.15). After the 1960s, export expansion was a decisive factor in rapid economic growth, and in the seventies its importance even outweighed domestic expansion. Economic growth due to import substitution was trivial, although it did register a slight contribution in the sixties.

Manufacturing Industries. It is of interest to examine closely the sources of output expansion of manufacturing, since it has been the leading industry. The subindustries of manufacturing are classified two ways—by trade patterns and by contribution to export growth.

The Four Groups. The classifications by trade patterns are divided into four groups: Export Competing, Export-Import Competing, Import Competing, and Nonimport Competing.[7] The following results can be observed from table 1.16:

1. The contribution of export expansion was greatest in the export-competing category throughout the whole period, 1956–76. Export expansion in the export-import-competing and import-competing categories was also very high. This result indicates that there was a close relationship between exports and imports in Taiwan; Taiwan's economy was highly processing-oriented.
2. The contribution of export expansion increased rapidly over time for each category, illustrating Taiwan's increasing dependence on exports.
3. The contribution of export expansion increased tremendously in the latest (1971–76) period relative to the earliest (1956–61) period. If we examine the results separately for each sector, we find them increasing by the following multiples: 2.1 (export competing), 3.1 (export-import competing), 3.5 (import competing), and 5.8 (nonimport competing times respectively. Thus, while the export-competing sector obviously became more sensitive to export expansion in the later period, the rest of manufacturing

---

7. See note 2.

Table 1.15. Relative Contribution of Various Sources to Output Expansion (%)

Period	Output Expansion due to Domestic Expansion	Output Expansion due to Export Expansion	Output Expansion due to Import Substitution	Output Expansion due to Changes in I-O Coefficient
1956–61	61.6	22.5	7.7	8.2
1961–66	63.2	35.0	0.5	1.3
1966–71	51.4	45.9	5.7	−3.0
1971–76	34.7	67.7	−2.4	n.a.

Source: Calculation based on the Input/Output data consistently deflated to 1971 constant domestic prices.

Notes: Calculated from 1971 constant domestic price I/O data of the 58 sectors for 1956, 1961, 1966, 1971, and 1976. All estimates of total contributions are arithmetical averages of the estimates derived by Laspeyres and Paasche versions. The estimates for 1961–71 in tables 1.16 and 1.17 are obtained by the chain measures of decomposition for the two periods, 1961–66 and 1966–71.

Table 1.16. Sources of Manufacturing Output Growth (classified by trade pattern; %)

Period and Category	Domestic Demand Expansion	Export Expansion	Import Substitution	Change in I-O Coefficients
1956–61				
Export competing	50.4	43.0	2.5	4.1
Export-import competing	46.2	24.3	23.4	6.1
Import competing	43.9	23.2	29.2	3.7
Nonimport competing	92.5	3.4	1.1	3.0
Manufacturing total	44.3	36.3	13.2	6.2
1961–71				
Export competing	35.6	67.1	1.6	−4.3
Export-import competing	38.4	53.1	4.8	3.7
Import competing	37.3	36.0	17.7	9.0
Nonimport competing	91.0	13.9	1.4	−6.3
Manufacturing total	36.9	51.5	7.6	4.0
1971–76				
Export competing	11.2	91.0	−2.2	n.a.
Export-import competing	23.9	76.3	−0.2	n.a.
Import competing	10.3	81.4	8.3	n.a.
Nonimport competing	82.1	19.6	−1.7	n.a.
Manufacturing total	19.8	80.6	−0.4	n.a.

Source and Notes: See table 1.15.

achieved gains in this external sensitivity at an even faster rate. In fact, the nonimport-competing sector gained at the highest rate.
4. A significant contribution made by import substitution was observed for the import-competing and export-import-competing categories in the first period. Although the contribution by import substitution in the import-competing category has been decreasing, it has always been positive.

Decomposition by Contribution to Export Expansion for Seven Manufacturing Categories. The classification in table 1.17 contains seven cate-

Table 1.17. Sources of Manufacturing Output Growth
(in percentages by industry group)

Period and Category	Domestic Demand Expansion	Export Expansion	Import Substitution	Change in I-O Coefficients
1956–61				
Food processing	40.9	54.0	4.6	0.5
Textiles	56.0	37.4	0.6	6.0
Steel, iron, & their products	3.8	41.4	41.9	12.9
Electrical machinery	54.5	23.4	21.5	0.6
Machinery	67.3	17.6	13.0	2.1
Intermediate goods	34.7	28.4	27.9	9.0
Final goods	62.5	17.3	8.0	12.2
Manufacturing	44.3	36.3	13.2	6.2
1961–71				
Food processing	65.9	28.0	2.0	4.1
Textiles	24.4	64.7	8.0	2.9
Steel, iron, & their products	43.1	49.6	10.9	−3.6
Electrical machinery	24.7	65.3	7.2	2.8
Machinery	54.7	30.8	9.0	5.5
Intermediate goods	43.1	42.1	8.1	6.7
Final goods	24.9	60.6	8.9	5.6
Manufacturing	36.9	51.5	7.6	4.0
1971–76				
Food processing	65.9	37.7	−3.6	n.a.
Textiles	−12.2	103.8	8.4	n.a.
Steel, iron, & their products	27.8	66.1	6.1	n.a.
Electrical machinery	16.7	82.8	0.5	n.a.
Machinery	52.0	58.5	−10.5	n.a.
Intermediate goods	57.0	57.2	−14.2	n.a.
Final goods	12.4	89.0	−1.4	n.a.
Manufacturing	19.8	80.6	−0.4	n.a.

Source: See table 1.15.

gories that add up to the manufacturing total. Interesting observable results are as follows:

1. The greatest export-expansion contribution was made by the food-processing industry in the first period, 1956–61. However, it shifted to textiles in 1961–71, and exceeded 100 percent in 1971–76. A closer inspection of this column indicates that of all industries at the present time, the textile industry is most sensitive to variations in external demand, while food processing has become the least sensitive (reversing its earlier external sensitivity). The sensitivity to variations in external demand of all industries should be examined in the same light.
2. The increase in the contribution of export expansion to electrical machinery was very significant, as it also was to final goods.
3. In the import-substitution period 1956–61, a large share of import substitution is observed in the categories of steel, iron, and their products; intermediate goods; and electrical machinery. The degree of contribution of import substitution, however, has been decreasing even in these industries. Particularly for the categories of machinery and intermediate goods, a negative import substitution was observed in 1971–76. This seems to indicate that the rate of secondary import substitution was not rapid enough to meet increasing requirements in the seventies.

Employment Expansion due to Export Expansion

One of the most important features of the Republic of China's economic development is the achievement of full employment in 1971. Employment data in an I-O classification are available only after 1961, and rapid labor absorption also occurred after that year. Therefore, the decomposition of employment growth will be carried out only for 1961–76.

Creation of Job Opportunities—Employment Expansion. In the period 1961–76, employment in Taiwan increased by 2.3 million persons, which is equivalent to 60 percent of the 1961 employment. The creation of job opportunities is closely connected with two essential factors—an advancement of labor productivity and an expansion of output markets. In production of a given quantity, an advancement in labor productivity will reduce the number of workers required. On the other hand, if labor productivity is kept unchanged, an expansion of output markets will, by increasing production opportunities, create more job opportunities. Therefore, the number of job opportunities a society can really create is actually dependent on the algebraic sum of the above two elements: the number reduced by the advancement of labor productivity and the number increased by market expansion. At the same time, we know that an expansion of production opportunities is caused by (1) expansion of domestic demand, (2) expansion of exports, (3) expansion due to import substitution, and (4) change due to change in I-O coefficients. An increase in these components will add to production opportunities and thus create job opportunities.

Causes of employment expansion are calculated in table 1.18. The actual increments of employment during the three periods 1961–66, 1966–71, and 1971–76 were, respectively, 377,000, 1,015,000, and 925,000. These increments were realized as the net results of employment expansion due to advancement in labor productivity and employment expansion due to output expansion. The table shows that the continuous advancement in labor productivity over the 15-year period produced a continuous labor release. During 1961–66, the advancement in labor productivity caused labor demand to decrease by 1,824,000 persons. The demand decrease in 1966–71 was 1,339,000 and that in 1971–76 was 1,681,000. It is obvious that if production opportunities had not been able to expand, the advancement of labor productivity would have carried large unemployment in its wake.

The increment of labor demand due to market expansion was crucial for employment expansion in all three periods. During 1961–66, market expansion (including domestic expansion, export expansion, import substitution, and change in I-O coefficients) caused labor demand to increase by

Table 1.18. Causes of Employment Expansion: An Aggregate Observation, 1961–76

Period	Actual Increment of Employment	Employment Release due to Advancement in Labor Productivity (If output did not expand)	Employment Expansion due to Output Expansion (If labor productivity did not increase)
	Increase in Employment (1,000 persons)		
1961–66	377	−1,824	2,201
1966–71	1,015	−1,339	2,354
1971–76	925	−1,681	2,606
	Increase in Employment as Percentage of Total Increase		
1961–66	100	−484	584
1966–71	100	−132	232
1971–76	100	−182	282

Source: See table 1.15.

2,201,000. The increase in labor demand due to market expansion was 2,354,000 in 1966–71, and 2,606,000 in 1971–76. It is evident that the additional job opportunities created by market expansion far exceeded the decrease in job opportunities caused by the advancement of productivity, thereby generating a net increase in employment.

How, then, was the market expanded? From table 1.19 we see that in the first period, domestic expansion and export expansion respectively explained 66 percent and 33 percent of the increment. The contribution to employment expansion made by domestic expansion was two times that made by export expansion in this early period. The contributions by import substitution and change in I-O coefficients were trivial. The importance of export expansion increased in the second period, and it increased further in the third period. The contribution to employment expansion by export expansion increased relatively in the second period. Thus, export expansion was the decisive factor in the economy's achievement of full employment in 1971. Furthermore, export expansion helped maintain this status after 1971. The increment of job opportunities due to export expansion in 1971–76 increased to 59 percent of employment expansion due to output expansion, a very significant portion, of which 45 percent was generated by export expansion to developed countries and the remaining 14 percent by export expansion to developing countries.

The advance in productivity, which tends to eliminate jobs, was most

Table 1.19. Causes of Employment Expansion: An Aggregate Observation, 1961–76

Period	Output Expansion	Domestic Expansion	Export Expansion	Exports to Developed Countries	Exports to Developing Countries	Import Substitution	Changes in I-O Coefficient
		Employment Expansion due to		Employment Expansion due to		Change in Employment due to	
		Employment (1,000 persons)					
1961–66	2,201	1,454	730	402	328	−10	27
1966–71	2,354	1,503	1,048	786	262	−21	−176
1971–76	2,606	1,185	1,533	1,172	361	−112	n.a.
		Employment as Percentage of Total					
1961–66	100	66	33	18	15	−1	2
			(100)	(55)	(45)		
1966–71	100	64	45	34	11	−1	−8
			(100)	(75)	(25)		
1971–76	100	45	59	45	14	−4	n.a.
			(100)	(76)	(24)		

Source: See table 1.15.

rapid in manufacturing, so more jobs were lost for that reason in manufacturing than in other sectors throughout the period 1961–76. On the other hand, manufacturing also created the greatest number of job opportunities through export expansion. Particularly during the second and third periods, the increase in employment due to export expansion in manufacturing was large enough to make up 60 percent of total employment. Employment opportunities created by export expansion far exceeded reductions generated by advancement in productivity, leading to employment increases that both absorbed newcomers and drew in the originally unemployed labor force.

In short, the successful absorption of 2.3 million laborers over the past 15 years can be attributed solely to market expansion. In the seventies, particularly, the contribution of export expansion far exceeded the contribution of domestic expansion.

Labor Utilization by Export Business. We have considered how much export expansion contributed to "increases" in employment over given periods of time. Here, we want to examine how much labor was "used" in the export trade at specific times. Therefore, instead of calculating the increment of employment, the amount of labor utilization will be examined through the following equations:

$$\left.\begin{array}{l} L^d = \hat{\ell}\,(I - A^d)^{-1}\,F^d \\ L^E = \hat{\ell}\,(I - A^d)^{-1}\,E \\ L^{E_k} = \hat{\ell}\,(I - A^d)^{-1}\,E_k \end{array}\right\} \quad (1.4)$$

where the symbols stand for:

L = the number of laborers, column vector
ℓ = labor coefficient, diagonal matrix
$(I - A^d)^{-1}$ = inverse matrix of domestic I-O coefficient
F^d = domestic final demand (including consumption and investment), column vector
d = domestic; ^ = diagonal matrix
E = export
k = area or country of destination

The calculations were based on I-O tables of 58 sectors consistently recompiled for four years in constant domestic prices. The allocation of labor utilization is shown in table 1.20. In this table, "direct employment" refers to the direct utilization of labor excluding the indirect effect. "Total employment" refers to the sum of direct and indirect employment including the indirect effect. Accordingly, the ratio of total employment to direct employment measures the relative size of indirect employment induced by a particular sector.

Table 1.20. Labor Utilization, Direct and Indirect (1961–76)

Year	Labor Used by Total Final Demand	Labor Used by Domestic Final Demand	Labor Used by Total Exports	Labor Used by Exports to Developed Countries	Labor Used by Exports to Developing Countries
	Employment (1,000 persons)				
1961					
Direct & indirect employment	3,353	2,953	400	238	162
Direct employment	1,920	1,739	181	105	76
1966					
Direct & indirect employment	3,731	2,969	762	454	308
Direct employment	2,150	1,761	389	240	149
1971					
Direct & indirect employment	4,746	3,523	1,223	836	387
Direct employment	2,923	2,241	682	489	193
1976					
Direct & indirect employment	5,670	3,746	1,924	1,385	539
Direct employment	3,492	2,437	1,055	771	284
	Percentage of Direct and Indirect Employment in Total Employment of the Economy				
1961	100.0	88.1	11.9	7.1	4.8
1966	100.0	79.6	20.4	12.2	8.2
1971	100.0	74.2	25.8	17.6	8.2
1976	100.0	66.0	34.0	24.5	9.5

Source: See table 1.15.

The characteristics of the allocation of labor utilization are as follows:

1. The labor force has been significantly utilized in export producing and related business. The number so employed was 400,000 in 1961, constituting 11.9 percent of that year's employment; it increased to 1,924,000, constituting 34.0 percent, in 1976. In other words, in 1976, export business provided 34 percent of employment opportunities.
2. The indirect effect of the production of export goods has been larger than that of domestic goods. In particular, the production of exports to developing countries came to have a greater indirect effect after 1966.

Table 1.21 is a more disaggregated presentation of the data in table 1.20. It depicts the allocation of labor utilization in the agricultural, manufacturing, and service sectors. We note that in 1976, the export business provided 34 percent of employment opportunities; out of this, manufacturing exports utilized 18.2 percent of employment, and manufacturing exports to

Export Expansion in the Republic of China

Table 1.21. Allocation of Labor Utilization (1961–1976)

Year and Industry	Labor Used by Total Final Demand	Labor Used by Domestic Final Demand	Labor Used by Total Exports	Labor Used by Exports to Developed Countries	Labor Used by Exports to the U.S.A.	Labor Used by Exports to Developing Countries
1961						
Agriculture	47.3	42.4	4.9	3.4	1.0	1.5
Manufacturing	13.3	9.7	3.6	1.8	0.9	1.8
Services	39.4	36.0	3.4	1.9	0.7	1.5
Whole economy	100.0	88.1	11.9	7.1	2.6	4.8
1966						
Agriculture	44.0	35.9	8.1	6.1	1.4	2.0
Manufacturing	15.7	9.3	6.4	2.9	1.5	3.5
Services	40.3	34.4	5.9	3.2	1.2	2.7
Whole economy	100.0	79.6	20.4	12.2	4.1	8.2
1971						
Agriculture	35.7	29.3	6.4	4.7	1.1	1.7
Manufacturing	22.7	10.7	12.0	8.0	5.1	4.0
Services	41.6	34.2	7.4	4.9	2.9	2.5
Whole economy	100.0	74.2	25.8	17.6	9.1	8.2
1976						
Agriculture	29.6	24.3	5.3	4.3	1.0	1.0
Manufacturing	28.1	9.9	18.2	12.7	7.0	5.5
Services	42.3	31.8	10.5	7.5	4.0	3.0
Whole economy	100.0	66.0	34.0	24.5	12.0	9.5

Source: See table 1.15.

developed countries alone provided 12.7 percent. In economic theory, and especially in pure theory, services are often treated as "non-tradables." In reality however, services are also exported indirectly. For example, employment opportunities provided by exports of the service sector in 1976 reached as high as 10.5 percent of total employment. That is to say, in 1976, the export of services brought Taiwan's economy more than 600,000 job opportunities, out of which the sectors of transportation and warehousing, communications, wholesale and retail trade, and miscellaneous services provided employment opportunities of 100,000, 95,000, 291,000, and 133,000, respectively.

In sum, the achievement and maintenance of full employment in the Republic of China depends greatly on exports. These business concerns utilized 34 percent of total employment in 1976, of which the utilization of agricultural exports was 5.3 percent, manufacturing exports 18.2 percent, and services 10.5 percent. Quantified, they were 300,000, 1,030,000, and 600,000, respectively totalling 1,930,000 employment opportunities.

In the 1971–76 period, the labor force was rapidly absorbed into the industries that were more labor-intensive and less productive. This made possible the use of more unskilled labor while it also caused the wage rate for unskilled labor to rise more rapidly than that of skilled labor. The greater relative earnings of lower-income families can be in great measure attributed to the rapid absorption of labor at low opportunity costs. Thus, industrialization and export expansion have also brought in their wake significant welfare benefits: a higher per capita income, a higher employment rate, and a higher standard of living.

Some Specific Features of the Seventies

In this section we shall highlight some specific features of the seventies (1971–81). Both internal and external conditions gave this period unique characteristics. Internally, it was a period when the Taiwan economy entered a later phase of external-orientation growth as it became fully export conscious. A dominant observable phenomenon of this period was the emergence of an export surplus, which was due to Taiwan's economic maturity as well as to deliberate government policies that encouraged exports.

Externally, the Republic of China's economy was affected by two exogenous events originating from the outside world. First, the oil crises exacted a particularly heavy toll on Taiwan, which imported 98 percent of the oil used domestically. A drastic increase in the price of oil amounted to a corresponding worsening of Taiwan's terms of trade. The second exogenous event affecting the Republic of China was the stagflation in its major trading partners, the industrially advanced countries. Because of Taiwan's great sensitivity to external conditions, the slow growth and high inflation rate abroad could not help being transmitted to its economy. By comparison with the sixties, the seventies were characterized by a fluctuation in inflation rates that were in part imported because of the worldwide inflation, and in part due to the export surplus.

Inflation and Terms of Trade

The quadrupling of oil prices in November 1973 had a significant effect on the Taiwan economy, since 98 percent of the island's petroleum was imported. Prices rose 22.9 percent in 1973 and 40.6 percent in 1974 (table 1.22). In the meantime, the GNP growth rate dropped to 1.1 percent in 1974. This was quite a new experience for the Taiwan economy. Various drastic government measures were taken. In 1974 inflation was controlled and dropped to a negative 5.1 percent, and the economy recovered to register a 4.2 percent growth. Thereafter, the Taiwan economy enjoyed renewed rapid growth with stable prices. For the three post-oil-crisis

Table 1.22. Fluctuations of Growth and Inflation Rates (%)

		Rate of Inflation		
Year	GNP Growth	Wholesale Prices	Consumer Prices	GNP Deflator
1961–71[a]	10.2	1.6	2.9	3.6
1971	12.9	0.02	2.8	3.1
1972	13.3	4.5	3.0	5.8
1973	12.8	22.9	8.2	14.9
1974	1.1	40.6	47.5	32.3
1975	4.2	−5.1	5.2	2.3
1976	13.5	2.8	2.5	5.6
1977	9.9	2.8	7.0	6.2
1978	13.9	3.5	5.8	4.7
1979	8.1	13.8	9.8	11.3
1980	6.6	21.5	19.0	16.1
1981	5.0	7.6	16.3	12.0
1982	3.9	−0.2	3.0	3.9

Sources: Directorate-General of Budget, Accounting and Statistics, Executive Yuan (1981b); Directorate-General of Budget, Accounting and Statistics, Executive Yuan (1982a); and Directorate-General of Budget, Accounting and Statistics, Executive Yuan (1982b).
[a]Annual average.

years, 1976–78, the average growth rate was a high 12.4 percent, and inflation a low 3.0 percent. Taiwan enjoyed a prosperous and stable period before the second oil crisis. But the rise of oil prices in 1979 and 1980 again sent shocks through the island's economy. Prices rose at annual rates of 13.8 percent in 1979 and 21.5 percent in 1980. On the other hand, the growth rate declined to 8.1 percent in 1979 and 6.6 percent in 1980. Thus, the inflation rate during the second oil crisis was about half that of the first crisis, and the reduction in the growth rate also was smaller. No widespread and drastic government measures were adopted at this time; only small monetary steps were taken. The economy adjusted itself gradually in the environment of tighter money. In 1981 the inflation rate was brought down to 7.6 percent; but the growth rate was not very high—5.0 percent. Although the recorded growth rate for 1982 was only 3.8 percent, the inflation rate became negative in June of that year.

The crux of the oil crises lay in the high price of petroleum, which not only increased costs of production but also resulted in a huge loss of real national income through adverse changes in the terms of trade. The loss due to unfavorable terms of trade in 1974 was 4.2 percent of the GNP (in 1971 prices), and the losses in 1979 and 1980 were equivalent to 2.4

Table 1.23. Major Items in Balance of Payments (US$ millions)

Year	Current Account Balance	Trade Balance	Basic Balance[a]	Overall Balance of Payments
1970	1	106	124	135
1971	173	292	262	254
1972	513	647	582	607
1973	566	734	764	610
1974	−1,113	−830	−726	−597
1975	−589	−255	−58	−149
1976	292	688	891	981
1977	920	1,177	1,269	1,132
1978	1,669	2,234	2,022	1,951
1979	241	1,408	724	96
1980	−965	147	241	−127
1981	497	1,970	1,336	1,299

Source: The Central Bank of China, Economic Research Department (January 1977; May 1981; and July 1982).

[a]Basic balance = current account balance + net direct investment + net long-term capital.

percent and 5.2 percent of the real GNP for each respective year in 1976 prices. The large outflow in the real GNP due to unfavorable terms of trade reduced demand for domestic commodities and imports. Thus, even if petroleum prices remain relatively stable in the near future, or if they decline, an efficient use of petroleum is still essential.

Trade Balance and Effective Exchange Rates

The Taiwan economy had favorable trade balances and favorable basic balances throughout the period 1970–81, except for 1974 and 1975 (table 1.23). One characteristic was that, in the four critical years of rapid monetary growth, the trade surpluses were particularly large in terms of their percentages of the GNP: 8.2 percent in 1972, 6.8 percent in 1973, 5.5 percent in 1977, and 8.3 percent in 1978. Such large trade surpluses not only created a vast pool of additional money, but also caused a large portion of domestic savings to flow out to foreign countries. Trade surpluses can be attributed to a superiority in export competitiveness. The competitiveness of exports is affected by two factors: relative prices and foreign exchange rates. Table 1.24 reviews these two factors in terms of purchasing power parity (PPP) and effective exchange rate (EER).

Purchasing power parity (PPP) measures the weighted average of the ratio of foreign prices to domestic prices. The year 1980 is used as the base because that year's trade balance and basic balance were both close to zero, i.e., equilibrium. When PPP is greater than 100, it means that foreign prices rise at a rate higher than domestic prices; when PPP is less than 100, it means that domestic prices rise at a higher rate. As can be seen from table 1.24, all figures for PPP were greater than 100 in the seventies, except in 1974, indicating that throughout the seventies, the inflation rate in Taiwan was lower than the aggregated inflation rates of Taiwan's trading partners. The relative price stability in 1970, 1971, 1972, and 1978 was particularly noteworthy. Another factor, the effective exchange rate (EER), is a weighted average of foreign exchange rates. For the same reason as that given above, 1980 is again used as the base year. An effective exchange rate greater than 100 means overvaluation of the domestic currency, while one less that 100 means undervaluation.

The change in the competitiveness of exports can be measured by EER/PPP, which is the real effective exchange rate. When the real effective exchange rate is greater than 100, competitiveness in that year is lower

Table 1.24. Purchasing Power Parity, Effective Exchange Rates, and Real Effective Exchange Rates (%)

Year	Purchasing Power Parity (PPP) Export Weighted	Purchasing Power Parity (PPP) Trade Weighted	Effective Exchange Rates (EER) Export Weighted	Effective Exchange Rates (EER) Trade Weighted	Real Effective Exchange Rates (EER/PPP) Export Weighted	Real Effective Exchange Rates (EER/PPP) Trade Weighted
1970	114.0	116.1	109.2	117.0	95.8	100.8
1971	116.1	118.1	103.9	113.2	89.5	95.9
1972	115.9	116.9	100.0	104.8	86.3	89.6
1973	107.3	108.1	101.0	103.1	94.1	95.4
1974	90.2	93.4	101.7	106.3	112.7	113.8
1975	103.3	105.1	102.9	106.5	99.6	101.3
1976	106.2	107.8	103.9	107.5	97.8	99.7
1977	108.5	109.6	101.3	103.2	93.4	94.2
1978	110.2	110.1	97.3	96.1	88.3	87.3
1979	106.8	106.2	99.6	99.1	93.3	93.3
1980	100.0	100.0	100.0	100.0	100.0	100.0
1981	100.4	99.4	100.1	99.3	99.7	99.9

Sources: International Monetary Fund (1982); Directorate-General of Budget, Accounting and Statistics, Executive Yuan (1981a); and Ministry of Finance, Department of Statistics (1981).

Notes: Export weights are based on the export value of the nine largest exporting countries in that year. Trade weights are based on trade value of the nine largest trading countries in that year.

than in the base year; when the real effective exchange rate is less than 100, competitiveness in that year is superior to that of the base year. From table 1.24 we know that whether we use exports or two-way trade as weights, the real effective exchange rates in the seventies were all less than 100—except in 1974, when prices skyrocketed. This shows that during the seventies, except for 1974, export competitiveness, in terms of relative price and foreign exchange rates combined, was favorable to exports when 1980 is used as the base year for comparison. We should also note that the real effective exchange rates in 1972 and 1978 were especially low, and generated large trade surpluses which in turn resulted in a great expansion of the money supply.

From the above observations, we know that Taiwan's economic environment immediately before the two oil crises was such that prices had been stable for some time, and that speedy export growth was creating a large physical demand on the one hand and inducing money supply growth on the other. Both oil crises occurred in this climate. Strong demand plus the available money supply easily absorbed the higher intermediate costs. The two periods of inflation in the seventies were thus caused by both demand-pull and cost-push.

The foreign exchange system was converted from a fixed system into a floating system in February 1979. Since then, the value of the New Taiwan dollar has fluctuated. The fluctuation has been very mild; during the period from February 1979 to June 1982, the New Taiwan dollar depreciated about 10 percent. The economic indicators did not reveal any obvious depreciation signals, for both current accounts and the basic balance were in surplus continuously over the six-year period of 1976–81. The real effective exchange rates were less than 100 (with 1980 as the base year) for the entire six-year period, indicating that in terms of the weighted foreign exchange rate, with the relative price change (domestic prices against foreign prices) taken into account, the value of the New Taiwan dollar was favorable for foreign trade during 1976–81.

In the coming years, the important goals in the foreign sector are the continuous expansion of exports and a net inflow of foreign capital. For continuous export expansion, the value of the New Taiwan dollar should be protected from overvaluation. The best way to do this is through import liberalization. Import liberalization is emphasized because it has an advantage for export expansion through its effects on cheaper acquisition of intermediate products and on the foreign exchange rate. A decrease in the trade surplus will make it easier to accept foreign capital inflow and direct foreign investment, which are important, among other things, for technical progress, structural change, and further export expansion.

Summary and Conclusions

Full employment, stable prices, and more equitable income distribution have characterized the rapid economic development of the Republic of China over the past three decades. Export expansion is considered to have been decisive to this achievement.

During the period 1952–70 Taiwan shifted from exporting mainly sugar and rice to exporting industrial products. Not only did exports and imports grow rapidly, but the commodity content of exports underwent swift diversification.

Successful trade expansion and structural changes in 1952–70 can be attributed to both environmental and resource factors. Changes in economic policies in the late fifties encouraged the full exercise of private entrepreneurial talent. The import-substitution strategy of the earlier fifties gave way to more liberalized externally oriented policies that allowed entrepreneurs to play a greater role in exploring the internal and especially the foreign markets. Export promotion schemes in the sixties were reflected in the enactment of the "Nineteen-point Supporting Measures" and the Statute for Encouragement of Investment, which offered various incentives: income tax holidays, tariff rebates, and reduction of the rate of protection. Also, the inflation of the fifties was brought under control. This change in the institutional environment was conducive to rational entrepreneurial calculation and efficiency.

Taiwan's capital and labor resources constituted the second factor that contributed to its success. A large portion of the funds for imports and investment came from exports of primary products (sugar and rice) and from U.S. aid in the early period. From the sixties on, however, investment funds were basically supported by domestic savings. During the course of this change, Taiwan instituted a "hidden rice tax" which created forced savings from the agricultural sector and made gains from favorable terms of trade derived from changes in the international sugar price. The availability of funds together with a high level of profits led to the rapid growth of imports and investments.

The quality of labor was relatively high in Taiwan. The decentralized industrialization pattern was favorable to efficient utilization of part-time farmers and commuting nonskilled workers. In particular, substantial numbers of young female workers were absorbed.

Originally, Japan was Taiwan's major trading partner. The United States replaced Japan as the largest market after 1967, however, which prompted a government policy to diversify markets in the seventies. As a result, the growth rates of exports to the United States declined and those to Japan,

Europe, and other destinations increased during that decade. Imports from the United States also increased.

The commodity content of exports reflected manufacturing product cycles of food processing, textiles, and subsequently electrical machinery. In the seventies, Taiwan's major markets for textiles and electrical machinery were the United States, Europe, Hong Kong, and Japan. During that decade, the market share of the United States for these exports decreased, Europe's share increased, and the market shares of Hong Kong and Japan changed very little. In the early period (1961–71) Taiwan developed a triangular trading structure in which it imported many of its needed producer goods from Japan while exporting its labor-intensive manufactures to the U.S. market. This triangle was modified in the period 1971–81; Taiwan's productive capacity advanced, allowing more exports to the European and Japanese markets. It also relied increasingly on the United States as a source of manufacturing and agricultural imports.

A calculation of factor intensity of competitive imports and exports based on input-output tables shows that the total capital intensity of competitive imports was higher than that of exports: Taiwan's exports required less capital per worker than did its import-competing goods. Because its exports were more labor-intensive than its import replacements, Taiwan's development proved to be in accord with its comparative advantage. Furthermore, a growing number of labor-intensive commodities were exported to the developed countries.

The share of import content in exports grew at a rapid rate, primarily because of a high rate of export expansion. A rapid rate of export expansion was possible only because of a rapid increase in imported intermediate goods. The economy became increasingly reliant on using domestic labor to process imported intermediate goods for re-export. Exports were crucial because they broadened the market and thus provided more productive opportunities and at the same time earned the requisite foreign exchange for the import of materials and equipment needed in processing.

The sources of output expansion may be classified into four categories—domestic expansion, export expansion, import substitution, and changes in I-O coefficients. In the early period, 1956–61, the contribution of export expansion to output expansion was 22.5 percent; it rapidly increased to 35.0 percent in 1961–66, 45.9 percent in 1966–71, and 67.7 percent in 1971–76. After the sixties, export expansion was decisive to rapid economic growth, and in the seventies its importance outweighed even domestic expansion. The role of import substitution in economic growth was negligible, although it did register a small contribution in the sixties.

In the 1961–76 period, the significance of export expansion to labor absorption has far exceeded that of domestic expansion. The achievement and maintenance of full employment in the Republic of China depends very much on production for export, which utilized 34 percent of total employment in 1976. In the latest period (1971–76), the labor force was rapidly absorbed into more labor-intensive and lower productivity industries; this made the use of more unskilled labor possible on the one hand, while it caused the wage rate of unskilled labor to go up at a higher rate than that of skilled labor on the other. The rapid absorption of labor at low opportunity costs contributed substantially to the rise in relative incomes of lower-income families.

During the seventies except for 1974, export competitiveness, measured as a combination of relative price and foreign exchange rates, was favorable to exports (using 1980 as the base year). Real effective exchange rates in 1972 and 1978 were especially low and generated large trade surpluses. In order to let foreign exchange rates move more freely, the foreign exchange system was converted from a fixed system into a floating system in 1979. Since then, import liberalization has been emphasized because it supports export expansion through reducing the costs of acquiring intermediate products, and stabilizing the foreign exchange rate. As the trade surplus decreases, it will become easier to accept foreign capital inflow and direct foreign investment, which are important, among other things, to technical progress, structural changes, and further export expansion.

References

The Central Bank of China, Economic Research Department. December, 1956, 1961, 1966, and 1971; January, 1977; May, 1981; and July, 1982. *Financial Statistics Monthly, Taiwan District, The Republic of China.*

Council for Economic Planning and Development, Executive Yuan. 1981. *Taiwan Statistical Data Book.* Taipei.

Directorate-General of Budget, Accounting and Statistics, Executive Yuan. 1981a. *Commodity-Price Statistics Monthly, Taiwan Area, the Republic of China* (December).

Directorate-General of Budget, Accounting and Statistics, Executive Yuan, 1981b. *National Income of the Republic of China.*

Directorate-General of Budget, Accounting and Statistics, Executive Yuan. 1982a. *Commodity-Price Statistics Monthly, Taiwan Area, the Republic of China* (November and June).

Directorate-General of Budget, Accounting and Statistics, Executive Yuan. 1982b. *Quarterly National Economic Trends, Taiwan Area, the Republic of China* (November).

Fei, John C. H., Gustav Ranis, and Shirley W. Y. Kuo. 1979. *Growth with Equity: The Taiwan Case.* London: Oxford University Press.

Hong, Wontack. 1975. "Capital Accumulation, Factor Substitution, and the Changing Factor Intensity of Trade: The Case of Korea (1966–1972)." Chapter 3 in Wontack Hong and Anne O. Krueger, eds, *Trade and Development in Korea*. Korea Development Institute.

International Monetary Fund. 1982. *International Financial Statistics Yearbook*. Washington, D.C.

Kuo, Shirley W. Y. 1970. *The Economic Structure of Taiwan, 1952–1969*. Taipei: Graduate Institute of Economics, National Taiwan University.

Kuo, Shirley W. Y. 1975a. "Effects of Land Reform, Agricultural Pricing Policy and Economic Growth in Multiple-Crop Diversification in Taiwan." *The Philippine Economic Journal* 14.27 (nos. 1 & 2, special issue on multiple-cropping in Asian development): 149–74.

Kuo, Shirley W. Y. 1975b. "Technical Change, Foreign Investment, and Growth in Taiwan's Manufacturing Industries, 1952–1970." In Shinichi Ichimura, ed., *The Economic Development of East and Southeast Asia*, 347–64. Honolulu: University Press of Hawaii.

Kuo, Shirley W. Y. 1983. *The Taiwan Economy in Transition*. Boulder, Colo.: Westview Press.

Lee, T. H. 1971. *Intersectoral Capital Flows in the Economic Development of Taiwan, 1895–1960*. Ithaca, N.Y.: Cornell University Press.

Lin, C. Y. 1973. *Industrialization in Taiwan, 1946–1972*. New York: Praeger Publishers.

Lewis, W. Arthur. 1954. "Economic Development with Unlimited Supplies of Labor." *The Manchester School of Economic and Social Studies* 22.2 (May): 139–91.

Ministry of Finance, Department of Statistics. 1982a. *Monthly Statistics of Exports and Imports, the Republic of China* (August).

Ministry of Finance, Department of Statistics, 1982b. *Yearbook of Financial Statistics of the Republic of China* (December).

Ministry of Finance, Department of Statistics. 1981. *Monthly Statistics of Exports and Imports, the Republic of China* (December).

Paauw, Douglas S., and John C. H. Fei. 1973. *The Transition in Open Dualistic Economies: Theory and Southeast Asian Experience*. New Haven: Yale University Press.

Ranis, Gustav, and John C. H. Fei. 1961. "A Theory of Economic Development." *American Economic Review* 51 (September).

Taiwan Sugar Corporation. 1981. *Managerial Analyses*.

Yeh, Ryh-Song. 1981. "Changes in the Economic Structure and Protection Policies (in Chinese)." In *Conference on Foreign Trade*. Taipei: Academia Sinica (August).

2 Direct Foreign Investment in Taiwan's Development
Gustav Ranis and Chi Schive

Introduction

The role of direct foreign investment (DFI) has been significant to the growth process in Taiwan, as the economy changed from that of a pre-World War II colony to its present status as one of the world's most successful cases of contemporary development. The exact significance of DFI remains one of the most controversial subjects in the development literature, partly because it has become a favorite North-South political football, with many observers more concerned with mounting emotionally laden attacks and defenses of the process than examining it dispassionately; partly because there are so many qualitative as well as quantitative dimensions that could be legitimately considered; and, most important, because it is conceptually as well as empirically extremely difficult to disentangle the contribution of this particular ingredient from that of so many others simultaneously at work within the total development broth.

We intend, therefore, not to aim, unrealistically, at any spuriously quantitative findings on precisely how much of the developmental success of Taiwan, in one dimension or another, can be laid at the doorstep of DFI. Instead, we shall have to be content with as objective an assessment as we can muster of the likely role this instrument played, in association with many other factors determining the economy's performance. While it seems clear that the role of DFI in the context of any particular economy cannot be assessed independently of the overall workings of the system, we must also guard against the temptation of simply retelling one more time the fascinating development story of Taiwan.[1]

The analysis of DFI in any particular societal context must clearly be sensitive both to the typological characteristics of the host (e.g., its size and

---

1. For one such effort see Walter Galenson, ed., *Economic Growth and Structural Change in Taiwan* (Ithaca, N.Y.: Cornell University Press, 1979).

resource endowment) and to historical time (i.e., DFI's possibly changing role in terms of the changing requirements of growth and the policies in place). Keeping one eye on the major controversy in the literature surrounding the costs and benefits of direct foreign investment, our basic premise, as we examine various dimensions of the problem, must be that it very much depends on the changing domestic resource and policy setting.

Direct foreign investment is not a blunt and homogeneous, but a complicated and finely differentiated, instrument. For example, investment focused on location-specific natural resources, such as oil and minerals, should be distinguished from the more footloose, manufacturing type based largely on imported raw materials. Within the latter category, domestic-market-oriented DFI may behave quite differently from the international-market or export-oriented types. Historically, natural-resources-linked DFI has generally tended to occur at an earlier stage in the development process, with domestic-market- and export-market-oriented manufacturing DFI following sequentially. Moreover, the relative "foreignness" of DFI, ranging from wholly owned subsidiaries through joint ventures to management contracts, is very much related to the process of domestic entrepreneurial maturation over various subphases of development and is relevant for any assessment of the contribution made.

Finally, a dimension of DFI which may be of special relevance to the various aspects of heterogeneity already cited is the country of origin. Geographical proximity, cultural relatedness, and source-country organizational/institutional features may make a difference. The modern theory of DFI stresses that a basic condition which must be satisfied for DFI flows to occur is that the foreign firm must have something special to offer which enables it to compete successfully with local firms which otherwise start out with the advantage of operating in familiar surroundings.[2] In the case of Taiwan, for example, it may, *ex ante*, seem useful to attempt to distinguish between "neighboring" DFI (i.e., mainly Overseas Chinese investments, entering rather competitive markets and constituting simple additions to domestic savings capacity) and the more traditional, more "distant" DFI, operating in increasingly noncompetitive markets emanating from the United States, Japan, and the West European countries.

The importance of natural-resources-linked DFI, for example, based mainly on initial endowment and geography, assumes a relatively unimportant role in the labor-surplus, natural-resources-poor East Asian type of less developed country, of which Taiwan is a prominent member. More

---

2. See, for example, J. H. Dunning, "Trade, Location of Economic Activity and the Multinational Enterprise: A Search for an Eclectic Approach," in *The International Allocation of Economic Activity*, ed. B. Ohlin et al. (New York 1977).

interesting is the analysis of the role of foreign investment in the footloose type of manufacturing-oriented DFI, where the size of the market, the supply of complementary domestic resources, and the policy framework each plays a major role in determining the contribution of foreign investment. This will itself change, presumably, from an early emphasis on helping to "get things done" via additions to scarce domestic capital, management, and entrepreneurial inputs, to providing a qualitatively different ingredient: access to specialized information and market channels within an increasingly noncompetitive setting. Broadly, this study will show that DFI itself should be seen as one particular form of foreign capital, relatively less important during the early postwar years than foreign aid and, once again, relatively less important than other forms of private foreign capital flows in the most recent period. But it also will show that DFI was of considerable quantitative importance to Taiwan, especially during the late sixties, and assumed growing qualitative significance, especially in the seventies and eighties.

Foreign Capital, DFI, and Transition Growth on Taiwan

While transition growth is a continuous historical process, a number of important subphases can be identified, between the epoch of colonial agrarianism, on the one hand, and the epoch of modern growth as described by Kuznets, on the other. Both the quantitative importance as well as the qualitative contribution of foreign capital, in general, and of DFI, in particular, are bound to change in the course of this transition. Briefly, during the colonial epoch, which for Taiwan is basically the period of Japanese control, we would expect relatively heavy emphasis on the exploitation of natural resources by the mother country, while in the post-independence era, industrialization can be expected to be the main focus of foreign investment. Finer demarcations become possible, depending on the particular combination of resource endowments and policy choices.

Capital Inflows in the Colonial Period

During the two centuries preceding its cession to Japan, Taiwan found itself in a typically agrarian situation, with population growth forcing expansion on the intensive margin in the Ricardian tradition. While some commercial exports, chiefly sugar and tea, had developed, traditional agriculture remained the dominant form of production.[3] In contrast, under the Japanese colonial administration, this agrarian quasi-equilibrium gave way to Taiwan's becoming a part of a mercantilist policy package, in which

---

3. For a detailed discussion of the precolonial and colonial periods see Samuel Ho, *Economic Development in Taiwan 1860–1970* (New Haven: Yale University Press, 1978).

one of the assigned roles of the colony was to produce a range of products required by Japan. Consequently, between 1895 and 1930 the colonial policies adopted were mainly focused on rice and sugar production, including the improvement of the agricultural infrastructure, a significant land reform, and the establishment of agricultural research institutes. As a direct result, exports of rice and sugar to Japan increased markedly, with Taiwan's share of total Japanese sugar imports, for example, increasing from 8.7 percent in 1903 to 81 percent in 1935.

This generally accepted view of Taiwan's economy under colonial rule, that of a principally agricultural appendix to the Japanese economy, is misleading in two important respects, however. First, although the traditional colonial exchange of rice and sugar for textiles and fertilizer represents the dominant flow, food processing on Taiwan, mostly in sugar refining but also in the processing of rice and pineapples, became increasingly important. By 1930, close to 20 percent of its national income was already being generated within industry, with food processing responsible for the lion's share, accounting for 75 percent of industrial output and 55 percent of industrial employment (HO 1978). The number of employees in all manufacturing and mining firms employing five or more persons had, in fact, increased from 24,600 in 1910 to 58,100 by 1930, an annual rate of increase of 4.4 percent (Mizoguchi 1979).

Much of this industrial expansion can be attributed to the particular technical conditions of sugar production, which strongly favor the location of large-scale refining facilities in close proximity to the supply of the raw material. Thus, food, drink, and tobacco processing accounted for more than 70 percent of total manufacturing output during this period, with sugar processing representing at least 60 percent (Lin 1973).

Furthermore, in the thirties Japan changed its colonial policies as it became remilitarized amid growing international tensions. This was accompanied by reevaluation of the strategic importance of Taiwan from a geopolitical point of view, leading to Japanese investments in such heavy industries as cement, chemicals, pulp, and paper, as well as in fertilizer, petroleum refining, and metallurgy. Manufacturing output, in fact, grew at 6.6 percent annually during the thirties. By the time of Japan's entry into World War II (1941), taking 1937 as an admittedly low base, the production index for metal and metal products, for example, stood at a remarkable 449 level, chemicals at 145, and textiles at 132. Employment in these activities doubled between 1930 and 1939, but food processing maintained its dominant position within total manufacturing.

Japanese DFI during the colonial period was defined as private, but was strongly encouraged by tariff protection and subsidies and viewed as part of colonial policy, providing substantial competitive advantages to the

Japanese capitalists relative to potential Taiwanese producers. In fact, prior to 1924 indigenous entrepreneurs were prevented from forming joint stock companies unless Japanese participation was assured; even after 1924 the selective maze of regulations and licensing procedures imposed by the colonial administration provided for the virtual exclusion of non-Japanese firms. Given this policy framework, we should not be surprised that, at the beginning of World War II, the bulk of large-scale industrial activity on the island was in Japanese hands (see table 2.1).

This combination of geographical factors and a heavy dose of Japanese colonial policies thus ensured that much of the industrial expansion of Taiwan during the colonial period was focused on sugar and rice processing and was financed by Japanese DFI. To the extent that Japanese investments deviated from the food-processing concentration typical of other colonial situations, it was related to the strategic considerations inherent in the thirties rearmament drive.

Capital Inflows during the Primary Import Substitution Subphase

A second subphase of development, almost invariably identified with the early post-independence policies of developing countries, is the well-known primary import-substitution (PIS) pattern, during which domestic industrialization, replacing previously imported nondurable consumer goods, becomes the focus of attention. In Taiwan, this phase was associated not only with political independence from Japan but also with the shock of substantial wartime destruction and the subsequent disruption occasioned

Table 2.1. The Role of Japanese Capital in Taiwanese Industry during the Colonial Period

Japanese Share of Paid-up Capital in All Companies[a]		
	1929	1941
Total paid-up capital value (T$ millions)	312	532
Japanese share (%)	76.3	91
Percentage of Factories Owned by Japanese Classified by Number of Employees[b]		
	1929	1939
5–49 employees	14.4	15.1
50–99	42.4	46.0
100–199	83.0	61.8
200+	85.2	96.5
All firms	18.2	18.4

[a]Chang (1980), pp. 49, 211–12.
[b]Mizoguchi and Yamamoto (1981).

by evacuation and severance from the Mainland. The severe runaway inflation of the late forties (price increases of 3400 percent in 1949 alone) was reined in (down to 9 percent by 1953) with the help of foreign aid inflows, and by 1951 the GNP had recovered its 1937 levels. The beginnings of independent transition growth via the PIS subphase on Taiwan is therefore generally dated as of 1952.

This subphase is customarily associated with policy changes differing markedly from the colonial period, all aimed at providing direct protection to a new indigenous industrial class and at transferring the proceeds from traditional export earnings, as well as domestic agricultural savings, to that class, either directly or indirectly.[4] Production in these rapidly growing PIS industries is bound to be costly and inefficient initially, with little chance for exports. In a small, natural-resources-poor country like Taiwan we can expect the overall scale of DFI in support of import-substituting industrialization to be modest in absolute terms, and certainly as a proportion of total capital inflows. Indeed, as is clear from table 2.2, during the decade of the fifties foreign capital mainly took the form of official concessional foreign aid, which was required to provide raw material imports so as to permit fuller utilization of existing industrial capacity. It also was needed to help overcome serious inflationary pressures in the context of a rather typical regime of extreme foreign exchange shortages.

The policy syndrome customarily deployed in this subphase is painfully familiar to observers of development; a mixture of protection, exchange controls, and import licensing, combined with substantial deficit financing, inflation, an increasingly overvalued exchange rate, and artificially low interest rates, all slated to assist the new industrial entrepreneurial class. However, by LDC standards, Taiwan experienced a relatively mild version of this PIS policy package, given the somewhat lower levels of effective protection of its industry, as well as the relatively shorter period during which the economy remained subject to this policy regime.

In any case, regardless of its severity and the efforts expended to prolong it, the PIS subphase must inevitably come to an end, once domestic markets for the nondurable consumer goods are saturated. This well-known phenomenon can be observed by the bottoming out of the proportion of the total supply of nondurable consumer goods still being imported, coupled with a decline in the growth rate of industrial output. At the micro level, it is indicated by a tendency toward excess capacity and increased competitiveness marked by falling prices and mounting pressures for cartelization and other government action. Between 1952 and 1957, the

---

4. The mechanism is through taxes and subsidies and/or overvalued exchange rates and artificially low interest rates.

Table 2.2. Foreign Capital Inflows: 1950s, 1960s, and 1970s[a] (US$ millions)

Period	Arrived DFI	Net Long-term Capital Inflow (excluding DFI)	Foreign Aid	Total	Total Foreign Capital as % of Total Investment
1952–60	41.5 (3.3)	188.0 (14.9)[a]	1028.5 (81.8)	1258.0 (100)	55.6
1961–70	241.6 (21.5)	430.3 (38.2)	453.7 (40.3)	1125.6 (100)	14.9
1971–80	940.0 (21.8)	3365.9 (78.2)[b]	0 (0)	4305.9 (100)	9.2

Sources: The Central Bank of China, *Balance of Payments*; Council of Economic Planning and Development (1983).
Note: Numbers in parentheses are percentages of total. Numbers may not add up exactly due to rounding.
[a]Not including actual data for 1953, 1954, and 1955, but estimated to provide a roughly comparable figure.
[b]Not including actual data for 1980, but estimated to provide a roughly comparable figure.

share of such consumer goods in total imports fell from 20 percent to 6.6 percent, indicating the rapid pace, the ultimate exhaustion, of primary import-substituting industrialization.

Capital Inflows during the Primary Export-Substitution Subphase

At the end of PIS, most developing countries are confronted with two choices: one is to continue import substitution, but now by shifting the manufacturing sector output mix towards durable consumer goods, capital goods, and the processing of raw materials, the so-called secondary import-substitution regime. The other is to attempt to shift the focus of industrial activity toward export markets, initially by exporting the nondurable consumer goods that previously were directed mainly toward the domestic market, a choice that we may label primary export substitution.

The majority of developing countries in Latin America and Asia have followed the first course, continuing to fuel industrial expansion by traditional raw material exports supplemented by foreign capital. Taiwan belongs to that small group of exceptions which shifted into a primary export-substitution pattern with the help of a substantial policy shift involving a general reduction of protection and a more market-oriented set of relative factor and commodity prices. The new path permits a gradually greater reliance on manufactured exports to replace the natural-resource-intensive exports of the earlier period; hence the export-substitution label.

The specific policy changes in Taiwan, popularly known as the 19 points, did not come over night, nor were they accomplished as part of an overall design or master plan. Nevertheless, looking back on it, we may note a formidable package of structural changes between 1959 and 1961, facilitated by the temporary ballooning of U.S. foreign assistance. Within a few years, the multiple exchange rate system was abolished; currency overvaluation, endemic in the controlled economy, was eliminated in the course of two consecutive devaluations. Import controls were gradually dismantled, inflation more or less brought under control, and tariffs on finished goods slowly brought down. Import tax rebates for industrial exports were established and gradually generalized; and a multifaceted package of fiscal incentives for both domestic and foreign investors was put in place. The aid flows provided Taiwan's policy makers with both psychological reassurance, in the face of such difficult decisions, and the necessary foreign exchange and counterpart domestic credit resources to tide them over a difficult period of adjustment.

In a relatively small country like Taiwan we would expect DFI to really become important only in the course of the new primary export substitution subphase of the sixties. As table 2.2 clearly indicates, this was, in fact, the case. Once the economy was safely on its export-substitution path, public capital from the outside could be phased out. In fact, negotiations for the termination of U.S. assistance began in the early sixties, leading to the virtual cessation of aid flows by the middle of the decade. As new official development assistance commitments came to an end and arrivals declined, it was DFI which increasingly took its place. (See table 2.2.) Unlike the primary import-substitution phase, when DFI may participate in exploring the domestic markets of large countries, its function now becomes increasingly one of providing information and access to international markets, and carrying increasing doses of foreign technology for purposes of assisting the industrial sector to achieve and maintain a competitive position in international markets.

In the initial export-substitution period in Taiwan, foreign capital inflow was mostly of the "sourcing" kind, focused on taking advantage of the large volume of cheap labor being released by agriculture in the course of a balanced intersectoral growth process. DFI provided an important augmentation of the domestic savings fund, as well as additional management, technology, and entrepreneurial capacity, basically as add-ons to the domestic industrial structure. Especially during the early or primary export-substitution subphase in the sixties, the preponderant contribution of DFI was in the labor-intensive light industries, such as textiles, as well as in electronic assembly based on value added, in the form of unskilled labor, to largely imported intermediate goods.

Capital Inflows during the Secondary Import- and Export-Substitution Subphase

Primary export substitution continued throughout the sixties, gradually giving way to secondary import and export substitution during the early seventies. By secondary import and export substitution we mean the slow shift, once the labor surplus had been exhausted, to more capital, skilled labor, and, ultimately, technology-intensive manufacturing industries. As the product mix changes with the march of the international product cycle, we may note two distinct shifts in Taiwan: (1), within DFI, a shift from pure sourcing investments to investments which focus on particular proprietary interests with an eye to both domestic and export markets; (2), especially during the late seventies and early eighties, a relative shift from DFI to other sources of foreign private capital—(portfolio capital, commercial bank loans, etc.). These figures demonstrate the culmination of the gradual displacement of foreign aid as the main source of capital inflows (82 percent in the fifties) by a combination of DFI and other long-term foreign capital in the latter half of the sixties and in the seventies. While DFI maintained its important absolute size and a respectable 22 percent share of a rapidly growing total in the seventies, it was now dwarfed by portfolio and longer-term capital movements. This resulted both from the gradual achievement of economic maturity and from the impact of the oil crisis, which led to petro-dollar recycling by commercial banks as an increasingly important phenomenon throughout the world.

Some Quantitative Dimensions of Foreign Capital Inflows and DFI during Transition Growth in Taiwan

The last column of table 2.2 indicates the initially large but rapidly declining importance of foreign capital as a proportion of Taiwan's total investment.[5] With respect to the overall quantitative contribution of DFI proper, table 2.3 shows the contribution of arrived DFI flows to both domestic private capital formation (column 2) as well as its specific contribution to manufacturing investment (column 6). Clearly the late sixties represented the heyday of DFI in this strictly quantitative sense, but its absolute importance continued to grow rather remarkably—along with the rest of the economy—during the seventies.

As far as DFI proper is concerned, the gradual shift from inward-looking, domestic-market-oriented foreign investment, participating—if in a minor way—in the primary import-substitution subphase, to export-oriented DFI, participating in a major way in the primary export-substitution subphase, was assisted not only by the aforementioned changes in the macroeconomic policy mix, but also by some specific institution building. What we are referring to here is the establishment of export processing zones and bonded factories, especially in the period after 1965. The export processing zones, or EPZs, were located in the port cities, with the more mobile bonded factories spread throughout the island. The purpose of the EPZs was the combination of a free port with the construction of standard plants complete with the necessary water, power, transport, and banking facilities, available for lease or purchase. The attraction was the easy application of various fiscal and investment incentives, via the one-stop avoidance of a cumbersome set of official procedures. It facilitated the routine importing of raw materials, the adding of value mainly in the form of unskilled labor, and the re-export of the more fully processed or finished goods, very often taking advantage of U.S. tariff code provisions 806 and 807.[6] More than 80 percent of the capital in EPZs was of the DFI type, its express purpose to facilitate the shift to a new mode of export-oriented manufacturing production, especially that based on imported raw materials. As we can see from table 2.4, however, while DFI

---

5. During the seventies, except for 1974 and 1975 (and again 1980), impacted by the two oil crises, Taiwan was, in fact, a net capital exporter in the balance of payments sense, that is, when the accumulation of foreign reserves is taken into account.

6. These provided that U.S. duty would be levied only on the value added abroad.

Table 2.3. Contribution of Direct Foreign Investment to Capital Formation: 1950s, 1960s, and 1970s (US$ millions)

Period	Arrived DFI (1)	Gross Domestic Private Capital Formation (2)	$\frac{(1)}{(2)} \cdot 100\%$ (3)	DFI Manufacturing Sector (4)	Part of (2) in Manufacturing Sector (5)	$\frac{(4)}{(5)} \cdot 100\%$ (6)
1952–60	41.45	1,065.3	3.89	32.11	290.4	11.06
1961–70	241.58	4,636.0	5.21	187.14	1,710.7	10.94
1971–80	940.0	33,315.5[a]	2.82	713.0[a]	12,210.1	5.84

Source: Council for Economic Planning and Development 1983.
[a] Estimated from 1972 survey data and assuming ratio stayed constant.

Table 2.4. Direct Foreign Investment in the Export Processing Zones

Period	(US$ millions) Total Arrived DFI[a]	(US$ millions) Arrived DFI in EPZ[b]	DFI in EPZs over Total Arrived DFI (%)	National	Overseas Chinese	U.S.A.	Japan	Europe	Others	Total
						\multicolumn{5}{c}{Sources of EPZ Capital Inflows(%)[c]}	
						\multicolumn{4}{c}{Non-Overseas Chinese}		
1966–70	143.0	32.7	22.87	19.94	20.59	19.58	31.50	8.38	0	59.46
1971–75	331.4	63.4	19.13	18.25	15.03	13.59	38.75	14.16	0.21	66.71
1976–80	608.6	95.9	15.76	16.87	9.97	13.65	41.22	14.59	5.36	74.82

Sources: Export Processing Zone Administration, *Export Processing Zone Essential Statistics*.
[a]Arrivals were calculated as the difference between the beginning and end of period capital stock.
[b]For 1966–70, the same DFI ownership structure in the EPZs as in 1975 was assumed.
[c]Sources of capital were calculated on the basis of end-period stock data.

in the export-processing zones grew substantially between the mid-sixties and 1980, its role relative to the total volume of direct foreign investment was never overwhelming, holding in the vicinity of 20 to 25 percent. Unfortunately, it is impossible to separate the bonded factories from the rest of the nonEPZ manufacturing activities for the entire period; but this form was clearly growing in importance.[7]

The export processing zones, tied into the countryside by a well-articulated internal transport network, permitted foreign investors to "reach out" to a very large catchment area of unskilled rural labor, with many members of rural families bicycling into the zones and returning to the rural households at night. The decentralized nature of most industrial activities, foreign and domestic, expanding in a balanced fashion with food-producing agriculture, permitted wages to remain relatively stable throughout the sixties and helped maintain a relatively strong international position for Taiwan's exports.

The dramatic increase in Taiwan's total industrial output, in its exports, and the even more startling shift in the composition of exports from agricultural to nonagricultural origin during the sixties has been fully documented elsewhere (Galenson 1979). The quantitative contribution of DFI to all this, however, while substantial, was by no means overwhelming. As we shall see, perhaps its major contribution has been in the qualitative domain. The EPZs were extremely helpful as a transitional device but still, as table 2.5 well illustrates, they made up no more than 6 to 8 percent of the country's total exports and manufacturing employment throughout the three decades under discussion. We should note, however, that bonded factories, embodying many of the EPZ features but dispersed throughout the island, represented an increasingly important share of total exports, especially of DFI related exports, and were heavily resorted to, especially by U.S. investors.[8]

The rapid growth of output and employment in Taiwan's increasingly export-oriented manufacturing industries brought an end to the labor surplus on the island by the end of the sixties. This is evidenced by the fact that real wages for female workers in textiles, which come closest to replicating an unskilled wage series, show more or less constancy in the sixties, and a marked rise in the seventies.[9] Higher unskilled wage rates,

---

7. It is interesting to note that the Japanese seemed to have a relative preference for EPZ investments, the United States for bonded factories.

8. In 1980, for example, more than 60 percent of total U.S. DFI exports emanated from bonded factories, compared to 25 percent for the Japanese. With respect to EPZ exports, the figures were reversed, 5 percent for the United States and 31 percent for the Japanese.

9. For a fuller discussion see Gustav Ranis, "Taiwan: Industrial Development," in *Economic Growth and Structural Change in Taiwan*, ed. Walter Galenson, (Ithaca, N.Y.: Cornell University Press, 1979).

Table 2.5. Share of Export Processing Zones in Total Exports, Imports, and Employment

Period	EPZ Exports (US$ millions)	% of Country's Total	EPZ Imports (US$ millions)	% of Country's Total	EPZ Employment[a] (1,000 persons)	% of Total Manufacturing Employment
1966–70	206.2	4.59	177.8	3.51	40.8	6.84
1971–75	1,779.6	8.69	1,156.0	5.49	66.1	5.30
1976–80	5,089.8	7.70	2,788.7	4.52	79.1	3.91

Sources: Export Processing Zone Administration Bureau, *Export Processing Zone Concentrates*.
[a] Data for the end of each period.

along with the continuing march of the Engel curve on the demand side, combined to yield a gradually more capital- and skill-intensive industrial output mix in the seventies as part of the rational use of resources. In other words, having first graduated from land-intensive output mixes in the fifties to unskilled-labor-intensive output mixes in the sixties, Taiwan now began to shift gradually to skill-technology and capital-intensive industries.

This process, a combination of secondary import and export substitution, constitutes a continuous move along the product cycle in response to continuing changes in endowment and demand patterns. In a small country we may expect an especially heavy emphasis on supply side changes in comparative advantage as well as a much shorter lag between secondary import and export substitution, mainly because of the relative narrowness of the domestic market.

The entire process of secondary import and export substitution is associated with the emergence of new consumer durable and producer goods industries with growing strength internationally, as manifested by their ability to compete successfully with foreign producers in domestic markets, and, subsequently, and usually quickly, taking them on in foreign markets. The phenomenon can be verified by the waves of industries moving into domestic production and then exports, described, for the Japanese historical case, as the "flying geese" pattern. Import substitution in these more sophisticated industries is thus almost always a prelude to export expansion, with the extent of the lag between the two very much a function of the importance of economies of scale. In a country like Taiwan, the wings of the flying geese are likely to be considerably shorter because of the relatively smaller size of domestic markets. DFI which is not fully aware of this restriction can become an expensive proposition, as in the case of motor car assembly in Taiwan.

In spite of the higher skill and capital intensity of the new industries of the seventies, and in spite of drastic shocks to the world economy from oil price increases, global recession, protectionism, and inflation, Taiwan's growth rate continued to be exceptionally high throughout the decade. The share of industry in national product, the share of exports in GDP, and the share of industrial exports in total exports all continued to show substantial increases.

The quantitative role of DFI in this context is well illustrated in table 2.6,[10] indicating that firms with DFI participation accounted for between 6 and 8 percent of value added, between 20 and 22 percent of exports, and approximately 16 percent of manufacturing employment. Weighting the "foreignness" of firms by the foreign ownership ratio we still obtain a

---

10. Unfortunately, reliable data on DFI arrivals are not available for earlier years.

Table 2.6. Contributions of Direct Foreign Investment to Growth and Employment

			Exports (US$ millions)			Employment (1,000 Persons)			
	Number of Firms (1)	Contribution to GNP (US$ millions) (2)	DFI Exports (3)	Exports Weighted by Foreign Ownership Ratio (4)	All Industries (5)	Manufacturing (6)	All Industries Weighted by Foreign Ownership Ratio (7)	Manufacturing Weighted by Foreign Ownership Ratio (8)
Foreign firms								
1975	749	917	1,140	n.a.	253	253	169	153
1977	747	1,492	1,961	1,386	298	288	189	183
1979	859	2,696	3,284	2,172	357	346	209	203
Country's total								
1975		14,401	5,302		5,521	1,501		
1977		19,490	9,348		5,952	1,735		
1979		32,337	16,092		6,424	2,101		
Foreign firms' share in country's total (%)								
1975		6.37	21.50	n.a.	4.58	16.86	3.06	10.19
1977		7.66	20.97	14.83	5.01	16.60	3.18	10.55
1979		8.34	20.40	13.49	5.55	16.47	3.25	9.66

Source: Ministry of Economic Affairs, Investment Commission, *An Analysis of the Operations and Economic Effects of Foreign Enterprises in Taiwan* (in Chinese), various issues.

contribution of 13 to 14 percent of total exports and 9 to 10 percent of manufacturing employment.[11]

The contribution of DFI to employment and exports varied substantially across industries. We can observe the heavy concentration of DFI in 1976 in electronics, textiles, and chemicals (see table 2.7), with traditionally labor-intensive industries like electronics, garments and footwear, rubber and rubber products, still contributing proportionately more to employment generation than textiles, which are beginning to shift toward the more capital-intensive synthetic-fibers-dominated output mixes. We can also observe that the relative dominance of DFI exports extends not only to labor-intensive electronics but to the capital-intensive chemical industry as well. But there is still a high rank-order correlation between relative labor intensities (implied by comparing columns 1 and 2) and the export/total sales ratio in column 5. The system is clearly in transition: DFI firms with a heavy domestic-market orientation, such as once important food processing, pulp and paper, and nonmetallic minerals, by now generally represent only trivial proportions of the total DFI presence on Taiwan. There are partial exceptions, such as (synthetic) textiles and chemicals, still at an early stage of their secondary import-/secondary export-substitution flying geese pattern. With the exception of chemicals, in one direction, and electronics, in the other, a comparison of columns 3 and 4 provides no surprises. For any real assessment of the role of direct foreign investment in the overall transition growth context, however, we must endeavor to go below the surface of these observations and try to ferret out the changing qualitative impact of this particular addition to the system's resources, an effort to which we now turn.

The Changing Anatomy of DFI on Taiwan

In this section we propose to examine more closely the qualitative contribution of DFI over time. While no very precise conclusions can be drawn, for reasons already stated, we hope at least to derive some strong circumstantial evidence on these matters from the changing sectoral allocation of DFI, from changes in the country of origin, as well as from what direct evidence we can muster on the differential behavior and impact of the investment itself over time. The general proposition we want to advance is that DFI is far from a homogeneous animal, and that its very heterogeneity over time gives evidence of a helpful responsiveness to the changing needs of the growing Taiwan economy. It is as difficult to assign

11. The weighting here is by the foreign/domestic equity-ownership ratio. Defining "foreign firms" as all those with *any* foreign capital participation undoubtedly overestimates the DFI impact, while the foreign capital participation weighted share probably underestimates it, since control does not relate to ownership in any linear or straightforward fashion.

Table 2.7. Direct Foreign Investment-Related Employment and Exports by Industry, 1976 (%)

Industry	Distribution of Foreign Firm Investment (1)	Distribution of Foreign Firm Employment (2)	Employment Share DFI/Total (3)	Export Share DFI/Total (4)	Exports/ Total Sales Ratios (5)	Average Foreign Ownership Ratio (6)
Food & beverage processing	3.03	2.41	5.72	6.24	25.00	51.64
Textiles	14.42	10.21	8.79	7.48	34.46	28.80
Garments & footwear	3.53	7.82	22.09	20.92	83.70	71.75
Lumber & bamboo products	2.17	1.91	5.62	19.30	69.05	75.68
Pulp paper & products	0.74	0.65	2.90	7.30	10.04	30.92
Leather & fur products	1.36	2.09	20.76	13.44	66.27	79.58
Plastic & rubber products	4.32	6.12	9.19	13.77	75.79	67.69
Chemicals	13.92	7.01	24.00	48.24	20.48	33.49
Nonmetallic minerals	2.73	3.21	11.54	9.28	7.45	12.48
Basic metals & metal products	5.39	4.23	8.76	11.36	42.67	55.59
Machinery equipment instruments	7.27	6.05	10.92	13.60	47.54	29.25
Electronics & electrical appliances	41.12	48.29	59.82	71.53	61.27	64.80
All manufacturing	100.00	100.00	17.60	20.07	46.06	42.42

Source: Ministry of Economic Affairs, Investment Commission, *An Analysis of the Operations and Economic Effects of Foreign Enterprises*, (in Chinese), various issues.

the role of "leading influence" versus "handmaiden" to DFI as it is to exports, but the timely and undoubtedly catalytic interaction with what was going on at the quantitative and macro level cannot be doubted.

Qualitative Dimensions of DFI: By Sector and by Country of Origin

Unfortunately, the breakdown of DFI by sectoral allocation and by country of origin is available on an arrivals basis only for the seventies. Thus, for the fifties and sixties we have to make do with government approved data, which tend to overstate totals, in addition to being subject to a substantial lag. However, an examination of the difference between approved and arrived data for the seventies indicates that no large errors are likely to be made in terms of the breakdown by sector of allocation or by country or origin.

Table 2.8 presents an overview of the changes in the allocation of DFI by sector as well as by country source over the three decades. We may note, first of all, as might be expected for the case of a small, relatively natural-resources-poor economy like Taiwan, that, taking the three decades as a whole, more than 90 percent of DFI was concentrated in the manufacturing sector. Second, it is clear that Overseas Chinese investment has been important from the outset and remains at between 30 and 37 percent of total DFI in Taiwan.[12] As early as September and October 1952 the new government on the island initiated regulations specifically encouraging the inflow of Overseas Chinese capital,[13] with a similar statute governing nonChinese foreign investors promulgated two years later. We should also note that the United States accounted for the major share, 62 percent of the total and 90 percent of the nonChinese DFI during the fifties, but that its predominance declined markedly in later decades, when Japanese and others, mostly European investors, began to play a larger role.

As far as the sectoral allocation of DFI is concerned, the Overseas Chinese initially invested 80 percent in construction and services, within which banking played a very important role, but over time they gradually shifted towards a relatively heavier emphasis on manufacturing, largely textiles. One may deduce from this, as well as from more direct evidence, that Overseas Chinese investors represented, in some respects, an extension of the domestic investor category, a closely "neighboring" type of foreign capital, which adds to scarce capital resources rather than having a particular special technological or marketing contribution to make. The virtual absence of non–Overseas Chinese DFI in construction and services

---

12. Overseas Chinese investors came mainly from Hong Kong, some from Japan, and some from other East and Southeast Asian countries.

13. During the fifties, Overseas Chinese investors were, for example, allowed to bring in import-controlled commodities as part of their initial capital.

Table 2.8. Approved Direct Foreign Investment by Source and by Sector: 1950s, 1960s, and 1970s (US$ millions; % in parentheses)

Sector	Overseas Chinese		U.S.A.		Japan		Others		Total	
1950s										
Primary	.8	(7.5)	0	(0)	.1	(4.0)	0	(0)	.1	(.3)
Manufacturing	8.1	(80.2)	18.8	(90.8)	2.3	(92.0)	.1	(100.0)	21.1	(91.0)
Construction and services	1.2	(12.2)	1.9	(9.2)	.1	(4.0)	0	(0)	2.0	(8.7)
Total	10.1	(100)	20.7	(100)	2.5	(100)	.1	(100)	23.2	(100)
[Share of DFI]	[30.3]		[62.2]		[7.5]		[.3]		[100]	
1960s										
Primary	4.2	(2.7)	.4	(.2)	0	(0)	1.0	(1.5)	1.4	(.5)
Manufacturing	65.2	(42.6)	193.2	(87.2)	82.3	(95.1)	63.5	(97.9)	239.0	(87.6)
Construction and services	83.6	(54.6)	27.8	(12.6)	4.3	(4.9)	.4	(.6)	32.5	(11.9)
Total	153.0	(100)	221.5	(100)	86.6	(100)	64.9	(100)	272.9	(100)
[Share of DFI]	[29.1]		[42.1]		[16.5]		[12.3]		[100]	
1970s										
Primary	8.0	(1.0)	.1	(0)	.2	(.1)	.1	(0)	.5	(0)
Manufacturing	459.0	(57.3)	475.0	(88.9)	347.2	(94.2)	419.0	(92.1)	1,241.1	(91.4)
Construction and services	334.6	(41.7)	58.9	(11.0)	21.2	(5.7)	35.7	(7.9)	115.9	(8.5)
Total	801.7	(100)	534.1	(100)	368.6	(100)	454.8	(100)	1,357.6	(100)
[Share of DFI]	[37.1]		[24.7]		[17.1]		[21.1]		[100]	

Source: Data before 1970 compiled on the basis of the primary data from the Investment Commission. Other data from Ministry of Economic Affairs (1980); and Liu (1971).

Direct Foreign Investment in Taiwan   105

Table 2.9. Export Ratios (exports/total sales) of Foreign and Domestic Firms by Industry, 1976 (%)

Industry	Foreign Firms Overseas Chinese	Foreign Firms Non-Overseas Chinese	All Foreign Firms	Domestic Firms
Food & beverage processing	38.12	17.68	25.00	33.12
Textiles	45.55	28.12	34.46	33.47
Garments & footwear	92.00	74.50	83.70	93.18
Lumber & bamboo products	61.69	77.24	69.05	94.47
Pulp paper & products	6.46	14.87	10.40	61.18
Leather & fur products	72.16	61.26	66.27	6.02
Plastic & rubber products	75.83	75.76	75.79	34.47
Chemicals	27.86	16.50	20.48	9.85
Nonmetallic minerals	4.55	12.47	7.45	14.50
Basic metals & metal products	60.26	40.68	42.67	14.76
Machinery equipment & instruments[a]	61.71	47.09	47.54	25.84
Electronics & electrical appliances	61.08	61.27	61.27	48.15
All manufacturing	38.57	48.18	46.06	33.90

Sources: Ministry of Economic Affairs, Investment Commission (1981); and Council for Economic Planning and Development (1980).

[a] Domestic production in the machinery industry does not include the repair subindustry data.

may be traced to early restrictions against branch banking by non-Chinese investors as well as to the fact that construction and public utilities were off limits to such foreigners unless they were willing to waive their foreign exchange settlement privileges. This is apparently the only area in which there was not completely equal treatment accorded to all foreign as well as domestic investors.

Qualitative Dimensions of DFI: Exports and Employment Creation

As we have already seen at the aggregative level, there can be little doubt that DFI, whether in the EPZs, in bonded factories, or elsewhere, was important for both export generation and job creation. As table 2.9 indicates rather clearly, however, it was more the characteristic of the particular industry than the ownership of the investment as between foreign and domestic which determined relative export orientation across industries. Moreover, while we might expect—and do find—the export orientation of DFI firms, especially in a small country, to be greater than that of domestic firms, the gap is not very pronounced.[14] To see the relationship between

14. Exceptions to the expected direction of differences, such as in pulp and paper, are based on special circumstances—for example, few firms and/or the overall small volume of exports.

the export and employment-generating functions of DFI both across and within industries, we can first weight each firm's employment by its export/sales ratio, giving us, on the assumption of identical technology, an indication of the extent to which its employment is associated with exports and with domestic sales. Summing these for each industry and dividing by the industry's total employment yields industry-level employment effects attributable to exports and domestic sales. If an industry's ratio of export-related employment to total employment is larger than the weighted average of exports over total sales, we may conclude that exports tend to create more jobs than production for domestic sale, or that firms hiring more labor per unit of sales tend to be more export-oriented. This is clearly indicated by the results of table 2.10. For total manufacturing, the ratio varies from 75.6 percent to 56.1 percent, while for the nonmetallic products industry alone, the gap is even larger, from 32.6 percent to 8.6 percent. A more disaggregated look at the data reveals that Overseas Chinese–invested cement firms were very much more local-market-oriented, lowering the average employment ratio, while a few of the nonOverseas Chinese DFI firms in the same category exported most of their output and used a relatively larger volume of labor.

The same data also permit us to calculate the number of employees per million dollars of DFI annual exports and of DFI domestic sales.[15] The results, shown in table 2.11, indicate that the overall employment effect per million dollars' worth of exports is 120 persons, compared to 67 persons per million dollars of domestic sales. In fact, except in the textile industry,[16] exports always create more employment than domestic sales; in the food and beverages, rubber and plastic products, nonmetallic products and machinery industries, the employment effect per million dollar of exports is about twice that of domestic sales.

To keep the contribution of DFI in perspective, however, we should really compare foreign and domestic firms whenever possible. This has been attempted in table 2.12, where we show the country's total exports in 1974 and 1980, and the proportion generated in DFI firms and in domestic firms. Except in electronics and electrical appliances and, to some extent, in chemicals, the preponderance of exports is generated by domestic firms, a situation which is quite different both from frequently held casual impressions about East Asia and from the actual situation in some other developing countries, such as Mexico. We might also note that, as between 1974 and 1980, the proportion of Taiwan's exports generated by domestic

15. Note again that we assume the use of the same technology in the production of goods for export and for domestic sale within given firms.
16. This is probably due to a difference in the output mix, as between cotton and synthetic materials.

Table 2.10. Direct Foreign Investment Employment in Relation to Export and Domestic Sales, 1975 (%)

Industry	All DFI — Export Ratio Weighted by Share in Employment	All DFI — Export Ratio Weighted by Share in Sales	Overseas Chinese DFI — Export Ratio Weighted by Share in Employment	Overseas Chinese DFI — Export Ratio Weighted by Share in Sales	Other DFI — Export Ratio Weighted by Share in Employment	Other DFI — Export Ratio Weighted by Share in Sales
Food & beverage processing	46.87	20.77	57.46	27.53	40.15	17.80
Textiles	75.51	77.61	78.62	78.26	73.08	77.35
Garments & footwear	97.38	96.84	98.11	98.27	96.60	95.38
Lumber & bamboo products	94.75	93.89	94.59	94.60	94.85	93.43
Pulp paper & products	22.90	16.69	22.88	12.01	22.93	20.54
Leather & fur products	99.99	99.96	0	0	99.99	99.93
Plastic & rubber products	94.42	85.29	92.95	88.16	95.11	84.45
Chemicals	54.70	43.17	72.14	71.53	37.96	29.10
Nonmetallic minerals	32.60	8.58	9.48	5.41	64.23	42.71
Basic metals & metal products	62.92	50.13	87.39	66.94	56.53	47.47
Machinery equipment & instruments	64.60	35.67	83.43	79.84	63.55	34.83
Electronics & electrical appliances	77.08	63.56	86.54	70.07	76.71	63.35
All manufacturing	75.57	56.09	78.61	50.01	74.74	57.96

Sources: Ministry of Economic Affairs, Investment Commission (1975); and Ministry of Economic Affairs, *Monthly Bulletin of Labor Statistics* (various issues).

Table 2.11. Number of People Employed per Million Dollars of Exports and per Domestic Sales of Foreign Firms, by Industry, 1975

Industry	Exports	Domestic Sales
Food & beverage processing	87.40	25.84
Textiles	77.14	86.64
Garments & footwear	184.68	152.38
Lumber & bamboo products	185.82	158.84
Pulp paper & products	112.86	76.00
Leather & leather products	264.10	42.01
Plastic & rubber products	197.98	68.02
Chemicals	57.76	36.48
Nonmetallic minerals	125.02	24.32
Basic metals & metal products	145.54	86.26
Machinery	120.08	36.48
Electronics & electrical appliances	126.92	65.74
All manufacturing	120.84	49.78

Source: Ministry of Economic Affairs, Investment Commission, 1975.

firms was not only high, but rising. One outstanding exception is textiles, which probably once again is related to a shift in the output and export mix toward synthetic fibers. The remarkable increase in the export contribution of domestic firms in the electronics and electrical appliances industry underlines the growing importance of secondary import- and export-substitution made possible by the growing levels of domestic ingenuity and capacity, especially in the production of increasingly sophisticated machinery, electronics equipment, and durable consumer goods. Thus, while the overall export-contribution percentages remain relatively constant over the six-year period, the industrial composition changes quite remarkably, in line with both the system's overall phasing experience and the march of the industrial product cycle.

Qualitative Dimensions of DFI:
Exports and Employment Relative to the Use of Capital

In assessing the relative contribution of DFI to exports and employment we should really examine performance in relation to the use of the system's scarcest input, presumably capital, over most of the period. Unfortunately, while we can examine performance across DFI industries and by country source, we do not have the requisite data for a full comparison with equivalent-sized domestic firms. Table 2.13 lists exports per unit of paid-up capital of foreign firms, by source, with the range of actual ownership ratios indicated explicitly. Since paid-up capital data admittedly have major weaknesses and industries differ markedly in the range of technol-

Table 2.12. Contribution to Exports of Foreign and Domestic Firms, by Industry and Source, 1974 and 1980

Industry	Total Exports (US$ millions)	% Foreign Firms Overseas Chinese	% Foreign Firms Non-Overseas Chinese	% Foreign Firms Total	% Domestic Firms
Food & beverage processing					
1974	636	3.53	2.34	5.87	94.13
1980	1,331	4.30	0.81	5.11	94.89
Textiles					
1974	586	5.74	5.53	11.27	88.73
1980	1,630	7.44	21.62	29.06	70.94
Garments & footwear					
1974	874	6.59	5.88	12.47	87.53
1980	2,844	2.25	3.41	5.66	94.34
Lumber & bamboo products					
1974	377	1.86	3.24	5.10	94.90
1980	1,120	1.42	1.30	2.72	97.28
Pulp paper & products					
1974	32	0.31	2.18	2.49	97.51
1980	149	2.73	1.81	4.54	95.46
Leather & leather products					
1974	132	6.39	2.67	9.06	90.94
1980	339	4.32	5.32	9.64	90.36
Plastic & rubber products					
1974	387	6.17	14.34	20.51	79.49
1980	1,770	3.24	8.33	11.57	88.43
Chemicals					
1974	149	15.00	21.41	36.41	63.59
1980	810	14.39	20.55	34.94	65.06
Nonmetallic minerals					
1974	67	19.67	6.15	25.82	74.18
1980	383	3.22	9.31	12.53	87.47
Machinery					
1974	419	0.67	7.85	8.52	91.48
1980	1,813	0.72	12.06	12.78	87.22
Basic metals & metal products					
1974	277	3.28	8.28	11.56	88.44
1980	1,257	1.92	9.98	11.90	88.10
Electronics & electrical appliances					
1974	997	1.93	68.75	70.68	29.32
1980	3,594	1.91	48.59	50.50	49.50
All manufacturing					
1974	4,933	4.46	19.22	23.67	76.33
1980	17,040	3.34	17.23	20.57	79.43

Source: Ministry of Economic Affairs, Investment Commission, *An Analysis of the Operations and Economic Effects of Foreign Enterprises in Taiwan*, various issues.

Table 2.13. Exports per Unit of Paid-up Capital by Foreign Ownership, by Industry and Source, 1975 (US$)

Industry	Overseas Chinese Firms X≥90%	90%>X ≥40%	40%>X	Total	Non-Overseas Chinese Firms X≥90%	90%>X ≥40%	40%>X	Total	All Foreign Firms X≥90%	90%>X ≥40%	40%>X	Total
Food & beverage processing	0	.44	2.32	1.32	1.82	1.55	1.53	1.57	0.52	1.34	2.28	1.46
Textiles	2.95	3.66	0.90	1.72	0	2.09	1.15	1.34	2.95	2.33	1.09	1.50
Garments & footwear	6.43	4.01	1.51	4.88	6.23	7.11	11.16	7.99	6.38	5.13	8.17	6.03
Lumber & bamboo products	4.62	1.18	0.63	3.14	5.97	4.06	1.82	2.97	5.03	2.71	1.73	3.04
Pulp paper & products	0.16	0.75	0.34	0.38	2.41	0.49	0.63	0.60	0.61	0.53	0.31	0.49
Leather & fur products	1.01	0	12.05	2.03	2.63	13.46	6.04	7.69	1.25	13.46	9.47	3.64
Plastic & rubber products	1.71	1.62	1.13	1.51	2.69	3.39	3.94	3.63	2.04	2.93	2.98	2.73
Chemicals	0.09	1.14	1.82	1.79	0.77	0.82	0.91	0.84	0.73	0.83	1.47	1.19
Nonmetallic minerals	0.55	0.12	0.20	0.19	0.08	1.16	2.09	0.92	0.19	0.63	0.23	0.29
Basic metals & metal products	2.12	2.14	1.11	1.82	1.67	1.29	0.51	1.14	1.79	1.33	0.59	1.22
Machinery equipment & instruments	0	2.55	0.16	1.95	3.71	0.45	0.03	1.49	3.71	0.59	0.03	1.51
Electronics & electrical appliances	1.75	6.79	1.20	1.91	5.12	1.82	0.75	3.19	5.03	1.93	0.81	3.11
All manufacturing	2.76	2.48	1.02	1.48	4.43	1.68	1.08	2.18	4.13	1.78	1.06	1.98

Source: Ministry of Economic Affairs, Investment Commission, An Analysis of Operations and Economic Effects of Foreign Enterprises in Taiwan, various issues.

Note: X denotes percentage of capital owned by foreigners.

ogy, conclusions based on such data should be treated with caution. Therefore, comparisons within industries are most likely to be useful here. It is interesting to note, in this context, that in 8 out of 12 industries there seems to be a positive relationship between the extent of participation of foreign capital and export intensity—although joint ventures with majority foreign ownership seem to do just as well as those approaching wholly owned subsidiary status.[17]

Table 2.13 also confirms the relatively high export intensity of certain labor-intensive industries, including garments and footwear, lumber and bamboo products, leather and fur products, as well as electronics and electrical appliances, as we would expect. Also, looking again at DFI across countries of origin, we see a general tendency for Overseas Chinese investors to be somewhat less externally oriented than non–Overseas Chinese investors taken as a whole. Furthermore, focusing especially on the U.S./Japanese comparison so frequently referred to in the literature (see table 2.14) we may note, in most industries, a somewhat higher export intensity per unit of capital for U.S. investors than for Japanese investors.

Turning to employment per unit of paid-up capital (tables 2.15 and 2.16), we get confirmation, first of all, that the highest labor intensities are almost invariably found in the industries which are also doing most of the exporting, those normally designated as nondurable consumer goods, plus electronics and electrical appliances. As expected, labor intensity, like export intensity, varies directly with the extent of foreign ownership. The propensity of Overseas Chinese investors to be somewhat more domestic-market-oriented means that they are also generally less labor intensive than other investors, showing the strength of the competitive forces of international trade. And in terms of the special pair-wise comparison between U.S. and Japanese DFI, we may note that overall, U.S. DFI appears to be only slightly less labor intensive than Japanese DFI. The extent of foreign versus local capital participation, however, seems to have a less marked impact on the choice of technology in the Japanese case.

We should not be surprised that foreign firms which export relatively more are also more job-intensive, because the motivation for the investment of DFI in Taiwan was initially related to the availability of low wage labor as the most important factor in providing international competitiveness via technology choices and the direction of technology change in both processes and products. Keeping in mind the fact that paid-up capital data are seriously deficient, we have also tried to assess capital/labor ratios

---

17. There seems to be some tendency, though we would not claim statistical significance, for the degree of foreign ownership to matter less in the more competitive industries such as garments, leather and fur products, and plastic and rubber products.

Table 2.14. Employment per Unit of Paid-up Capital of United States and Japanese Firms by Foreign Ownership and Industry, 1975 (US$)

Industry	United States Firms				Japanese Firms			
	$X \geq 90\%$	$90\% > X$ $\geq 40\%$	$40\% > X$	All DFI Firms	$X \geq 90\%$	$90\% > X$ $\geq 40\%$	$40\% > X$	All DFI Firms
Food & beverage processing	0.02			0.00		2.98		2.98
Textiles		7.34	1.11	1.11	8.63	2.09	1.20	1.61
Garments & footwear	13.42	1.26	14.70	14.17	4.48	7.49	4.59	7.14
Lumber & bamboo products		0.83		7.34	2.41	1.75	1.82	2.20
Pulp paper & products				0.83	2.37	0.12	0.63	0.41
Leather & fur products		8.87		8.87		19.42	6.04	7.05
Plastic & rubber products	0.42	0.43	6.72	1.90	2.69	5.07	6.04	4.65
Chemicals	0.43	0.69	0.29	0.59	1.94	0.11	1.04	0.89
Nonmetallic minerals		1.20		1.20		1.10	2.09	1.33
Basic metals & metal products	2.48	0.03	0.78	0.82	1.13	1.77	0.48	1.22
Machinery equipment & instruments	4.32		0.02	0.81	4.52	0.83	0.05	2.44
Electronics & electrical appliances	5.76	1.90	0.38	5.18	5.03	1.64	0.76	2.19
All manufacturing	5.06	0.84	1.26	2.44	4.51	2.00	0.99	1.98

Source: Ministry of Economic Affairs, Investment Commission, *An Analysis of Operations and Economic Effects of Foreign Enterprises in Taiwan,* various issues.

Note: X denotes percentage of capital owned by foreigners.

Table 2.15. Employment per Paid-up Capital by Foreign Ownership, by Industry and Source, 1975 (employees/US$ millions)

Industry	Overseas Chinese Firms X≥90%	Overseas Chinese Firms 90%≥X≥40%	Overseas Chinese Firms 40%>X	Overseas Chinese Firms All DFI Firms	Non-Overseas Chinese Firms X≥90%	Non-Overseas Chinese Firms 90%≥X≥40%	Non-Overseas Chinese Firms 40%>X	Non-Overseas Chinese Firms All DFI Firms	All Foreign Firms X≥90%	All Foreign Firms 90%≥X≥40%	All Foreign Firms 40%>X	All Foreign Firms All DFI Firms
Food & beverage processing	91	290	274	237	190	364	145	346	120	350	267	297
Textiles	450	396	196	274	1,724	160	93	113	450	197	118	153
Garments & footwear	1,343	658	446	940	1,815	1,216	1,778	1,492	1,437	861	1,364	1,143
Lumber & bamboo products	722	400	240	575	1,815	566	322	608	1,050	488	316	595
Pulp paper & products	339	277	247	282	385	202	600	224	348	214	237	241
Leather & fur products	573		2,470	750	401	2,629	1,369	1,489	547	2,629	1,997	959
Plastic & rubber products	555	420	303	436	511	626	1,232	675	540	573	620	574
Chemicals	290	201	167	169	93	81	102	90	104	83	142	118
Nonmetallic minerals	373	101	67	74	187	337	1,026	353	230	219	81	112
Basic metals & metal products	548	744	178	472	309	259	214	256	374	282	209	282
Machinery equipment & instruments		612	317	538	439	196	158	272	439	224	162	280
Electronics & electrical appliances	462	893	228	352	666	430	326	521	661	441	312	512
All manufacturing	636	420	154	261	598	292	198	337	605	309	179	316

Source: Ministry of Economic Affairs, Investment Commission, *An Analysis of Operations and Economic Effects of Foreign Enterprises in Taiwan*, various issues.

Note: X denotes percentage of capital owned by foreigners.

Table 2.16. Employment per Paid-up Capital of United States and Japanese Firms by Foreign Ownership and Industry, 1975 (employees/US$ millions)

Industry	United States Firms				Japanese Firms			
	X ≥ 90%	90% ≥ X ≥ 40%	40% > X	All DFI Firms	X ≥ 90%	90% ≥ X ≥ 40%	40% > X	All DFI Firms
Food & beverage processing	17	207		192		509		509
Textiles			74	74		160	114	135
Garments & footwear		1,310	2,211	2,146	1,846	1,305	974	1,314
Lumber & bamboo products	8,000	370		4,185	578	360	322	365
Pulp paper & products		199		199	385	204	600	246
Leather & fur products		4,167		4,167	175	820	1,367	878
Plastic & rubber products	90	175	1,232	421	475	879	1,233	815
Chemicals	76	70	78	72	101	212	107	129
Nonmetallic minerals		194		194		512	1,026	633
Basic metals & metal products	516	46	214	204	152	340	214	266
Machinery equipment & instruments	328		136	172	381	281	212	315
Electronics & electrical appliances	780	415	325	726	791	412	326	478
All manufacturing	696	179	153	345	656	361	220	349

Source: Ministry of Economic Affairs, Investment Commission, *An Analysis of Operations and Economic Effects of Foreign Enterprises in Taiwan*, various issues.

Note: X denotes percentage of capital owned by foreigners.

directly utilizing two sets of data, one for fixed assets, the other for machinery and equipment. In calculating the capital/labor ratios of foreign firms in each industry, we first divided firms into export- and domestically oriented firms according to their actual sales performance; then we summed each firm's capital data to obtain the industry's total, assuming that within any given company, products sold for exports and into the domestic market use identical technology. The results, which are not shown here, indicate, not very surprisingly, that, on the average, each employee in DFI firms focused mainly on exports was equipped with US$9,000 worth of fixed assets, with more than double the amount of fixed assets in firms focused on producing commodities for the local market. The export-oriented firms had lower capital/labor ratios than the domestically oriented firms throughout the sixties as well as the seventies, whether or not capital is measured in terms of fixed assets or in terms of machinery and equipment.[18] This result is consistent with the notion that export-oriented firms are exposed to greater competitive pressure, leading to the adoption of more labor-intensive processes and product mixes.

Looking across individual industries, we may note that fixed assets per worker in relation to domestic sales were at least twice as large as those related to exports in food and beverages, garments, plastic and rubber products, nonmetallic products, and the machinery industries, while in the electronics and electrical appliances industry the capital/labor ratio for exports was only 30 percent lower than that linked to local sales. Our general findings hold up if we measure capital alternatively in terms of machinery and equipment, with textiles and paper and paper products the only exceptions. The seemingly perverse result that foreign textile producers use more capital-intensive techniques in exports than in supplying domestic markets is consistent with the shift to synthetic fiber, especially by non–Overseas Chinese investors producing for export markets in recent years, and would undoubtedly disappear at a higher level of disaggregation.

It may be worthwhile to pay some additional special attention to the frequently discussed contrast between Japanese and U.S. DFI. The well-known Kojima thesis states that Japanese firms are more likely to be interested in competitive sourcing, and are therefore bound to be more labor-intensive and to concentrate in assembly, processing, and mainte-

---

18. These findings are also consistent with those of Liang, "Employment and Distribution Effects of Export Promotion in Taiwan," *Proceedings of Conference on Income Distribution in Taiwan*, (Taipei: Academia Sinica, 1978), where he found that the capital/labor ratio in 1971 in the export industries was NT$124,000 per employee, compared to NT$356,000 in import competing industries. Export industries were defined as exporting at least 10 percent of the total product. Similar results have been found in studies by Anne Krueger and others.

nance, while U.S. firms in the same industries are likely to be more interested in earning rents on their special "noncompetitive inputs" derived from trademarks, patents, market power, etc. (Kojima 1977). The Japanese, in fact, do seem to have been more labor-intensive in virtually every industry, with the exception of chemicals.[19] In exporting activities, workers in U.S. firms in 1975 were equipped with approximately US$7,700 worth of machinery and equipment as compared with US$2,300 in Japanese DFI firms. If we alter the definition of capital to include buildings and all other fixed assets, the relevant numbers become US$10,400 compared with US$6,800. If one looks at the activities in the domestic market, similar results are obtained even though the overall capital/labor ratios are higher. Unlike our earlier findings, this seems to lend some support to Kojima's thesis.

With respect to market orientation, however, which is another and essential dimension of the Kojima thesis, the data, at least for 1975, do not indicate that Japanese DFI is clearly more export-oriented than U.S. DFI. In fact, U.S. subsidiaries or joint ventures in Taiwan exported 65 percent of their total manufacturing product in 1975, while the figure for the Japanese was only 53 percent, and that for the European investors, almost 96 percent. It is true, however, that the Japanese were initially more heavily concentrated in the more homogeneous-product, price-competitive areas relative to the U.S. investors in that particular year. But how much of this is due to the fact that they started later is still an open question. Japanese DFI in the fifties was small in volume but concentrated in the electrical appliances and electronics industry, at that time almost entirely domestic-market-oriented. In the seventies, Japanese DFI moved into chemicals and other heavier industries, with a composition very similar to that of U.S. DFI. One would find it easier to conclude that both types of DFI were overwhelmingly affected by Taiwan's phase of development, plus transport costs, rather than by some pervasive difference in home country industrial structure or motivation.

An important and hitherto neglected dimension of the qualitative impact of DFI is a comparison not just among DFIs by origin but also between DFI and domestic firms in the same industries. On this subject we have assembled two sets of data, one for 1966 and 1971 based on samples from the census, and the other a special study done in 1977 based on 1976 data. As indicated in table 2.17, fixed assets per employee appear to be consistently (except in the garment industry) higher for DFI than for domestic firms. However, we have a statistical problem once again in that the domestic firms were not of equivalent size, even if we do not include the

---

19. The comparison is less clear-cut when paid-in capital is used (see table 2.15).

Table 2.17. Capital Labor Ratios of Domestic and Foreign Firms, by Industry, 1966, 1971 (US$ thousands)

	1966				1971					
	Number of Firms		Fixed Assets per Employee		Number of Firms		Fixed Assets per Employee		Machinery and Equipment per Worker	
Industry	Domestic	Foreign	Domestic	Foreign	Domestic	Foreign	Domestic	Foreign	Domestic	Foreign
Plastic products	9	6	0.25	1.55	9	9	0.77	1.90	0.39	1.32
Pharmaceuticals	8	8	0.99	2.18	13	7	2.15	3.67	0.53	0.91
Machinery	50	5	0.50	1.82	41	15	1.49	3.05	0.74	2.02
Electronics	15	7	0.43	2.68	13	16	0.75	1.76	0.33	1.07
Electrical equipment	37	8	0.74	1.60	10	6	1.03	1.70	0.70	0.64
Garments	34	3	0.34	0.30	9	12	0.47	0.71	0.19	0.25

Sources: 1966 and 1971 census data.
Note: Domestic and foreign firms with similar size and product lines were selected randomly.

really small-scale firms not captured in the census. The 1976 special study data (table 2.18) yields the opposite (and more expected) relationship, but with much smaller gaps and more "noise," (i.e., with variations across industries). In food and beverages, for example, as well as in apparel, wood products, leather and leather products, rubber and plastic products, chemicals, basic metals, and electrical equipment and electronics, we find that foreign firms have a lower capital/labor ratio than domestic firms. Whether this reflects a real shift from 1966 to 1976 or simply the use of a different data base is hard to establish. It is possible that foreign firms, especially in the light industry category, made relatively greater efforts over time to take advantage of the cheap labor supply on Taiwan while it lasted. This is certainly a picture consistent with the notion that multinational companies may begin operating with cheap labor and then gradually learn to export

Table 2.18. Fixed Assets per Employee of Domestic and Foreign Firms by Industry, 1976 (US$ thousands)

		Foreign Firms		
Industry	Domestic Firms	Overseas Chinese	Non-Overseas Chinese	Total
Food & beverage processing	11.68	4.32	6.13	5.10
Textiles	7.61	10.29	25.66	17.74
Garments & footwear	1.53	1.32	1.13	1.24
Lumber & bamboo products	3.87	3.79	1.87	2.79
Pulp paper & products	6.89	12.13	9.58	10.92
Leather & leather products	1.74	1.63	0.97	1.32
Plastic & rubber products	3.58	2.29	2.05	2.13
Chemicals	21.84	15.05	11.66	13.32
Nonmetallic minerals	7.39	33.13	22.21	27.53
Basic metals & metal products	9.42	1.74	4.42	3.79
Machinery	6.87		17.32	16.32
Electronics & electrical appliances	4.55	2.58	2.60	2.60
All manufacturing[a]	7.15	8.20	5.77	6.49

Sources: Ministry of Economic Affairs, Investment Commission (1977); and the Committee on Industrial and Commercial Census of Taiwan-Fukien District (1978).

Note: Figures are weighted averages.

[a]The figure for the national manufacturing total was US$8,390. It included some industries with no DFI, such as refinery and miscellaneous ones.

competitively with the help of labor-using adaptations of imported technology.[20] The large body of literature on the impact of DFI on technology choice remains inconclusive, but much of it does seem to indicate that multinationals with long-term experience and a number of subsidiaries, which therefore have superior capacities to scan across countries, manage to "learn by doing" and to make better adjustments in terms of product and process mixes. Somewhat stronger support for the basic notion that more competitive environments induce lower capital/labor ratios is provided by comparing technology choices within the EPZs with those outside the EPZs, whether we are dealing with domestic or foreign firms. Table 2.19, based on a 1971 census survey, indicates that fixed assets per employee were consistently lower in the EPZs than outside the EPZs, with the differences larger for foreign than for domestic firms.

When comparing 1966 and 1971 census data (see table 2.17) it is not, however, surprising that all capital/labor ratios (except for electronics), measured by fixed assets per employee, rose consistently over time in each of the industries selected. This is an indication of the changes in relative endowments and factor/price ratios as labor surplus gradually ended in the late sixties, and rapidly growing incomes spurred increased domestic savings, augmented by foreign capital inflows.

Qualitative Dimensions of DFI: The Transfer of Technology

The impact of DFI on Taiwan's technology is broader and more complicated than the simple question of relative capital/labor ratios, itself an imperfect index, especially in light of the aforementioned problems with measuring capital. What one would really like to know is the extent to which foreign firms have greater access to foreign technology than domestic firms, and whether this technology is more or less "appropriate." A survey conducted in 1972 comprising 311 exporting firms[21] provides one indirect approach to this problem, although we recognize the difficulty of obtaining a good proxy for the breadth of technological choice. As table 2.20 indicates, 86 percent of the 126 foreign firms sampled actually claim to have applied foreign technology in their production, via either patents, licensing, or technical assistance contracts. The use of foreign machinery by itself was not accepted as a proxy. By contrast, only 8 percent of domestic firms "used" foreign technology in this sense. Furthermore, if we break down foreign firms into majority- versus minority-owned we find that the ownership ratio among foreign firms affects the behavior in the use of foreign technology; more than 90 percent of majority-owned foreign

20. Singer's operation in Taiwan, discussed more fully below, is a case in point.
21. Samples were taken from a list of firms with a minimum of US$1 million of exports or a "high growth rate" of exports.

Table 2.19. Capital/Labor Ratios of Domestic and Foreign Firms, by Source, 1971 (US$ thousands per worker)

	In EPZs			Outside EPZs		
Status	Number of Firms	Fixed Assets per Employee	Machinery and Equipment per Worker	Number of Firms	Fixed Assets per Employee	Machinery and Equipment per Worker
Domestic firms	11	1.14	0.75	151	1.44	0.75
Foreign firms	60	1.74	0.95	30	2.59	1.57
Overseas Chinese	14	1.42	0.72	19	3.28	1.48
Non-Overseas Chinese	46	1.84	1.02	11	2.34	1.69

Source: 1971 census survey data.
Note: Firms were selected randomly from five industries: plastic products, pharmaceuticals, electrical equipment and electronics, and garments.

firms used foreign technology, as opposed to only 61 percent of minority-owned foreign firms. This pattern seems to hold for every one of the industries sampled, with only two exceptions; in textiles, minority-owned

Table 2.20. Foreign Technology Participation between Foreign and Domestic Exporting Firms, 1972 (number of firms)

Industry	Firms with Foreign Technology Participation (1)	Total (2)	% (1)/(2)
Textiles			
Domestic firms	7	76	9
Foreign firms	13	17	76
Majority-owned[a]	8	10	80
Minority-owned	5	7	71
Garments & footwear			
Domestic firms	2	47	4
Foreign firms	15	22	68
Majority-owned	14	18	77
Minority-owned	1	4	25
Plastic & plastic products			
Domestic firms	1	34	3
Foreign firms	24	27	89
Majority-owned	22	24	92
Minority-owned	2	3	66
Metal & metal products			
Domestic firms	2	11	18
Foreign firms	13	15	87
Majority-owned	12	13	92
Minority-owned	1	2	50
Electrical equipment & electronics			
Domestic firms	4	17	24
Foreign firms	43	45	96
Majority-owned	38	38	100
Minority-owned	5	7	71
All industries			
Domestic firms	14	185	8
Foreign firms	108	126	86
Majority-owned	94	103	91
Minority-owned	14	23	61

Source: Data were provided by Professor Yen Hwa and Yung-sun Lee, based on a survey of the manufacturing exporting firms in Taiwan conducted and sponsored jointly by the Graduate Institute of Economics, National Taiwan University and Kiel Institute for World Economics.

[a] 50% or above.

firms seemed to behave not very differently from majority-owned firms; and in the metal and metal products industry, domestic firms applied foreign technology just as frequently as minority-owned foreign firms.[22]

The more competitive industries like textiles and apparel seem to have resorted somewhat less to this measure of foreign technology participation than the less competitive plastics and electronics industries, especially as far as the DFI firms are concerned. This seems to support the notion that the use of foreign technology as measured in this way, excluding the use of modification of imported machinery, may understate the deployment of foreign technology in the more competitive industries. The real difference may well be between technology imports directed to the sourcing motivation of DFI and the growing technology imports over time directed to the specialized noncompetitive motivation of DFI. We may also note (see table 2.21) that DFI firms are of uniformly larger average size than domestic firms in the same industry, and thus presumably have greater market power. Not unexpectedly, U.S. DFI firms tend generally to be larger than others, but, surprisingly at first blush, Overseas Chinese DFI firms are, on the average, slightly larger than the average non–Overseas Chinese firms. We should remember, however, that Overseas Chinese investors favored the more domestically oriented activities in each industry, counting less on technological superiority than other DFI investors. One would expect a lower rate of foreign technology participation as defined here—though not necessarily of technology change overall—in these activities.

At any moment of time (e.g., in the late sixties), we would expect the "later," more technology or capital intensive industries to be less competitive and to embody more of the specialized noncompetitive resource arguments for DFI, in contrast to the "earlier" more competitive industries likely to carry more of the straight "cheap labor" sourcing motivation. Over time as well, comparing the sixties and seventies, we would expect, within any given industry, an increasing importance to be attached to the specialized resources contribution of DFI as the economy moves into the more sophisticated range of industrial products. Access to specialized information and marketing channels, for example, represents an important, often noncompetitive, skill not sufficiently emphasized by many economists.[23] It embodies knowledge, difficult to patent and imitate and clearly not available to all comers, especially not domestic firms. Marketing networks

22. The textiles exception may be due to the more competitive nature of that industry at that time, while the second is probably due to the very small population of minority-owned foreign firms in this industry.

23. For example, R. Caves, *International Corporations, Industrial Economics and Foreign Investment* as well as Stephen Hymer, *The International Operation of National Firms: A Study of Direct Foreign Investment* (Cambridge: MIT Press, 1976).

Table 2.21. Average Size of Foreign and Domestic Firms, by Country of Origin and Industry, 1975 (number of employees)

Industry	Overseas Chinese	Non-Overseas Chinese					Domestic Firms
		U.S.A.	Japan	Europe	Other	All	
Food & beverage processing	199	187	248		69	205	17
Textiles	673	1,137	534		563	610	63
Garments & footwear	442	1,002	263	261	280	381	31
Lumber & bamboo products	138	419	177	12		216	16
Pulp paper & products	147	319	74			109	68
Leather & fur products	1,075	1,250	134	246	508	363	9
Plastic & rubber products	144	396	265	38	143	267	12
Chemicals	520	172	107	822	496	149	28
Nonmetallic minerals	448	621	154		253	193	23
Basic metals & metal products	127	176	108		168	118	12
Machinery equipment & instruments	162	319	153	191	871	226	18
Electronics & electrical appliances	70	1,060	682	1,002	420	789	15
All manufacturing	386	676	335	458	423	362	23

Sources: Ministry of Economic Affairs, Investment Commission, *An Analysis of the Operations and Economic Effects of Foreign Enterprises* (various issues); and Directorate-General of Budget, Accounting, and Statistics, Executive Yuan (1976).

usually require larger fixed costs and rather small marginal costs. As a result, they become increasingly valuable rent-yielding assets. This is illustrated by the fact that in the electronics and electrical appliances industry, for example, firms whose exports were completely handled by their parent companies had an average export value approximately double that of other majority-owned foreign firms of equivalent size.

Table 2.22 summarizes the extent to which a total of 314 exporting firms in 1972 experienced some foreign technology participation as well as the source of their export-marketing information and channelization. First of all, foreign-owned firms, in general, relied much more heavily on their foreign partners to obtain access to market information, with the tendency even stronger among majority-owned foreign firms. On the other hand, contacts with foreign customers provided most of the export market information and access for domestic firms. Among foreign firms, the minority-owned utilized this more competitive channel more heavily. Moreover, we can see that foreign firms had their own sales agents more frequently than domestic firms, while domestic firms more often received information from industrial associations and trading companies. While we do not present the data here, the same pattern holds for each of the major DFI industries. In general, then, minority-owned foreign firms seem not to behave so differently from domestic firms. A clear relationship appears to exist between the relative amount of foreign ownership and the less competitive, specialized kinds of trade information and marketing channels, along with the more extensive use of foreign technology imports.

Technology Transfer and the Learning Process

In order to provide a little more flesh for the DFI technology-transfer contribution story, the history of the Singer sewing machine on Taiwan may briefly be cited.[24] Singer Sewing set up its first fully owned subsidiary in Taiwan in 1963. At the time of the investment Taiwan already had a group of small domestic sewing machine companies, producing a total of 39,000 units annually, using a rather primitive production process and almost no quality control. More serious, the precision of the specifications and the interchangeability of the parts was limited and not uniform among producers. Critical components such as shuttle bodies and bobbin cases had to be imported.

When Singer first applied to enter Taiwan during the last years of the primary import-substitution policy subphase, the domestic firms strongly

---

24. For a fuller account see Chi Schive, "Technology Transfer Through Direct Foreign Investment: A Case Study of Taiwan Singer," *Proceedings of the Academy of International Business, Asian-Pacific Dimensions of International Business* (December 1979).

Table 2.22. Foreign Technology Participation and the Export Marketing Methods of Exporting Firms; 1972

	Total Number of Firms	Firms with Foreign Technology Participation	Foreign Sales Agents	International Firms	Customer Sales Relations	Foreign Partners	Industrial Associations	Trading Companies
						\multicolumn{3}{c}{Export Marketing Methods (%)[a]}
Domestic firms	187	8	29.9	11.8	86.6		36.9	13.9
Foreign firms	127	86	40.9	12.6	66.9	74.8	16.5	3.9
Majority-owned	104	93	39.4	11.5	62.5	80.8	15.4	1.9
Minority-owned	23	61	47.8	17.4	87.0	47.8	21.7	13.0

Sources: Data were provided by Professors Yen Hwa and Yung-sun Lee, based on a survey conducted in the fall of 1972, sponsored jointly by the Graduate Institute of Economics, National Taiwan University, and the Kiel Institute for World Economics.
[a] Since each firm uses more than one marketing method, the percentages do not add up to 100.

opposed the idea; they were afraid that Singer, given its world-famous brand name, technological leadership, advantages in capital, in installment credit, and marketing, would constitute a major threat to local producers. Nevertheless, the government, in transition toward a more competitive, export-oriented growth phase, did approve the Singer application but imposed a gradually increasing domestic procurement of supplies requirement, as well as a general caveat to "export as much as possible, as quickly as possible." Table 2.23 clearly shows the success of Singer's sales and export performance during a period when local content was raised from zero in 1964 to 50 percent in 1965, 75 percent in 1966, and 80 percent in 1967. By 1969, Taiwan Singer used only locally made parts except for the needles for the regular straight-stitch model. Moreover, Singer initiated the production of shuttle bodies and bobbin cases within Taiwan; that is, backward linkages took place. In 1970, the company sold these two parts to local assemblers at a price about 20 percent lower than the imported price. Later on, other domestic manufacturers were able to produce the same parts competitively. Taiwan Singer's volume of exports increased at a stable annual rate of 12 percent as it shifted its markets; while in 1964, roughly 25 percent of the total volume had been exported, by 1975, 86 percent of total output was exported. Thus, Singer's participation in Taiwan's export-substitution subphase was quite pronounced. While the attractive local market had clearly been a key factor in bringing this particular DFI to Taiwan initially, it was the export market to which it became the important contributor thereafter.

What is even more interesting is the impact of Singer's coming to Taiwan on the sewing machine industry in general. When Singer was first established, its experts in the areas of accounting, production, and management from other parts of the Singer organization around the world came in and helped organize the management team and also trained local employees. Once the plan was operational, Singer personnel began to give technical assistance, free of charge, to other members of the sewing machine industry, providing blueprints and measuring gauges to parts producers, and a variety of other services to individual firms to help solve their technical problems in casting and plating. Most of the early staff actually consisted of Taiwan Singer's local technicians, and only later were some foreign experts brought in for specific assistance to local parts suppliers.

Taiwan Singer's willingness to provide free technical assistance to parts suppliers was in its own interest, to ensure the quality of the parts to its own rigid specifications. The indirect by-product, however, was that the industry as a whole, which had been stagnant previously, grew at an average rate of more than 23 percent after 1964. The technological upgrading of the industry in the mid-sixties, aided by Singer's technical assistance to other

Table 2.23. Sales and Exports of Taiwan Singer, Lihtzer, and the Sewing Machine Industry in Taiwan (1,000 units)

	Taiwan Singer[a]		Lihtzer[a]	Total Sewing Machine Industry		
Year	Domestic Sales Volume	Export Volume	Export Volume	Production	Exports Volume	Exports Value (US$ millions)
1954–57	n.a.	n.a.	n.a.	188	0.5	0.04
1959–61	n.a.	n.a.	n.a.	227	0.3	0.01
1962–63	n.a.	n.a.	n.a.	87	1.5	0.03
1964	5.0	1.3 (22.9)	n.a.	91	5.5	0.18
1965	11.1	6.2 (52.0)	n.a.	79	11.9	0.20
1966	8.5	17.1 (21.8)	n.a.	125	78.6	1.99
1967	12.0	26.1 (14.5)	n.a.	212	180.4	2.52
1968	9.7	40.4 (13.8)	n.a.	361	293.1	4.40
1969	8.7	41.6 (11.8)	140 (39.7)	519	352.2	6.08
1970	10.0	42.4 (11.1)	180 (47.0)	629	383.3	5.75
1971	10.3	68.7 (9.7)	240 (33.9)	788	707.1	10.69
1972	10.4	80.5 (8.1)	280 (29.1)	916	962.3	16.19
1973	13.2	93.5 (9.1)	360 (35.1)	1,256	1,026.2	19.55
1974	18.0	116.1 (9.8)	400 (35.7)	1,222	1,186.3	31.32
1975	18.2	104.6 (10.7)	320 (32.7)	1,047	977.9	27.11
1976	18.7	129.2 (7.4)	400 (23.0)	1,379	1,733.7	43.06
1977	n.a.	n.a.	452 (29.3)	1,546	1,541.1	44.87
1978	n.a.	n.a.	509 (24.9)	2,458	2,042.4	69.42

Sources: Ministry of Economic Affairs, *The Monthly Bulletin of Industrial Production* (various issues); Ministry of Finance, *The Trade of China* (various issues); Singer Industries (Taiwan) Ltd. company reports; and Lihtzer Sewing Machine Company reports.

[a] Figures in parentheses are shares in total sewing machine industry exports. Lihtzer is the largest domestic firm and exports 100 percent of its output. Data for Lihtzer before 1969 and for Taiwan Singer after 1976 were not available.

parts suppliers, seems to have been responsible in large part for this remarkable growth. Having first obtained the cooperation of parts manufacturers because of its international reputation, Singer thus assisted the growth of competitors who gradually supplanted the company's own dominance. In this particular instance, DFIs absolute technological superiority, coupled with the strong marketing skills of the parent organization, provided Taiwan Singer with the opportunity to move in, do well, and not be concerned about the diffusion of technology to domestic firms.

At the same time, local firms, with Lihtzer as a leading example (see table 2.23), were able to take advantage of the assistance offered and upgrade their own technological standards. The competitive pressure exercised by Singer's presence gradually forced a choice between upgrading production lines or shutting down. The fact that Singer's share in exports in terms of value was twice as high as its contribution in terms of volume indicates that its products probably shifted toward the higher (more expensive) end of the product line, with domestic producers moving into the medium- and lower-quality range, all constituting an intra-industry, or micro, example of the so-called flying geese pattern.

Singer, of course, had its own motivation; by upgrading local parts suppliers it helped itself, but at the same time it indirectly helped other assemblers. Singer might not have been permitted to come in at all had it not complied with the government regulations requiring domestic procurement of parts. It should also be remembered that without supply side capacities, managerial and marketing, as well as the high quality of skilled labor, the domestic industry would not have been in a position to adapt and compete successfully and might instead have been eliminated. By not appropriating the technology, Taiwan Singer's investment helped to spur the growth of the entire industry and to make Taiwan a major producer and exporter in this particular domain. More recently, Singer has asked local producers to produce sewing machines carrying Singer's name for export, indicating that its competitive strength is now more in the trademark and marketing areas rather than in production proper, as we might expect.

It is not claimed that all instances of DFI technology transfer are equally successful. For example, the motor car assembly industry, in which heavily protected and cartelized production, plus operating scales well below optimal size, was endemic, has consistently been one of the least efficient industries in Taiwan, as in other developing countries, with very little export capacity, certainly not of the relatively unsubsidized, competitive variety. But all too often DFI in manufacturing is accused of maintaining its "enclave"[25] characteristics, with very few spillover or linkage effects for the

---

25. Defined by Charles Kindleberger, *American Business Abroad* (New Haven: Yale University Press, 1969), p. 46, as having "little or limited economic contact with the local

rest of the economy. As the Taiwan experience indicates, even if we were to assume only employment effects, especially in the export-processing zones, this would have constituted no mean contribution in a labor-surplus economy. In fact, as the Taiwan Singer case demonstrates, the contribution of DFI usually extends substantially beyond creating jobs, especially when the time dimension is taken into account.

One indicator of the increased impact of DFI on the domestic economy over time is the proportion of intermediate goods procured domestically. It is, therefore, interesting to note that the local procurement ratio of DFI firms stood at 41 percent in 1972, rising to 47 percent in 1975 and 50 percent in 1978 (see table 2.24). It is even more interesting that even in the export-processing zones, specifically designed for adding value to imported raw materials and not subject to minimum local content requirements, these ratios were substantial and rising (29 percent in 1975 and 35 percent in 1978). Not surprisingly, in terms of their presumably superior knowledge of local sources of supply, Overseas Chinese DFI ratios were at high levels, but the gap narrowed over time.

Table 2.25 renders the analysis more dynamic by disaggregating firms' local procurement ratios by their date of establishment. Thus, in 1978, for non-EPZ foreign firms, those established before 1972 had a procurement ratio of 54.8, and those established before 1975 a ratio of 56.7. In general, the longer a firm has been in existence, *ceteris paribus*, the more it will be inclined to purchase from the local market. If, for example, we plotted the local procurement ratios in 1975 and 1978 in the foreign-invested electrical appliances and electronics industry by individual year of the firms' establishment, we would note that each curve follows something of a U-shaped pattern, indicating that, after a brief initial preference for imported inputs, the more recently established the firm, the higher its domestic-content ratios. Moreover, this must be voluntary, since this particular industry, especially over the past decade, has not only been an important component of total DFI but was also very heavily represented in EPZ activity, which is free of domestic procurement requirements. A second observation is that the 1978 procurement ratios are all higher than the 1975 ratios, indicating that, for each vintage of firms, local procurement ratios increased over time. We may thus conclude that the backward-linkage effects of DFI were indeed at work, even in the so-called export platforms of Taiwan, and that their effect increased cumulatively with time.

Government policy encouraged the indigenous industrial maturation process, or at least accommodated and did not obstruct it. By keeping the

---

economy—tightly bound to the home country, far away, but only loosely connected, except geographically, to the local scene."

Table 2.24. Local Purchase Ratios of Foreign Firms, by Location (US$ millions; %)

Status of Investors	1972 Firms outside EPZ Local Purchases	1972 Firms outside EPZ Ratio	1975 Firms outside EPZ Local Purchases	1975 Firms outside EPZ Ratio	1975 Firms in EPZ Local Purchases	1975 Firms in EPZ Ratio	1975 Total Firms Local Purchases	1975 Total Firms Ratio	1978 Firms outside EPZ Local Purchases	1978 Firms outside EPZ Ratio	1978 Firms in EPZ Local Purchases	1978 Firms in EPZ Ratio	1978 Total Firms Local Purchases	1978 Total Firms Ratio
Overseas Chinese	99.2	64.50	163.4	58.16	15.3	29.04	178.7	53.57	345.0	55.83	27.2	36.43	372.2	53.74
Non-Overseas Chinese	265.1	35.84	515.9	49.00	65.3	29.59	581.2	45.63	1,243.3	51.56	161.7	35.30	1,405.0	48.96
Total	364.3	40.78	679.3	50.94	80.6	29.48	759.9	47.28	1,588.3	52.43	188.9	35.46	1,777.2	49.89

Sources: Primary data from Ministry of Economic Affairs, Investment Commission, *Economic Effects of Foreign Enterprises*, various issues.

Direct Foreign Investment in Taiwan

Table 2.25. Local Purchase Ratios of Foreign Firms Not in Export Processing Zones, by Years of Establishment (%)

Status of Investors	1972 All Firms	1975 Firms Established before 1972	1975 All Firms	1978 Firms Established before 1972	1978 Firms Established before 1975	1978 All Firms
Overseas Chinese	64.50	57.73	58.16	54.81	56.72	55.83
Non-Overseas Chinese	35.84	48.55	49.00	52.04	51.96	51.56
Total	40.78	50.43	50.94	52.41	52.65	52.43

Source: Ministry of Economic Affairs, Investment Commission, *An Analysis of Operations and Economic Effects of Foreign Enterprises* (in Chinese), various issues.

primary import-substitution phase of the fifties relatively short and mild, the shift to a labor-intensive industrial export regime in the sixties was rendered relatively less painful. By the seventies, as Taiwan entered its unskilled-labor-shortage era and policies shifted toward secondary import cum export substitution, the levels of effective protection in the industrial sector were rather low by international standards (see table 2.26).[26] We should also note that there appears to be a positive rank-order relationship between the level of effective protection and the share of DFI in total industry investment, especially as far as Overseas Chinese investors are concerned. On the other hand, non–Overseas Chinese investors seem to relate their share of sales in domestic markets to the level of effective protection. This supports our contention that Overseas Chinese investors represent something of an extension of domestic investors.

The theory of comparative advantage teaches us that the trade pattern of a country in transition to modern growth can be expected to provide a mirror image of the policy-tinged subphases referred to. In fact, between 1962 and 1970, during the height of labor-intensive primary export substitution, Taiwan's total industrial exports shifted from a 42 percent concentration on developed countries to a 70 percent concentration. Since then, as Taiwan has moved well into her secondary import-/secondary export-substitution subphase, this has meant improved opportunities not only for taking full advantage of foreign technology imports but also for routinely generating its own indigenous process and product innovations. It also has meant a wider range of industrial production and export activities as the "special" scarce-resource characteristics of DFI increasingly gain ascendancy over the simple sourcing motivation. In terms of product

26. Unfortunately, there are no comparable estimates for effective rates of protection for other, especially earlier, years.

Table 2.26. Effective Protection Rates and Direct Foreign Investment Structure, 1974 (%)

Industry	Effective Protection Rates[a]	DFI Shares Overseas Chinese	DFI Shares Non-Overseas Chinese	Local Sales Shares Overseas Chinese	Local Sales Shares Non-Overseas Chinese
Food & beverage processing	16.06	7.70	12.76	21.73	7.21
Textiles	65.21	34.62	8.15	2.91	9.25
Garments & footwear	50.66	17.40	6.32	0.54	0.57
Lumber & bamboo products	−4.75	3.50	1.12	0.25	0.18
Pulp paper & products	−14.00	0.65	0.88	0.97	0.82
Leather & fur products	−37.78	2.81	1.35		
Plastic & rubber products	2.13	8.18	14.28	13.03	1.59
Chemicals	49.94	4.89	12.93	8.93	17.90
Nonmetallic minerals	2.28	7.92	33.29	47.17	1.01
Basic metals & metal products	23.98	3.72	1.85	0.55	3.64
Machinery equipment & instruments	30.14	1.77	0.83	0.23	9.36
Electronics & electrical appliances	32.62	6.84	6.23	3.70	48.48
Rank correlation coefficients between effective protection rates and measures of DFI		.573	.301	.154	.650

Sources: Lee et al. (1975) Appendix Table 4; Ministry of Economic Affairs, Investment Commission (1975).

[a]For 1969.

mix, this is accompanied by a shift toward more sophisticated products as well as by a change in trading partners. By 1980, manufactured DFI exports to the advanced countries had once again declined to 66 percent of the total, with exports to LDCs across a wide variety of industries increasing proportionately. Once again, the DFI country of origin matters less for export destination than the combination of industry characteristics and historical time.

Concluding Remarks

Our examination of the role of DFI in Taiwan's development indicates that it undoubtedly provided important assistance to the success story that has evolved over the past three decades on that island; nevertheless, it probably does not deserve to receive star billing from either friend or foe. Crucial to Taiwan's overall performance, which is without parallel anywhere in the third world, were both her relatively favorable initial conditions and her subsequent policies which accommodated, rather than obstructed, the metamorphosis of the system in line with changing domestic capacities and international conditions. Foreign capital, especially that of the official concessional type, was clearly helpful in easing the system's path of policy adjustment from a natural-resources-based and inward-looking import-substitution subphase in the fifties to an unskilled-labor-based and export-substitution-oriented subphase in the sixties. Foreign capital, now mainly of the private DFI type, again undoubtedly helped Taiwan's entry into new, more sophisticated and capital-intensive product lines and markets in the seventies, once her labor surplus had been eliminated. And finally, foreign capital of the private portfolio and commercial bank variety has helped her overcome some of the difficulties of consecutive oil shocks, global stagflation, and the "new protectionism."

But it would be difficult to draw firmer conclusions. Foreign capital, mainly aid, financed more than 50 percent of total investment in the fifties, but became insignificant by the seventies. DFI itself never amounted to more than 10 percent of total manufacturing investment. Clearly, the critical policy decisions were domestic, as were the overwhelming contributions to the quantitative side of the ledger, in terms of savings rates and growth rates, as well as to the qualitative side, in terms of technology choice, adaptation, and the search for competitive entry into new markets. Direct foreign investment dances to the tune of the domestic economy. Where that tune is well composed, flexible, and agreeable as in Taiwan, DFI can add considerably to the overall effect. Where policies, on the other hand, are adverse to and obstructive of the underlying economic forces working themselves out in the course of the transition growth process, DFI can equally well have a negative impact by encouraging the system to persevere in its nonoptimal growth pattern.

The Japanese colonial regime in Taiwan, in contrast to that of most other colonial experiences, left behind a rather strong rural infrastructure as well as a not inconsiderable industrial base. Given her relative natural-resources scarcity as well as her small size, Taiwan's postindependence DFI was focused heavily on participating in the labor-intensive, export-oriented subphase of the sixties as well as in the more diversified and sophisticated industrial output and export mixes of the seventies and eighties. If flexibility in response to changing endowment and demand patterns is but another name for successful development—as we believe it is—DFI has helped provide Taiwan with additional flexibility, in the sixties mainly by adding substantially to her capacity to quickly absorb and thus export her abundant supply of labor, and in the seventies by adding a technological and market-scanning capacity, gradually moving away from a pure sourcing motivation and toward more sophisticated output mixes and imperfect markets.

The export-processing zones and bonded factories are an important example of the "lead" role played by DFI in helping to assist the economy in its transition growth. They represent an important "switching device" between the primary import-substitution and primary export-substitution subphases and were heavily populated by foreign firms at the outset. The combination of government-provided physical infrastructure and administrative flexibility with foreign investors' specialized knowledge of technologies and markets, especially for such intermediate goods as electronics, substantially helped Taiwan move into unfamiliar new export markets in the sixties. It contributed not only to one of the most dramatic industrial labor absorption processes ever witnessed—and the exhaustion of the labor surplus—but also to the gradual integration of the export enclave into the rest of the economy, as growing indigenous capacity permitted a continuous relative expansion in domestic intermediate product procurement to take place. DFI's contribution via backward-linkage effects undoubtedly became even more pronounced outside the special zones, whose relative importance declined with the end of labor surplus and extended to the entire system, as demonstrated by the Singer case we have cited. While DFI never occupied a dominant position in total manufacturing investment—though it was quantitatively important in certain specific industries—we should not underestimate its qualitative contribution in leading the way, under competitive pressure, in initial technology choices or technology adaptation, and in export-market orientation.

The sectoral allocation of DFI over time seems to have reflected the evolution of the economy's changing comparative advantage position. Overseas Chinese investors who had the advantage of familiarity were initially relatively more heavily involved in consumer goods production for domestic markets. Nevertheless, we can detect no very pronounced or lasting differences in the allocation pattern or, indeed, in the quantitative or qualitative performance of various kinds of DFI depending on the country of origin. This is especially significant in comparing U.S. and Japanese DFI. While Japanese investments seem to have been on a somewhat smaller scale, more prone to seeking local partners, and more labor-intensive than their U.S. counterparts in the same industries, their industrial allocation pattern is not markedly different, nor are they more export- as opposed to domestic-market-oriented. Especially when we adjust for the fact that the Japanese postwar re-entry into Taiwan occurred later than that of the United States, it is difficult to find strong support for the Kojima thesis, which has U.S. DFI concentrating much more on the non–price-competitive, appropriable advanced-technology end of the industrial spectrum, relative to the price-competitive, unskilled-labor-based, and homogeneous-products-focused Japanese type.

Our findings indicate that export-oriented firms, whether DFI or domestic, tend to be more labor-intensive than domestic-market-oriented firms in the same industry. We also found some evidence that the extent of export orientation and labor intensity varies directly with the extent of foreign capital participation up to a point, and that these majority-owned DFI firms seem to rely more heavily on foreign technology imports and on specialized information and access to marketing channels. This leads us to the tentative conclusion that it is the combination of the opportunities offered by the international technology shelf with domestic adaptations which is really crucial, especially in the early stages, when sourcing is the predominant DFI motive and the competitiveness of the environment induces the required flexibility in process choice. As the economy moves into the more sophisticated output mixes characteristic of secondary import and export substitution, the product choice, specialized information, and access contributions of DFI gain in importance.

References

Caves, Richard E. 1971. "International Corporations: The Industrial Economics of Foreign Investment." *Economica* 38 (February): 1–27.

The Central Bank of China. *Balance of Payments Yearbook* (in Chinese), various years. Taipei.

Chang Chung-Han. 1980. *Industrialisation in Taiwan During the Colonial Period* (in Chinese). Taipei: United Economics.

Committee on Industrial and Commercial Census of Taiwan-Fukien District. 1978. *The Report of the 1976 Committee on Industrial and Commercial Censuses of Taiwan-Fukien District of the Republic of China.* Taipei.

Council for Economic Planning and Development, Executive Yuan. 1983. *Taiwan Statistical Data Book.* Taipei.

Council for Economic Planning and Development, Executive Yuan. 1980. *Taiwan Input-Output Tables, 1976.* Taipei.

Directorate-General of Budget, Accounting and Statistics, Executive Yuan. 1976. *Year Book of Labor Statistics.* Taipei.

Dunning, John H. 1977. "Trade, Location of Economic Activity and the Multinational Enterprise: A Search for an Eclectic Approach." Chapter 12 in B. Ohlin et al., eds., *The International Allocation of Economic Activity*, 395–431. New York: Holmes & Meier Publishers.

Export Processing Zone Administration Bureau. *Export Processing Zone Concentrates*, various issues. Taipei.

Export Processing Zone Administration Bureau. *Export Processing Zone Essential Statistics*, various issues. Taipei.

Galenson, Walter, ed. 1979. *Economic Growth and Structural Change in Taiwan.* Ithaca, N.Y.: Cornell University Press.

Ho, Samuel. 1978. *Economic Development in Taiwan 1860–1970.* New Haven: Yale University Press.

Hwa, Yen and Hung-sun Lee. 1972. Primary data from a survey of the manufacturing exporting firms in Taiwan, sponsored jointly by the Graduate Institute of Economics, National Taiwan University, and the Kiel Institute for World Economics.

Hymer, Stephen. 1976. *The International Operations of National Firms: A Study of Direct Foreign Investment.* Cambridge, Mass.: MIT Press.

Kindleberger, Charles. 1969. *American Business Abroad.* New Haven: Yale University Press.

Kojima, Kiyoshi. 1977. "Transfer of Technology to Developing Countries—Japanese Type versus American Type." *Hitotsubashi Journal of Economics* 17.2 (February): 1–14.

Krueger, Anne O., ed. 1981. *Trade and Employment in Developing Countries.* Chicago: University of Chicago Press.

Krueger, Anne O., et al. 1974–75. *Foreign Trade Regimes and Economic Development: A Special Conference Series on Foreign Trade and Economic Development.* New York: National Bureau of Economic Research.

Lee, T. H., K. S. Liang, C. Schive, and R. S. Yeh. 1975. "The Structure of Effective Protection and Subsidy in Taiwan." *Economic Essays* 6.

Liang, Kuo-Shu. 1978. "Employment and Distribution Effects of Export Promotion in Taiwan." *Proceedings of Conference on Income Distribution in Taiwan.* Taipei: Academia Sinica.

Lihtzer Sewing Machine Company. Company interview data.

Lin, Ching Wang. 1973. *Industrialization in Taiwan 1946–1972.* New York: Praeger.

Liu Min-Cheng. 1971. "Economic Development and Direct Foreign Investment in Taiwan" (in Chinese). *Bank of Taiwan Quarterly* 22 (December): 4.

Ministry of Economic Affairs. *The Monthly Bulletin of Industrial Production, The Republic of China,* various issues. Taipei.

Ministry of Economic Affairs, Investment Commission. 1975. *An Analysis of Operations and Economic Effects of Foreign Enterprises in Taiwan 1974* (in Chinese). Taipei.

Ministry of Economic Affairs, Investment Commission. 1977. *An Analysis of Operations and Economic Effects of Foreign Enterprises in Taiwan, 1976* (in Chinese). Taipei.

Ministry of Economic Affairs, Investment Commission. 1980. *Statistics on Overseas Chinese Foreign Investment.* Taipei.

Ministry of Economic Affairs, Investment Commission. 1981. *An Analysis of Operations and Economic Effects of Foreign Enterprises in Taiwan, 1980* (in Chinese). Taipei.

Ministry of Finance. *The Trade of China, Taiwan District,* various years.

Mizoguchi, Toshiyuki. 1979. "Economic Growth of Korea under the Japanese Occupation—Background of Industrialization of Korea 1911–1940." *Hitotsubashi Journal of Economics* 20.1 (June): 1–19.

Mizoguchi, Toshiyuki, and Yuzo Yamamoto. 1981. "Colonial Investments of Japan." In Mataji Umemura and Toshiyuki Mizoguchi, eds., *Quantitative Stud-*

ies on the Economic History of the Japanese Empire 1890–1940. Tokyo: Institute of Economic Research, Hitotsubashi University.

Ranis, Gustav. 1979. "Industrial Development." Chapter 3 in Walter Galenson, ed., *Economic Growth and Structural Change in Taiwan*. Ithaca, N.Y.: Cornell University Press.

Singer Industries (Taiwan), Ltd. Company interview data.

Schive, Chi. 1979. "Technology Transfer Through Direct Foreign Investment: A Case Study of Taiwan Singer." *Proceedings of the Academy of International Business: Asian-Pacific Dimensions of International Business* (December).

II The Republic of Korea

3 The Role of Foreign Trade in the Economic Development of Korea
Bela Balassa

Introduction

The role of foreign trade was key to the economic development of the Republic of Korea (for short, Korea) during the two decades between 1960 and 1980. Korea experienced rapid economic growth during this period, with per capita incomes rising at an average rate of 7 percent a year, matching the performance of Hong Kong, Singapore, and Taiwan, and surpassing that of any other developing country.[1]

In the same period, per capita incomes increased at an average annual rate of 4 percent in the middle-income developing countries, defined as countries having per capita incomes between US$420 and US$4500 in 1980. Korea was at the bottom of this group in 1960 and in the upper third in 1980. Furthermore, while per capita incomes were lower in Korea than in Ghana, Senegal, Liberia, Zambia, Honduras, Nicaragua, El Salvador, and Peru in 1960, Korea had more than three times the average income of the four sub-Saharan African countries and more than twice that of the four Latin American countries 20 years later. The Republic of Korea also came to surpass, by a considerable margin, income levels in North Korea (the Democratic Republic of Korea), which retained much of Korean industry after partition in 1947 and had per capita incomes one and a half times those in the South in 1960.

_{The author is Professor of Political Economy at the Johns Hopkins University and Consultant at the World Bank. He is indebted to Messrs. Gary Fields, Walter Galenson, Kim Kihwan, Kwang Suk Kim, Gerhard Pohl, and Larry Westphal for helpful comments. The author alone is responsible for the contents of the paper, which should not be interpreted to reflect the views of the World Bank.}

_{1. Unless otherwise noted, data for Korea originate in the *Economic Statistics Yearbook* and in other publications of the Bank of Korea. Data for foreign countries derive from the *World Development Report, 1982*; for Taiwan, they originate in Taiwan District, *Financial Statistics*.}

The period of rapid growth was one of structural change in Korea, transforming a backward, primary-product-based economy into a newly industrializing developing country. This transformation occurred following the adoption of an outward-oriented development strategy, which permitted the exploitation of Korea's comparative advantage in international trade and contributed to rapid increases in productivity.

This study will examine the conditions existing in Korea after World War II, the changes in the principal macroeconomic relationships between 1960 and 1980, and the transformation of the structure of exports during the two decades. It also will analyze Korea's trade policies and economic performance in the course of three successive periods in comparison with other developing countries.

Next, the study will describe Korea's adoption of an outward-oriented development strategy between 1960 and 1973, and will investigate the economic effects of this strategy compared with development strategies followed in other semi-industrial countries. After some hesitation, Korea maintained its outward-oriented stance in the 1973 to 1978 period, when the rapid expansion of the world economy was followed by a recession aggravated by the quadrupling of oil prices. The study will analyze the development strategies followed, and their economic effects, during this period. Finally, it will consider the implications of the policy reversals that occurred in Korea between 1978 and 1980, with increased emphasis on import substitution followed by renewed export orientation.

Economic Growth and Foreign Trade, 1960–80

The Initial Conditions

Between 1910 and 1945, Korea was a Japanese colony and its economic ties were largely with Japan. Korea had originally been called upon to furnish Japan with rice, which accounted for about half of its exports, as well as with fish, silk, and various minerals. Subsequently, some heavy industries, including iron and steel, cement, and paper, were developed to aid the Japanese war effort. Industries producing nondurable consumer goods were discouraged, however, as Japan wished to conserve market outlets in Korea for its own industries.

The severing of economic ties with Japan, the subsequent partition of the country, and the Korean War led to considerable economic dislocation. Furthermore, while the South had much of the agricultural land and some light industry, much of industry and, in particular, the majority of the heavy industrial plants, remained in the North. The end of the Korean War in 1953 thus left the Republic of Korea with a war-damaged economy based largely on agriculture, fishing, and minerals.

The period following the Korean War was characterized by import substitution in nondurable consumer goods and their inputs. Exports were discouraged by overvalued exchange rates, with balance-of-payments equilibrium being maintained through large inflows of foreign aid. Import substitution accounted for 24 percent of industrial growth in the second half of the fifties, while exports contributed only 5 percent (Westphal-Kim 1982, p. 258).[2]

In 1960, Korea engaged in little foreign trade, had low rates of investment, and generated practically no domestic savings. The exports of goods and services were about 3 percent of its gross domestic product and the share of merchandise exports did not reach even 1 percent, with services performed for the United States military forces accounting for much of the remainder. As the imports of goods and services were 13 percent of the gross domestic product, capital inflow equalled 10 percent of GDP (table 3.1). In the same year, the exports and the imports of goods and services, averaged 16 percent and 17 percent respectively of the gross domestic product in the middle-income developing countries, and the inflow of foreign capital amounted to 1 percent.

Notwithstanding the large inflow of foreign capital, the share of investment in Korea's GDP was only 11 percent in 1960, indicating that domestic savings were negligible. In contrast, in the middle-income developing countries, investment and domestic savings shares, respectively, were 20 percent and 19 percent of the gross domestic product.

In the same year, agriculture, inclusive of forestry and fishing, accounted for 40 percent of Korea's gross domestic product, exceeding the average 24 percent share in the middle-income developing countries. In contrast, the share of manufacturing was only 12 percent in Korea, compared with the average share of 20 percent in those countries.

In 1960, primary commodities dominated Korea's export structure, accounting for 86 percent of merchandise exports. Agricultural, forestry, and fishery products represented 56 percent, and fuels, minerals, and nonferrous metals 30 percent. The share of primary products in the exports of the middle-income developing countries was 87 percent, with agricultural, forestry, and fishery products accounting for 60 percent, and minerals, fuels, and nonferrous metals for 27 percent of the total.

Developments in the 1960–80 Period

These relationships changed in Korea during the following two decades. The share of the export of goods and services in the gross domestic product increased from 3 percent in 1960 to 14 percent in 1970, and reached 36

2. The estimates refer to the direct contribution of import substitution and exports to increases in the manufacturing output; the contribution of increase in domestic demand, representing the residual, was 71 percent.

Table 3.1. Principal Macroeconomic Relationships, 1960–80 (% in current prices)

	1960	1965	1970	1975	1980
Composition of GDP[a]					
Private consumption	85.2	84.2	72.6	69.8	64.2
Government consumption	14.8	9.4	10.5	10.3	12.2
Total consumption	100.0	93.6	83.1	80.1	76.4
Gross fixed capital formation	11.1	14.9	24.5	25.6	30.9
Increase in stocks	0.0	0.3	2.4	3.4	−0.6
Total investment	11.1	15.2	26.9	29.0	30.3
Exports of goods & services	3.3	8.6	14.3	27.6	35.7
Imports of goods & services	12.8	16.0	24.1	36.3	42.7
Net foreign investment	9.5	7.4	9.8	8.7	7.0
Domestic savings	0.0	6.4	16.9	19.9	23.6
Share of trade in GDP[a]					
Merchandise exports (fob)	0.9	5.8	9.7	24.7	29.6
Merchandise imports (fob)	8.2	14.0	21.0	32.8	34.9
Service exports	2.4	2.8	4.6	2.9	6.1
Service imports	4.4	2.0	3.1	3.5	7.8
Sectoral shares in GDP[b]					
Agriculture, forestry, & fishing	39.6	40.2	29.5	26.0	20.0
Industry	18.7	24.2	27.3	31.9	39.0
Manufacturing	12.1	17.3	18.2	23.4	27.0
Services	41.7	35.6	43.2	42.1	41.0
Export composition[c]					
Agriculture, forestry, & fishing	56.0	25.2	16.6	15.7	10.0
Minerals & nonferrous metals	30.0	15.4	6.7	2.8	1.0
Manufactured products	14.0	59.4	76.7	81.5	89.0

Sources: [a]International Monetary Fund (1981).
[b]World Bank data base.
[c]Table 3.2.

percent in 1980. The share of merchandise exports rose from 1 percent to 30 percent, while that of service exports increased from 2 percent to 6 percent.

In interpreting these figures, it should be noted that merchandise exports embody imported inputs; adjusting for these inputs, the share of net exports was about 17 percent in 1980. In turn, after a decline following the end of the Vietnam War, the acceleration of the growth of service exports toward the end of the period is largely explained by the rapid rise of construction contracts in the Middle East.

The share of the imports of goods and services in GDP rose from 13 percent in 1960 to 43 percent in 1980, with merchandise imports accounting for 35 percent in 1980. Adjusting for imports that enter into export production, the net share of merchandise imports was 17 percent.

In conjunction with changes in export and import shares, the inflow of foreign capital declined from 10 percent of GDP in 1960 to 7 percent in 1980. Notwithstanding this decline, investment nearly tripled, rising from 11 percent in 1960 to 30 percent in 1980. This occurred as domestic savings reached 24 percent in 1980 from virtually zero in 1960.

As a result of these changes, export, import, investment, and domestic savings shares in Korea have come to exceed those in the middle-income developing countries, where the respective shares averaged 25 percent, 27 percent, 27 percent, and 25 percent in 1979.[3] Korea also surpassed these countries in the relative importance of the manufacturing sector, raising its share from 12 percent in 1960 to 27 percent in 1980 as against a decline from 20 percent to 19 percent in the latter group. Finally, manufactured products have come to account for 90 percent of Korea's merchandise exports, compared to 38 percent in the middle-income developing countries, while two decades earlier the corresponding shares had been 14 percent and 13 percent respectively.

Changes in the Composition of Merchandise Exports

The transformation of the Korean export structure is shown in greater detail in table 3.2. The data indicate that the largest drop occurred in the export share of industrial materials, from 48 percent of the total in 1960 to 2 percent in 1980. The declining relative importance of tungsten ores and concentrates (14 percent of exports in 1960), raw silk, and ginseng (3 percent each) were largely responsible for this outcome. The exports of seaweed, which accounted for 4 percent of merchandise exports in 1960, also greatly declined in importance. By 1980, these four products, taken together, represented less than 1 percent of Korean exports.

During the sixties, Korea's major exports were relatively simple manufactured goods. In 1970, wigs were the largest single export, accounting for 12 percent of the total, followed by plywood and veneer (11 percent), cotton yarn and fabrics (5 percent), electronic parts and components (4 percent), noncotton fabrics and clothing (3 percent each), and footwear (2 percent). Plywood, veneer, and wigs increasingly lost their importance during the seventies; altogether, they accounted for less than 3 percent of Korean exports in 1980. Clothing assumed first place in 1975, with 23 percent of exports, followed by cotton yarn and fabrics (8 percent), noncotton fabrics (6 percent), electronic parts and components (5 percent), and footwear (4 percent).

The relative shares of textiles and clothing declined after 1975, although

---

3. Export and import shares refer to trade in goods and services. For lack of information, no adjustment has been made for the import content of exports.

Table 3.2. The Composition of Merchandise Exports (%)

	1960	1965	1970	1975	1980
Food & live animals (0)	29.6	16.1	7.9	11.9	6.5
Beverages & tobacco (1)	1.5	0.5	1.7	1.3	0.7
Inedible crude materials (2)	48.2	21.1	12.0	3.0	1.9
Mineral fuels (3)	3.3	1.1	1.0	2.1	0.2
Animal & vegetable oils & fats (4)	0.6	0.1	0.0	0.0	0.1
Chemicals (5)	1.2	.2	1.4	1.5	4.4
Manufactured goods by material (6)	11.9	37.9	26.4	29.2	35.2
Nonferrous metals (68)	2.8	1.7	0.7	0.2	0.6
Wood & cork products (63)	0.0	10.4	11.2	4.5	2.3
Textiles (65)	0.0	6.0	10.2	12.8	12.4
Nonmetallic mineral manufactures (66)	0.0	1.6	0.8	2.1	2.5
Iron & steel (67)	0.0	7.3	1.6	4.6	9.3
Manufactures of metal (69)	0.0	1.3	1.5	2.4	4.2
Others (61 + 62 + 64)	0.0	9.6	0.4	0.6	3.9
Machinery & transport equipment (7)	0.3	3.1	7.4	13.8	20.7
Nonelectrical machinery (71)	0.0	1.4	1.0	1.5	2.0
Electrical machinery & appliances (72)	0.0	1.1	5.3	8.7	12.2
Transport equipment (73)	0.0	0.6	1.1	3.6	6.5
Miscellaneous manufactured articles (8)	0.3	19.7	42.2	37.1	29.9
Clothing (84)	0.0	11.8	25.6	22.6	16.7
Footwear (85)	0.0	2.3	2.1	3.8	4.9
Miscellaneous (89)	0.0	5.1	13.7	7.5	4.9
Others (81 + 82 + 83 + 84)	0.0	0.5	0.8	3.2	3.4
Unclassified (9)	3.0	0.1	0.0	0.2	0.4
Primary products (0 + 1 + 2 + 3 + 4 + 68)	86.0	40.6	23.3	18.5	10.0
Manufactured goods (5 + 6 + 7 + 8 + 9 − 68)	14.0	59.4	76.7	81.5	90.0
Total	100.0	100.0	100.0	100.0	100.0
Value of merchandise exports (US$ millions)	33	175	835	5,081	17,685

Source: Bank of Korea, *Economic Statistics Yearbook,* various issues.

Note: The figures shown here are based on customs clearance data and thus exclude exports not cleared through customs, such as sales of goods to military forces overseas and offshore sales of fish.

Numbers in parentheses are SITC Codes.

these products continue to have an important place in Korea's exports. With a shift occurring from cotton to noncotton fabrics and the increasing exports of footwear, the 1980 shares in merchandise exports were: clothing, 17 percent; noncotton fabrics and cotton yarn and fabrics, 6 percent each; and footwear, 5 percent. In turn, the share of machinery and transport equipment in total exports, 7 percent in 1970, doubled by 1975 and tripled by 1980. This category continued to be dominated, however, by relatively simple products, with radio and television sets accounting for 5 percent and electronic parts and components for 4 percent of the total. Korea's exports of nonelectrical machinery increased slowly, not exceeding 2 percent of merchandise exports in 1980, while the exports of ships, accounting for over 3 percent of the total, incorporated largely Japanese machinery. Korea has been unsuccessful in gaining a foothold in world markets for passenger automobiles.

After having declined from 7 percent in 1965 to 2 percent in 1970, the export share of iron and steel attained 5 percent in 1975 and 9 percent in 1980, reflecting the effects of large investments undertaken during the seventies. The combined export shares of fertilizer and cement reached 3 percent in 1980, while investments in petrochemicals and chemicals did not lead to the expected increase in exports.

The Implementation of an Outward-Oriented Development Strategy, 1960–73

Trade Policies during the Import-Substitution Phase, 1945–60

After World War II, Korea embarked on the first stage of import substitution characteristic of developing countries in the early period of industrialization. The application of this policy led to the expansion of industries producing nondurable consumer goods and their inputs. At the same time, exports were discouraged by the increased over-valuation of the exchange rate, as rapid domestic inflation was not fully offset by the depreciation of the Korean won.

The overvaluation of the exchange rate was especially pronounced toward the end of the Korean War, when the currency was devalued from 6 to 18 won to the U.S. dollar. With continuing rapid inflation, however, the effects of the devaluation wore off by August 1955, when a new exchange rate of 50 won to the dollar was adopted. This rate remained in effect until January 1960, notwithstanding continued domestic inflation. The real exchange rate, estimated by adjusting the official exchange rate for changes in wholesale prices at home and abroad, fell to half of its 1949–50 value (Frank, Kim, and Westphal 1975, pp. 30–33).

The government attempted to reduce the adverse effects of the overvaluation of the won on exports by alloting certificates to the holders of foreign exchange which allowed them to import certain popular items, essentially establishing a multiple exchange rate system. But exporters received preferential credits only on a limited scale, and tariff exemptions on the import of raw materials were not instituted until 1959. Altogether, the measures only compensated to a small extent for the overvaluation of the won, and exports were further discouraged by fluctuations in the real exchange rate that created considerable uncertainty as to the domestic currency value of export earnings.

The process of import substitution continued behind high protection, with increasing use made of quantitative import restrictions. By 1957, however, possibilities for first-stage import substitution were increasingly exhausted, since domestic production accounted for nine-tenths of the consumption of nondurable consumer goods and their inputs. The economy stagnated after 1957, setting the stage for the student revolution that overthrew President Syngman Rhee in April 1960.

Transition towards Outward Orientation, 1960–63

After a small devaluation to 65 won to the U.S. dollar in February 1960, the won was devalued substantially in the aftermath of the student revolution, reaching 130 won to the dollar in February 1961. At the same time, exchange rates were unified and import controls liberalized. An export subsidy scheme was put into effect, a 50 percent tax reduction was provided on profits derived from exports, and exporters received full exemption from indirect taxes on their inputs, as well as on export sales.

These measures reflected the liberalization philosophy of the civilian government established in April 1960 and of the military government that replaced it in May 1961. However, the real exchange rate declined again after February 1961 as rapid inflation was not compensated for by a further devaluation. The resulting deterioration in the balance of payments in turn led to the adoption of increased import restrictions and the reestablishment of a multiple exchange rate system.

A far-reaching reform was undertaken after the election in August 1964 of the government of Park Chung Lee, who retained power until his assassination 15 years later. In the trade area, the reform involved a devaluation from 130 to 257 won to the U.S. dollar, the unification of the exchange rate, import liberalization, and increased incentives for exports. The practice of giving preference to exporters in the granting of import licenses was expanded and formalized; exporters were given the automatic right to import their inputs duty free, and were permitted high wastage allowances on raw materials used in export production. Furthermore, the types and the volume of preferential loans were substantially increased and a governmental export promotion agency, KOTRA, was established.

The reform further included measures aimed at increasing public and private savings. Revenue collections were reorganized to increase the ratio of government revenue to GNP, steps were taken to hold down government expenditures, and interest rates on deposits were raised substantially to encourage private savings. With the successful application of anti-inflationary measures, real interest rates reached 10 percent a year.

The Policy of Outward Orientation

The policy package introduced after the August 1964 elections translated into practice the philosophy of liberalization that first emerged in the early sixties. This philosophy reflected the understanding that the liberalization of restrictions is necessary for the unhindered operation of economic forces; that Korea's poor resource endowment called for economic growth based on manufacturing activities; and that the limited domestic market could not provide opportunities for further import substitution, so that industrial expansion had to be sought in exporting.

The emphasis on exports represented a break with the policies applied by many developing countries in Latin America and South Asia which, upon the completion of the first stage of import substitution, moved to a second stage that entailed replacing by domestic production the imports of producer and consumer durables and the intermediate goods used in their manufacture. Korea thus joined Singapore and Taiwan in applying an outward-oriented development strategy.

Under inward orientation, production for domestic markets is favored over exports, while outward orientation involves providing similar incentives for exports and for import substitution. In Korea, a free-trade regime was applied to exports, supplemented by some additional incentives to nontraditional exports in the form of preferential export credits, generous wastage allowances on imported inputs, reductions in direct taxes, and preferential electricity and transportation rates. Exporters had the freedom to choose between domestic and imported inputs; they were exempted from indirect taxes on their output and inputs; and they paid no duty on imported inputs. The same privileges were extended to the producers of domestic inputs used in export production.[4]

The application of these rules provided similar treatment to all nontraditional exports. Furthermore, production for foreign and domestic markets received similar incentives, on the average. Uniform overall incentives were provided to primary and to manufacturing activities as well.

The application of the free-trade regime to exports was in no way contingent upon the fulfillment of export targets that were established for individual firms. Preferential export credits were provided according to predetermined rules, and wastage allowances were set for each product rather than for each firm. Thus, fulfillment of export targets did not affect the firm's access to export incentives, although successful Korean exporters reportedly enjoyed advantageous treatment in pending tax cases, and, in a few instances, wastage allowances were renegotiated between the government and industry representatives simultaneously with export targets. The

---

4. For an early discussion, see Balassa 1971.

commitment of the government to exports and the honors bestowed on exporters had a positive psychological impact. The monthly export meetings held by various levels of the administration also may have had a stimulating effect on exports, and exporters were given assistance in solving the administrative problems they encountered.

The export promotion measures were, throughout the period under consideration, imparting stability to the incentive system. Stability was further served by periodic devaluations that neutralized the effects of differential inflation rates in Korea and abroad. At the same time, the government followed a policy of "even keel," avoiding inflationary excesses and increasing nominal interest rates to keep real interest rates approximately constant.

The import liberalization measures adopted in 1964 and 1965 were followed in 1967 by the replacement of a positive list of items whose importation was allowed, by a negative list of items which required specific authorization to import. Import licenses were thus automatically granted, except for specifically prohibited or restricted items. Little change in import regulations occurred in subsequent years as decreases in the number of quota items were accompanied by increases in the number of restricted items (Balassa 1976, p. 147).

The System of Incentives and Its Economic Effects

The System of Incentives in 1968

Westphal and Kim (1982) have estimated nominal and effective protection and effective subsidy rates in Korea for 1968. Their study was undertaken within the framework of a research project directed by the present author, which also covered Argentina, Colombia, Israel, Singapore, and Taiwan. These developing economies have established an industrial base and can be classified as semi-industrial; they all belong to the upper range of middle-income developing economies. Differences in their incentive systems indicated by the structure of nominal and effective rates of protection and effective rates of subsidies reveal differences in their development strategies.

Nominal protection rates show the effects on domestic prices of import tariffs, export subsidies, and quantitative import restrictions. Effective protection rates relate the effects of these protective measures on the price of the product and on the price of its inputs in relation to value added in the production process. Effective subsidy rates indicate the relationship of the combined effects of protective measures and credit and tax preferences to value added. Average nominal protection, effective protection, and effective subsidy rates in the six semi-industrial economies, for primary and for manufacturing activities, are shown in table 3.3.

Table 3.3. Indicators of Incentives in Six Semi-Industrial Economies (%)

	Average Incentive Rates			Relative Incentives to Domestic and Foreign Markets		
	Primary Activities	Manufacturing	All Industries	Primary Activities	Manufacturing	All Industries
Argentina 1969						
Nominal protection	3	70	36	1.16	1.75	1.53
Effective protection	0	112	47	1.24	3.41	1.94
Effective subsidy	2	110	47	1.22	2.92	1.86
Colombia 1969						
Nominal protection	−8	30	3	1.11	1.16	1.22
Effective protection	−10	35	−2	1.13	1.42	1.23
Effective subsidy	−9	31	−2	1.06	1.20	1.13
Israel 1968						
Nominal protection	18	42	31	1.12	1.30	1.26
Effective protection	48	76	62	1.26	1.63	1.50
Effective subsidy	47	76	62	1.54	1.63	1.50
Korea 1968						
Nominal protection	10	16	13	1.11	1.12	1.14
Effective protection	9	13	10	1.16	0.95	1.10
Effective subsidy	11	8	10	1.11	0.81	1.01
Singapore 1967						
Nominal protection	3	3	3	1.05	1.05	1.05
Effective protection	9	4	6	1.13	1.09	1.09
Effective subsidy	12	2	6	1.11	1.08	1.08
Taiwan 1969						
Nominal protection	6	12	9	1.07	1.18	1.12
Effective protection	0	14	5	1.03	1.34	1.10
Effective subsidy	−2	13	5	0.89	1.01	0.89

Source: Balassa et al. (1982), Table 2.4.
Note: Agriculture is defined to include forestry and fishing; mining comprises mining and energy. Petroleum products are regarded as traditional exports in Colombia while diamonds are regarded as traditional exports in Israel. In all other countries, these products are classified as nontraditional. − Negative numbers show that the product group in question was discriminated against by the system of incentives.

Korea provided roughly similar incentives to primary and to manufacturing activities. Singapore appeared to favor primary over manufacturing activities, but the former had little importance in its economy. And while the manufacturing sector appears to be favored over primary activities in Taiwan, the estimates do not allow for the preferential tax treatment of agriculture. Furthermore, on the average, Korea, Singapore, and Taiwan gave similar incentives to exports and to import substitution, reflecting the application of an outward-oriented development strategy. In Argentina, Colombia, and Israel, which, to a greater or lesser extent, followed an inward-oriented development strategy, there was a considerable bias against primary activities as well as against exports. The anti-export bias was the most pronounced in the countries where manufacturing activities received considerable protection.

Development Strategies, Exports, and Economic Performance

The choice of development strategies influenced export performance to a considerable extent. This is shown by the experience of 11 semi-industrial economies in the 1960–73 period. In addition to the countries listed in table 3.3, the group includes Brazil, Chile, Mexico, Yugoslavia, and India.

The relationship between economic policies and exports is particularly evident in the case of Korea, where the adoption of an outward-oriented development strategy in the early sixties led to the highest export growth rates among the 11 semi-industrial economies in both the 1960–66 and the 1966–73 periods. Within total exports, the same result was obtained for manufactured goods and for primary products (table 3.4). Korea was followed by Singapore and Taiwan in terms of export growth rates in both groups of commodities.

Argentina, Brazil, Colombia, and Mexico followed traditional inward-oriented policies, but provided incentives to exports after 1966 as these policies led to a slowdown in economic growth. Correspondingly, exports accelerated in the 1966–73 period. By contrast, export growth rates declined in Chile and changed little in India, both of which persisted in the application of an inward-oriented development strategy. Finally, Israel and Yugoslavia experienced some deceleration in the growth of exports as earlier efforts at export promotion gave place to increased import protection.

Outward-oriented development strategies also have favorable effects on productivity and economic growth. These effects operate through resource allocation according to comparative advantage, greater capacity utilization, the exploitation of economies of scale, and technological improvements in response to competition abroad. Furthermore, exports under outward orientation may permit breaking the foreign exchange bottleneck that hinders economic growth. Finally, in the case of labor-surplus economies, employment increases as exports generate demand for domestic products through higher incomes, while higher employment is supported by savings in capital, as noted below.

The experience of the 11 semi-industrial economies in the 1960–73 period demonstrates the favorable effects of exports on economic growth. In Korea, rapid export expansion was followed by the acceleration of

Table 3.4. Export Growth in Eleven Semi-Industrial Economies (average annual percentage growth rate)

	Argentina	Brazil	Chile	Colombia	India	Israel	Korea	Mexico	Singapore	Taiwan	Yugoslavia
Primary products											
1953-60	0.2	-3.1	2.5	-3.5	3.7	20.5	-5.4	3.8	n.a.	-1.2	12.4
1960-66	6.3	4.7	9.7	0.3	4.5	15.5	24.0	6.9	29.5	17.3	5.7
1966-73	7.8	17.0	5.5	10.7	6.5	16.8	26.0	4.3	19.5	17.0	9.8
Manufactured goods											
1953-60	-11.7	9.9	3.2	0.0	1.3	18.0	14.0	5.6	n.a.	29.5	28.0
1960-66	14.6	27.5	15.6	35.0	6.7	15.3	80.0	12.7	24.5	36.5	21.5
1966-73	33.5	38.5	0.0	27.5	7.7	17.5	50.0	20.0	42.0	47.0	14.9
Total exports											
1953-60	-0.6	-2.8	2.6	-3.4	2.6	19.6	-3.2	3.9	n.a.	2.2	17.2
1960-66	6.7	5.4	10.1	1.5	5.5	15.3	40.0	7.8	28.5	23.5	13.6
1966-73	10.8	19.9	5.3	12.7	7.0	17.0	44.0	8.1	28.5	35.5	13.8

Source: Balassa (1982), Table 3.1.
Note: Data have been expressed in terms of U.S. dollars.

economic growth, with GNP growth rates reaching 7.3 percent in 1960–66 and 10.7 percent in 1966–73. Output growth rates were especially high in manufacturing (13.0 percent and 21.0 percent, respectively), where much of the export expansion was concentrated. At the same time, Korea was surpassed by few countries in agricultural growth.

The correlation between export expansion and the rate of output growth is also apparent in intercountry relationships. Such a relationship has been established for agriculture as well as for manufacturing. The Spearman rank correlation coefficient was 0.67 in the first case and 0.71 in the second, statistically significant at the 1 percent level. Correlating manufacturing exports with the growth of manufactured output net of exports, a rank correlation coefficient of 0.74 was obtained. The latter result presumably reflects the indirect effects of exports through demand for domestic products as well as technological improvements. Furthermore, the Spearman rank correlation coefficient between the intercountry rate of growth of total exports and that of GNP was 0.89 for the entire 1960–73 period. The coefficient was only slightly lower, 0.77, if export growth was correlated with the growth of GNP net of exports, statistically significant at the 1 percent level.

Export expansion also appears to have had a positive effect on economic growth in a production-function type of relationship, after allowance is made for increases in capital and labor. Thus, adding an export variable to domestic and foreign capital and labor increases the explanatory power of the regression equation by one-third. From the estimated relationships, it further appears that the increase in per capita income would have been 43 percent lower in Korea if it had had export growth rates identical to the average for the group as a whole.

In a production-function type of relationship, one considers the effects of export expansion on economic growth from the supply side, and the coefficient of the export variable is interpreted to express the favorable effects of outward orientation on total productivity. An alternative approach examines the effects of export expansion on economic growth from the demand side, with domestic demand and import substitution included as additional demand variables. Results obtained for Korea in the 1960–68 period, show the total[5] contribution of export expansion to the increase in aggregate output to be 38 percent, that of import substitution 2 percent, and that of domestic demand expansion 60 percent (Frank, Westphal, and Kim 1975, p. 40). However, the contribution of exports is underestimated by excluding indirect effects that operate through increases in incomes and technological change. The same conclusion applies to more recent esti-

---

5. Inclusive of indirect effects operating through input-output relationships.

mates for the period 1963–73, which further separate the contribution of changes in input-output coefficients to output growth. The relevant results are: export expansion, 36 percent; import substitution, 10 percent; domestic demand expansion, 35 percent; and changes in input-output coefficients, 19 percent (Kim and Roemer 1979, pp. 114–15).

Comparative Advantage, Employment, and Income Distribution

The next question concerns specialization according to comparative advantage. Estimates of the factor intensity of Korean production, exports, and imports were first made by Westphal and Kim. The estimates reported in table 3.5 show manufactured exports to be substantially more labor-intensive than imports, while the opposite is true for total trade if only direct coefficients are considered. The reversal occurs because Korea's exports of primary products are much more capital-intensive than are the primary products it imports.

Westphal and Kim suggest that the high capital intensity of Korea's primary exports, consisting mainly of minerals, may be explained by complementarity between capital and natural resources, whereas Korea imports labor-intensive agricultural products (1982, p. 262). The same observation applies to results obtained by Hong (1979), who excluded noncompetitive imports from his estimates reported in table 3.5. Correspondingly, attention should be focused on trade in manufactured goods. This will be done by reference to direct factor intensities, which provide a more appropriate test of specialization according to comparative advantage than total (direct and indirect) factor intensities, since intermediate products are tradable.

According to the estimates by Westphal and Kim, Korean manufactured exports became increasingly labor-intensive relative to manufactured imports as well as to manufactured output during the 1960–68 period. Hong does not provide data on manufactured imports but shows even larger differences between the labor intensity of manufactured exports and that of output, with little change taking place during the sixties and a trend towards lesser labor intensity for manufactured exports apparent in the early seventies.

The cited estimates define capital in terms of physical assets and labor in terms of man-years. In an earlier study, Hong also considered the skill intensity of Korea's trade. The results show exports to be relatively skill-intensive compared to competitive imports throughout the 1967–72 period (1976, table 10.3). Estimates for manufactured exports and imports are not available, however, and competitive imports include agricultural products that tend to use unskilled and semiskilled labor.

A different procedure has been utilized by the present author, who

Table 3.5. Capital/Labor Ratios in Domestic Output, Exports, and Imports

	Westphal and Kim						Hong				
	10 million won per man-year						US$ millions per man-year				
	1960	1962	1966	1968	1960	1963	1966	1968	1970	1973	1975
Direct factor requirements											
Manufactured products											
Domestic outputs	3.37	3.46	3.75	3.79	1.62	1.53	1.81	1.63	2.00	2.62	3.00
Exports	3.68	3.31	3.09	2.82	.82	.78	.86	.86	1.07	1.67	3.40
Imports	4.78	5.18	5.05	4.29	n.a.	n.a.	n.a.	n.a.	n.a.	n.a.	n.a.
All goods & services											
Domestic output	2.28	2.18	2.24	2.43	.58	.62	.70	.84	1.06	1.28	1.48
Exports	3.08	3.97	4.15	4.76	.47	.58	.78	.86	1.08	1.73	2.86
Imports	2.21	2.05	2.47	2.33	.34	.70	1.40	.98	1.05	1.57	1.72
Total factor requirements											
Manufactured products											
Domestic output	1.84	1.85	1.99	1.95	n.a.	n.a.	n.a.	n.a.	n.a.	n.a.	n.a.
Exports	2.67	2.70	2.44	2.33	1.00	.97	1.13	1.15	1.49	2.17	3.80
Imports	3.61	4.17	4.17	3.65	n.a.	n.a.	n.a.	n.a.	n.a.	n.a.	n.a.
All goods & services											
Domestic output	2.28	2.18	2.24	2.43	n.a.	n.a.	n.a.	n.a.	n.a.	n.a.	n.a.
Exports	2.92	3.28	3.08	2.17	.59	.71	1.00	1.51	1.48	2.13	3.13
Imports	2.65	2.73	3.07	2.87	.54	.95	1.58	1.46	1.55	2.60	2.75

Sources: Westphal and Kim (1982), table 8.22; Hong (1979), tables 2.7, 2.8, and 2.1.

examined the relationship between "revealed" comparative advantage and capital/labor ratios in developed and developing countries (Balassa 1979). This was done by regressing "revealed" comparative advantage ratios for 184 industrial product categories, defined in terms of relative export shares, on capital/labor ratios, defined in terms of stocks as well as flows and with distinction made between physical and human capital using U.S. coefficients. The stock measure of physical capital was represented by the value of fixed capital; the stock measure of human capital was taken to equal the discounted value of the difference between the average wage and the unskilled wage; and the flow measures of physical and human capital were defined as nonwage and wage value added, respectively.

In the case of Korea, the regression coefficients of "revealed" comparative advantage ratios on capital/labor ratios have the expected negative signs, indicating that Korea is relatively poor in physical and human capital. The coefficients of both the stock and the flow measures of human capital are significant at the 5 percent level, while the coefficient of the flow measure of physical capital is significant at the 10 percent level.

Subsequently, estimates have been made for the same year, using the same methodology but Korean coefficients, by Chungsoo Kim (1983). Kim's estimates also have a negative sign and are statistically significant at the 5 percent level in the case of the flow measure of human capital and at the 10 percent level for the stock measure of total capital (table 3.6). Kim has further estimated regression equations for Korean imports by taking the relative import shares for individual commodity categories as the dependent variable. All the regression coefficients have the expected positive signs, and are significant at the 5 or 10 percent levels.

The results indicate that Korea's manufactured exports tend to be labor-intensive compared with its imports. Kim's estimates for Korean bilateral trade support this conclusion. The regression coefficients of Korea's relative export shares on total capital/labor ratios, estimated for bilateral trade with 18 developed and 17 developing countries, are negatively correlated with the physical capital endowments and the human capital endowments of the individual countries, while a positive correlation obtains with regard to Korean imports. The estimates are statistically significant for the physical and human capital endowment variables, taken individually, at the 5 percent level, although the results for human capital endowment lose their statistical significance if the two endowment variables are included jointly in the equation (1979, tables 21 and 22).

Specialization according to comparative advantage raises national income directly by reducing the domestic resource cost of foreign exchange. In fact, in 1968, the domestic resource cost of earning foreign exchange through exports was less than half of the domestic resource cost of saving

Table 3.6. The Factor Intensity of the Pattern of Exports

	Regression Results Obtained by Using		
	U.S. Input Coefficients	Korean Input Coefficients	
	Export	Export	Import
Stock measure of capital			
Physical capital	−.46	−.43	.02
Human capital	−1.24*	−.18	1.25**
Total capital	−1.67	−.66**	.66*
Flow measure of capital			
Physical capital	−.69**	.13	.03
Human capital	−3.91*	−1.06*	1.25*
Total capital	−3.02	−.43	.65*

Sources: Balassa (1979), pp. 121–56; Kim (1983), pp. 14–15.

Note: Regression coefficients have been estimated by regressing the "revealed" comparative advantage ratio for 184 product categories, defined in terms of relative export (import) shares, on capital/labor ratios. The stock measure of physical capital is represented by the value of fixed capital. The stock measure of human capital is taken to equal the discounted value of the difference between the average wage and the unskilled wage. The flow measures of physical and human capital, respectively, equal nonwage and wage value added. Regression coefficients that are significant at the 5 percent level have been denoted by *; those significant at the 10 percent level by **.

foreign exchange through import substitution (Westphal and Kim 1982, p. 247).[6]

In labor-surplus economies, specialization according to comparative advantage also raises national income indirectly, since savings in capital make it possible to increase employment. There are further savings in capital in that exporting permits increased capacity utilization and the exploitation of economies of scale. It has been reported that average utilization rates in Korean manufacturing nearly doubled between 1962 and 1971. Furthermore, the productivity of capital and labor in manufacturing doubled between 1960 and 1973, representing an annual average rate of increase of 5.5 percent (Westphal and Kim 1982, pp. 263–64).

Notwithstanding the rapid rise of labor productivity, manufacturing employment more than quadrupled between 1960 and 1973, corresponding to an average annual rate of growth of 12 percent. Nineteen percent of the increase in manufacturing employment was in production for exports;

---

6. This is not to say that there would not have been high-cost exports in Korea, supported by export incentives. But such cases are few in number and represent an exception rather than the rule.

this proportion rises to 26 percent if account is taken of the indirect effects of exports through input-output relationships (Cole and Westphal 1975, table 8). The estimates do not allow, however, for the employment effects of exports through demand for domestic products generated at higher income levels.

The rapid increase in manufacturing employment led to a fall in the rate of unemployment from 8 percent in 1963 to 4 percent in 1973, with the decline being concentrated in urban areas. It further created considerable pressure in labor markets, contributing to a near-doubling in real wages between 1960 and 1973. With rapid increases in employment and real wages, the share of the poorest 60 percent of the population in national income increased from 34.5 percent in 1950 to 42.4 percent in 1970 (Ahluwalia, Carter, and Chenery 1978, p. 28).[7] Greater interest attaches, however, to changes in the absolute, rather than the relative, incomes of the poor. In this connection, it is instructive to compare the experience of Korea with that of Sri Lanka, which adopted an inward-oriented development strategy and followed egalitarian policies. The incomes of the poorest 60 percent of the population rose 20 percent faster than the national average in Korea between 1958 and 1970, while the incomes of the same income group rose 130 percent faster than the national average in Sri Lanka between 1967 and 1973. But, with much more rapid overall growth, the per capita incomes of the poor increased at an average annual rate of 9.8 percent in Korea, compared to 4.6 percent in Sri Lanka (ibid.).

External Shocks and Policy Responses to These Shocks, 1973–78

The Policies Applied

The favorable effects of outward orientation were observed in 1960–73, a period that was characterized by the rapid growth of the world economy. At the time the question was repeatedly raised whether an outward-oriented development strategy would retain its advantages over inward orientation if world economic conditions deteriorated. In the years after 1973 such a deterioration did in fact occur.

Oil prices quadrupled in 1973–74 and aggravated the world recession that was to follow the 1972–73 boom. The recession deepened further as all major industrial countries more or less simultaneously adopted anti-inflationary policies. As a result, the industrial countries' GDPs remained stationary in 1974 and in 1975, compared to a 4.6 percent rate of growth in the 1963–73 period. Also, following increases of 16.5 percent a year be-

---

7. Professor Gary Fields has pointed out to me, however, that the data are subject to considerable error.

tween 1963 and 1973, the volume of the industrial countries' imports of manufactured goods from the developing countries increased by only 4.2 percent in 1974 and declined by 1.5 percent in 1975 (Balassa 1981a, p. 265).

The initial reactions in Korea to the deterioration of the world economic environment took the form of proposals to modify the outward-oriented development strategy of the previous decade. These reactions were expressed in the preliminary documents for the Fourth Five-Year Plan, covering the period 1977–81, prepared in June 1975. The *Discussion Paper on the Development Strategy for the Fourth Five-Year Plan, 1977–81*, prepared by the Korea Development Institute, suggested the need for "defending the economy from various international instabilities" (1975, p. 24). It further added: "In the past Korea has pursued a course which left foreign trade to reach any level achieved by comparative advantage in world markets. It is only judicious to reduce Korea's vulnerability to the trade effects of foreign countercyclical policies and to the growing imperfections in the world market for basic commodities" (ibid.). In accordance with the proposed change in strategy, the *Guidelines for the Fourth Five-Year Economic Development Plan*, prepared by the Korea Economic Planning Bureau, envisaged "the increase of import substitution and conservation of resources in order to reduce the growth rate of imports to the level of the GNP growth rate" (1975, p. 15).

In an advisory report prepared for the government of Korea, the present author objected to the proposals for increased inward orientation and recommended maintaining Korea's outward orientation. As stated in the report, "the author's recommendations reflect the fact that, following the 1974–75 recession, developed nations will again experience relatively high rates of economic growth, leading to rapid increases in their imports from developing countries. It is further assumed that the flexibility of its economy, the existence of excess capacity in its export industries, and favorable domestic supply and foreign demand conditions in potential new exports would enable Korea to continue increasing its share in LDC exports of manufactured goods, albeit at a lower rate than beforehand" (Balassa 1975, p. 136).

In fact, GDP of the industrial countries increased by 4.3 percent annually between 1975 and 1978, while the volume of their manufactured imports from the developing countries grew by 16.5 percent a year during this period (Balassa 1981a, p. 265). Korea also continued to increase its market share in industrial countries' imports from the developing countries as a result of the continued outward orientation decided upon by the Korean policy makers in preparing the final version of the Fourth Five-Year Plan. These found expression in the trade policies followed in the 1975–77 period.

To begin with, reductions in import protection through the lowering of tariffs and the liberalization of import restrictions appear to have been greater than reductions in export subsidies through the elimination of tax benefits on income derived from exports and decreases in wastage allowances on imported inputs used in export production. Also, new facilities were established for medium-term and long-term export credits and the subsidy equivalent of export credits increased.[8] At the same time, although the real exchange rate declined from its 1973 all-time high when wholesale prices in Korea rose less rapidly than in other countries, it was above the 1970 level in 1978.

Singapore and Taiwan, too, continued their outward-oriented strategies, further reducing import protection. These countries also promoted savings and investment through high real interest rates, government budget surpluses, and incentives to private investment. Similar measures to promote domestic savings and investment were taken in Korea.

Among inward-oriented countries, Chile and Uruguay turned toward outward orientation in response to external shocks. Both of these countries devalued the exchange rate in real terms, liberalized imports, reduced tariffs, and ended price controls. They also established positive interest rates, liberalized financial markets, and virtually eliminated the government budget deficit.

On the other hand, Brazil and Colombia increased the bias of the incentive system against exports through greater import protection and reduced export subsidies. Furthermore, Colombia let its exchange rate appreciate in real terms to a considerable extent. In the early part of the period, the exchange rate was also overvalued in Argentina and Mexico, and while there was little change in their relative incentives for exports or for import substitution, both countries followed excessive expansionary policies and had large budgetary deficits. Finally, both Israel and Yugoslavia raised the level of import protection and let their exchange rates appreciate in real terms, while India continued its inward-oriented development strategy.

The Balance-of-Payments Effects of External Shocks and of Policy Responses to These Shocks

The estimated balance-of-payments effects of external shocks, in the form of the deterioration of the terms of trade and the slowdown in world demand after 1973, for the 11 semi-industrial countries discussed earlier, as well as for Uruguay, are reported in table 3.7. It further shows the

---

8. These measures provided incentives to capital-intensive exports. In fact, the capital intensity of manufactured exports increased after 1973 (table 3.5).

Table 3.7. Balance-of-Payments Effects of External Shocks and of Policy Responses to these Shocks, 1974–1978 Average (%)

	Argentina	Brazil	Colombia	Mexico	Chile	Uruguay	India	Korea	Singapore	Taiwan	Israel	Yugoslavia
External shocks												
Terms of trade effects/ average trade	2.5	38.2	−21.3	14.8	54.8	55.7	34.7	27.6	16.1	7.9	46.1	56.1
Export volume effects/ exports	1.1	9.4	13.5	13.3	4.9	5.9	14.1	9.9	8.0	10.8	14.1	23.4
External shocks/GNP	0.2	2.7	−0.7	1.3	8.0	6.1	2.1	6.9	23.3	6.5	11.9	7.8
Policy responses												
Additional net external financing/ average trade	−8.0	12.7	5.7	47.8	−3.6	44.0	65.6	−34.2	15.2	−14.7	32.2	47.1
Increase in export market shares/ exports	−3.0	7.9	−1.8	−10.2	25.5	20.4	−9.5	34.6	6.4	1.9	−15.3	−9.4
Import substitution/ imports	18.2	28.3	−11.4	−17.5	18.1	2.4	−6.5	47.9	−8.0	7.1	6.8	11.0
Import effects of lower GNP growth/ imports	0.7	−4.0	−0.5	4.4	26.7	−7.3	−0.8	−11.4	9.8	26.7	21.6	16.9

Source: Balassa (1981b), pp. 158–59.

estimated balance-of-payment effects of policy responses to external shocks, including additional net external financing, as well as domestic policy measures in the form of export promotion, import substitution, and (temporarily) reducing the rate of income growth.[9]

While outward-oriented economies suffered relatively large external shocks, they did well in increasing their export market shares and, with the exception of Singapore, also experienced positive import substitution. Again with the exception of Singapore, these countries placed little reliance on additional net external financing, as domestic policy measures generally sufficed to offset the adverse balance-of-payments effects of external shocks.

Korea holds first place among the 12 national economies in export promotion as well as import substitution, with export shares increasing by one-third and import coefficients declining by one-half. Korea experienced losses in export market shares and negative import substitution in 1978, however, as its real exchange rate appreciated and a shift in policies occurred favoring large, capital-intensive investments in intermediate products and heavy machinery.[10]

All inward-oriented economies other than Brazil experienced a decline in export market shares between 1973 and 1978. Furthermore, apart from Argentina, where a considerable amount of import substitution occurred, all of these countries relied on additional net external financing, since domestic policy measures were not adequate to cope with the balance-of-payments effects of external shocks.

Adjustment Policies and Economic Growth

It appears, then, that while outward-oriented economies suffered substantially greater external shocks than most inward-oriented economies, they have been more successful in surmounting these shocks through domestic adjustment. In particular, the policies which were applied permitted outward-oriented economies to increase their export market shares. The extent of reliance on export promotion, in turn, favorably affected the rate of economic growth.

Although the original response might have been to apply deflationary policies, as in Singapore and Taiwan, outward-oriented economies eventually surpassed or approached the GNP growth rates of the earlier period. By contrast, although some of the inward-oriented economies, such as Brazil and Yugoslavia, attempted to maintain high economic growth rates

9. Detailed results, a description of the methodology, and a discussion of the policies applied can be found in Balassa 1981b.
10. Changes in the policies applied and their economic effects in 1979–80 are examined in detail in a subsequent section of this chapter.

in the face of external shocks, they eventually experienced a slowdown in economic expansion. For the group as a whole, the Spearman rank correlation coefficient between the extent of reliance on export promotion and the rate of economic growth was 0.70, statistically significant at the 1 percent level.[11]

Various considerations may be introduced to explain these results. To begin with, imports include goods competing with domestic production under an outward-oriented strategy and extend from raw materials to final consumer goods. By contrast, economies that pursue inward-oriented policies generally exclude imports which compete with domestic production and limit imports to material inputs and machinery. Correspondingly, there is greater latitude to reduce imports in response to external shocks under an outward-oriented than under an inward-oriented strategy, and the loss of production due to the decline in the capacity to import tends to be larger in the latter case than in the former. This observation is supported by an analysis of the effects of external shocks in archetypes of alternative development strategies in a general equilibrium framework (de Melo and Robinson 1980).

The flexibility of the national economy is also greater under an outward-oriented than under an inward-oriented strategy. In the former case, firms have been exposed to competition in world markets and have acquired experience in changing their product composition in response to shifts in foreign demand. By contrast, under inward orientation, there is generally limited competition in the confines of the narrow domestic market and firms have little inducement to innovate, which is necessary under outward orientation in order to meet competition from abroad.

Finally, the low extent of discrimination against primary activities, the relatively low degree of variation in incentive rates, and cost reductions through the exploitation of economies of scale in export industries contribute to efficient exporting and import substitution in outward-oriented economies, whereas import substitution behind high protection—aggravated by the variability of incentive rates—becomes increasingly costly and brings diminishing returns in terms of net foreign exchange savings. This proposition receives support from the observed high correlation between the extent of reliance on export promotion and the reciprocal of the incremental capital/output ratio. The Spearman rank correlation coefficient between the two variables was 0.75 in the 1973–79 period.

11. The extent of reliance on export promotion in response to external shocks was defined as the ratio of the increment in exports associated with increases in market shares to the balance-of-payments effects of external shocks. In order to allow for the delayed effects of the reforms undertaken in Chile and Uruguay, the rate of growth of GNP for the 1975–79 period was used in the calculations.

Economic growth was further influenced by the rate of domestic savings and investment that was promoted by the policies followed in outward-oriented economies. In an intercountry context, a 10 percent increase in the reciprocal of the incremental capital/output ratio was associated with a 9–10 percent increase in the GNP growth rate, and a 10 percent increase in the domestic savings ratio with a 3–4 percent increase in growth.

Policy Reversals in the Second Period of External Shocks, 1979–80

Exchange Rates and Investment Allocation in Korea

Between 1975 and 1978 oil prices rose less than world inflation, but the real price of oil in 1978 nevertheless exceeded its 1973 level by two and a half times. The price of oil doubled between 1978 and 1980, representing increases by more than four-fifths in real terms. The inflationary pressures generated by the doubling of oil prices led to the adoption of deflationary policies in the developed countries, which aggravated the direct effect of the oil price increase on their national economies.

The new policies, however, were more favorable to profits and to investment than those of the years 1974–75, and the rate of growth of GDP in the developed countries declined only from 3.8 percent in 1978 to 3.4 percent in 1979 and to 1.3 percent in 1980. Imports of manufactured goods from the developing countries fared even better, rising by 12 percent in 1979 and 10 percent in 1980 in volume terms. This result was achieved despite the existence of protectionist pressures in the developed countries; moreover, the increase occurred from a base nearly twice that of five years earlier.

The volume of Korean exports, however, fell by 1 percent in 1979 (table 3.8). This decline represented a continuation of the slowdown of export expansion in Korea in the preceding year. While the average rate of growth of the exports of manufactured goods by the developing countries to the developed countries rose from 8 percent in 1977 to 16 percent in 1978, in Korea a 19 percent rise in 1977 was followed by a 14 percent increase the following year.[12]

The contrast is even more marked with Hong Kong, Singapore, and Taiwan, whose export volume increased by 17 percent, 20 percent, and 7 percent respectively in 1979, following improvements in 1978, in the cases of Hong Kong and Taiwan. Had Korea matched average increases in export volume in the three other Far Eastern countries in 1978 and in 1979, its exports would have been US$2.2 billion higher in the latter year. And

---

12. It should be recalled that manufactured goods account for nine-tenths of Korea's exports.

Table 3.8. Export Performance 1974–79: Korea, Taiwan, Singapore, and Hong Kong (% change)

	1974	1975	1976	1977	1978	1979	1980	1981
Korea								
Export value[a]	38.5	13.9	51.6	30.4	26.5	15.7	17.1	21.3
Export volume index	9.3	22.9	35.9	19.0	14.2	−1.1	10.9	18.2
Unit value index	26.6	−7.3	11.7	9.5	10.7	16.9	5.3	2.4
Taiwan								
Export value[a]	25.2	−5.8	53.8	14.6	31.9	23.6	23.0	14.5
Export volume index	−4.3	0.2	50.2	7.8	24.1	6.6	10.6	10.1
Unit value index	30.9	−5.9	2.4	6.4	6.1	16.0	11.2	3.6
Singapore								
Export value[a]	60.2	−7.9	21.8	24.9	23.5	39.9	35.5	8.0
Export volume index	10.1	−8.3	19.0	15.1	12.4	20.1	16.8	n.a.
Unit value index	45.5	0.4	2.4	8.5	9.9	16.5	16.0	n.a.
Hong Kong[b]								
Export value[a]	0.0	0.0	41.7	12.9	19.5	31.8	30.2	10.4
Export volume index	0.0	0.0	30.0	4.6	11.0	16.6	10.9	8.7
Unit value index[c]	0.0	0.0	9.0	7.9	7.7	13.0	17.5	1.6

Sources: International Monetary Fund, *International Financial Statistics* and World Bank data bank.
[a]In billions of U.S. dollars; based on balance of payments accounts.
[b]Trade figures from IMF Data Bank.
[c]Derived from export value and volume figures.

Korea's exports would have been US$8.2 billion higher had it maintained the advantage in export growth rates it experienced in 1976 and in 1977 vis-à-vis the other three Far Eastern economies.

An important factor contributing to the deterioration of Korea's export performance was the appreciation of the real exchange rate. With the official exchange rate being maintained at 484 won to the U.S. dollar in the face of domestic rates of inflation in excess of inflation rates abroad, the real exchange rate appreciated by 5 percent between 1975 and 1978, and by 7 percent between 1978 and 1979.

At the same time, calculations of real exchange rates derived by the use of wholesale price indices underestimate the decline in Korea's competitive position. This is because increases in the prices of goods that enter international trade are limited by foreign competition, and hence do not fully reflect the rise in production costs. Interest attaches, therefore, to changes in unit labor costs, which show the extent of cost pressures on the firm due to increases in wages, adjusted for variations in labor productivity. Differential changes in wholesale prices and in unit labor costs, in turn, provide an indication of changes in profit margins.

As shown in table 3.9, unit labor costs in Korean manufacturing rose less rapidly than wholesale prices until 1975, thereby raising profit margins. The situation was subsequently reversed; between 1975 and 1979, unit labor costs doubled while wholesale prices increased by 62 percent. Correspondingly, Korea's labor-cost-adjusted real exchange rate appreciated by 29 percent between 1975 and 1979.[13]

These calculations have been made with reference to Korea's principal markets, the United States and Japan, in order to indicate changes in the competitiveness of Korean producers in these markets. Further interest attaches to comparisons of unit labor costs in Korea and in the Far Eastern economies competing with Korea. The data in Table 3.9 indicate that unit labor costs, expressed in terms of U.S. dollars, increased by 101 percent in Korea between 1975 and 1979, while the increase was 34 percent in Japan, 25 percent in the United States, and 35 percent in Taiwan.

Through its impact on exports, the deterioration of the competitiveness of Korean industry adversely affected economic growth, albeit with a time lag. This is indicated by the reversal of the pattern of year-to-year changes in real GNP between the four quarters of 1977 (9.7, 9.2, 11.2, and 13.7 percent) and of 1978 (17.1, 16.7, 13.8, and 4.9 percent), the subsequent decline in the rate of growth of GDP to 1.9 percent between the fourth quarters of 1978 and 1979, and the absolute fall in GDP by 2.0 percent in the first half of 1980. Exports and economic growth were also adversely affected by the sectoral allocation of investment. While the original version of the 15-Year Social and Economic Development Plan for the 1977–91 period, calling for a shift toward import substitution, was revised in response to criticisms (Balassa 1977), policy changes favoring capital-intensive industries producing intermediate goods and heavy machinery were much greater than envisaged in the revised plan.

Capital-intensive industries producing intermediate products, such as ferrous and nonferrous metals, petrochemicals and chemicals, and heavy machinery, such as electrical power generators and heavy construction and engineering equipment, were given priority in the allocation of domestic credit and in access to foreign credit. "Directed" credit assumed increased importance during the period, when the cost of credit to the industries in question was reduced through preferential interest rates. Fiscal incentives in the form of exemptions from corporate income taxes and accelerated depreciation provisions also lowered the cost of capital to these industries. At the same time, the government applied "moral suasion," often practi-

---

13. Owing to lack of information for all the countries concerned, wholesale price indices rather than indices of unit labor costs have been used in the calculations for Korea's principal trading partners.

Table 3.9. Nominal and Real Exchange Rates (1975 = 100)

		1970	1971	1972	1973	1974	1975	1976	1977	1978	1979	1980	1981	1979 IV	1980 IV	1981 IV
Nominal & real exchange rates, Korea																
(1) Nominal exchange rate, won per US$		310.4	350.1	394.0	398.5	406.0	484.0	484.0	484.0	484.0	484.0	607.6	681.0	484.0	651.3	690.1
(2) Wholesale prices, Korea		42.1	45.7	52.0	55.6	79.0	100.0	112.1	122.2	136.5	162.1	225.3	275.8	175.4	245.9	283.6
(3) Unit labor costs, Korea		62.4	66.7	71.8	72.3	85.8	100.0	124.2	144.0	168.6	200.5	239.3	249.2	235.2	258.6	274.8
(4) Foreign wholesale prices, US$		58.8	61.4	66.0	78.6	93.6	100.0	104.3	112.8	129.9	143.3	163.5	170.0	147.7	173.4	169.1
(5) Relative wholesale prices	(2):(4)	71.6	74.4	78.8	70.7	84.4	100.0	107.5	108.3	105.1	113.1	137.8	162.2	118.8	141.8	167.7
(6) Relative unit labor costs	(3):(4)	106.1	108.6	108.8	92.0	91.7	100.0	119.1	127.7	128.6	139.9	146.4	146.6	159.2	149.1	162.5
(7) Real exchange rate (wholesale prices)	(1):(5)	433.5	470.6	500.0	563.6	481.0	484.0	450.2	446.9	460.5	427.9	441.0	419.9	407.4	459.3	411.5
(8) Real exchange rate (unit labor costs)	(1):(6)	292.6	322.3	362.1	433.2	442.7	484.0	406.4	379.0	376.4	346.0	415.2	464.5	304.0	436.8	424.7
Unit labor costs (US$)																
(9) Korea		97.3	92.2	88.2	88.9	100.6	100.0	124.1	143.5	167.1	200.5	239.3	174.8	235.2	191.9	192.7
(10) U.S.A.		n.a.	n.a.	74.6	76.7	84.9	100.0	100.7	107.3	115.7	125.4	142.1	153.6	130.1	146.9	161.9
(11) Japan		n.a.	n.a.	58.0	67.5	80.4	100.0	99.4	113.2	144.0	133.7	129.1	137.9	121.7	143.0	135.1
(12) Taiwan		n.a.	n.a.	52.3	64.2	93.6	100.0	104.7	115.3	117.6	132.7	153.4	176.1	142.4	157.0	n.a.
(13) Singapore		n.a.	n.a.	53.7	64.4	90.7	100.0	107.0	113.0	127.9	138.1	152.0	171.3	n.a.	n.a.	n.a.
Unit labor cost & real wages, Korea																
(14) Nominal wage		37.9	45.2	52.4	58.2	78.7	100.0	134.7	180.2	242.1	311.4	383.1	458.9	356.8	421.4	502.8
(15) Manufacturing output		35.3	41.1	47.8	64.8	83.7	100.0	131.8	158.7	196.4	220.2	215.8	238.8	214.2	222.3	247.4
(16) Manufacturing employment		58.2	60.6	65.5	80.5	91.2	100.0	121.5	126.9	136.8	141.8	134.8	129.7	141.2	136.4	135.2
(17) Labor productivity	(15):(16)	60.7	67.8	73.0	80.5	91.8	100.0	108.5	125.1	143.6	155.3	160.1	184.1	151.7	163.0	183.0
(18) Unit labor costs	(14):(17)	62.4	66.7	71.8	73.2	85.7	100.0	124.1	143.5	168.6	200.5	239.3	249.3	235.2	258.6	274.8
(19) Consumer prices		49.1	55.7	62.2	64.2	79.8	100.0	115.3	127.0	145.3	171.9	221.3	272.9	182.0	243.0	282.2
(20) Real wages	(14):(19)	77.2	81.1	84.2	90.7	98.6	100.0	116.8	141.8	166.6	181.2	173.1	168.2	196.0	173.4	178.2

Sources: International Monetary Fund, *International Financial Statistics*, and Bank of Korea *Monthly Economic Statistics*.

cally forcing firms in labor-intensive export industries to invest in the favored industries.

The effects of these measures are apparent in changes in the pattern of investment. While the amount of industrial investment undertaken in the first three years of the Fourth Five-Year Plan (1977–81) was 80 percent of that planned for the entire five-year period, the corresponding figures were 130 percent for basic metals and 101 percent for chemicals and other intermediate products. By contrast, only 50 percent of planned investment was undertaken in the textile industry and 42 percent in the other light industries. Machinery, electronics, and shipbuilding occupied a middle position, the corresponding figure being 101 percent, with larger than planned increases for heavy machinery.

With the overfulfillment of plan targets for capital-intensive intermediate goods and heavy machinery, in the 1977–79 period 26.8 percent of manufacturing investment was in basic metals; 28.8 percent in chemicals and other intermediate goods; 23.3 percent in machinery, electronics, and transport equipment; 12.6 percent in textiles and clothing; and 8.5 percent in other light industrial goods. This contrasts with the relative shares of the same industries in industrial production in the base year of the plan, 1975: 7.7 percent, 25.8 percent, 14.7 percent, 25.4 percent, and 26.4 percent respectively.

The new emphasis lowered the productivity of capital in Korean manufacturing. This is evidenced by the rise in the incremental capital/output ratio from 1.34 in 1970–73 and 1.46 in 1973–76 to 1.63 in 1976–78 and 2.73 in 1979. This increase reflects high costs in the industries that produced intermediate goods and heavy machinery. Apart from the capital intensity of the production process, firms in these industries could not fully utilize their capacity in the confines of the domestic market and were not sufficiently specialized. These industries' unused capacity contrasted with the lack of sufficient new capacity in traditional labor-intensive export industries that were disadvantaged by the system of credit allocation and suffered the adverse consequences of the increased overvaluation of the won. The scarcity of new investments in the latter industries, in turn, hindered the expansion and the upgrading of Korea's labor-intensive exports.

Policy Changes in 1980 and 1981

The turn toward import substitution in capital-intensive industries could not be rationalized by the slow growth of the manufactured imports of the developed countries or by the resumption of the rise in oil prices that occurred only in mid-1979. Rather, it can be attributed to decisions taken by President Park, reflecting considerations of national prestige, which may also largely explain the maintenance of an increasingly unrealistic exchange rate.

At the same time, the share of gross fixed investment in GDP was increased from about 25 percent in the mid-seventies to more than 30 percent in 1978 and 1979, in part to finance investments in capital-intensive industries. Feverish construction activity, in turn, created pressures in labor markets, leading to an 81 percent rise in real wages between 1975 and 1979. The high import intensity of industries producing intermediate goods and heavy machinery, together with the deterioration of the competitiveness of Korean industry, also contributed to the acceleration of the growth of imports, with average annual increases of 21 percent in volume between 1977 and 1979, compared to 14 percent in the 1970–77 period. The acceleration of import growth is even greater if one excludes the import content of exports; the relevant figures are 11 percent in 1970–77 and 25 percent in 1977–79.

Following the assassination of President Park, the won was devalued by 20 percent in terms of the U.S. dollar in January 1980. With small exchange rate adjustments during the rest of the year, the exchange rate reached 656 won to the U.S. dollar, representing an additional devaluation of 13 percent. As a result, the real exchange rate depreciated by 13 percent between the fourth quarters of 1979 and 1980, although it remained only 5 percent lower than in 1975.

Greater improvements occurred in labor costs as pressures on profit margins, relatively high unemployment, and exhortation by the government led to a slowdown of wage increases, with real wages declining by 12 percent between the fourth quarters of 1979 and 1980. Correspondingly, the real exchange rate, calculated by the use of unit labor cost indices, depreciated by 44 percent between the fourth quarters of 1979 and 1980. In the same period, unit labor costs expressed in terms of U.S. dollars declined by 18 percent, compared with increases of 13 percent in the United States, 12 percent in Japan, and 15 percent in Taiwan, although Korea did not regain the competitive position it enjoyed in 1975 (table 3.9).

The depreciation of the real value of the won led to increases in the volume of Korea's merchandise exports by 11 percent in 1980, approximately matching estimated changes in Taiwan and Hong Kong, although falling short of the 17 percent increase in Singapore. With the depreciation of the won limiting increases in export unit values,[14] however, the dollar

---

14. In 1980, average export unit values in Korea relative to other countries approximated the 1975 level. For manufactured goods, the export unit value index was 162 in Korea on a 1975 basis, compared to an average of 158 for the industrial countries as reported by the United Nations and an average wholesale price index of 164 in Korea's major markets. At the same time, the decline of the export unit value index compared to the domestic wholesale price index (179 in 1980) points to the existence of a profit squeeze in Korea.

value of exports increased substantially less in Korea (17 percent) than in the other three Far Eastern economies (Taiwan, 23 percent; Hong Kong, 30 percent; and Singapore, 36 percent).

In turn, the volume of imports declined by 13 percent in Korea, reflecting in part the 4 percent fall of GDP in 1980 and in part the favorable effects of the depreciation of the real exchange rate. But the rise in the price of imports, in particular oil, led to a 15 percent increase in the dollar value of imports.

In 1980, the Korean economy was adversely affected by a disastrous harvest. Even adjusted for the decline of agricultural production, the Korean economy stagnated in 1980, compared with GDP growth rates of 10 percent in Singapore and 7 percent in Taiwan. Measures were taken in early 1980 to undo the inflationary excesses of previous years and the disruptions caused by the uncertain political situation, but the poor performance of exports which continued until mid-1980, largely explains the outcome.

With rapid increases in productivity and continued wage restraint, the real exchange rate calculated by the use of unit labor cost indices depreciated further in the first half of 1981, representing a 4 percent devaluation in real terms compared to 1975. However, a change in the opposite direction occurred in the second half of 1981 and, by the fourth quarter, there was an appreciation of 12 percent in real terms over 1975. An even larger appreciation (15 percent) is observed if calculations are made in terms of wholesale prices. Part of the explanation is that the 6 percent devaluation of the won in terms of the U.S. dollar between the fourth quarters of 1980 and 1981 was not sufficient to offset the 7 percent appreciation of the dollar vis-à-vis the Japanese yen. This outcome raises questions about the appropriateness of determining the value of the won with respect to the U.S. dollar.

More generally, there is a need to maintain a realistic exchange rate in Korea that provides appropriate incentives to exports as well as to import substitution. The rapid increase of exports in the first six months of 1981 (the volume of exports increased by 25 percent between the second quarters of 1980 and 1981) shows the favorable effects of the depreciation of the real exchange rate during the period. The subsequent appreciation, however, adversely affected Korean exports and the increase was only 7 percent between the fourth quarters of 1980 and 1981. Nevertheless, with labor costs declining in dollar terms, Korea was able to increase its export market shares in 1981, taken as a whole.

The choice of a realistic exchange rate is part of an outward-oriented development strategy. In an advisory report prepared for the Korean government in August 1980, the author recommended that Korea fully re-establish this strategy, including reductions in, and the rationalization of, tariffs, the elimination of quantitative import restrictions, the abolition of credit preferences favoring capital-intensive industries, and the simplification and unification of investment incentives. Proposals were further made for restoring positive real interest rates, relying on interest rates as a rationing device in the place of credit allocation, abolishing price control, and reducing government involvement in economic life in general (Balassa 1980).

The *Preliminary Outline of the Fifth Five-Year Economic and Social Development Plan of the Republic of Korea* (1982–86), issued in June, 1981, called for a return to a full-fledged outward-oriented development strategy. It stated that "the basic strategy Korea will follow . . . will be to promote competition at home and liberalize its external economic policies" (p. 10). The document added that "there is no escape from the conclusion that during the Fifth Five-Year Plan period export expansion should continue to be the major engine of growth for Korea" (p. 13). The preliminary plan further indicates the general orientation of policies to serve these objectives:

> In order to expand exports during the Fifth Five-Year Plan period, the government will make every effort to strengthen the competitiveness of Korea's export industries (p. 16).
>
> In order to sustain long-term growth of exports and the economy as a whole, import liberalization is essential. There is a limit to which a country can improve its industrial structure without import liberalization. Furthermore, a country cannot possibly hope to improve its price competitiveness while its cost of living rises due to import restriction . . . (p. 17).
>
> The single most important change in government industries policy during the Fifth Five-Year Plan period will be the reduction of the government's role in promoting so-called strategic industries. Investment choices will be left to the initiative of the private sector and the government will provide only the general framework in which such choices will be made by private entrepreneurs in cooperation with their bankers and financiers. Stated differently, during the 1980's government industrial policy will aim at reducing preferential treatment for selected industries and expose domestic producers to foreign competition in order to enhance their international competitiveness (pp. 22–23).
>
> During the Fifth Five-Year Plan period the government will make special efforts to make greater use of the market mechanism and private initiative for continued social and economic progress (p. 30).

In addition, special efforts will be made to maintain the real interest rate on bank loans and deposits at a positive level and gradually reduce the scope of policy preference loans (p. 31).

Making a greater use of the market mechanism also implies equalizing the terms of competition and policy incentives for all industries. ... During the Fifth Five-Year Plan period the government plans to gradually phase out specific incentives and provide instead generalized uniform incentives for investment in all industries (p. 31).

Concluding Remarks

The preliminary outline of the Fifth Five-Year Plan indicates the determination of the government to reverse recent tendencies toward greater inward orientation and government intervention. This is based on the perception that outward orientation is not only the best guarantee for long-term economic growth, but also helps overcome the effects of external shocks. The rationale is spelled out in the preliminary plan:

It is true that the above assessment of the world economic environment expected to prevail in the 1980's does not spell an optimistic outlook for a trade-oriented economy such as Korea's. But one should be careful not to draw from such an assessment a policy conclusion that the country should in any way compromise its outward-looking development strategy. If anything, the only way for Korea to meet effectively the challenges posed by external uncertainties is to pursue a development strategy that is even more outward-looking than in the past. The validity of this view has been underlined by Korea's own experience in dealing with the severe impact of two rounds of oil price increases during the 1970's and also the experiences of such other countries as Japan. Both Korea's and other countries' experiences clearly show that an open, trade-oriented economy can alleviate the initial impact of higher oil prices first by increasing exports and then by shifting the burden of higher oil prices through subsequent improvement in terms of trade (pp. 12–13).

This study has provided evidence of the validity of the above propositions. It has been shown that the adoption of an outward-oriented development strategy permitted Korea to reach rapid rates of growth of exports and GDP. It has further been established that Korea, along with other outward-oriented economies, has been better able to overcome the effects of external shocks than countries pursuing an inward-oriented development strategy. In turn, the policy reversals that occurred in 1979–80 had adverse effects on Korea's economy, while the re-establishment of a full-fledged outward-oriented strategy may be expected to bring benefits in the future.

References

Ahluwalia, M. S., N. G. Carter, and H. B. Chenery. 1979. "Growth and Poverty in Developing Countries," World Bank Staff Working Paper No. 309 (December).

Balassa, Bela. 1971. "Industrial Policies in Taiwan and Korea." *Weltwirtschaftliches Archiv* 1: 55–57.

Balassa, Bela. 1975. "Korea's Development Strategy for the Fourth Five-Year Plan Period (1977–81)," an Advisory Report prepared for the Government of Korea. Published as Essay 8 in Bela Balassa, *Policy Reform in Developing Countries*, 119–138. Oxford: Pergamon Press, 1977.

Balassa, Bela. 1976. "Incentives for Economic Growth in Korea," an Advisory Report prepared for the Government of Korea. Published as Essay 9 in Bela Balassa, *Policy Reform in Developing Countries*, 139–64. Oxford: Pergamon Press, 1977.

Balassa, Bela. 1977. "The 15 Year Social and Economic Development Plan for Korea," an Advisory Report prepared for the Government of Korea. Published as Essay 15 in Bela Balassa, *The Newly Industrializing Countries in the World Economy*, 365–80. New York: Pergamon Press, 1981.

Balassa, Bela. 1979. "A 'Stages' Approach to Comparative Advantage." Chapter 11 in Irma Adelman, ed., *Economic Growth and Resources*, Volume 4, *National and International Issues*, 121–56. London: Macmillan. Republished as Essay 6 in Bela Balassa, *The Newly Industrializing Countries in the World Economy*, 149–68. New York: Pergamon Press, 1981.

Balassa, Bela. 1980. "Korea During the Fifth Five-Year Plan Period (1982–86)," an Advisory Report prepared for the Government of Korea, October. To be published in a collection of advisory reports by the Korea Development Institute.

Balassa, Bela. 1981a. "Trade in Manufactured Goods." *World Development* (March): 267–75. Republished as Essay 11 in Bela Balassa, *The Newly Industrializing Countries in the World Economy*, 193–210. New York: Pergamon Press, 1981.

Balassa, Bela. 1981b. "The Newly-Industrializing Countries After the Oil Crises." *Weltwirtschaftliches Archiv* 1: 142–94. Republished as Essay 2 in Bela Balassa, *The Newly Industrializing Countries in the World Economy*, 26–82. New York: Pergamon Press, 1981.

Balassa, Bela. 1982. "Development Strategies and Economic Performance: A Comparative Analysis of Eleven Semi-Industrial Economies," Chapter 3 in Bela Balassa, et al., *Development Strategies in Semi-Industrial Economies*, 38–62. Baltimore, Md.: The Johns Hopkins University Press.

Balassa, Bela, et al. 1982. *Development Strategies in Semi-Industrial Economies*. Baltimore, Md.: The Johns Hopkins University Press.

Bank of Korea. *Economic Statistics Yearbook*. Various issues.

Chenery, H. B., S. Shishido, and T. Watanabe. 1962. "The Pattern of Japanese Growth, 1919–1954." *Econometrica* (January): 98–129.

Cole, D. C., and L. E. Westphal. 1975. "The Contribution of Exports in Korea." Chapter 4 in Wontack Hong and Anne O. Krueger, eds., *Trade and Development in Korea*, 89–102. Seoul: Korea Development Institute.

de Melo, Jaime, and Sherman Robinson. 1980. "An Economic and Political Analysis of Alternative Trade Adjustment Policies in Three Archetype Developing Economies," World Bank Staff Working Paper No. 442 (December).

Frank, C. R., Jr., Kwang Suk Kim, and L. E. Westphal. 1975. *Foreign Trade Regimes & Economic Development: South Korea*. New York: National Bureau of Economic Research.

Hong, Wontack. 1976. *Factor Supply and Factor Intensity of Trade in Korea*. Seoul: Korea Development Institute.

Hong, Wontack. 1979. *Trade, Distortions and Employment Growth in Korea*. Seoul: Korea Development Institute.

International Monetary Fund. 1982. *International Financial Statistics Yearbook*. Washington, D.C.

Kim, Chungsoo. 1983. *Evolution of Comparative Advantage: The Factor Proportions Theory in a Dynamic Perspective*. Tubingen: J. C. B. Mohr, 1983.

Kim, Kwang Suk, and Michael Roemer. 1979. *Growth and Structural Transformation*. Cambridge, Mass.: Harvard University Press.

Korea Development Institute. 1975. *Discussion Paper on the Development Strategy for the Fourth Five-Year Plan 1977–81*. Seoul.

Korea Economic Planning Board. 1975. *Economic Guidelines for the Fourth Five-Year Development Plan* Seoul. 193–210

Korea Economic Planning Board. 1981. *Preliminary Outline of the Fifth Five-Year Economic and Social Development Plan of the Republic of Korea*. Seoul (June).

Westphal, L. E., and Kwang Suk Kim. 1982. "Korea." Chapter 8 in Bela Balassa, et al., *Development Strategies in Semi-Industrial Economies*, 212–79. Baltimore, Md.: The Johns Hopkins University Press.

World Bank. 1981. *World Development Report, 1981*. Washington, D.C. (August).

4 The Role of Direct Foreign Investment in Korea's Recent Economic Growth
Bohn Young Koo

Introduction

Korea has achieved remarkable economic growth during the past two decades, with an almost 10 percent average annual GNP real growth, and a rise in its per capita GNP from US$87 in 1962 to US$1,636 in 1981.

The major contributors to this process have been the existence of a large and relatively well-educated labor force and its full utilization through development of labor-intensive industries; government policies which maintained a relatively open economic system; and political and social stability throughout the period, except during 1979–80.

The international environment has also been relatively favorable. World trade volume grew at a phenomenal pace throughout the sixties and the seventies, although its growth slowed down at the end of the last decade. The international capital market also expanded continuously during the period, enabling Korea to borrow necessary investment funds from abroad.

Unlike some other developing countries which have achieved growth with mostly domestic resources (e.g., Taiwan), Korea has depended heavily on foreign resources for its development. At the end of 1981, Korea's total outstanding foreign debt, including short-term trade credits, amounted to US$32.5 billion, making Korea one of the biggest borrowers in the international capital market. On the other hand, the prevalence of direct foreign investment has not been as great, at least on the surface, as in many Latin American countries.

This study will first briefly review the Korean government's policies relating to foreign investment during the past two decades, since government policy appears to be one of the most important factors influencing the effects of DFI in a country. Then, we will examine DFI in Korea in terms of the countries where it originated and the industries to which it was distributed. The effects of DFI on the recent economic growth of Korea will then be examined, through its influence on employment, the balance of payments, and technological development. Finally, we will examine the role of DFI in greater detail by looking at the status of DFI in major sectors.

A Brief Review of Foreign Investment Policies in Korea

Until the late fifties, Korea was a war-devastated country, absorbed with reconstruction activities and offering few investment opportunities, especially for foreign investors. The economy was completely dependent on foreign aid, mostly from the United States, and domestic savings were negligible. In 1959, the investment rate (gross domestic capital formation in GDP) remained at the low level of 11 percent, and most of the investment was financed by U.S. aid. In addition, Korea was deficient in most natural resources. Finally, revolutions in 1960 and 1961 further damaged whatever investment climate existed at that time.

The first attempt by the Korean government to provide a legal basis for the attraction of foreign capital was made in January 1960, through enactment of the Foreign Capital Inducement Promotion Act. The act provided various incentives, including equal treatment with domestic firms, tax holidays, guarantee of profit remittances and withdrawal of principal, and tax rebates for technology licensees. But until the end of 1961, not a single foreign investor came in, mainly because of the political and social instability of the country.

In 1962, as the First Five-Year Economic Plan began, the government realized the importance of foreign capital, and thus adopted more concrete measures to encourage its inflow. The basic principle from 1962 to 1966 was to permit the entrance of any form of bona fide foreign capital, if it was considered conducive to the objectives of the Five-Year Plan.

All foreign capital was to receive government protection and relevant government support. Participation of domestic firms in the form of joint ventures was not required, provided that their absence did not adversely affect the national interest. Foreign technologies were also encouraged. Not much foreign investment, however, came in during this period, again mainly because the political stability of the country was uncertain.

In 1965, Korea normalized its diplomatic relations with Japan after 20 years of rupture, and Japanese investment gradually began to flow in. The government, expecting a surge of Japanese investment, had revised the Foreign Capital Inducement Promotion Act in August 1966, and adopted a "Comprehensive Measure for Rationalization of Foreign Capital Inducement" in 1967. The 1967 act was the Korean government's first attempt to regulate the quality of foreign capital, but it was directed primarily to foreign loans rather than to direct investment. In any case, because of inefficient administration, the measure was not effectively implemented.

In 1969, the government announced another "Measure to Promote the Inflow of Direct Foreign Investment and to Foster the Activities of Foreign Subsidiaries," improved administrative procedures, and reinforced the support system for foreign investors. And in 1970 the first Free Export Zone (FXZ) was established in Masan.

As a result of these various incentives, considerable foreign investment came into Korea during the early seventies. However, the government began to feel that unlimited approval of foreign investment might create some adverse effects on the domestic economy, such as the control of domestic industry by foreign firms and the resultant problem of implementing development strategies, an increase in vulnerability in times of external shocks due to potential massive withdrawals, and a hindrance to the development of indigenous firms. Thus, to maximize the contribution of foreign investment to economic growth, major changes were made in 1973. The most important was that joint ventures were to receive higher priority than firms wholly owned by foreign investors. A similar practice had existed informally even before the revision of the act in 1973, but the new act further reinforced this trend.

In addition, a specific general guideline for direct foreign investment was adopted in the same year, which became the backbone of Korean foreign investment policy until the late seventies, though some minor revisions were made from time to time. The guideline consisted of criteria for project eligibility, foreign ownership, and investment scale.

The eligibility criteria designated the following projects as noneligible: (1) those that disrupted domestic demand and supply of raw materials and intermediate products; (2) those that competed in overseas markets with domestic firms; (3) those aimed solely at financial support for existing domestic enterprises; and (4) those that sought to profit solely from land use.

The foreign participation ratio was basically limited to 50 percent, except in the following cases: (1) entirely export-oriented projects that did not compete with domestic firms in overseas markets; (2) technology-intensive projects that produced or induced production of important exporting or import-substituting products; (3) multinational projects that invested only in the form of wholly owned subsidiaries in other countries; (4) projects that contributed to the rationalization of domestic industrial structure and were beyond the capacity of domestic investors, because of large capital or advanced technology requirements; (5) projects from a country that had made little investment in the past but which was expected to increase investment in the future; (6) projects by Korean residents abroad; and (7) projects in Free Export Zones, and some other specific industrial estates designated by the government. In addition, local participation of more than 50 percent was required for the following types of projects: (1) purely labor-intensive; (2) purely bonded-processing; (3) dependent on domestic resources for major raw materials; and (4) oriented toward local market sales.

The minimum amount of investment was set in 1973 at US$50 thousand per project, and was gradually raised to US$100 thousand in 1974, to US$200 thousand in 1975, and to US$500 thousand in 1979, to discourage small investors who came only to utilize low-cost labor. But here too, exceptions were allowed for investments by Korean residents abroad and for projects deemed necessary by the government.

With such detailed and sometimes conflicting regulations, the government was able to exert comprehensive influence on the pattern of foreign investment. As will be discussed in later sections of this chapter, competition with domestic firms was seldom allowed in either domestic or world markets; export requirements were very stringent until 1979; and foreign ownership limitations were very firm, rendering Korea one of the few countries with very restrictive foreign investment regulations.

In September 1980, the Korean government reversed its policy and substantially liberalized foreign investment guidelines, allowing foreign investment in many new areas, permitting firms to be majority-owned or wholly owned by foreign investors in many additional cases, and reducing the minimum amount of investment to US$100 thousand to induce small-scale but technology-intensive investors. Such reversal of policy was caused in part by the government's concern over the deteriorating balance of payments, but its more basic objectives were to provide increased competition for domestic firms, to enhance the efficiency and productivity of protected firms, and to promote the technological development of sophisticated industries.

Characteristics of DFI in Korea

Korea's rapid growth during the preceding two decades was achieved through ever-increasing investment. The average investment rate rose from 14.4 percent of GNP during 1962–66 to 35.8 percent during 1977–81.[1] Because of the relatively low domestic savings rate in the initial stage, the investment had to be financed in large measure by foreign savings. Gradually, the dependence on foreign savings was reduced, and by 1977 accounted for only 2 percent of total savings. The massive investment in heavy industry and the chemical industry, added to the second oil crisis,

---

1. Since 1962, the Korean government has carried out four Five-Year Economic Plans during the plan periods 1962–66, 1967–71, 1972–76, and 1977–81. Many of the statistics in this chapter used the same convenient divisions of the period.

Table 4.1. Outstanding Foreign Loans in Korea (US$ millions)

Characteristic of Loan	1972	1977	1981
Long-term (3 years and over)	2,834	8,583	20,127
Public & commercial loans[a]	2,671	7,477	14,349
Bank loans[b]	155	602	4,174
IMF credit	8	341	1,246
Bonds	0	163	358
Medium-term (1 to 3 years)	116	350	623
Trade credit	114	335	564
Cash loans	2	15	59
Short-term (less than 1 year)	559	2,923	8,465
Trade credit	253	1,492	3,454
Refinance	164	695	3,892
Others	142	736	1,119
Foreign banks' A account[c]	40	792	3,275
Total	3,549	12,648	32,490

Source: Ministry of Finance.
[a] Loans induced by the Korean government or private companies.
[b] Loans induced by the Korean banks to relend to private Korean companies.
[c] Foreign banks' capital and operating funds swapped against Korean currency.

however, once again increased Korea's dependence on foreign savings. Thus in 1981, foreign savings accounted for 30 percent of total savings.

Foreign borrowing to supplement the deficient domestic resources took a variety of forms.[2] Public and commercial loans were the major source throughout the period, but later the importance of other loans, such as bank loans, IMF credit, and short-term trade credit increased. Particularly, bank loans increased tremendously in the past few years, as Korea's balance of payments position deteriorated badly in 1979 (table 4.1).

Compared to the magnitude of foreign borrowing, the amount of foreign direct investment has been very small. At the end of 1981, a total of 1,464 separate foreign investments had been made in Korea, amounting to US$1,758 million on the approval base, or US$1,202 million on the arrival base.[3] Among these, 444 projects were cancelled, and 185 projects local-

2. Foreign borrowing includes not only borrowing to finance the balance-of-payments deficit, but also to repay the principal of foreign loans, to increase foreign exchange reserves, and to allow exports on a deferred payment base. As such, it differs from foreign savings, which refers mainly to the balance-of-payments deficit, or the sum of commodity and invisible trade deficits.

3. Amounts approved and arrived differ because of the lag between the time of approval and actual receipt of investment funds, and also because of some cancellations after projects were approved.

ized, leaving 835 companies in operation at the end of 1981, with the approved amount of US$1,276 million.

The scale of annual DFI inflow fluctuated widely, depending on such factors as general economic conditions in Korea and around the world, Korean government policy, and the size of individual investments in each year. Until 1973 there was a general upward trend, the scale of annual flow increasing from a meager US$600 thousand in 1962 to US$317 million in 1973 on the approval base. Nevertheless, the scale dropped sharply in 1974, and thereafter it fluctuated widely, showing no apparent trend either upward or downward.

Several factors appear to have been behind this relative stagnation in the inflow of DFI into Korea after 1974. First, as noted earlier, the Korean government tightened up its entry regulations for foreign investors in 1973, particularly regarding ownership restrictions and export requirements. Thus, potential foreign investors who wanted to retain management control or to develop a domestic market went to other countries where restrictions were more lenient. Second, Korean wage rates began to rise sharply in the middle of the seventies, particularly in relation to competing countries such as Singapore, Hong Kong, and Taiwan. Foreign investors who wanted to utilize low-cost labor went to these countries. Consequently, the annual DFI flow into Korea stagnated during 1974–81, particularly in terms of new entrants.[4]

Establishment of the Masan Free Export Zone in 1970 and the Iri Free Export Zone in 1974 helped to increase the annual scale of DFI inflow, but once fully occupied, the importance of FXZs in total DFI decreased. At the end of 1981, the FXZs were responsible for only 8.4 percent of total DFI approved, and their weight is expected to further diminish, as creation of new FXZs or expansion of the existing FXZs is not expected.

Home Country Distribution

At the end of 1981, Japan ranked first among investor countries, both in terms of the amount of investment (55 percent of total DFI) and the number of firms (76 percent of total) (table 4.2). This preponderance of Japanese investment can be attributed to several factors. First, Korea is the country nearest to Japan, not only in terms of geographical proximity, but also in terms of its unhappy historical colonial ties with Japan. Second, Korea has an abundant and relatively well-educated labor force, with wages considerably lower than those in Japan, and Japan badly needed

---

4. Total flow of DFI from advanced to developing countries also fluctuated widely every year during the period, but no other country experienced the sharp drop in average annual flow that Korea underwent after 1973. The Korean phenomenon appear to be unique, explainable mostly in terms of policy and environment in Korea.

Table 4.2. Distribution of Investor Countries by Amount of Investment (%)

Period	Japan	U.S.A.	Europe	Others	Total	Amount (US$ millions)	Number of Firms
1962–66	21.1	75.0	1.8	2.1	100.0	43	37
1967–71	45.3	39.8	4.9	10.0	100.0	206	347
1972–76	72.2	11.0	8.8	8.0	100.0	872	845
1977–81	36.8	34.2	18.6	10.4	100.0	636	235
Average/Total	55.0	24.3	11.6	9.1	100.0	1,757	1,464
Amount (US$ millions)	966	427	206	158	1,757		
Number of firms	1,108	235	68	53	1,464		

Source: Ministry of Finance.
Note: Distribution based on total approved amount.

such labor for relocation of its declining industries, particularly in the early seventies. Third, Japan has more than 600,000 Korean residents who emigrated there before World War II, and many Korean businessmen in Japan made considerable investments in their mother country.[5]

Beginning in the mid-seventies, however, Japanese investments declined in relative terms, while U.S. and European investments gained in importance. This trend occurred apparently because of the different characteristics of Japanese and U.S. or European investment. Much Japanese investment in the early seventies was concentrated in the labor-intensive industries in order to utilize the low-cost labor in Korea. This factor diminished in importance as labor costs began to rise in Korea from about the middle of the seventies. For more advanced industries, relocation was not easy because of both resistance at home and possible competition by Korean subsidiaries in the world market.

On the other hand, U.S. and European investments were relatively less concentrated in labor-intensive industries, compared with Japanese investment, so that the rise of labor costs did not become as serious an obstacle for them. Thus, the Japanese share in total DFI inflow declined sharply from 72.2 percent during 1972–76 to 36.8 percent during 1977–81,

---

5. Among all foreign investors in Korea, 84 (10 percent of all foreign investors) were Korean residents abroad. They invested US$238 million on the current approval base, or 19 percent of total foreign investment, as of the end of 1981. Of these investors, Korean residents in Japan accounted for 83 percent of the amount of investment. One important feature of investment by Korean residents abroad was that 70 percent of their total investment was in 13 projects in the hotel business.

Direct Foreign Investment in Korea

while the share of the U.S. and European DFI together increased from 19.8 percent to 52.8 percent during the same period[6] (table 4.2).

Industrial Distribution

Korea is endowed with few natural resources, so little DFI was made in primary industries. At the end of 1981, only 1 percent of total DFI was made in primary industries; the manufacturing sector accounted for 75 percent and the service sector, 24 percent of total DFI inflow (table 4.3).

The distribution of investment in the service sector was almost entirely determined by government policy, which allowed foreign investment in this sector only in very special circumstances. To promote tourism, DFI in the hotel business was approved with few restrictions. To facilitate the inflow of foreign loans, some joint venture merchant banks were approved. The remaining areas included several data-processing companies, computer and other machinery-leasing companies, special-purpose storage companies, and a few engineering companies. Except for these, DFI in the service sector had not been allowed in the past.

The distribution of investment in the manufacturing sector was also greatly influenced by government policies. According to Ray Vernon's (1966) product cycle theory, DFI in a country like Korea can be expected to be concentrated in industries that produce technologically standardized products. Richard Caves's (1971) industrial organization approach would predict that DFI in Korea should concentrate in oligopolistic industries that produce differentiated products (in horizontal investment). When severe entry restrictions prevail, however, the power of such theories is limited in explaining the overall industrial distribution of DFI.

The pattern of DFI in Korea's manufacturing sector appears to have followed the direction of the government's industrial policies closely. At the early stage of Korean industrialization, foreign investments were concentrated in areas like fertilizers, petroleum refining, and chemicals, to substitute for imports of major raw materials. At the next stage, such import-substituting DFI expanded into areas like synthetic fibers and petrochemicals.

As Korean export growth gained momentum, however, a large amount of DFI also began to flow into areas like garments, electronics, and machine tools. And during the latter half of the seventies, DFI also came into

---

6. The scale of annual Japanese DFI flow to Asian countries fluctuated widely during 1974–81, but nowhere else did it decline as sharply from the level achieved in 1973 as it did in Korea. Moreover, the proportion of Japanese DFI to Korea in total Japanese DFI to Asian countries (excluding the Middle East) dropped sharply around 1974, reflecting a major shift in locational preferences on the part of Japanese investors. Thus, the decreasing Japanese share appears to have been a unique Korean phenomenon.

Table 4.3. Distribution of Direct Foreign Investment Inflow by Industry, 1962–81 (%)

	1962–66	1967–71	1972–76	1977–81	Average/ Total	Amount (US$ millions)
Agriculture, fishery, & forest	0.3	0.9	1.4	1.1	1.2	21.4
Mining	0.0	0.2	0.4	0.2	0.3	5.5
Manufacturing	98.5	84.9	75.5	68.3	74.6	1,310.2
Food	7.9	1.5	0.9	4.7	2.2	44.5
Textile & garments	2.2	10.2	18.9	0.6	11.0	191.0
Chemical	0.9	10.9	19.5	19.4	18.2	316.1
Pharmaceuticals	0.7	1.4	0.2	1.5	0.6	14.7
Fertilizer	57.2	0.0	2.4	0.0	2.7	46.0
Petroleum refining	11.7	18.3	3.7	1.3	4.6	83.5
Metal	0.0	10.0	4.0	3.8	4.6	79.4
Machinery	4.7	8.0	5.7	10.0	7.6	132.0
Electrical & electronics	8.7	13.5	11.9	17.9	14.2	249.3
Transport equipment	0.4	1.2	4.9	4.2	4.2	72.0
Service	1.2	14.1	22.7	30.4	23.9	420.4
Banking	0.0	1.3	1.4	8.2	3.8	67.0
Construction & business services	0.0	6.8	2.2	5.9	4.1	70.8
Hotels	1.2	3.1	18.6	11.9	13.9	244.7
Total	100.0	100.0	100.0	100.0	100.0	1,757.5
Amount (US$ millions)	42.8	206.3	871.8	636.6	1,757.5	

Source: Ministry of Finance.
Note: Distribution based on total approved amount.

the heavy electrical and nonelectrical machinery industries, as Korea began her second-stage import substitution. About that time, DFI in the textile industry had almost completely ceased, since Korea was beginning to lose its comparative advantage in that industry. Nevertheless, DFI continued in the chemical and electronics industries for further import substitution and for the development of more sophisticated products.

Throughout the sixties and seventies, very few DFI entrants were allowed to compete with domestic firms in the domestic consumer goods market. Relatively small investments were made in areas like food processing, pharmaceuticals, cosmetics, and distribution services. With few exceptions, those foreign producers of consumer goods that were allowed

Direct Foreign Investment in Korea

Table 4.4. Industrial Distribution of Direct Foreign Investment by Country (%)

	Japan[a]	U.S.A.[a]	Europe[b]	Others	Average/Total
Agriculture, fishery, & forest	1.2	0.9	0.5	0.9	1.0
Mining	0.3	0.0	0.1	0.0	0.2
Manufacturing	67.5	82.8	85.7	60.5	72.7
Food	1.8	3.7	0.0	5.6	2.5
Textile & garments	10.6	0.2	0.7	1.3	5.6[c]
Chemical	16.4	21.0	64.9	3.7	22.0
Pharmaceuticals	0.2	1.7	3.8	1.4	1.1
Fertilizer	0.1	7.5	0.0	11.1	3.3
Petroleum refining	0.0	0.2	0.5	18.9	2.5[c]
Metal	7.2	0.8	1.7	5.9	4.8
Machinery	8.9	3.4	7.9	7.0	7.2
Electrical & electronics	16.4	26.8	4.5	4.5	16.0
Transport equipment	1.1	12.7	0.0	0.0	3.7
Service	27.6	16.3	13.8	38.6	26.2
Banking	0.2	1.4	13.7	24.3	5.2
Construction & business services	4.6	8.1	0.0	0.6	4.4
Hotels	25.1	1.3	0.0	9.1	14.1
Total	100.0	100.0	100.0	100.0	100.0
(Amount)	(645.2)	(314.7)	(157.7)	(158.582)	(1,276.1)

Source: Ministry of Finance.

Note: Based on current approved amount for remaining firms as of the end of 1981; thus the total distribution differs slightly from that which appears in table 4.3.

[a] Some investments made by subsidiaries of the United States and Japanese multinationals in other countries have been treated as investments from those countries rather than from the United States or Japan because of identification problems.

[b] Industrial distribution of European DFI was calculated using only Germany, England, France, and the Netherlands as the sample. The DFI from these countries accounted for 84 percent of total DFI from European countries.

[c] Weight reduced in recent years due to divestment.

entrance were asked to export their entire product or to substitute for imports.

The industrial distribution of investment by country (table 4.4) shows that Japanese investment was relatively heavy in the textile, machinery, and hotel industries, while U.S. investment predominated in transport equipment and business services. Both countries invested heavily in the chemical and electronics industries. The indication in table 4.4 that European investments were concentrated in the chemical industry is due to a large investment by a Dutch subsidiary of the U.S. Dow Chemical firm. Apart from the investment by Dow, European investments were mainly in machinery industries.

In terms of market orientation, Japanese investments have been relatively more concentrated in export industries, while U.S. and European investments have been more import-substitution or domestic-market-oriented. These patterns of investment appear to confirm Kojima's (1973) argument that Japanese investments have been trade-oriented while U.S. investments have been anti-trade-oriented. Kojima argued that most Japanese investments were directed toward natural resources development and labor-intensive manufacturing industries in which Japan was losing its comparative advantage. He said that Japanese foreign investments help host countries open wider markets while promoting structural adjustment in Japan.

On the other hand, Kojima argues, most U.S. investments have been concentrated in highly technology-intensive and oligopolistic industries where the United States had the strongest comparative advantage. Such investments were not complementary to the exploitation of the host countries' potential comparative advantage and also worsened the balance of payment difficulties and unemployment problems in the United States by decreasing its exports to these countries.

This generalization, however, appears to be too sweeping. First, there have been many cases of Japanese investment in technically advanced industries. Second, much of U.S. investment in Korea was made in essential import-substituting industries, with little adverse effect on resource allocation. Third, for a fast-growing economy like Korea, the scope of so-called complementary investments becomes limited as its comparative advantage position changes rapidly. For example, Korean comparative advantage has moved from simple labor-intensive products like wigs, plywood, garments, and consumer electronics (assembly) to more capital- and skill-intensive products like steel, ships, electronic parts and components, and machinery. And for many of these skill-intensive products, Korean products compete directly with Japanese products in the world market, so Kojima's argument regarding complementary investments by Japanese producers becomes difficult to sustain.

Foreign Ownership Patterns

As stated earlier, Korea was one of the few countries that until very recently enforced local participation in the form of joint ventures strictly. Thus, in a study of 180 U.S. multinationals as of the end of 1975, Korea was

Direct Foreign Investment in Korea 187

the country with the smallest proportion (less than 30 percent) of wholly owned subsidiaries, among 66 countries.[7]

Table 4.5 shows the ownership distribution of foreign firms in Korea by investor countries, dividing ownership into four categories: minority-owned (less than 50 percent), co-owned (50 percent), majority-owned (more than 50 percent, but less than 100 percent), and wholly owned (100 percent). Reflecting the government's strong enforcement of local participation, the proportion of wholly owned subsidiaries among all approved firms remained at only 14.6 percent in 1981. And if we further exclude Free Export Zones, where there has been no restriction of foreign ownership, the proportion is further reduced. On the other hand, the proportion of less-than-majority-owned (minority-owned and co-owned) firms amounted to 73 percent of all foreign firms.

Table 4.5. Ownership Distribution of Foreign Firms, End of 1981 (%)

Country	Minority-owned Firms	Co-owned Firms	Majority-owned Firms	Wholly owned Firms	Total	Number of Firms
Japan	45.3	27.9	11.9	14.9	100.0	612
U.S.A.	38.5	29.6	14.8	17.0	100.0	135
Europe	36.5	40.4	11.5	11.5	100.0	52
Others	50.0	33.3	11.1	5.6	100.0	36
Average/Total	43.8	29.2	12.3	14.6	100.0	835

Source: Ministry of Finance.
Note: The distribution has been calculated using remaining firms as the sample.

The United States had the lowest proportion of less-than-majority-owned firms, and Japan the highest proportion of minority-owned firms. Feldman (1978) suggested the following four factors to explain the reluctance of U.S. firms to form joint ventures, particularly less-than-majority-owned ones: (1) the large U.S. home market gives U.S. firms a viable alternative to overseas investment, and U.S. firms also enjoy greater access to capital than their foreign competitors, obviating the need for joint ventures; (2) more U.S. than Japanese or European firms possess proprietary technologies, and they do not want to share such assets with firms in other countries; (3) the long tradition of an arms-length relationship be-

---

7. J. P. Curhan, W. H. Davidson, and R. Suri, 1977, p. 314, chapter 6, section 2, table 3. Next in line were Israel with 30 percent, Japan with 33 percent, and Saudi Arabia with 36 percent.

tween the government and the business community in the United States predisposes U.S. managers to resist host government pressures more strongly than do Japanese or European managers; and (4) the management system of the U.S. firms, particularly the multinationals, is more centrally oriented than that of firms in other countries, so minority-owned firms create difficult management problems.

Mason (1980) has also pointed out that the less sophisticated nature of Japanese technology, with fewer economic rents to be appropriated from superiority in technology compared to that of U.S. or European technology, may have been one of the major factors explaining the greater receptiveness of Japanese firms to joint venture agreements with host country firms. In addition, he argues that Japanese manufacturing firms are, on the average, more likely to be in direct competition with local firms, and the joint venture form may serve the purpose of protective collaboration.

On the other hand, Lee (1980) has argued that the difference in characteristics of the intangible assets possessed by U.S. and Japanese firms may be the main reason for differences in behavior. United States firms invest abroad with greater advantages in production and management techniques, while Japanese firms invest more with marketing advantages in home or world markets. When the purpose of investment is to sell in the home or world market, rather than the host country market, the investor enjoys more leverage in the pricing of both imported inputs or exported outputs, so that the need for majority ownership becomes less compelling.

Although an element of truth is contained in all three arguments, it appears to the author that the phenomena could better be explained in terms of the different industrial distribution of U.S. and Japanese investment. United States and Japanese firms should behave similarly in the same industry, particularly in the same product category. As Japanese industrial structure and its overseas investment pattern becomes similar to that of the United States, differences in ownership patterns are likely to disappear.[8]

Scale of Investments

There have been many small-scale foreign investors in Korea, particularly from Japan. During the early seventies, many small and medium-sized Japanese firms moved their plants to Southeast Asian countries, including Korea, to utilize the low-cost labor there, sometimes under the umbrella of general trading companies in Japan. That has made the average size of DFI in Korea very small.

8. In fact, Japanese firms are said to favor more and more majority ownership not only in advanced but also in developing countries. In Korea, the difference between ownership by U.S. and Japanese firms has been reduced considerably in recent years.

In terms of the number of firms, those with investments of less than US$1 million constituted 75 percent of foreign investment, while those with more than US$5 million constituted only 6 percent. The big multinationals with investments of over US$5 million, however, accounted for more than 60 percent of total DFI inflow (table 4.6).

Over time, the average scale increased for investments from every country, both because the government had continued to increase the minimum scale of investment until 1980, and because the DFI by small- and medium-sized Japanese firms has declined relatively in importance in recent years. In addition, several large investments in heavy industry and the chemical industry during the latter half of the seventies have contributed to the trend of increasing the average size of investments. The scale of Japanese investment, however, remains the smallest among major investing countries in Korea (table 4.7).

Table 4.6. Distribution of Investment by Scale, End of 1981

Scale (US$ millions)	Number of Firms	%	Amount (US$ millions)	%
<0.5	516	61.8	83.0	6.5
0.5–1	111	13.3	78.5	6.2
1–5	155	18.6	344.5	27.0
>5	53	6.3	770.0	60.9
Total	835	100.0	1,276.0	100.0

Source: Ministry of Finance.
Note: Sample based on firms existing as of the end of 1981.

Table 4.7. Changes in the Average Scale of Investment (US$ millions)

	1962–66	1967–71	1972–76	1977–81	Average/Total
Japan	1.5	0.4	0.9	1.8	0.9
U.S.A.	1.5	1.0	1.4	3.4	1.8
Europe	0.2	1.3	3.3	3.7	3.0
Others	0.2	1.4	3.2	5.5	3.0
All Countries	1.2	0.6	1.0	2.7	1.2

Source: Ministry of Finance.
Note: Sample based on all government-approved investment.

Effects of Direct Foreign Investment in Korea

It is well known to empirical research workers that a rigorous cost-benefit analysis of DFI is out of the question, chiefly because of two factors: there is an inherent logical problem involved in determining the probable alternative economic state in the absence of direct foreign investment, and there is the notorious paucity of data. Thus, analyses tend to be qualitative and, in most cases, hazy about the net effect of DFI, and this study is no exception. In the case of Korea, however, the two problems were not complete obstacles to the analysis.

The foreign investment policies of the Korean government have been very restrictive until 1980, so competition with existing domestic firms was seldom allowed. Consequently, most foreign investments have been either in highly technology-intensive, import-substituting industries, such as fertilizer, petroleum refining, petrochemicals, and heavy machinery where no domestic firms existed before, or in the form of off-shore assembly or processing for purely export purposes as in electronics. For both groups of industries, investment by domestic firms alone would have been a difficult problem, either because Korean firms lacked necessary technology and capital or because they were global sourcing type investments. Thus, even though there were exceptions, it appears to be a generally valid assumption about Korea that the alternative to DFI would have been the absence of domestic investment.

As for the data problem, the minimum necessary information on the performance of foreign firms was available in Korea, through comprehensive surveys by the government and detailed foreign exchange statistics. The government carried out two special surveys in 1976 and 1979, containing such valuable information as domestic and foreign sales, procurement of raw materials by source, number of domestic and foreign employees, and various financial statements. Although individual company data were not available, most of the data for detailed industry groups were available.

This analysis of the effects of direct foreign investment on the Korean economy is based mainly on the government's special survey of 1979, which included performance statistics of foreign firms for the period 1974 to 1978. In addition, various other published and unpublished statistics have been used.

Costs of Foreign Investment

Before we consider the contributions made by DFI, we first need to know its costs. The direct costs of foreign investment consist of profit remittances, reinvested earnings, royalties and other service fees, and foreign claims on undistributed profits. Reinvested earnings and foreign claims on undistributed profits, however, do not constitute true social costs from the national economic viewpoint, since both funds can be assumed to be used for productive activities in the host countries, and no real transfer of resources takes place until profits are remitted abroad. So we included only profit remittances and royalties and other service fees sent by foreign firms as direct costs of foreign investment.[9]

In addition, there can be indirect costs, such as reduced competitiveness of domestic firms, reinforcement of dualistic social structure, distortions in financial resource allocation because of the privileged position of foreign firms, or other external diseconomies not internalized. And there is also the possibility of overcharge for imported inputs in intracompany transactions. But these indirect costs are hard to ascertain or quantify, just as with indirect benefits, so we have limited our analysis to the direct costs.

Table 4.8 shows the costs of foreign investment as the ratio of profit remittances (and royalties) sent abroad by foreign firms to the total remaining balance of foreign investment in Korea.[10] The ratios do not show any definite trend, which is quite understandable in view of the inherent instability of profit rates. The profitability of foreign firms is influenced not only by general business conditions, but also by such factors as exchange rates, the host government's trade and industrial policies, and new foreign entrants.

The substantial reductions in profit ratios in the years 1971, 1972, 1975, and 1980 appear to have been caused by worldwide recessions and by the devaluations in Korea in mid-1971, the end of 1974, and early 1980. In general, royalties constituted about a third of total remittances, but their proportion has been rising in recent years, implying increasing use of licensing agreements by foreign firms.

Profitability of foreign firms naturally differed among countries due to different industrial distribution and different motives for DFI. Table 4.9 shows the ratio of profit remittances sent abroad by firms from individual countries to the average remaining balance of investment by these firms in

---

9. An argument can be made that royalties for technology licensing or management and other fees should not be considered an element of foreign investment costs, since the payment would have been made even without direct foreign investment. But this argument does not appear to be valid in the case of Korea. If, in the absence of direct foreign investment, domestic firms had set up the plants with foreign technologies and management contracts, the contention would be generally valid, even though the possibility of overcharge by foreign investors still would have remained. But when the host country would not have made the investment, then the royalties and other service fees paid by foreign firms definitely constitute a portion of total costs. Thus, regarding Korea, it seems relevant to include these payments as part of total costs of DFI.

10. The management and other service fees have not been included because of the lack of data, but their inclusion would not affect the analysis, since they constitute only a small portion of total remittances.

Table 4.8. Cost of Direct Foreign Investment in Korea (US$ millions)

Year	Cumulative Arrivals (A)	Cumulative Withdrawals (B)	Remaining Balance (C) = (A − B)	Profit Remittance (D)	Royalties[a] (E)	Profit Ratios[b] I (D)/(C)	Profit Ratios[b] II ((D) + (E))/(C)
1966	16.7	0.0	16.7	0.2	n.a.	1.0	3.0
1967	29.3	0.0	29.3	0.2	0.5	1.6	2.8
1968	44.1	0.0	44.1	0.6	0.4	11.7	13.2
1969	51.0	0.2	50.8	5.5	0.7	12.8	20.8
1970	76.3	0.4	75.9	8.1	5.1	8.9	12.2
1971	113.0	1.0	112.0	8.3	3.1	4.7	7.6
1972	174.3	3.9	170.3	6.7	4.1	6.2	9.1
1973	332.7	8.1	324.6	15.4	7.0	6.7	8.6
1974	495.3	14.2	481.1	26.8	7.9	4.7	7.1
1975	564.5	20.1	544.3	24.0	12.6	6.3	8.8
1976	670.1	24.6	645.5	37.7	14.8	7.1	11.5
1977	772.4	35.6	736.8	49.3	30.1	5.6	9.2
1978	872.8	47.3	825.5	44.1	27.7	6.5	n.a.
1979	999.8	138.2	861.6	54.7	n.a.	5.4	n.a.
1980	1,096.4	228.4	867.5	46.8	n.a.	5.3	n.a.
1981	1,206.5	231.8	974.7	49.0	n.a.		

Source: Ministry of Finance.

[a] The royalties paid to foreign investors have been calculated by identifying individual foreign firms among all firms paying royalties abroad.
[b] The ratios have been calculated as the ratio of profit (or profit plus royalties for profit ratio II) remitted in the year to the average of remaining balance at the beginning and end of the year.

Table 4.9. Differences in Profitability among Countries

Year	U.S.A.	Japan	Europe	Others	Average
1977	23.8	2.7	7.4	2.6	7.1
1978	12.0	3.9	6.8	3.7	5.6
1979	14.7	3.9	4.5	7.3	6.5
1980	11.2	2.8	5.2	8.8	5.4
1981	10.3	2.3	5.2	12.3[a]	5.3

Source: Author's calculations using raw data from the Ministry of Finance.

Note: The profitabilities here refer to the ratio of profit remittances in the year to the average remaining balance of investment; the other ratios (profit ratio II in table 4.8) are not presented here, but show similar differences among countries.

[a]The sudden increase in the ratio was caused by the unusually large profit remittance by a U.S. chemical subsidiary in Panama, and thus is not considered to be a normal figure.

Korea for the years 1977–1981. The profit remittance ratios have been the highest for the U.S. firms, and the lowest for Japanese firms. European investors' profit ratios were between these two countries.[11]

The major reason for the difference in profitability between U.S. and Japanese firms in Korea appears to have been variance in market orientation. As noted earlier, relatively more Japanese investments have been made in export industries with advantages in marketing skills either in Japan or abroad, while more U.S. investments have been domestic-market-oriented. Thus, to Japanese investors who imported most of their inputs and exported most of their products either to Japan or world market (in many cases with the Japanese investor working as the sales agent), the retention of profits in Korea was neither desirable nor necessary.

On the other hand, U.S. investors who sold their products in the Korean market had to earn a return in the form of either profits or royalties. In addition, there were cases at the earlier stage of industrialization when high profits had been guaranteed by the government to induce U.S. investors in such key industries as fertilizer and petroleum refining. These factors appear to explain the relatively high profit ratios for the U.S. firms.

The next step is to compare the costs of DFI with those of commercial loans. We sometimes hear the argument that DFI is the more desirable form of foreign capital, since it does not entail prefixed costs to the host country, as is the case with commercial loans, and thus exerts less pressure on the balance of payments to host countries.

---

11. In the study by Reuber et al. (1973), Japanese investments appear to be the most profitable ones, when compared with U.S. and European investments. However, those conclusions were based on total accounting profit over equity, while here we calculated profit remitted home over equity. Thus, depending on the tax system in the host country, and the propensity to pay dividends and to reinvest, the ratios may differ widely.

Table 4.10. Average Costs of Commercial Loans and Foreign Investment (%)

Year	Commercial Loans	Foreign Investment Ratio I	Foreign Investment Ratio II
1967	3.5	1.0	3.0
1968	2.9	1.6	2.8
1969	3.5	11.7	13.2
1970	5.4	12.8	20.8
1971	6.0	8.9	12.2
1972	6.8	4.7	7.6
1973	7.8	6.2	9.1
1974	8.4	6.7	8.6
1975	8.1	4.7	7.1
1976	7.6	6.3	8.8
1977	8.1	7.1	11.5
1978	8.6	5.6	9.2
1979	9.5	6.5	n.a.
1980	11.3	5.4	n.a.
1981	12.8	5.3	n.a.

Source: Ministry of Finance.

Note: In the case of commercial loans, the average costs of capital have been calculated as the ratio of interest payments in the year to the average of the remaining balance of total commercial loans at the beginning and end of the year; and the costs of foreign investment are the same profit ratios as in table 4.8.

Table 4.10 shows the average cost of commercial loans, expressed as the ratio of interest payments to the average remaining balance of commercial loans in the year. That cost rose almost consistently from 1967 to 1981, reflecting interest rate changes in the international capital market, while the average cost of foreign investment, in terms of average profit remittance ratios, fluctuated widely.

In general, the ratios of profit remittances alone to the average remaining balance of DFI (ratio I) have been lower than the average costs of commercial loans, while the combined ratios (ratio II) have been higher. Thus, the argument that DFI is the less expensive form of foreign capital in terms of financial burden does not seem to be generally valid.

Linkage Effect

To measure the contribution of DFI to economic growth, we should take into account not only the activities of foreign firms themselves, but also activities of those domestic firms that are directly or indirectly affected by the foreign firms. If the foreign firms had not existed, the activities of those domestic firms would have been either considerably reduced or nonexistent.

Direct Foreign Investment in Korea 195

The extent of such local linkage creation depends, as noted by Lall (1978), on such diverse factors as the stage of industrial development, technical capabilities, trade and industrial policies in the host countries, and host country firms' bargaining power vis-à-vis multinationals. Thus, the outcome should be widely different from country to country, depending on situations in particular host countries.

Table 4.11 shows the linkage effect measured by domestic raw materials purchased per unit of production by foreign firms in Korea during 1974–78.[12] The linkage effect measured this way overstates the true magnitude of linkages because of several factors. Some of the raw materials might have been produced even without foreign investment (e.g., to export); many of the foreign firms have minority foreign ownership; and some of the transactions have been between foreign firms. On the other hand, first-round backward linkages create additional backward linkages, and there should have been some forward linkages too, through supply of better-quality components and parts by foreign subsidiaries to local firms. These two effects cancel each other out, so the estimates presented in the table, though inadequate, may show the probable magnitude of the linkage effect.

Table 4.11. Linkage Effects of Foreign Firms in Korea (US$ millions)

		1974	1975	1976	1977	1978
1.0	Production	2,895	3,541	5,106	6,541	8,630
2.0	Raw materials purchased	2,375	2,725	3,749	4,471	5,958
2.1	from domestic firms	431	472	793	995	1,786
3.0	Linkage effect (2.1/1.0)	0.149	0.133	0.156	0.153	0.207
4.0	Share of domestic raw materials (2.1/2.0)	0.181	0.173	0.212	0.223	0.300
5.0	Raw materials ratio (2.0/1.0)	0.820	0.770	0.734	0.684	0.690

Note: Estimated by the author, using the survey data provided by the government. Detailed estimation procedures appear in the appendix.

The table shows that by 1978, one unit of production by foreign firms in Korea was generating 0.2 unit of additional production in other domestic firms for the whole economy, and almost 0.3 unit of additional production in other domestic firms for the manufacturing sector, excluding petroleum refining (not shown in the table). The table also indicates that linkages have been increasing overall during the period, mainly because of increasing

---

12. Lall (1978) has correctly pointed out the inadequacy of the measures in examining the linkage effect, but we had no choice but to use these measures, because of conceptual and data problems.

procurement of domestic raw materials by foreign firms. The proportion of raw materials purchased by foreign firms from domestic sources has increased from 18 percent (32 percent for manufacturing firms, excluding petroleum refining) in 1974 to 30 percent (47 percent for manufacturing firms excluding petroleum refining) in 1978. Therefore, even though the raw materials ratio decreased considerably during the period, the linkages increased. Without taking into account such linkage effects, any analysis of the effects of DFI on the host country economy would be inadequate.

Employment Effects

DFI creates new jobs by establishing new firms and by expanding the operations of existing firms. Nevertheless, the effect of DFI has generally been very small on the creation of employment in relation to the size of the total labor force in most host countries, mainly because of the relatively small size of the modern sector. Korea was no exception. In 1978, the total number of domestic employees in foreign firms is estimated to have been about 315,000, while total Korean employment in the year was 13.5 million. Thus, about 2.3 percent of total labor force was employed in foreign firms in that year.

Foreign investment in Korea, however, has been concentrated in the manufacturing sector, so the weight of foreign firms in total manufacturing employment has been considerably higher (table 4.12). For example, in 1978, foreign firms employed almost 10 percent of the total labor force in the manufacturing sector. In addition, the importance of foreign firms has been increasing consistently because of the continuing flow of new foreign investment and the expanded activities of existing foreign firms. Further-

Table 4.12. Employment Status of Foreign Firms in Korea (1,000 persons)

	1974	1975	1976	1977	1978
Employed by foreign firms[a]					
Total	159	180	225	257	315
Manufacturing industries	153	174	218	245	288
Total Korean employment[b]					
Total	11,586	11,830	12,556	12,929	13,490
Manufacturing industries	2,012	2,205	2,678	2,798	3,016
Weight of foreign firms (%)					
Total	1.4	1.5	1.8	2.0	2.3
Manufacturing industries	7.6	7.9	8.1	8.8	9.5

[a]Number of employees in foreign firms refers only to domestic employees excluding expatriate foreign workers; detailed estimation procedures appear in appendix.
[b]Data for total employment from Bank of Korea (1982).

Direct Foreign Investment in Korea 197

Table 4.13. Industrial Distribution of Employment by Foreign Firms in Manufacturing Industries, 1978 (1,000 persons)

Industry	Total Employed[a]	Employed by Foreign Firms[b]	Proportion Employed by Foreign Firms (%)
Textile & garments	635.8	38.2	6.0
Industrial & other chemicals	101.7	24.5	24.1
Petroleum refining	3.7	3.7	100.0
Metal	83.3	9.7	11.6
Nonelectrical machinery	336.3	43.3	12.9
Electrical & electronics	232.2	82.2	35.4
Others	718.9	55.5	7.7
Total	2,111.9	257.1	12.2

Sources: Author's estimate (for foreign firms) and Economic Planning Board (1980).

[a]The number of employees in manufacturing industries in this table (2,111,900) differs from that in table 4.12 (3,016,000), because only firms with more than five employees are accounted for in the Manufacturing Census.

[b]The number employed by foreign firms in this table (257,100) differs from the number employed in manufacturing industries in table 4.12 (288,000), because Masan Free Export Zone had to be excluded from the sample, on account of insufficient breakdown of data.

more, if we also take into account the indirect employment creation effect through linkages, foreign investment in Korea appears to have had a considerable employment creation effect in manufacturing industries.

Table 4.13, showing the distribution of employment by foreign firms in manufacturing industries, indicates that the largest contribution was made by foreign firms in the electronics, machinery, textile and apparel, and chemical industries. These four industries accounted for about two-thirds of total manufacturing employment by foreign firms.

Effects on the Balance of Payments

DFI affects every major item in the balance of payments, through various activities of foreign firms. We first examined the direct effect on the balance of payments, considering only financial flows directly related to DFI.

Table 4.14 presents DFI arrivals, withdrawals, profit remittances, and royalties sent by foreign firms annually and compares their net effect on the balance of payments (investment arrivals − investment withdrawals and profit and royalty remittances) with total foreign exchange expenditure of the economy for the year. The table clearly shows that the positive balance of payments effect of direct foreign investment has been almost negligible in relative terms.

Table 4.14. Direct Balance-of-Payments Effects of Foreign Firms in Korea (US$ millions)

Year	Investment Arrivals (A)	Investment Withdrawals (B)	Profit Remittances (C)	Royalties[a] (D)	Net Direct Effect on Balance of Payments (E) = (A − B − C − D)	Current Foreign Exchange Expense of Whole Economy[b] (E)	Proportional Effect of Foreign Firms (G) = (E)/(F)
1967	12.7	0.0	0.2	0.5	12.0	1,060.0	1.1
1972	61.2	2.9	6.7	4.1	47.5	2,767.8	1.7
1977	102.3	11.0	49.3	30.1	11.9	13,284.1	0.1
1978	100.5	11.8	44.1	27.7	16.9	18,717.5	0.1
1979	126.0	90.9	54.7	n.a.	n.a.	24,120.8	n.a.
1980	96.6	90.2	46.8	n.a.	n.a.	28,347.3	n.a.
1981	105.4	3.4	49.0	n.a.	n.a.	32,496.9	n.a.

Source: Ministry of Finance.
[a]Royalties here refer to only those paid by foreign firms.
[b]Current Foreign Exchange Expense of Whole Economy refers to total import value plus invisible expenditures by the Korean economy in the year.

In addition, the table shows that the direct effects should have been negative in 1979 and 1980, even though the exact magnitudes cannot be calculated because of insufficient royalty data. The negative effects in 1979 and 1980 were caused by the withdrawal of a few large foreign investors, so they cannot be considered normal situations. Nevertheless, the argument that DFI has no significant positive balance-of-payments effect, and that it may even create negative effects in the long run, appears to be valid, when we look only at the direct balance-of-payments effect in the narrowest sense.

The picture changes, however, if we take into account the impact on the balance of payments through the export and import activities of foreign firms. Table 4.15 shows the estimated values of total exports and imports of foreign firms during 1974–78 in Korea. If we assume that none of the domestic sales by foreign firms was import-substituting, the balance-of-payments effect (I) of foreign firms appears to have been consistently negative. On the other hand, if we assume that all domestic sales by foreign firms have been import-substituting, the balance-of-payments effect (II) of foreign firms appears to have been substantial and increasing.

The latter assumption appears nearer to reality than the former, so the substantial positive effect appears to be the more plausible conclusion than the negative effect. This can be seen clearly if we exclude petroleum refining, an import-substituting industry. In that case, the balance-of-payments effect of foreign firms appears to have been positive and increasing, even though none of the other domestic sales by foreign firms is

Table 4.15. Export and Import Activities of Foreign Firms in Korea (US$ millions)

	1974	1975	1976	1977	1978
1.0 Total exports by foreign firms	1,024	1,135	1,962	2,332	2,899
(excluding petroleum)	923	1,040	1,830	2,232	2,869
2.0 Domestic sales by foreign firms	1,853	2,406	3,144	4,209	5,731
(excluding petroleum)	801	1,007	1,473	2,047	3,075
3.0 Total imports by foreign firms	1,932	2,253	2,956	3,476	4,172
(excluding petroleum)	823	909	1,311	1,439	1,889
4.0 Balance-of-payments effects I					
(1.0 − 3.0)	−908	−1,118	−994	−1,144	−1,273
(excluding petroleum)	100	131	519	793	980
5.0 Balance-of-payments effects II					
(1.0 + 2.0 − 3.0)	945	1,288	2,150	3,065	4,458
(excluding petroleum)	901	1,138	1,992	2,840	4,055
6.0 Total current account expenditures	7,598	7,997	10,120	13,284	18,718

Note: Exports, domestic sales, and imports of foreign firms have been estimated, using the survey data provided by the Korean government.

regarded as import-substituting. Thus, even though the exact magnitude of the balance-of-payments effect by foreign firms cannot be measured, it appears to have been positive, substantial, and increasing in recent years.

Effects on Export

The propensity of foreign firms to export has been considerably higher than that of domestic firms, both because the government seldom allowed foreign firms to compete in domestic markets (except for import-substituting purposes) and because many foreign firms came into Korea to exploit low-cost labor for their off-shore assembly operations. During 1974–78, the average propensity of foreign firms to export in the manufacturing sector was about 36 percent, while that of domestic firms was 23 percent (table 4.16). If we further exclude petroleum refining, the average propensity of foreign firms to export was about 57 percent (not shown here).

During the period of our examination, however, the propensity of domestic firms to export has increased steadily, while that of foreign firms has stagnated. As a result, the foreign firms' share of total exports stabilized around a 25 percent level. An older survey indicated that foreign firms' share in total exports had grown consistently from the early sixties to the early seventies. The implication of our new finding is thus that since about the middle of the seventies, import-substituting activities of foreign firms have grown as fast as export activities. This trend appears to have occurred because Korea had embarked on a massive investment program for her second-stage import substitution from about that time.

Table 4.16. Export Propensity of Foreign and Domestic Firms in Manufacturing Industries

	1974	1975	1976	1977	1978
1.0 Total production	18,334	20,336	27,441	33,514	43,123
1.1 by foreign firms	2,829	3,462	5,009	6,309	8,311
1.2 by domestic firms	15,505	16,874	22,432	27,205	34,812
1.3 Foreign firms' share (1.1/1.0)	15.4	17.0	18.3	18.8	19.3
2.0 Exports	4,253	4,791	7,283	8,795	11,420
2.1 by foreign firms	1,004	1,096	1,927	2,271	2,810
2.2 by domestic firms	3,249	3,695	5,356	6,524	8,610
2.3 Foreign firms' share (2.1/2.0)	23.6	22.9	26.5	25.8	24.6
3.0 Export propensity	23.2	23.6	26.5	26.2	26.5
3.1 of foreign firms (2.1/1.1)	35.5	31.7	38.5	36.0	33.8
3.2 of domestic firms (2.2/1.2)	21.0	21.9	23.9	24.0	24.7

Sources: Bank of Korea (1982); Economic Planning Board (1982).

Note: Performance of foreign firms has been estimated by the author, using survey data provided by the government. Detailed estimation procedures appear in the appendix.

Effects on Growth

In a simple neoclassical world, where capital and labor are the only factors of production, the contribution of DFI to growth can be measured only through its contribution to the increase in capital stock. But in the real world where unemployment, taxation, imperfect competition, technological development, and varying efficiency of production invalidate the assumptions of neoclassical theory, the increase to the capital stock is only the tip of the iceberg in analyzing the effects of direct foreign investment on overall economic growth.

It has been pointed out by many students of DFI that the amount of DFI is typically relatively small compared to the total capital stock of a nation, and Korea is no exception in this respect. The proportion of direct foreign investment in gross domestic capital formation fluctuated between 0.2 percent and 4.7 percent during 1962–81. The contribution of DFI was greatest in 1973 (4.7 percent), but since then its relative importance has been gradually decreasing. In recent years, its contribution has been less than 1 percent of total capital formation. Of course, the contribution is greater if we confine the comparison to the manufacturing sector, but even there, the share of DFI was mostly less than 5 percent, except during 1972–74.

As to the impact on growth, we were able to measure the direct effect of DFI, since there are detailed statistics on the performance of foreign firms. Assuming that total sales minus total raw material purchases represented a rough estimate of value added, we estimated total value added created by foreign firms and compared it with the GNP.

Table 4.17 shows that the value added ratio of foreign firms increased during the period 1974–78, from 18 percent in 1974 to 31 percent in 1978. This appears to have been the result of several factors: the weight of the petroleum-refining industry, where the value-added ratio is very small, decreased in relative importance because of the inflow of other DFIs; the relative importance of off-shore assembly type DFIs decreased because of wage increases; and DFI in high value-added industries increased as Korea began to pursue second-stage import substitution.

Because of the increase in the value-added ratio and the expansion and new entry of foreign firms, the weight of foreign firms in the economy in terms of value added increased considerably during the period, reaching 5.6 percent in the entire economy, and 18.9 percent in the manufacturing sector, in 1978.[13]

---

13. Comparison of tables 4.13 and 4.17 tells us that foreign firms have been on the average less labor-intensive than domestic firms. In addition, comparison of tables 4.16 and 4.17 tells us that foreign firms' share in manufacturing increased considerably faster in terms of value added than in terms of production value. In 1974, the foreign firms' share in manufacturing

Table 4.17. Value Added by Foreign Firms (US$ millions)

	1974	1975	1976	1977	1978
1 Total sales by foreign firms[a]	2,895	3,541	5,106	6,541	8,630
(manufacturing)	2,829	3,462	5,009	6,309	8,311
2 Total raw material purchases by foreign firms[a]	2,375	2,725	3,749	4,471	5,958
(manufacturing)	2,360	2,707	3,721	4,422	5,897
3 Value added created by foreign firms (1 − 2)	520	816	1,357	2,070	2,672
(manufacturing)	469	755	1,288	1,887	2,414
4 Value-added ratio (3/1)	18.0	12.0	26.6	30.6	31.0
(manufacturing)	16.6	21.8	25.7	29.9	29.0
5 Gross National Product	18,062	20,234	27,424	35,167	47,351
(manufacturing)	4,704	5,351	7,566	9,492	12,798
6 Weight of foreign firms (3/5)	2.0	4.0	4.9	5.9	5.6
(manufacturing)	9.9	14.1	17.0	19.9	18.9
7 Contribution to growth by foreign firms (%)[b] ($\Delta 3/\Delta 5$)		13.8	7.5	9.2	5.0
(manufacturing)		44.5	24.1	31.2	15.9

Source: Data for GNP from Bank of Korea (1981).

Note: Prices are all in current prices, so there remains the possibility of bias in calculation of the contribution of foreign firms.

[a]Total sales and raw material purchases by foreign firms have been estimated, using the survey data provided by the Korean government: detailed estimation procedures appear in the appendix.

[b]The contribution to growth by foreign firms has been calculated as the proportion of increase in GNP explained by foreign firms. In other words, $\Delta 3$ is the difference between the value added created by foreign firms in the year and that in the preceding year, and $\Delta 5$ is the difference between GNP in the year and that in the preceding year, and the contribution of foreign firms to GNP has been measured as the raio of $\Delta 3$ over $\Delta 5$.

According to the estimates presented in the table, DFI's contribution to Korea's growth ranged from 5 percent of total growth in 1978 to 13.8 percent in 1975 (the contribution to growth of the manufacturing sector has been greater). Multiplication of these contributions to Korea's economic growth rate during the period indicates that about one percentage point of

---

was 15.4 percent in terms of production value (table 4.16, 1.3), but only 9.9 percent in value added. However, both shares were about equal, beginning in about 1977. This implies that the value-added ratio of foreign firms had been lower than that of domestic firms until 1977.

the growth rate annually during the period is explainable by the contribution of DFI.[14]

The significance of this calculation should not be overemphasized, since there are many logical and data problems involved. In addition, many indirect effects of DFI on growth which may be more important than direct effects have not been accounted for. Thus we will complete our analysis on the role of DFI in Korea's growth with a discussion of the indirect effects.

Table 4.18. Licensing Agreements by Industry (end of 1978)

Industry	Number of Agreements All (A)	Foreign (B)	Share of Foreign Firms (%) (B)/(A).100
Chemical	192	68	35.4
Petroleum refining	17	17	100.0
Glass & glass products	7	5	71.4
Nonferrous metal	13	8	61.5
Fabricated metal products	60	14	23.3
Machinery	399	62	15.5
Electronics	237	87	36.7
Other manufacturing	195	27	13.8
Nonmanufacturing	60	14	23.3
Total	1,180	302	25.6

Source: Economic Planning Board (1979).

Note: Licensing agreements by foreign firms have been identified by looking at individual company names from Economic Planning Board data on all licensing agreements in Korea.

Diffusion of Technology and Other Indirect Effects

With respect to technology, the only data available were the number of licensing agreements made by foreign firms. Table 4.18 presents the licensing agreements made by all Korean and foreign firms, by industry. Licensing agreements made by both Korean and foreign firms have been heavy in the chemical, machinery, and electronics industries, and foreign firms accounted for a considerable portion of total licensing agreements in many industries, including those three.

14. We have included in the value added by foreign firms profits, royalties, and interest sent abroad by these firms. These payments were a little less than 20 percent of total value added by these firms. Their contribution should thus accordingly be discounted. We have at the same time omitted the linkage effect of DFI, however, to simplify the discussion. Thus, the probable scale of direct contribution to growth appears not grossly biased.

With the limited data available, it was not possible to draw any firm conclusions about the contribution DFI made to technological development in Korea. It cannot be determined whether the technologies which foreign investors brought in were the appropriate ones, whether they were effectively spread to local producers, or whether foreign firms without licensing agreements made the same contribution as those with the agreements. Similarly, we could not determine whether U.S. or Japanese technologies were better suited to the Korean economy. But at least for those foreign firms that were involved in off-shore assembly or sourcing-type operations with imported inputs, it appears true that they had little incentive to help develop the technological capabilities of local producers, whether competitors or manufacturers of components and parts.

Through interviews with managers of foreign firms and field trips, the present author concluded that the training effects were significant in some industries, even though there was no noticeable transfer of high-level technology. Overall, however, the contribution of DFI to technological development appears to have been marginal, in the sense that it was not critical in bringing about Korea's current state of technological development. Many domestic firms were able to exploit the international technology market through licensing agreements, and they were able to refine their technologies through export activities. In addition, the technology contributions of Korean scientists and engineers, many of them educated abroad, have been substantial, and there has been relatively little local research and development effort by foreign firms.[15]

DFI also affects the host country economy in various other ways. For example, it has an impact on industrial structure through backward and forward linkages, on market structure through competition with domestic firms, and on domestic financing activities. In addition, competition with DFI often affects the efficiency and productivity of domestic firms, as well as research and development efforts. These efforts, however, could not be discussed because of both data and conceptual problems.

Some Sectoral Observations

Electronics

Foreign investment in electronics in Korea began with off-shore assembly of transistors and integrated circuits by U.S. multinational firms. First

15. Westphal, Rhee, and Pursell (1981) made a similar observation regarding the contribution of DFI to technological development in Korea when they examined the sources of Korea's industrial competence acquired in recent years. According to them, DFI has been an important primary source of technology in only a few sectors, primarily in chemicals, electronics, and petroleum refining. For other sectors, licensing agreements or, to a greater extent, machinery imports and turnkey plant construction have been important. They argue, however, that the effective assimilation or adaptation of most technologies has been achieved in Korea chiefly by local effort.

came the Komy Corporation in 1965, followed by Fairchild Semiconductors, Signetics, and Motorola. Soon afterwards, computer firms such as IBM, Control Data, Univac, and Sperry Rand began leasing operations in Korea.

The major wave of DFI in electronics began with the coming of Japanese firms in the early seventies to manufacture various kinds of electrical and electronic components and parts. The most common examples were switches, resistors, condensers, transformers, and meters. Some assembly operations of final consumer equipment also began about that time, but investment in final consumer equipment was relatively small compared to investment in components and parts.

Foreign investment in industrial equipment, another major area of electronics, also began as early as 1970 with the establishment of joint ventures to manufacture telephone switching systems and copying machines for the domestic market. But investment in this area was relatively small until after the mid-seventies, mainly because of the domestic-market orientation of these products and the underdevelopment of domestic communications and office equipment markets. Coming into recent years, however, several new major investments have been made in this area too, as the domestic market expanded and export possibilities grew.

Of the investor countries in the electronics industry, Japan far outweighed the others. Table 4.19 shows investor country distribution in the industry for 192 firms remaining as of the end of 1980. The average size of Japanese investment has been much smaller than that of the United States, reflecting the relative importance of small and medium-sized firms in Japanese investment.

The phenomenal growth of foreign, and particularly Japanese, investment in electronics beginning in the early seventies reduced the share of production of domestic firms from 68 percent in 1970 to 36 percent in 1975,

Table 4.19. Foreign Investment in the Electronics Industry

Investor Country	Firms[a] Number	Percent	Investment[b] Amount (US$ millions)	Percent	Amount per Firm (US$ thousands)
Japan	153	79.7	104.5	61.6	683
U.S.A.	32	16.7	51.5	30.4	1,609
Others	7	3.6	13.6	8.0	1,943
Total	192	100.0	169.5	100.0	883

Source: Ministry of Finance.
[a]As of the end of 1980.
[b]On approval basis for existing firms as of end of 1980.

as shown in table 4.20. But, after 1975, the proportion of production by domestic firms rose, reaching 58 percent in 1981. The share of domestic firms in the exports of electronic products was small until 1975, but it began to rise rapidly thereafter, and constituted 53 percent of total exports by 1981. Table 4.20 also shows that both the export propensity of domestic firms and the domestic-market orientation of foreign firms have increased during the period.

The increase in the share of domestic firms in total production and exports in recent years has been achieved mainly through an increase in their production of consumer equipment rather than of industrial equipment or parts and components. DFI has been relatively small in the consumer equipment area. This can best be explained by the government policy mentioned earlier. There were already several indigenous firms producing most lines of consumer equipment in the protected domestic market, and the government did not want foreign firms to compete with them. DFI was rarely permitted in the consumer equipment area, except with the condition of 100 percent export.

Even though the domestic market was closed to foreign investors in this area, foreign investors nevertheless earned considerable rent through licensing agreements for products oriented toward local market sales; and for their home or world markets they placed orders through subcontracting agreements. In both cases, they maintained a good deal of leverage in both production and sales, because they supplied essential parts and components either through joint venture firms in Korea or the mother companies at home, and because they were working as licensors or sales agents in their home or world markets. Domestic electronics firms in Korea have thus grown mainly as assemblers of consumer equipment and have lagged in production of parts and components. Many joint ventures in parts and components were also assemblers of completely knocked-down parts, rather than manufacturers of the parts.

Thus, the contribution of DFI in the electronics industry appears to have been rather limited. Foreign firms created 70,000 to 80,000 jobs in the industry and have, to a certain extent, contributed to the balance of payments through their export activities. But since many of them were involved with simple assembly jobs using imported inputs, the contribution to technological development appears to have been small.

Textiles

The dominance of Japanese firms as foreign investors has been most prevalent in the textile industry. Among 71 foreign investors remaining in the industry as of the end of 1980, only six firms were non-Japanese. The Japanese textile industry has long been internationally competitive, and

Table 4.20. Electronics Production and Exports by Firm Characteristics

	Production (US$ millions)	Distribution (%) Domestic	Distribution (%) Foreign	Total	Exports (US$ millions)	Distribution (%) Domestic	Distribution (%) Foreign	Total
1970	105.4	67.8	32.2	100.0	55.0	26.4	73.6	100.0
1973	462.9	48.1	51.9	100.0	369.3	31.3	68.7	100.0
1975	860.2	36.4	63.6	100.0	581.9	26.1	73.9	100.0
1978	2,271.0	45.5	54.5	100.0	1,359.0	38.6	61.4	100.0
1980	2,852.5	48.5	51.5	100.0	2,003.8	47.6	52.4	100.0
1981	3,790.9	57.5	42.5	100.0	2,195.6	52.8	47.2	100.0

Source: Electronics Industries Association of Korea (1982).

historical ties appear to have further facilitated Korean joint ventures with them.

The foreign investments were made in all areas of the textile industry: fiber, fabrics, and garments, but they were the most prominent in the synthetic fiber area, the most capital-intensive part of the industry. As of 1980, 80 percent of nylon and 76 percent of polyester manufacturing were owned by joint venture firms. These foreign investments in synthetic fibers accounted for 47 percent of total DFI in the textile industry (table 4.21).

The remainder of foreign investments were made mainly by small and medium-sized Japanese firms to manufacture garments such as knitwear, lingerie, jackets, and hosiery. There were also some joint ventures in silk fabrics. However, DFI in these areas was small in relation to indigenous industry.

The contribution of DFI in textiles appears to have been limited to some employment creation and foreign exchange earnings through import-substituting and exporting activities. However, some positive contribution appears to have been made to technological development in the synthetic fiber industry.

Petroleum Refining

Petroleum refining was the only industry in Korea where foreign firms originally dominated domestic production. Petroleum refining began in 1964 with the construction of a 35,000 barrels per day refinery, 75 percent of its equity being owned by the state and 25 percent by Gulf. At a later stage, Gulf was joined by Caltex, Union Oil, and National Iranian Oil Co. (NIOC) in the Korean market. These four companies represented the petroleum refining industry in Korea (table 4.22).

The state originally was the major shareholder of the Korea Oil Co., but it divested itself in 1980 through sale of its share to the general public.

Table 4.21. Status of Foreign Investment in the Textile Industry

Area of Investment	Number of Foreign Investors[a]				Amount of Investment[b] (US$ millions)			
	Japan	Others	Total	(%)	Japan	Others	Total	(%)
Synthetic Fiber	6	2	8	11.3	29.8	4.7	34.5	47.4
Others	59	4	63	88.7	36.9	1.4	38.3	52.6
Total	65	6	71	100.0	66.7	6.1	72.7	100.0

Source: Ministry of Finance.
[a]As of the end of 1980.
[b]On current approval basis.

Table 4.22. The Petroleum Refining Industry in Korea

Company[a]	Year Established	Foreign Investor	Foreign Ownership (%) Initial	Foreign Ownership (%) End 1981	Capacity at 1981 Year End (thousand barrels per day)
Korea Oil[b]	1964	Gulf (U.S.A.)	25	0	280
Honam Oil	1969	Caltex (Bahamas)	50	50	280
Kyungin Energy	1972	Union Oil (Bahamas)	62	62	60
Ssang Yong Oil	1980	NIOC (Iran)	50	0	60

Source: Ministry of Finance.
[a]There were two other foreign investors, Dutch Shell and Mobil. But since their product is confined mainly to lubricating oil, they have been excluded.
[b]Gulf participated in petrochemical projects in 1970, thus increasing its share to 50 percent in that year, but it divested itself completely in 1980.

However, it has controlled and still controls all refinery operation in Korea by means of price and trade regulations.

As of 1981, Korea had a refining capacity of 780,000 barrels per day, 44 percent being owned by domestic producers and the rest by joint ventures. The four firms were originally all joint ventures, but Gulf divested itself in 1980 by agreement with the government, and NIOC divested itself voluntarily in the same year.[16]

The major contribution of DFI in petroleum refining was in training technicians and engineers, who later, together with those trained in fertilizer firms, supplied the necessary skills for the operation and construction of petrochemical plants. Gulf also directly participated in the first Korean petrochemical complex project with the construction of a naphtha cracker.

A relatively stable supply of crude oil during the oil crises may have been another contribution of the foreign investor. But in employment creation and the balance of payments, the DFI impact was minimal because of the capital-intensive nature of the industry and because Korea imports all of its crude oil.

Petrochemicals

The petrochemical industry is another in which foreign firms have dominated. The Korean petrochemical industry began with the construction of the first petrochemical complex in 1973. As noted earlier, a naphtha cracker was built by Gulf, and most other downstream producers were also joint ventures with major foreign chemical producers. In the case of the second petrochemical complex, which was completed at the end of 1979, there were more purely domestic firms with licensing agreements and fewer joint ventures. The status of major foreign producers in the petrochemical industry is shown in table 4.23. The first thing to note is that more Japanese than U.S. or European firms have participated in the petrochemical industry, unlike other chemical industries such as petroleum refining, fertilizers, or pharmaceuticals, where U.S. or European firms have dominated. This appears to be due to equally efficient Japanese technology in the field and the preference of Korean businessmen for forming joint ventures with the Japanese. The second interesting thing to note from table 4.23 is that most joint ventures have been on a 50-50 basis. Since the petrochemical industry is one of the most basic raw-materials-producing industries, the Korean government did not want it under foreign control.

The contribution of foreign investment in petrochemicals may be defined as follows: first, the experience of building and operating the first

---

16. Union Oil also withdrew from Korea in early 1984.

Table 4.23. Foreign Firms in the Petrochemical Industry

Name of Firm	Year Approved	Foreign Investor	Foreign Ownership (%) Initial	Foreign Ownership (%) End 1981	Major Products
Korea Oil	1963	Gulf (U.S.A.)	25	0	Ethylene
Lucky Continental Carbon	1968	Continental Carbon (U.S.A.)	50	50	Carbon black
Korea Pacific	1969	Dow Chemical[a] (Netherlands)	50	50	LDPE
Tong Suh Petrochemical	1969	Asahi Kasehi (Japan)	50	34	AN
Korea Petrochemical	1970	Marubeni (Japan)	50	50	PP
Korea Synthetic Rubber	1971	Mitsui (Japan)	50	50	SBR
Taesung Methanol	1973	Mitsubishi (Japan)	50	50	Methanol
Samsung Petrochemical	1974	Mitsui (Japan) Amoco (U.S.A.)	50	50	TPA
Korea Polyol	1974	Tomen (Japan); Sanyo Chemical (Japan)	50	50	PPG
Dai Nong Petrochemical	1974	Mitsui Toatsu (Japan)	50	50	MA
Dow Chemical—Korea[a]	1974	Dow Chemical (Netherlands)	100	100	Chlorine
Honam Petrochemical	1975	Dai-ichi Chemical (Japan)	50	50	PP
Kolon Petrochemical	1976	Nippon Petrochemical (Japan); PICA (Panama)	45	45	Petroleum resin
Hyosung BASF	1980	BASF (Germany)	50	50	PS

Source: Korea Petrochemical Industry Association.
[a]Dow Chemical withdrew from Korea in 1982.

complex facilitated the development of the Korean engineering industry, thus enabling some engineering companies to participate in the construction of a second complex. This has also helped Korean plant exports at a later stage by providing necessary experiences. Second, the existence of a domestic petrochemical complex enhanced the negotiating leverage of manufacturers of textiles, tires, and footwear in securing stable supplies of raw materials from abroad. Third, through import substitution and by using domestic naphtha which would have been exported if there had been no petrochemical producers in Korea, the foreign investment made a positive contribution to the balance of payments.

But, as in petroleum refining, the contribution to employment creation was minimal and research and development efforts have also been almost nonexistent. The contribution to local technological development appears to have been small.

Machinery

Japanese firms also dominated the machinery industry (table 4.24).[17] Several major European producers made considerable investments as well, thus raising the average scale of investment per European firm.

Table 4.24. Status of Foreign Investment in the Machinery Industry

Investor Country	Firms[a] Number	Firms[a] Percent	Investment[b] Amount (US$ millions)	Investment[b] Percent	Amount per Firm (US$ thousands)
Japan	93	76.9	55.1	58.1	592
U.S.A.	10	8.3	10.4	11.0	1,040
Others	18	14.9	29.3	30.9	1,628
Total	121	100.0	94.8	100.0	783

Source: Ministry of Finance.
[a]As of the end of 1980.
[b]On current approval basis.

In line with the industrialization strategy pursued by Korea, foreign investments in the machinery industry in the earlier years were concentrated in machine tool manufacturing and some simple parts and components. Beginning in the middle of the seventies, as Korea began heavy industrialization, foreign investment also began to flow into such areas as turbines and generators, boilers, and heavy industrial machinery. Some of

17. The machinery industry includes fabricated metals, industrial machinery, professional and scientific equipment, and their parts and components. Electrical and electronic machinery and transport equipment have been excluded.

these products have been exported, but the main orientation of foreign investment in machinery has been to the domestic market. In 1978, the propensity of foreign firms to export is estimated to have been about 26 percent, a considerably lower figure than the average propensity of other foreign firms.

Compared with other industries, there have been relatively more licensing agreements than foreign investments in the machinery industry. The world machinery market is still dominated by advanced country multinationals, and it is very difficult for developing country producers, whether they are indigenous or joint ventures, to penetrate world markets because of the high degree of product differentiation and economies of scale necessary for efficient production. Thus, domestic-market orientation is almost inevitable for foreign investment in the machinery industry, and the Korean domestic market has been too small for efficient production. But licensing agreements could earn returns for potential foreign investors' intangible assets without entailing worry about the efficiency of domestic production or about potential competition from the licensees in the world market.

Future contributions of DFI may be very important in this area, since Korea needs to develop its machinery industry to continue its growth, and since DFI plays a key role here for both final goods and components and parts. Thus, the Korean government's recent emphasis on DFI in the machinery industry, particularly in components and parts, appears well directed.

Conclusion

Cohen (1975), after surveying 10 foreign and 10 Korean firms, argued that there was very little net gain from direct foreign investment and that Korea would have been better off with foreign commercial loans financing the expansion of its indigenous firms. His argument appears to be overstated and to be based on inadequate empirical evidence.

Many joint ventures in Korea, particularly those with less than majority foreign ownership (which constitute almost three-quarters of all investment) were initiated by Korean entrepreneurs who approached potential foreign investors. Positive results may be attributed to such initiatives and it is dangerous to take a position without analyzing those results.

Purely private decisions to outcompete other domestic firms might well have proved beneficial both to private firms and to the Korean economy in areas such as increased efficiency, greater international competitiveness, and upgraded technology. Particularly because of the high quality of both domestic entrepreneurs and workers, joint ventures may have created considerable external economies, though they are not readily measurable.

When we consider the background of foreign investment in Korea, the ill effects often cited by critics of foreign investment, such as the reinforcement of dualism, the introduction of inappropriate products and technologies, and the weakening of domestic entrepreneurship, appear to have been minimal. Rather, the foreign investment seems to have made a positive contribution to employment creation and the balance of payments through its import-substituting and exporting activities.

In addition, foreign investment appears to have made important indirect contributions to Korea, although perhaps not as comprehensively as Korea may have wished. In some cases, foreign investors appear to have provided their domestic partners with technologies and markets that were crucial to the development of the industry.

Furthermore, the mere existence and continuous flow of foreign investment may have affected the overall performance of the domestic economy in many ways. The tapping of the international capital market may have been made easier, partly because the presence of prominent foreign investors enhanced the credibility of Korea's economic stability in the opinion of international bankers. Similarly, the efficiency of domestic entrepreneurs may have increased faster, and their research and development efforts may have been heightened, because of potential competition from foreign investors.

All the benefits arising from DFI, however, could not have been realized without the presence of dynamic and efficient domestic entrepreneurs, the diligent labor force with its capacity to absorb training, and the relevant industrialization strategy followed by the government. The effects of DFI in a country depend not so much on the good intentions of foreign investors as on the ability of the host country to maximize its contribution to economic growth.

Appendix

Estimation Procedure of the Performance of Foreign Firms

The 1979 survey of the performance of foreign firms by the Economic Planning Board was expected to include all 856 foreign firms investing in Korea as of the end of 1978. However, replies came from only 593 firms, 69.3 percent of the total. Thus, it was inevitable that some estimates had to be made to deduce the activities of all foreign firms. Fortunately, most of the data for the firms in the Masan Free Export Zone were available separately, so estimates were done only for the firms inside the country.

As an example, let us consider the estimating procedure for the number of domestic employees of foreign firms in 1978. First, we excluded from the total sample of 856 firms those in the Masan Free Export Zone (114), those approved by the government during the year 1978 (47), and those which did not operate in 1978, though they had been approved earlier (10). The exclusion of the latter two groups was made to prevent possible overestimation due to inclusion of nonoperating firms. The remaining sample included 685 firms; the number of firms submitting the survey replies was 468, and those with employment data, 442.

Using the status report of the Economic Planning Board, which includes approval and arrival data for all firms, we calculated the amount of total capital in U.S. dollar terms for 685 firms by industry. Next, we calculated the total capital for 442 firms for which we had employment data, by industry. The industrial classification system used was at the three-digit level. Using the data on employment for the 442 firms, and the ratio of total capital for 442 and 685 firms, we estimated total employment for all 685 firms. Finally, we added employment in the Masan Free Export Zone to arrive at total employment by all foreign firms by three-digit industries.

In calculating total capital, we used the remaining balance and the foreign ownership ratio in 1978. Thus, the later the actual timing of the investment arrival, the greater the overestimation of total capital in a relative sense. However, since this bias is present in the calculation of the capital stock for both samples of the 685 firms and the 442 firms, the margin of error due to this bias does not appear to be great.

The estimates of employment in other years, and sales and raw materials during 1974–78, have all been calculated using a similar methodology, though sample sizes differed in individual estimates.

References

Bank of Korea. 1982. *Economic Statistics Yearbook*.
Bank of Korea. 1982. *National Income in Korea*.
Caves, Richard E. 1971. "International Corporations: The Industrial Economics of Foreign Investment." *Economica* 38 (February): 1–27.
Cohen, B. 1975. *Multinational Firms and Asian Exports*. New Haven: Yale University Press.
Curhan, J. P., W. H. Davidson, and R. Suri. 1977. *Tracing the Multinationals*. Cambridge, Mass.: Ballinger Publishing Co.
Economic Planning Board. 1979. *Status of Licensing Agreements: 1978*.
Economic Planning Board. 1980. *Report on Mining and Manufacturing Census: 1978*.
Economic Planning Board. 1982. *Major Statistics of Korean Economy*.
Electronics Industries Association of Korea. 1982. *Statistics of Electronic and Electrical Industries*.
Feldman, G. M. 1978. "Coping with New Challenges to Investment Ventures Abroad." *Commerce America* (July 3 and 17).
Kojima, Kiyoshi. 1973. "A Macroeconomic Approach to Foreign Direct Investment." *Hitotsubashi Journal of Economics* 14.1 (June): 1–21.

Lall, Sanjaya. 1978. "Transnationals, Domestic Enterprises, and Industrial Structure in Host LDCs: A Survey." *Oxford Economic Papers* (July).

Lee, Chung H. 1980. "United States and Japanese Direct Investment in Korea: A Comparative Study." *Hitotsubashi Journal of Economics* 20.2 (February): 26–41.

Mason, R. Hal. 1980. "A Comment on Professor Kojima's 'Japanese Type versus American Type of Technology Transfer'." *Hitotsubashi Journal of Economics* 20.2 (February): 42–52.

Reuber, G. L., et al. 1973. *Private Foreign Investment in Development*. Oxford: Clarendon Press.

Vernon, R. 1966. "International Investment and International Trade in the Product Cycle." *Quarterly Journal of Economics* (May).

Westphal, L. E., Y. Rhee, and G. Pursell. 1981. "Korean Industrial Competence: Where It Came From," World Bank Staff Working Paper No. 469 (July).

III   Hong Kong

5 Trade, Foreign Investment, and Development in Hong Kong
Tzong-biau Lin and Victor Mok

Introduction

For both the newly industrialized countries (NICs) and the less developed countries (LDCs), economic development is generally accompanied by a quest for manufactured exports. This is a recent phenomenon, about two decades old. For most of these countries, export orientation was usually preceded by a phase of import substitution. The shift signified a need for a growing industrial capacity to find markets beyond national boundaries in order to sustain further development.

In this respect, Hong Kong was an exception. For one thing, it is not an independent country. Having been an entrepôt under British rule for more than a century, it had a tradition of free trade. In the early fifties, when its industrialization started, Hong Kong's political future was uncertain. Laissez-faire was just a way of letting things run their natural course. Hong Kong's industrialization did not come by design. It was a textbook case of the operation of the market mechanism and the principle of comparative advantage.

An import-substitution policy for Hong Kong would not have been desirable simply because Hong Kong was so small and deficient in natural resources. In the days of entrepôt trade, it had little industry. Most goods were imported and paid for by earnings derived from trading for others. When this way of making a living came to an end, Hong Kong turned to manufacturing. Its products had to be exported, since its domestic market was small and imports were required for its industries and people. Hong Kong's industrialization was export-oriented from the very beginning, and its development made it more outward-looking than ever before.

Free trade made it possible for Hong Kong to obtain in the cheapest way the raw materials and capital goods required for a competitive edge. On this basis, Hong Kong soon developed its labor-intensive industries and penetrated into the markets of the developed countries. In the fifties, when the world market for labor-intensive products was expanding and the other LDCs were busy implementing their import-substitution programs, Hong Kong rapidly capitalized on the golden opportunity to develop through trade by the sheer force of comparative advantage. Hong Kong thus had a head start; its outward-looking attitude towards trade and foreign investment made it a giant in manufactured exports among the LDCs, despite its small size.

Trade and Development

Background of Economic Development

The economic history of Hong Kong is essentially a history of trade. For almost a century under British rule following the mid-1850s, Hong Kong thrived as the entrepôt of South China, channeling imports en route to China and re-exporting Chinese products to various parts of the world. Manufacturing industries were few in number, elementary in character, and mainly catered to domestic consumption. During World War II, entrepôt trade came to a virtual standstill. It revived rapidly afterward, only to be disrupted again by two major developments around 1950.

The first was the change of government in Mainland China. Although it left Hong Kong politically untouched, it brought a massive inflow of people from China, some of them entrepreneurs bringing capital and expertise, others just bringing any skills they may have had. The second development was the United Nations' embargo on China during the Korean War. This dealt a heavy blow to Hong Kong's entrepôt trade. With its traditional means of making a living largely gone and with increasing millions to feed, Hong Kong simply had to break new ground in order to survive. Given the extreme lack of natural resources, industrialization along the lines of nonresource-based, labor-intensive manufactures was the only answer.

As a result, there was a rapid transformation of the Hong Kong economy. Entrepôt trade had left Hong Kong with an efficient network of banking, communications, and transportation facilities, and trade connections continued despite the decline of the China trade. On the other hand, the inflow of capital and labor changed the basic complexion of Hong Kong's factor endowment. There were entrepreneurs with previous industrial experience in China, most notably textile manufacturers from Shanghai, and there was an abundant supply of immigrant workers who were willing to work long hours at low wages. Hong Kong continued to trade, but now mainly traded its own manufactures instead of the products of others.

There was no division between domestic exports and re-exports in Hong Kong's trade statistics before 1959. In the early fifties, Hong Kong's exports were primarily re-exports. The United Nations' embargo of the mainland and China's increased trade with countries in the Communist bloc caused

Hong Kong's total exports to dwindle in the first half of the fifties. By the end of that decade, however, Hong Kong's exports were back to the level of the early fifties, but well over two-thirds were domestic goods. The transformation of Hong Kong from an entrepôt into an industrial city was complete, and from then on, re-exports never accounted for more than one-third of Hong Kong's total exports.

This development is reflected in the city's manufacturing employment. In 1950, it was only about 82,000, but it grew to around 216,000 in 1960 and 907,000 in 1980, representing 18 percent and 37 percent of Hong Kong's labor force respectively. Table 5.1 provides an overall picture of Hong Kong's rapid economic growth through the development of manufacturing for exports. Growth rates of its GDP, both total and per capita, domestic exports, and manufacturing employment, are all impressive by any standard.

Table 5.1 also shows that the growth record was more impressive in the sixties than in the seventies. Like the rest of the world, Hong Kong's development was slowed by the oil crisis plus keen competition and growing protectionism. An open economy has to live with developments beyond its borders, and Hong Kong has stood up quite well.

The city's economic development was not based on manufacturing alone. It also had a large tertiary sector which gained increasing importance. But that came at a much later stage: it was only in the latter part of the seventies that Hong Kong emerged as a financial center. The principal driving force behind its sustained economic growth for three decades was manufacturing for export. Trade was the engine of growth.

Pattern and Structure of Trade

Table 5.2 shows the development of Hong Kong's trade pattern since 1960. Several observations can be made. First, in value terms all components of trade grew tremendously.[1] This was particularly true of domestic exports

---

1. During the postwar period up to 1980, the Hong Kong dollar appreciated somewhat against the U.S. dollar. It was first pegged to the British pound, then went through several independent adjustments in the turbulent years of the late sixties and early seventies, and was finally floated in November 1974. Changes of the exchange rate (to the U.S. dollar) are as follows:

Up to Nov. 19, 1967	HK$5.71
Nov. 20, 1967, to Nov. 22, 1967	6.67
Nov. 23, 1967, to Dec. 17, 1971	6.06
Dec. 18, 1971, to July 5, 1972	5.58
July 6, 1972, to Feb. 13, 1973	5.65
Feb. 14, 1973, to Nov. 25, 1974	5.09
1976	4.67
1978	4.80
1980	5.13

Table 5.1. Indicators of Growth in Hong Kong (% per annum)

Indicators	Nominal Growth Rates 1960–70	1970–80	1960–80	Real Growth Rates 1960–70	1970–80	1960–80	1980 Level
Population (mid-year)				2.88	2.44	2.66	5,040,000
GDP (at market prices)							
Total GDP	13.73[a]	18.71	16.32[a]	10.24[a]	9.18	9.68[a]	HK$106,770,000
Per capita	10.94[a]	15.88	13.52[a]	7.54[a]	6.58	7.03[a]	HK$ 21,191,000
International trade							
Total exports	14.49	20.49	17.45	11.93	10.24	11.08	HK$ 98,243,000
(Per capita)	11.28	17.62	14.41	8.79	7.62	8.20	HK$ 19,499,000
Domestic exports	15.72	18.63	17.17	13.13	8.54	10.81	HK$ 68,171,000
Re-exports	10.45	26.39	18.15	8.24	15.89	12.00	HK$ 30,072,000
Imports	11.62	20.29	15.87	9.63	10.53	10.08	HK$111,651,000
Manufacturing							
Employment				9.79	5.15	7.44	907,463
Establishments				13.18	10.56	11.86	45,025

Sources: Census and Statistics Department, Hong Kong, *Hong Kong Statistics 1947–1967* (1969); *Hong Kong Trade Statistics* (various issues); and *Estimates of Gross Domestic Product* (various issues).

Note: All growth rates used here are compound rates.

[a]Because of the lack of official GDP data, the initial year of the covered period for these figures is 1961 instead of 1960.

Trade, Investment, and Development in Hong Kong 223

Table 5.2. Pattern of Hong Kong's External Trade

	1960	1965	1970	1975	1980
Value (HK$ millions)					
Total exports	3,937	6,530	15,239	29,832	98,243
Re-exports	1,070	1,503	2,892	6,973	30,072
Domestic exports[a]	2,867	5,027	12,347	22,859	68,171
Manufactured exports[b]	2,571	4,694	11,839	22,168	65,463
Total imports	5,864	8,965	17,607	33,472	111,651
Total trade	9,801	15,494	32,845	63,304	209,984
Total balance	−1,926	−2,435	−2,369	−3,640	−13,408
Proportion (%)					
Re-exports/total exports	27.18	23.02	18.98	23.37	30.61
Domestic exports/total exports	72.82	76.98	81.02	76.63	69.39
Manufactured exports/domestic exports	89.68	93.38	95.89	96.98	96.03
Total exports − imports/total exports	−48.92	−37.29	−15.55	−12.20	13.65
Total exports/GDP	n.a.	62.10	79.31	73.52	92.01
Manufactured exports/GDP	n.a.	85.25	91.64	82.50	104.57
Total exports + imports/GDP	n.a.	147.34	170.94	156.02	196.59

Sources: Census and Statistics Department, Hong Kong, *Hong Kong Trade Statistics* (various issues); *Estimates of Gross Domestic Product* (various issues);
[a] Domestic Exports equal to Total Exports minus Re-exports.
[b] Manufactured Exports refer to exports of domestically manufactured goods which fall into SITC sections 5–8.

except during the last two years, when there was a phenomenal upsurge of re-exports due to the change in Chinese foreign policy. Nevertheless, domestic exports remained at more than two-thirds of total exports.

Second, the proportions of Hong Kong's exports, imports, and total trade to its GDP demonstrate the trade-dependent nature of its economy. By any standard, these proportions were already high at the beginning, and they moved to even higher levels in the process of industrialization. Economic development had made Hong Kong more trade-dependent than ever as a result of its outward-looking strategy.

Third, the growth of Hong Kong's domestic exports was due exclusively to its manufactured exports. Limited by its resource base, Hong Kong itself had little else to offer in nonmanufactures. As early as 1960, close to 90 percent of Hong Kong's domestic exports were in manufactures. In the subsequent periods, the proportion of manufactured to total domestic exports increased further, to more than 95 percent.

Finally, Hong Kong has always had a deficit in its merchandise trade because it has had to import most of the goods necessary for consumption and production. In absolute terms, this deficit widened tremendously, but at a rate much slower than the growth of its exports. At its peak in 1962, the deficit amounted to an alarming 51.7 percent of total exports, but the proportion was rapidly cut in following years. In 1976, when Hong Kong experienced a 43 percent increase in domestic exports as a result of its rebound from the recession caused by the oil crisis, it was almost able to finance all its imports by exports.

This persistent merchandise trade deficit raises the question of financing. Presumably it was covered by the inflow of capital, and earnings from banking, shipping, insurance, and other financial services as well as tourism. But detailed official statistics in these areas are scanty. To the best of our knowledge, Hong Kong's invisible trade surplus (the services account) was more than enough to cover its deficit in visible trade (the goods account) from 1971 to 1977. But this was reversed during 1978, leaving a trade gap, that is, the proportion of the value of imports of goods and services not covered by the value of exports of goods and services, of approximately 5 percent in the early eighties.[2]

A further picture of Hong Kong's development can be seen in the changing structure of its external trade. Table 5.3 classifies the contents of its retained imports (total imports minus re-exports) and domestic exports according to SITC Commodity Sections and gives them as percentages of their respective total values.

In general, Hong Kong's retained imports were more diversified in comparison with its domestic exports. This is natural for a small, open economy which had to import foodstuffs, raw materials, and manufactures as well as machinery to support its people and its export industries. But the relative importance of commodities also changed over time. Except for fuel, the share of foodstuffs and other primary products declined sharply, while that of manufactures and semimanufactures increased. This is to be expected in the process of economic development, according to Engel's Law.

On the side of domestic exports, the structure is simple. Limited by its lack of resources, Hong Kong had few nonmanufactured goods to export. Indeed, most of its manufactured goods fell into the category of miscellaneous manufactured articles, a situation that was accentuated by further industrialization. Moreover, there was also a decline in the relative importance of resource-based manufactures which were generally found in SITC Section 6, and their place was rapidly taken up by machinery. In the end, Hong Kong's domestic exports had become even more lopsided in nonresource-based manufactures.

The finer commodity composition of Hong Kong's major domestic ex-

2. See *1982 Economic Prospects*, Census and Statistics Department, Hong Kong, 1982.

Table 5.3. Structure of Hong Kong's External Trade (%)

SITC section code & description	Imports (Excluding Re-exports)					Domestic Exports				
	1960	1965	1970	1975	1980	1960	1965	1970	1975	1980
0 Food & live animals	24.6	23.7	18.7	21.0	11.1	4.6	2.7	1.6	1.5	1.2
1 Beverages & tobacco	2.2	2.7	2.1	2.0	1.4	0.5	1.3	0.4	0.2	0.2
2 Crude materials, inedible, except fuels	10.8	10.3	7.9	7.4	3.2	4.8	2.2	1.9	1.0	1.6
3 Mineral fuels, lubricants & related materials	4.0	3.5	3.2	7.7	8.2	—	—	—	—	0.1
4 Animal & vegetable oils & fats	1.0	0.7	0.6	0.8	0.4	0.1	0.1	—	—	—
5 Chemicals	7.0	5.8	6.3	6.0	5.6	1.8	1.1	0.8	0.8	0.8
6 Manufactured goods classified chiefly by material	32.5	29.8	31.5	28.6	38.1	27.0	22.1	15.0	13.5	11.4
7 Machinery & transport equipment	11.2	14.8	17.8	17.4	20.0	4.8	6.9	11.8	14.6	18.3
8 Miscellaneous manufactured articles	6.7	8.7	11.9	9.1	12.1	58.6	63.7	68.9	68.3	66.3
Total	100.0	100.0	100.0	100.0	100.0	100.0	100.0	100.0	100.0	100.0

Source: Census and Statistics Department, Hong Kong, *Hong Kong Trade Statistics* (various issues).

Table 5.4. Commodity Composition of Hong Kong's Domestic Exports (%)

SITC division code & description	1960	1965	1970	1975	1980
65 Textiles	19.4	16.7	10.4	9.4	6.7
69 Manufactures of metal	4.1	3.1	2.8	2.7	3.0
71 Machinery other than electrical	0.4	0.5	0.8	2.1	4.0
72 Electrical machinery	1.7	5.9	10.5	12.2	14.7
83 Travel goods	0.7	0.9	1.4	2.0	2.2
84 Clothing	35.4	35.4	35.2	44.8[a]	34.4
85 Footwear	4.0	3.0	2.5	1.1	0.9
86 Professional goods	0.6	0.8	1.8	3.9	10.8
89 Miscellaneous manufactured goods	13.8	20.5	25.5	14.7	16.3
Others	19.9	13.2	9.1	7.1	7.0
All merchandise	100.0	100.0	100.0	100.0	100.0
(Value: HK$ millions)	(2,867)	(5,027)	(12,347)	(22,859)	(68,171)

Source: Census and Statistics Department, Hong Kong, *Hong Kong Trade Statistics* (various issues).

[a]The big increase in the percentage of clothing in 1975 was due to the upsurge in world demand for denims in the mid-seventies. The U.S. market was especially buoyant in that period.

ports is given in table 5.4. There are three different trends in development concerning these commodity divisions.

The first trend was the rapid decline in the relative importance of some industries, notably footwear and textiles. Both of these belonged to Hong Kong's traditional manufacturing sector, established at the very beginning of its industrialization. Indeed, footwear was Hong Kong's most labor-intensive industry and its decline was not surprising, as Hong Kong began to experience a labor shortage toward the end of the sixties. Textiles, especially in weaving and spinning, were comparatively capital-intensive. Their relative decline can be attributed to two factors. One was competition from other LDCs, which usually established textile industries first in the process of industrialization. Compared to Hong Kong, they had cheaper labor and larger resource bases. The second factor was quantitative restrictions imposed by the importing countries. These restrictions first covered cotton textiles and then expanded to all textiles in the Multi-Fibre Arrangement. Hong Kong's exports of footwear to a number of countries also were placed under quantitative restrictions.

The second trend was large gains among industries such as machinery, electrical machinery, and professional goods. These were Hong Kong's newer industries and were not founded until the mid-sixties, and some even in the early seventies. They generally required more modern technology and skilled labor than the older industries. Their rapid development signified Hong Kong's move into manufactures of higher capital and skill intensity under the pressure of rising wages and keen competition. They soon replaced textiles in importance in Hong Kong's export basket. Within electrical machinery and professional goods, the performance of electronic products and watches and clocks was spectacular. These two groups had both surpassed textiles by 1980.

The third trend was the maintenance of position by some products despite year-to-year fluctuations. The notable ones were clothing, toys, and plastic products within the miscellaneous manufactured goods classification. They also belonged to Hong Kong's traditional industries and were labor-intensive, but unlike footwear and textiles, they fared quite well. Indeed, Hong Kong had become the world's largest exporter of garments and toys, mainly because these industries were able to rely on the quality of Hong Kong's labor so that labor intensiveness did not become a liability.

A comparison of garments with textiles illustrates this point. Both had a long history in Hong Kong and were subject to quantitative restrictions abroad. The textile industry, especially in its weaving and spinning sectors, was relatively capital-intensive and operated on the basis of mass production of more or less standardized goods. Once the other LDCs had mastered the basic technology, Hong Kong had little advantage. The labor intensity of garment production, on the other hand, had its advantages. In its many years of garment production, Hong Kong had built up a huge and continuing supply of labor skilled in this trade. Despite the abundance of labor in LDCs, it is difficult for them to train a labor force adequately in a short period of time.

Moreover, when little capital and much skilled labor is required, economies of scale have little significance. Large and small manufacturers can operate side by side and production can easily be expanded. When capital equipment is not very specialized, manufacturers, large or small, can easily change their product lines according to market conditions. In good times, many small operators join in, and in bad times, they simply leave, waiting for another chance. These possibilities impart a great deal of flexibility to Hong Kong's garment industry. Furthermore, there is much room for product diversification. There are many varieties of garments, and fashions change fast. Manufacturers can specialize and cater to their own customers to keep the market fully exploited. Finally, a labor-intensive process can capitalize on labor skills by improving the quality of its product. Hong Kong's garment industry has continued to move into high-priced, high-quality products, so that, despite quantitative restrictions, its exports have retained their value.

The geographical distribution of Hong Kong's trade has changed somewhat over the years. With respect to imports, the combined share of the four major traditional sources, namely Japan, China, the United States, and the United Kingdom, remained at around 40 percent. The Japanese share expanded at the expense of the British share within this group. By the second half of the seventies both Taiwan and Singapore had surpassed the United Kingdom as Hong Kong's major suppliers. The contents of the imports reflected the nature and development of these exporting countries. Singapore mainly supplied fuels, while Taiwan and Japan exported machinery, miscellaneous manufactures, and chemicals to Hong Kong. In addition, China supplied substantial amounts of foodstuffs, crude materials, and fuel, and the United States provided foodstuffs and raw materials.

Table 5.5 indicates the direction of Hong Kong's domestic exports. The United States, the United Kingdom, and West Germany remained its top three markets, though the British share was rapidly overtaken by West

Table 5.5. Geographical Distribution of Hong Kong's External Trade (%)

Source and Destination	1960	1965	1970	1975	1980
		Imports			
U.S.A.	12.3	11.1	13.2	11.8	11.8
U.K.	11.3	10.7	8.6	5.1	4.9
China	20.2	25.9	16.1	20.3	19.7
Japan	16.1	17.3	23.8	20.9	23.0
All others	40.1	35.0	38.3	41.9	40.6
(Singapore)		(2.7)	(2.0)	(5.7)	(6.6)
(Taiwan)		(1.7)	(4.7)	(5.8)	(7.1)
Total	100.0	100.0	100.0	100.0	100.0
		Domestic Exports			
U.S.A.	26.0	34.2	42.0	32.1	33.1
U.K.	20.4	17.1	12.0	12.2	10.0
West Germany	3.7	7.4	8.0	12.5	10.8
Japan	3.5	2.6	4.0	4.2	3.4
Canada	2.7	2.7	3.2	3.4	2.6
Australia	3.0	2.7	2.9	4.5	2.9
Singapore		2.8	2.3	2.7	2.6
All others	40.7	30.5	25.6	28.4	34.6
Total	100.0	100.0	100.0	100.0	100.0
(North America and Western Europe)	(57.1)	(69.4)	(74.2)	(71.9)	(69.8)

Source: Census and Statistics Department, Hong Kong, *Hong Kong Trade Statistics* (various issues).

Germany. At least up to the early seventies, Hong Kong was increasingly catering to markets in the developed countries. The rapid expansion of these markets, especially in manufactures, under the impact of economic growth and tariff liberalization, had led Hong Kong in this direction: an export-oriented economy must go where the markets are. In the early sixties, some of the LDCs in Southeast Asia, such as Thailand, Malaysia, and Indonesia, were still among Hong Kong's top 10 markets. But by the seventies, only Singapore remained on the list. The shares of the Asian countries were replaced by those of Switzerland, the Netherlands, and Sweden.

In terms of the balance of trade, Hong Kong had large deficits with its neighboring Asian countries, such as Japan, China, Taiwan, and Singapore. These deficits were largely financed by Hong Kong's surpluses with countries in the West.

Analyses of Trade in Relation to Development

In a study of export-led growth, the first task is to establish the link between export expansion and economic growth. Specifically, it is essential to show that production is caused by export demand rather than home demand or import substitution, so that it becomes clear that the direction of causation is from trade to growth and not vice vesa. By relating production, imports, exports, and home demand, Chenery (1960, pp. 624–54) formulated a method of evaluating the relative effects of export expansion, home demand, and import substitution on output growth. Following this approach, a study was made of Hong Kong for the period from 1964 to 1974 (Lin, Mok, and Ho 1980). Some of the results are reported in table 5.6.

Due to a paucity of statistics on domestic demand and production, the study was limited to four manufacturing industries and foodstuffs production. Of the four manufacturing industries, three were "traditional," namely, clothing, footwear, and furniture, and one was "modern," namely, precision instruments. For the three traditional industries, the effect of import substitution was negligible. By the very nature of these industries, they would have seemed to be prime candidates for home consumption. The evidence indicated that this was only moderately true for footwear and furniture. For all three, the bulk of effect came from export expansion.

The precision instruments (scientific, medical, optical, measuring and control instruments and apparatus, watches, and clocks) industry needs more explanation. During the period under review, this industry was in its infancy, but expanding rapidly. It was mainly engaged in assembling and processing. As output grew and new products emerged, large numbers of components had to be imported as inputs for final products, resulting in a sharp decrease in the degree of self-sufficiency. This accounted for the huge negative import-substitution effect, which was balanced by the other two effects caused by rapid increases in both exports and home demand, especially the former.

These industries can be considered fairly representative of Hong Kong's manufacturing sector. As a whole, the effect of export expansion was overwhelming and that of import substitution negligible. By way of contrast, food production was wholly for home demand. This is fully expected,

Table 5.6. Relative Effects of Export Expansion, Home Demand, and Import Substitution of Production 1964–74 (%)

Industry	Export Expansion	Home Demand	Import Substitution	Total
Clothing	89.23	5.07	5.70	100.00
Footwear	71.69	34.27	−5.95	100.00
Furniture	67.46	38.76	−6.21	100.00
Precision instruments	627.25	241.88	−769.13	100.00
All four manufacturing industries	89.41	10.20	0.38	100.00
Footstuffs	2.31	102.74	−5.05	100.00

Source: Adapted from Lin, Mok, and Ho (1980), p. 129, Table 5.2.
Note: The relative effects are derived as follows:
Let Y = domestic production
M = retained imports (total imports minus re-exports)
X = domestic exports (total exports minus re-exports)
H = home demand
$S = Y + M$, total supply
$D = X + H$, total demand
$u = Y/S$, the share of domestic production in total supply, or the degree of self-sufficiency.

Thus, the change in domestic production can be written as
$$\Delta Y = Y_2 - Y_1 = u_2 S_2 - u_1 S_1$$
where the subscripts 1 and 2 refer to the initial and final years respectively.
Since
$$\Delta Y = (u_2 - u_1)S_2 + u_1(S_2 - S_1) \text{ and}$$
$$S_2 - S_1 = \Delta S$$
$$\Delta S = \Delta D = \Delta H + \Delta X$$
By substitution, we get
$$\Delta Y = (u_2 - u_1)S_2 + u_1 \Delta H + u_1 \Delta X$$
Therefore, output change ΔY can be broken down into
import substitution $(u_2 - u_1)S_2$
increase in home demand $u_1 \Delta H$ and
export expansion $u_1 \Delta X$

The effects in the table above are expressed in relative terms. When $u_1 > u_2$, i.e., the degree of self-sufficiency decreases over time, the import substitution effect becomes negative.

as there was little likelihood of advantageous export expansion and import substitution in these commodities for an economy like Hong Kong's.

We come next to the basis of trade, the first principle of which is comparative advantage. According to the Heckscher-Ohlin factor-proportions theory, a labor- (capital-) abundant economy tends to export labor- (capital-) intensive goods and import capital- (labor-) intensive goods. A standard way to test this hypothesis, as developed by Leontief (1953), is to compare the labor and capital requirements of a country's exports and imports. In the case of Hong Kong, it was found that indeed its imports were more capital-intensive than its exports (Lin, Mok, and Ho 1980, chapter 6). Over a period of 10 years, in fact, there was little change in the labor/capital requirement ratio of its exports, while that of its imports had substantially declined. As table 5.7 shows, the pattern hypothesized by the Heckscher-Ohlin theory had become more definite in the process of Hong Kong's economic development.

Moreover, the total labor requirement was greatest, the same study found, in the exports of the clothing, footwear, miscellaneous manufacturing, textiles, electrical products, and metal products industries. These exports accounted for 87 percent of the total employment creation in Hong Kong's manufacturing in 1964, and rose to more than 90 percent in 1974. When total labor requirements were separated into direct and indirect portions, shares of the latter were found to be generally low. Overall, they were less than 10 percent of the total, indicating the lack of linkage among Hong Kong's manufacturing industries. This is not surprising in view of

Table 5.7. Total Labor/Capital Requirement Ratios of Hong Kong's External Trade

Year	Labor/Capital Ratio of Exports (1)	Labor/Capital Ratio of Imports (2)	(1)/(2)
1964	2.69	2.23	1.21
1970	2.92	2.31	1.26
1974	2.86	1.74	1.64

Source: Lin, Mok, and Ho (1980), p. 147, table 6.12.

Note: In the calculation, the 1970 Singapore input-output table was used to derive the labor/output and capital/output ratios for 1964 and 1970, while the ratios for 1974 were derived from Hong Kong's own industrial census in 1973. The reason for using the Singapore input-output table is the lack of Hong Kong input-output tables for 1964 and 1970, and the high degree of similarity in the industrial structures of these two economies. As in similar studies, labor/capital requirements for imports are only those for import replacements, and the level of imports has been adjusted to that of exports for comparison.

Hong Kong's poor resource endowment and high degree of export orientation.

An alternative way of testing the Heckscher-Ohlin hypothesis is to relate the degree of export orientation to various definitions of factor intensity in a cross-industry study. This was done for Hong Kong's 22 manufacturing industries in 1973 (Mok 1980, pp. 1–16). The degree of export orientation, measured by the ratio of exports to total sales, was regressed on value added per person, the so-called Lary definition of total capital intensity; on fixed assets per person, representing physical capital intensity; and on the proportion of operative to total man-hours as an inverse measure of labor skills. The degree of export orientation was found consistently to be significantly and inversely related to capital intensity, whether the latter was measured directly by fixed assets per person, or by value added per person, which includes the effects of both physical and human capital. The most powerful explanatory variable turned out to be the inverse of labor skills. The export-oriented industries were indeed using high proportions of operative to total man-hours, indicating the labor-intensive nature of their manufacturing processes.

The relationship between exports and employment in manufacturing can be investigated at the industry level. A number of instability indices were constructed for the export earnings and employment of 12 manufacturing industries which accounted for some 80 percent of Hong Kong's manufacturing employment for the period 1959–73.[3] When the employment instability indices were regressed on the export earnings instability indices, it was found that the relationship was positive and highly significant. In most cases, more than 70 percent of the variation in employment could be explained by the variation in export earnings, and the functional relationship was stable. Moreover, all indices showed that the degree of fluctuation for manufacturing as a whole was significantly less than for most individual industries. This suggests that while the export earnings and employment of Hong Kong's various manufacturing industries did experience a certain degree of instability over the years, the variations tended to offset one another, so that for the sector as a whole, both export earnings and employment had become quite stable. This is a reflection of the flexibility of the Hong Kong economy, which enabled it to adjust its production according to changing demand conditions. The result was that Hong Kong's overall export earnings were much more stable than those of other LDCs, especially the primary-producing ones.

3. These indices are: Coppock's log variance, normalized standard error, semi-log standard error, modified log variance, and five-year moving average deviation instability indices. See Lin, Mok, and Ho 1980, chapter 4.

Still another type of analysis was the decomposition of the effects of various factors on export expansion. The technique was first developed by Tyszynski (1951, pp. 272–304) and later widely used in the analysis of trade expansion. In this method, the effect of world trade expansion is the amount by which a country's exports would have increased if it had shared proportionately in total world exports. Any deviation is attributed to changes in commodity composition, market distribution, and competitiveness. The commodity composition effect is determined by calculating the amounts by which a country's exports of each commodity group would have increased if each group had increased by the same percentage as world exports of the respective commodity group, and then deducting from their sum the total of the amounts by which each group would have increased if it had increased by the same percentage as total world exports. The result would be positive if world demand expansion were more than proportionate in the commodities in which the country specializes. A similar calculation is made for market distribution. The residual is the effect of increased competitiveness.

Table 5.8 shows the results of such a computation for Hong Kong's exports and some of its components (Lin, Mok, and Ho 1980, chapter 5). Had Hong Kong's exports grown at the same pace as world exports from 1964 to 1974, the increase would have been HK$7,781.34 million. But the actual increase was HK$18,483 million. The difference was then attributed to the other factors, as shown. In all cases except footwear, Hong Kong's exports grew faster than those of the world at large. The commodity composition effect was very strong, indicating Hong Kong's ability to supply the kind of manufactures for which world demand was rapidly increasing. In comparison, the market distribution and competitiveness effects did not perform well. Hong Kong's exports were concentrated in markets of slower expansion and suffered from keen competition in virtually all traditional products.

Table 5.9 shows the same calculation for Hong Kong's exports to the United States during the period 1968–80. There is no market distribution effect since only one market is involved. Had Hong Kong's exports been able to maintain their market share in the United States, they should have done better. But the strong trade expansion effect was undercut by adverse effects from commodity composition and competitiveness. For the first subperiod, the commodity composition effect was in fact positive and strong, but competitiveness suffered considerably from internal labor shortages and the worldwide inflation which adversely affected an open economy like Hong Kong's. Effects of the oil crisis were evident in the second subperiod, 1972–76. The actual increase in exports, HK$5,112

Table 5.8. Decomposition of Effects of Hong Kong's Domestic Exports (HK$ millions)

	Textile Products	Metal Manu-factures	Clothing	Electrical Products	Footwear	Miscellaneous Manu-factures	Others	Total
Increase in exports from 1964 to 1974	2,030.00 (100.0)	495.00 (100.0)	7,132.00 (100.0)	3,110.00 (100.0)	136.00 (100.0)	2,834.00 (100.0)	2,746.00 (100.0)	18,483.00 (100.0)
Of the above								
Due to trade expansion	1,520.05 (74.9)	266.31 (53.8)	3,480.42 (48.8)	399.90 (12.9)	376.25 (277.7)	1,859.75 (65.6)	96.11 (3.5)	7,781.34 (42.1)
Due to commodity composition	2,128.05 (104.9)	373.23 (75.4)	4,878.30 (68.4)	230.60 (7.4)	526.75 (387.3)	2,603.65 (91.9)	−101.60 (−3.7)	10,315.51 (55.8)
Due to market distribution	−116.68 (−5.7)	−62.37 (−12.6)	−292.41 (−4.1)	28.42 (0.9)	−268.05 (−197.1)	132.85 (4.7)	−5.49 (−0.2)	−572.97 (−3.1)
Due to increased competitiveness	−1,501.42 (−74.0)	−82.17 (−16.6)	−934.29 (−13.1)	2,451.08 (78.8)	−498.95 (−367.9)	−1,762.25 (−62.2)	2,756.98 (100.4)	961.12 (5.2)

Source: Adapted from Lin, Mok, and Ho (1980), p. 124, table 5.1.
Note: Figures in parentheses are percentages of totals.

Table 5.9. Decomposition of Effects of Hong Kong's Domestic Exports to the United States (HK$ millions)

	1968–80	1968–72	1972–76	1976–80
Increase in exports	19,104.0	2,637.0	5,112.0	11,355.0
	(100.0)	(100.0)	(100.0)	(100.0)
Of the above				
Due to trade	21,787.8	2,346.4	7,208.6	11,125.9
expansion	(114.0)	(89.0)	(141.0)	(98.0)
Due to commodity	−1,513.8	1,174.9	−2,499.8	−911.6
composition	(−7.9)	(44.6)	(−48.9)	(−8.0)
Due to increased	−1,170.0	−884.3	403.3	1,140.7
competitiveness	(−6.1)	(−33.6)	(7.9)	(10.0)

Source: Computed from data given by the Census and Statistics Department, Hong Kong, in *Hong Kong Trade Statistics* (various issues); and by the United States Department of Commerce in *Survey of Current Business* (various issues).

Note: Figures in parentheses are percentages of totals.

million, was substantially lower than what it would have been, at HK$7,208.6 million, had Hong Kong been able to keep its market share. Despite a tremendous increase in clothing, Hong Kong's exports were no match for oil in the U.S. import bill. Therefore, the commodity composition effect was large and negative. The flexibility of the Hong Kong economy, however, enabled it to regain some of its competitiveness during the recession, in which real wages fell considerably. For the last subperiod, Hong Kong was just about maintaining its share of the U.S. market. The negative commodity-composition effect due to the oil shock was not yet over. But this was balanced by the positive competitiveness effect, probably due to the depreciation of the Hong Kong dollar and the massive immigration from China, which kept wages in the manufacturing sector from increasing rapidly in those years.

Overall Assessment

The economic development of Hong Kong since World War II can be roughly described in periods of decades. The first decade, that of the fifties, marked the initiation of its industrial development. Starting with the textile, clothing, footwear, plastics, and metal manufacturing industries, this process resulted in building up the manufacturing sector as the backbone of the economy. The sixties were characterized by a further expansion of the manufacturing sector, which rapidly absorbed the large labor force. New industries such as electrical and electronic products were established and some traditional industries were already on the decline. At the end of the decade, the importance of the manufacturing sector in terms of its relative contribution to GDP reached a peak, and there were signs of a labor shortage. The seventies saw another change in the structure of Hong Kong's economy. Despite the emergence of new industries and increasing employment, the importance of the manufacturing sector, in terms of GDP contribution, began to level off, from 30.9 percent in 1970 to 26.7 percent in 1978.[4] Overall, the pattern of industrial development in Hong Kong is not unfamiliar in the experience of the developed countries.

There is no doubt that Hong Kong's industrial development was export-led. In terms of contribution to employment, output, and value added, industries such as apparel, textiles, plastic products, fabricated metal products, electrical machinery, and professional goods (e.g., watches and clocks), were simply overwhelming. They were all highly export-oriented except textiles, which also served the apparel industry, in addition to exports. Across industries, the degree of export orientation was positively related to labor intensity.

Hong Kong's labor-intensive industries catered mainly to markets in the developed countries. Since the markets of the other LDCs for manufactures were limited by income and protected by import-substitution policies, Hong Kong had to turn to the high-income developed countries where markets were expanding under the impact of tariff liberalization. As a result, Hong Kong relied on Asian countries for the provision of foodstuffs and raw materials and the advanced countries for the supply of capital goods, and specialized in the manufacture of standardized consumer goods for the West. This was Hong Kong's model of industrialization.

This pattern of trade and specialization led to a high degree of concentration in Hong Kong's exports, measured by concentration coefficients. As shown in table 5.10, there was little discernible change over the years, despite changing commodity composition and market distribution. Starting in the early seventies, however, there were outcries for diversification when some markets were found to be slow in expansion and traditional industries began to decline.

As a result, the Hong Kong government appointed an Advisory Committee on Diversification in 1977, whose report defined diversification as "a process whereby resources are continually redeployed in response to shifting market conditions, to changes in the availability and relative costs of factors of production, and to technological innovations."[5] As far as diversification goes, this definition is a misnomer because the process

4. See *The 1981–82 Budget: Estimates of Gross Domestic Product, 1966 to 1979*, Census and Statistics Department, Hong Kong, 1981, p. 35.
5. See *Report of the Advisory Committee on Diversification 1979*, government secretariat Hong Kong, 1979, p. 7.

Table 5.10. Hirschman-Gini Concentration Coefficients of Hong Kong's Domestic Exports

	1964	1966	1968	1970	1972	1974	1976	1978
Commodity concentration index	40.5	39.7	40.0	40.1	43.2	40.9	45.5	41.4
Market concentration index	36.4	40.6	45.3	45.1	44.4	37.5	39.1	41.0

Source: Lin and Ho (1981), pp. 82–83.
Notes: The algebraic formula and mathematical limits of a concentration coefficient C are:
$$100(n^{-1/2}) \leq C = 100[\Sigma(X_i/X)^2]^{1/2} \leq 100$$
Where X_i is the export value of commodity i (or to market i), X is total value of exports, and n is the number of commodities (or markets). A smaller C signifies a lower degree of concentration. For the calculation above, three-digit SITC commodity groups and the actual number of countries are used.

The increase in the commodity concentration index for 1976 was due to a big increase in clothing exports, and the decrease in the market concentration index for 1974 was due to the slump in the American market.

described might well lead to further specialization and concentration. But the committee did have a clear understanding of the nature of the Hong Kong economy and its problems. The overriding issue is not diversification per se. For an export-oriented economy, diversification may or may not follow as a result of industrial development. The most important thing is the ability to keep abreast of technological development and adjust to changing market conditions. A small, open economy must live with a certain degree of export concentration in both commodity composition and market distribution, for that is the only way to take full advantage of specialization. The experience of Hong Kong has demonstrated that specialization and trade in labor-intensive manufactures is an effective road to economic development.

Foreign Investment And Development

Problems and Limitations

The fundamental problem in the study of foreign investment in Hong Kong is the definition of what is foreign. Having been under British rule for well over a century, the city naturally abounds with British capital, much of which has long been resident. Many of the locally incorporated large companies that dominate the banking, insurance, utilities, trading, and real estate fields are controlled by British nationals. In addition, there are those with head offices in Britain and those of recent arrival. The other side of the coin is Chinese capital. For a number of political and economic reasons, Hong Kong provides a great attraction for Overseas Chinese capital, both short and long term. Over the years, many Overseas Chinese established businesses in Hong Kong and eventually settled there, while local Chinese continue to run firms there after acquiring foreign citizenship or residency. To make the picture more complicated, the Chinese government in recent years has sharply increased its involvement in the Hong Kong economy by making investments directly or through its affiliated business concerns. All these defy a consensus on what is foreign: foreign investment means different things to different people.

It is possible to tackle the problem from a geographical point of view. But under Hong Kong's policy of laissez-faire, there is little from which to trace the source of capital. Except for public utilities and the banking sector, business licensing is open. Little information is required concerning ownership, which can easily change hands. Even for public companies, the issue of requiring the major owners to disclose their holdings has recently encountered considerable objection. Under such circumstances, statistics concerning business ownership, especially those differentiating local and nonlocal interests, are extremely meager.

The fact that Hong Kong is rapidly emerging as a financial center makes the matter even more complex. The Hong Kong dollar was floated and exchange controls were abolished after 1974. Many financial institutions have since set up offices there, and dealings in foreign exchange have become increasingly active. Many of these dealings are short term in nature, but it is also known that considerable funds have been channeled into the local stock and real estate markets. There is no way to distinguish between portfolio and direct investment. As far as the balance of payments is concerned, reliable information can be found only in the trade account.

Even if there were agreement on what is foreign, Hong Kong provides little in the way of statistics for a study on the overall foreign involvement in its economy. Officially, the term "overseas investments" is used. But that does not help much under the condition of very limited statistical information.

Since the early seventies, the Commerce and Industry Department (which has recently become the Trade, Industry and Customs Department) has conducted an annual survey of manufacturing establishments in Hong Kong known to have overseas interests. The 1973 and 1978 industrial censuses also provide some information on these establishments. These sources, though incomplete, do provide some quantitative information on the development, role, and contributions of foreign establishments in Hong Kong.

Admittedly, this is far from a complete picture of foreign investment in

Hong Kong because it neglects the tremendous involvement in the financial sector, a significant part of Hong Kong's overall economic development. But Hong Kong's emergence as a financial center is recent. It was the development of the manufacturing sector that transformed Hong Kong into an industrial city and put it on the map as one of the fastest growing NICs.

The Pattern of Overseas Investment in Manufacturing

There are two special features that distinguish Hong Kong from the other LDCs at the initial stage of industrialization. The first is the complete absence of foreign aid. There was no capital inflow at the government level for the purpose of capital formation. The second is the relative unimportance of private foreign investment in manufacturing. Industrialization was initiated primarily by the effort of local entrepreneurs. The reason was that politically Hong Kong was not a country, and in the fifties its future was very unclear. Private foreign capital did flow in, but it was generally concentrated in the financial and trading sectors and shied away from manufacturing. Even local British capital, with its long history in Hong Kong, avoided these investments. At that time, investment in manufacturing in the LDCs had yet to be proved a viable proposition. In Hong Kong, the initial test was made by local Chinese industrialists. By the sixties, Hong Kong had become a profitable exporter of labor-intensive manufactures, and an increasing number of overseas investors seized the opportunity to join in.

Table 5.11 shows the state of overseas investment in the Hong Kong manufacturing sector up to 1970. This is all the information available for that period. In 1960, there were only 27 such establishments, amounting to

Table 5.11. Overseas Investments in Hong Kong Manufacturing, 1960–74

Year	Number of Establishments	Total Capital Investment as of December 1974 (HK$ millions)
1960	27	473.7
1965	67	1,330.5
1970	149	1,871.5
1974	236	2,150.5
(1974) excluding local interest in joint ventures:		(1,633.2)

Source: Commerce and Industry Departments, Hong Kong (1975).

0.6 percent of all manufacturing establishments in Hong Kong. By 1970, the number had grown to 149, up to 0.9 percent. That seemed to be the period of the greatest growth, because the number of overseas establishments stabilized at 1 percent of all manufacturing establishments. In terms of capital investment, the amount quadrupled in that decade. But the amounts shown in the table include local interests and are not entirely comparable to those reported later. For lack of detailed information, there is little more that can be said about these investments. From what can be deduced from the pattern that emerged later, however, it is clear that the bulk of capital came from the United States and Japan, and was concentrated in the electronic products, textile, watch and clock, metal, electrical, and plastic products industries, all export-oriented.

There is somewhat more detailed information for the seventies. Overseas investment figures are available from the Trade, Industry and Customs Department by industry and country, but care must be exercised in using these figures. First, they exclude local interests in joint ventures, and are thus not entirely consistent with the information on their employment and output. Second, figures are presumably totals of inflow of overseas investments when they first arrived, and do not take into account their expansion and revaluation. Third, since Hong Kong is a free economy and there is no lack of capital, overseas firms of respectable standing generally have little difficulty in seeking local financing for expansion once they are established. Finally, the figures are based on surveys covering firms known to have overseas interests. They are necessarily incomplete, especially where overseas investors have minor interests. In sum, the investment figures substantially underrepresent the role of overseas firms in Hong Kong's manufacturing sector.[6]

Bearing these qualifications in mind, table 5.12 indicates that overseas investment more than tripled in the seventies. In general, the rate of growth was greater in the early part of the decade. Electronics and textiles (including garments) continued to account for the largest amounts, but, like the toy and metal products industries, their relative shares decreased. On the other hand, there were significant increases in a number of indus-

---

6. Based on its latest survey, the Trade, Industry and Customs Department recently reported that as of the end of 1981 there were 426 manufacturing establishments with overseas interests. This was less than the number for 1980 as previously reported because some establishments had closed down or were completely taken over by local interests. For 391 establishments which provided full information, total capital investment was given as just over HK$7,000 million, which was some 1.7 times more than the old figure reported for 1980. Since new investments could hardly account for this tremendous increase, explanations must be sought in the method of reporting, such as expansion not previously reported, revaluation, and inclusion of local interests. But no official explanation was provided.

Table 5.12. Distribution of Overseas Investments in Hong Kong's Manufacturing Industries, Excluding Local Interests, 1971–80 (HK$ millions at end of year)

Industry	1971	1975	1980	Average Annual Rate of Growth (%)
Electronics	264.7	587.5	549.5	12
	(34.9)	(34.7)	(21.6)	
Textiles	160.9	253.1	415.7	18
	(21.2)	(14.9)	(16.3)	
Chemicals	11.6	96.5	304.9	281
	(1.5)	(5.7)	(12.0)	
Electrical products	16.3	97.2	270.3	173
	(2.1)	(5.7)	(10.6)	
Printing & publishing	22.7	61.5	156.9	66
	(3.0)	(3.6)	(6.2)	
Watches & clocks	26.2	188.2	181.4	66
	(3.4)	(11.1)	(7.1)	
Food manufactures	5.4	59.9	122.6	241
	(0.7)	(3.5)	(4.8)	
Metal products[a]	38.4	49.7	104.9	19
	(5.1)	(2.9)	(4.1)	
Toys	36.4	58.2	65.7	9
	(4.8)	(3.4)	(2.6)	
Metal rolling, extrusion, etc.		46.8	57.9	4
		(2.8)	(2.3)	
Building & construction materials		51.9	34.5	11
		(3.1)	(1.4)	
Others	176.9	144.4	283.8	7
	(23.3)	(8.5)	(11.1)	
Total	759.9	1,694.9	2,548.1	26
	(100.0)	(100.0)	(100.0)	

Source: Trade, Industry, and Customs Department, Hong Kong.
Note: Figures in parentheses are percentages of totals.
[a] Metal and metal products for 1971.

tries, including electrical products which were mainly for export markets; the chemical, printing and publishing industries, which were more capital-intensive and served both export and local markets; and the food industry, which was capital-intensive and served primarily the local market. The pattern indicates a general movement away from the traditional into the more sophisticated industries which required more capital. At the same time, even though export remained their major objective, overseas investments seemed to be increasingly designed for local markets, such as the chemical and food industries. In general, overseas investments became more diversified in the seventies.

Table 5.13 presents data on the number of firms. A comparison of tables 5.12 and 5.13 indicates that, on the one hand, the chemical and food industries grew much faster in terms of investment than in the number of firms, suggesting the growing size and capital intensity of firms in these industries, while on the other hand, the difference was much smaller in the watch and clock industry. For those industries which experienced slow

Table 5.13. Distribution of Overseas Firms in Hong Kong's Manufacturing Sector (in number of firms)

Industry	1973	1976	1980	Average Annual Rate of Growth (%)
Electronics	48	59	75	8
	(22.9)	(20.4)	(16.3)	
Textiles	56	71	105	12
	(26.7)	(24.6)	(22.8)	
Chemicals	8	11	23	27
	(3.8)	(3.8)	(5.0)	
Electrical products	8	18	34	46
	(3.8)	(6.2)	(7.4)	
Printing & publishing	6	8	12	14
	(2.7)	(2.8)	(2.6)	
Watches & clocks	10	22	41	44
	(4.8)	(7.6)	(8.9)	
Food manufactures	4	10	18	50
	(1.9)	(3.5)	(3.9)	
Metal products	9	18	34	40
	(4.3)	(6.2)	(7.4)	
Toys	8	9	11	5
	(3.8)	(3.1)	(2.4)	
Metal rolling, extrusion, etc.	4	5	6	7
	(1.9)	(1.7)	(1.3)	
Building & construction materials	4	5	5	4
	(1.9)	(1.7)	(1.1)	
Others	45	53	96	16
	(21.4)	(18.3)	(20.9)	
Total[a]	210	289	460	17
	(100.0)	(100.0)	(100.0)	

Source: Trade, Industry, and Customs Department, Hong Kong.
Notes: All figures are for December. Figures in parentheses are percentages of totals.
[a]Some others are known but no detailed information is available.

growth of overseas investment, such as electronics, textiles, and toys, growth rates in investment and number of firms were quite similar.

As a source of overseas investment, the United States led all countries, but its share declined from well over 50 percent at the beginning of the seventies to around 40 percent in 1980. Japan barely maintained its share, while that of the United Kingdom also declined. As seen from table 5.14, significant increases occurred in the shares of Switzerland, the Netherlands, Singapore, Thailand, West Germany, and the Philippines. There was a gradual process of diversification in which an increasing number of

Table 5.14. Distribution by Source of Overseas Investments in Hong Kong's Manufacturing Sector, Excluding Local Interest, 1971–80 (HK$ millions at end of year)

Source	1971	1975	1980
U.S.A.	406.3	800.2	1,025.4
	(53.5)	(47.2)	(40.2)
Japan	169.9	261.3	579.1
	(22.4)	(15.4)	(22.7)
U.K.	85.9	159.0	203.8
	(11.3)	(9.4)	(8.0)
Switzerland	13.5	42.3	136.4
	(1.8)	(2.5)	(5.4)
Netherlands	17.4	22.7	102.8
	(2.3)	(1.3)	(4.0)
Australia	31.5	93.8	94.5
	(4.1)	(5.5)	(3.7)
Singapore	8.7	61.0	75.8
	(1.1)	(3.6)	(3.0)
Thailand	2.5	134.5	63.4
	(0.3)	(7.9)	(2.5)
West Germany	6.2	19.3	51.1
	(0.8)	(1.1)	(2.0)
France		23.9	23.6
		(1.4)	(0.9)
Taiwan	9.5	31.0	27.1
	(1.3)	(1.8)	(1.1)
Philippines	6.3	15.8	8.50
	(0.8)	(0.9)	(3.3)
Others	1.8	30.1	80.1
	(0.2)	(1.8)	(3.1)
Total	759.5	1,694.9	2,548.1
	(100.0)	(100.0)	(100.0)

Source: Trade, Industry, and Customs Department, Hong Kong.
Note: Figures in parentheses are percentages of totals.

Table 5.15. Distribution by Source of Overseas Firms in Hong Kong's Manufacturing Sector, 1974–80 (in number of firms)

Source	1974	1977	1980
U.S.A.	95	110	141
	(35.8)	(30.0)	(28.0)
Japan	67	88	123
	(25.3)	(24.0)	(24.5)
U.K.	26	31	38
	(9.8)	(8.4)	(7.6)
Switzerland	7	12	21
	(2.6)	(3.3)	(4.2)
Netherlands	3	7	7
	(1.1)	(1.9)	(1.4)
Australia	14	23	26
	(5.3)	(6.3)	(5.2)
Singapore	8	16	21
	(3.0)	(4.4)	(4.2)
Thailand	5	16	21
	(1.9)	(4.4)	(4.2)
West Germany	4	15	23
	(1.5)	(4.1)	(4.6)
France	3	2	3
	(1.1)	(0.5)	(0.6)
Taiwan	12	13	24
	(4.5)	(3.5)	(4.8)
Philippines	7	3	8
	(2.6)	(0.8)	(1.6)
Others	14	31	46
	(5.3)	(8.4)	(9.2)
Total[a]	265	367	502

Source: Trade, Industry, and Customs Department, Hong Kong.
Note: Figures in parentheses are percentages of totals.
[a] Some firms have several investors. Therefore total numbers here are larger than elsewhere reported.

Western Europeans and Overseas Chinese became interested in Hong Kong's manufacturing industries. Table 5.15 shows the number of firms from various countries and their shares in the total. Basically it shows the same pattern as that of the amount of investments.

In 1978, the four largest overseas investing countries, the United States, Japan, the United Kingdom, and Switzerland, accounted for more than 75 percent of overseas investments in Hong Kong. Table 5.16 shows the distribution of their investments in various industries. By sheer size, the United States dominated a number of industries. It has been pointed out that U.S. foreign investment tends to be market-oriented (Kojima 1977,

Table 5.16. Sources and Distribution of Overseas Investment in Hong Kong, 1978, Excluding Local Interests (HK$ millions)

Industry	U.S.A.	Japan	U.K.	Switzerland	Others	Total
Electronics	343.5	61.0	10.5	3.3	103.1	521.4
Textiles	90.9	109.5	21.1	8.0	85.4	314.9
Chemicals	171.7	24.4	28.9	6.1	24.7	255.8
Electrical products	138.3	47.6	0.3	0	17.1	203.3
Printing & publishing	33.5	52.2	3.5	50.0	2.6	141.8
Watches & clocks	18.2	32.4	16.8	4.1	65.9	137.4
Food manufactures	7.4	13.5	0	37.1	64.5	122.5
Metal products	58.4	21.5	0	0	19.5	99.4
Toys	56.6	0	8.5	0.3	2.2	67.6
Metal rolling, extrusion, etc.	1.0	20.6	0	0	33.3	54.9
Building & construction materials	0	0	4.5	0	30.0	34.5
Others	29.5	18.1	59.1	0	45.9	152.6
Total	949.0	400.8	153.2	108.9	494.2	2,106.1

Source: Trade, Industry, and Customs Department, Hong Kong.

chapter 4), while Japanese foreign investment tended to be trade-oriented. This was not borne out in the case of Hong Kong, because much U.S. investment was found in the export-oriented industries such as electronics and electrical products, while the Japanese investors were substantially interested in the local demand for textile products.

Table 5.16 also shows that British investment in Hong Kong spread out in a wide variety of industries, while Swiss investment concentrated in the printing and publishing and food industries. As for other major investors, Thai capital dominated the watch and clock industry; Singaporean capital was found mainly in the food industry; Australians had substantial interests in basic metals and building and construction materials; and Taiwanese capital was strong in building and construction materials.

In general, U.S. investors preferred complete ownership whereas Japanese investors preferred joint ventures. Since there is no apparent reason for investors of different countries to prefer one form of ownership over another, the explanation must be sought in the pattern of investment. The bulk of U.S. investment was in electronics and chemicals. The development of the electronics industry was initiated by U.S. investors who found Hong Kong an excellent off-shore base for the production of computer components and consumer electronics in the late sixties. United States technology was brought in when the local industry was in its infancy. The same was true for the chemical industry, when U.S. investors started the highly capital-intensive production of plastic materials. Neither industry required local participation, which accounted for the larger number businesses that were wholly owned by U.S. firms.

Other industries had different experiences. The garment industry, for example, had a long history in Hong Kong and was highly labor-intensive. Having a local partner made it much easier for a foreign investor to get into such an industry and to deal with its local work force. To some extent, this was also true for other labor-intensive industries such as electrical products, watches and clocks, metal products, and toys.

This pattern seemed to apply to investors from other countries as well. In electronics and chemicals, the number of wholly owned foreign firms exceeded joint ventures, whereas the reverse was true in textiles, especially garments. The only case that requires explanation is the food industry, which was capital-intensive and yet dominated by joint ventures, probably because its products were mainly for local consumption and therefore required expertise in local marketing.

In summary, overseas investment in Hong Kong's manufacturing sector was insignificant in the initial stage of Hong Kong's industrialization, and was not substantial until Hong Kong successfully founded labor-intensive industries for exports. As overseas investment poured in, it brought new industries and technology, in addition to supplementing old ones. It contributed to broadening the industrial base of Hong Kong, so that both the sources and distribution of overseas investment became more diversified.

The Significance of Overseas Investments in Manufacturing

Hong Kong has had an abundant supply of labor, especially in the initial stage of its industrialization. Under a policy of free trade, the principle of comparative advantage worked to develop its labor-intensive industries for export markets. Overseas investment in manufacturing were subject to the same effect. These firms naturally had particular foreign characteristics; but in a laissez-faire economy, they worked side by side with local firms and constituted an integral part of the manufacturing sector. In comparing them with the manufacturing sector of Hong Kong as a whole, some of their distinguishing qualities will become evident.

The fact that Hong Kong is full of small industrial enterprises necessarily limits the numerical size of the overseas investment sector. Firms with overseas interests constituted only 1 percent of Hong Kong's manufacturing establishments. In the electronics industry, the relative share of foreign firms, at one time 16.3 percent of that industry, was reduced. The same was true in watches and clocks. As table 5.13 indicates, this was not due to an actual reduction in the number of overseas firms but rather to the tremendous growth in the number of local firms. In those industries where substantial overseas investment moved in later, such as chemicals, electrical products, food and metal products, the share of foreign firms actually increased.

The number of firms is not a good measure of the relative importance of overseas firms because, in general, those firms are much larger than the domestic ones. According to Hong Kong's 1973 Census of Industrial Production, if we include only industrial establishments engaging at least 10 persons, the share of overseas firms was around 2.5 percent, and if 20 persons is used as the lower limit, the share of overseas firms went up to 5 percent. The percentage would be even higher if we refer to larger-sized firms. But this should not be interpreted as indicating the dominance of large overseas firms in Hong Kong's manufacturing. It might be true, say, in the case of chemicals. But Hong Kong itself has no lack of large local manufacturing establishments in almost all industries.

Another measure of the relative importance of overseas firms in Hong Kong's manufacturing sector is the number of persons they employ (see table 5.17). It is interesting to note that from 1973 to 1980, employment in overseas electronics firms did not increase at all, while that in almost all other industries did.

A comparison of tables 5.12 and 5.17 indicates that, among overseas firms, those in the electronics, textile, and toy industries tended to be labor-intensive while those in the rest were capital-intensive. The data also suggest that overseas firms in electronics and toys were engaged in assembly processing, a labor-intensive type of production on a large scale based on the relatively cheap labor in Hong Kong. To some extent, this was also true of the electrical products industry.

The relative importance of overseas firms in Hong Kong's overall manufacturing employment, as shown in table 5.18, does not appear to be very great. The overall share of overseas firms was around 10 percent and actually decreased toward the end of the seventies. They were not able to keep up with the local firms in absorbing Hong Kong's rapidly increasing labor force. Overseas electronics firms, the largest employer among all overseas firms, at one time employed well over half of Hong Kong's labor force in the industry. Their share dropped to less than a third because of the rapid development of local firms.

Table 5.19 provides a summary estimate of the role of overseas firms in Hong Kong manufacturing. Overseas firms, as we have noted, accounted for 1 percent of Hong Kong's manufacturing establishments and approximately 10 percent of their employment. But in terms of output, value added, and fixed assets, their shares were higher, suggesting that indeed they used more capital and were more productive. The productivity differ-

Table 5.17. Employment in Overseas Firms in Hong Kong, 1973–80 (1,000 employees)

Industry	1973	1976	1980
Electronics	30.2	24.6	28.9
	(48.0)	(39.0)	(33.1)
Textiles	9.7	13.5	22.1
	(15.4)	(21.5)	(25.3)
Chemicals	0.7	0.7	1.2
	(1.1)	(1.2)	(1.3)
Electrical products	3.9	4.2	6.1
	(6.2)	(6.7)	(7.0)
Printing & publishing	1.2	1.2	2.0
	(1.8)	(1.9)	(2.3)
Watches & clocks	4.9	5.6	7.2
	(7.7)	(8.9)	(8.3)
Food manufactures	0.9	1.7	2.4
	(1.5)	(2.6)	(2.7)
Metal products	1.4	1.8	2.5
	(2.3)	(2.9)	(2.8)
Toys	4.5	4.4	5.8
	(7.1)	(7.0)	(6.7)
Metal rolling, extrusion, etc.	0.9	0.9	0.9
	(1.5)	(1.4)	(1.1)
Building & construction materials	0.3	0.5	0.6
	(0.5)	(0.7)	(0.7)
Others	4.4	4.0	7.5
	(6.9)	(6.3)	(8.7)
Total	63.0	63.0	87.3
	(100.0)	(100.0)	(100.0)

Source: Trade, Industry, and Customs Department, Hong Kong.
Notes: Figures in parentheses are percentages of totals. All employment figures are for December.

ence was even greater in 1978 than in 1973. However, in the value of fixed assets and addition to fixed assets, overseas firms fell behind. One explanation is that while local firms preferred to own their factory premises, overseas firms preferred to rent theirs.

Relatively little is known about the export share of overseas firms. Presumably they were at least as export-oriented as their local counterparts. A 1975 survey by the Commerce and Industry Department estimated their total production at HK$2,724 million and HK$3,310 million for 1973 and 1974, with 69.8 percent and 73.7 percent exported respectively,[7] representing 9.7 percent and 10.6 percent of Hong Kong's domes-

---

7. The survey also provided estimates of the proportion of exports in the production of overseas firms in various manufacturing industries. These proportions were quite similar to those of Hong Kong as a whole.

Table 5.18. Share of Overseas Firms in Total Manufacturing Employment in Hong Kong (%)

Industry	1973	1976	1980
Electronics	53.9	34.6	32.2
Textiles	3.4	3.5	5.6
Chemicals	11.4	13.4	14.7
Electrical products	27.2	24.6	18.9
Printing & publishing	6.0	5.3	7.4
Watches & clocks	49.2	43.3	17.9
Food manufactures	6.4	10.9	13.3
Metal products	2.7	2.8	3.2
Toys	11.3	9.5	10.7
Metal rolling, extrusion, etc.	30.3	23.4	19.1
Building & construction materials	32.4	36.2	30.0
Others	3.6	3.0	4.7
Total	10.1	8.1	9.6

Sources: Census and Statistics Department, *Employment Statistics* (various issues); and Trade, Industry, and Customs Department, Hong Kong.

Note: For overseas firms, figures used are numbers of employees, whereas for total manufacturing, figures used are numbers of persons engaged.

Table 5.19. Contribution of Overseas Firms to Hong Kong's Manufacturing Sector (%)

	1973	1978
Number of establishments	1.0	1.0
Average number of persons employed	11.0	9.7
Gross output	12.9	16.2
Census value added	12.7	15.1
Value of fixed assets	13.9	13.4
Gross addition to fixed assets	19.9	11.6

Sources: Census and Statistics Department (1976 and 1981).

Note: There is some underestimation of the role of overseas firms because, in the data used, the manufacturing sector includes all establishments, while the overseas firms include only those that engaged 20 or more persons. Since very few overseas firms engage fewer than 20 persons, the underestimation is insignificant.

tic exports. Since the survey is known to be incomplete, these percentages tended to underestimate their shares in Hong Kong exports. They should be somewhat higher and more consistent with their shares in gross output, which was estimated at 12.9 percent for 1973. On the other hand, it might be noted that overseas investors played only a small role in Hong Kong's garment industry, which was highly export-oriented and accounted for some 35 percent of Hong Kong's domestic exports in 1973. Therefore, a rough estimate of around 12 percent would not be far off the mark. By the same token, it should be around 16 percent in 1978.

To further analyze the role of overseas firms, a comparison between overseas firms and their local counterparts of similar size is shown in table 5.20. It is interesting to note that over the years the average size of both overseas and local manufacturing establishments in Hong Kong actually decreased to a considerable extent, partly because of the proliferation of small factories.

There were some areas in which overseas firms were similar to local firms. The small difference in labor cost per person indicates that both overseas and local firms recruited their work force from the same competitive labor market. It is sometimes argued that direct foreign investors in the processing industries of the LDCs tend to take advantage of cheap labor and contribute little in terms of value added. In the case of Hong Kong, it was true that overseas firms were mostly engaged in processing; but in terms of value added per dollar of output, they were on a par with their local counterparts. Overseas and local manufacturing establishments worked side by side and in a similar manner, competing for the same labor force, processing largely imported materials, mainly for export markets.

On the other hand, overseas firms were more capital-intensive. Their output per person was higher, and as a result their labor cost was lower as a percentage both of output and value added. What is interesting is that over the years differences between overseas and local firms in these respects

Table 5.20. Comparison of Overseas and All Manufacturing Establishments in Hong Kong with 20 or More Persons Engaged, 1973 and 1978

	1973		1978	
	Overseas Firms	All Manufacturing	Overseas Firms	All Manufacturing
Number of persons per establishment	283.2	106.0	225.6	93.3
Fixed assets per person (HK$ thousands)	10.2	9.0	18.9	14.9
Labor cost per person (HK$ thousands)	9.5	9.7	17.0	16.4
Output per person (HK$ thousands)	53.9	49.9	134.2	87.6
Labor cost per HK$ of output (%)	17.6	19.3	12.6	18.7
Value added per HK$ of output (%)	35.5	35.6	32.0	33.3
Labor cost per HK$ of value added (%)	49.7	54.4	39.5	56.2

Sources: Census and Statistics Department, Hong Kong (1976 and 1981).

have grown larger. The ratios of labor cost to output and value added for Hong Kong as a whole changed little, but these ratios were markedly reduced for overseas firms, suggesting that they had become even more capital-intensive than their local counterparts.

Assessment of the Overall Foreign Investment Contribution

Initially, Hong Kong's industrialization was essentially based upon local effort. It was not until the mid-sixties, after Hong Kong had already established its manufacturing industries, that overseas investors started to move into that sector at an accelerated rate. They were drawn to Hong Kong by its favorable investment climate. According to some surveys, Hong Kong's most attractive factors were its laissez-faire and nondiscriminatory policies, free foreign exchange, low tax rates, excellent supporting facilities, and good labor relations (Mun and Ho 1979, pp. 275–96; Hung 1980, pp. 200–233).

In quantitative terms, overseas investments accounted for 1 percent of Hong Kong's manufacturing establishments, 10 percent of their employment, and some 16 percent of their output and exports. These were modest by the standard of the LDCs in general. They did not dominate any of Hong Kong's manufacturing industries, but in some cases, such as the production of plastic materials, where local producers were still technically incompetent, they were predominant.

The effect on the balance of payments is very often a major consideration in foreign investment. This is difficult to gauge for Hong Kong, since its dollar floats[8] and there are no restrictions on foreign exchange remittances. As far as trade is concerned, many of the overseas investments in the manufacturing sector are export-oriented. They help promote Hong Kong's exports in various ways, such as by supplying components to parent firms at home and selling final products in their home or third markets. Conversely, those overseas investments catering to the local market also tend to save foreign exchange for Hong Kong by replacing imports. Overseas investments do not seem to create a problem for Hong Kong in the balance of payments.

Since the investment figures that have been shown only record initial inflows from overseas, there is no way to assess the contribution of overseas firms in terms of total resource augmentation. In any case, Hong Kong does not lack capital, and overseas firms have had ample opportunity to resort to local financing. If foreign sources have contributed substantially to capital accumulation, it has been mainly via the financial sector and not directly through investment in manufacturing.

8. The Hong Kong dollar was again pegged to the U.S. dollar on October 17, 1983, at the rate of HK$7.8 to US$1.

In view of Hong Kong's own industrial capacity and high rate of economic growth, it is fair to assume that Hong Kong could have maintained full employment in the absence of overseas investments. The fact that overseas firms were found mainly in the newer, more capital-intensive and higher-technology industries suggests that they contributed to higher productivity, especially in the use of labor.

It was pointed out earlier that some of Hong Kong's new industries, such as electronics and watches and clocks, were first brought in by overseas investors. In this process, they helped broaden Hong Kong's industrial base. This has been an important development, since Hong Kong is facing keen competition and trade barriers in its traditional export markets. How much foreign firms can contribute to the LDCs sometimes seems doubtful, because new technology tends to remain in their own hands. But the situation in Hong Kong is an entirely different story. In an environment where overseas and local firms work competitively side by side, imitation is almost immediate. Hong Kong is a compact industrial city where labor mobility is high and information travels fast, and where there are numerous entrepreneurs ready to come in at the sight of a profit, so that the diffusion process is very swift. The electronics and watches and clocks industries serve as an example. At one time they were dominated by overseas firms. But in just a few years, numerous local firms sprang up like mushrooms and eventually took over the bulk of the business. The overseas firms served as a catalyst to Hong Kong's further industrialization, and this was their greatest contribution.

Conclusion And Prospects

The economic performance of the NICs in East Asia during the last two decades has become the envy of the world. The process of rapid transformation in these economies had one thing in common—the export of manufactured goods was the prime mover in growth. Considerable rethinking has occurred about outward-looking strategies toward economic development, which at one time had fallen into disfavor.

For Hong Kong, which had long experienced free trade, an outward-looking policy could hardly be called a strategy. It was a way of life under the general umbrella of a laissez-faire policy. The government generally refrained from intervening in economic affairs. Growth was a major objective, but no specific measures were taken to shape development into a "desired" pattern. Promotion was directed toward providing favorable background conditions, and the market was relied upon to work out the details. Industrial growth was the result of a natural process rather than contrived efforts.

This philosophy also found expression in another feature which distinguishes Hong Kong from some other NICs. The regime of free trade is complete. There are neither protective tariffs nor any form of nontariff trade barriers. Exports are not promoted by subsidies, tax rebates, or other means frequently found elsewhere. The free flow of merchandise is abetted by free foreign exchange.

Hong Kong's openness can further be seen in its attitude toward foreign enterprise. Overseas investors are not attracted to Hong Kong by concessions or tax holidays, but neither are they discriminated against. Like their local counterparts, they are free to choose their line of business, form of ownership, technology, and employees. Repatriation of capital and profit is unlimited.

Hong Kong remains a bastion of free enterprise where the market works in full force. The development of its manufacturing exports was a result of this mechanism, while in some other NICs such success was the result of deliberate policy.

The postwar world was characterized by a long period of trade expansion resulting from economic growth and tariff liberalization. Accordingly, the markets that developed countries offered for manufactured goods increased significantly, with the United States in the lead. This led to a change in comparative advantage. The location for production of labor-intensive manufactures began to shift to LDCs where labor was cheap. This was just the right time for Hong Kong's industrialization. There were two additional factors working in Hong Kong's favor. One was that it happened to be the first among the LDCs to embark on the production of labor-intensive manufactures for the developed countries. Hong Kong initially encountered little competition from its peers, and by the time others began to follow, Hong Kong had firmly established itself in the business. The second was Hong Kong's size. This we might call the advantage of being insignificant.

Hong Kong produced what the world demanded, according to comparative advantage. When demand conditions changed, it had to adjust production. This required the flexibility that only a market economy could provide, for which the free enterprise system had proved most suitable. Survival of the fittest was the name of the game.

So much for history. In the eighties, Hong Kong seems to be going through another transformation. The major feature is its rapid emergence as a regional financial and service center. In fact, this process started in the early seventies, but its pace accelerated after China embarked upon its program of "four modernizations" and adopted more liberal economic policies. In terms of contribution to GDP, Hong Kong's manufacturing sector declined from 30.9 percent in 1970 to 27.6 percent in 1979, whereas the finance, insurance, real estate, and business services sector climbed from 14.9 percent to 21.4 percent during the same period.[9] This pattern of development is not inconsistent with the experience of the developed countries, but it has raised questions about the prospects for Hong Kong's industrial development.

There is no doubt that manufacturing will remain the backbone of the Hong Kong economy. It is the major provider of employment and foreign exchange. The problem it faces is deeper than the current world recession. It is one of changing comparative advantage in the course of economic development, which all NICs are encountering. They have all recognized the need to restructure their industries to a level of higher skill and technology, and efforts are being made toward this goal. In the case of Hong Kong, mention was made earlier of the appointment of the Advisory Committee on Diversification, in 1977. In its 1979 report,[10] the committee recommended in very general terms the supply of more industrial land, the introduction of modern technology, the promotion of overseas investments, the training of manpower, and the provision of supporting facilities. The basic philosophy is still essentially one of laissez-faire: the government broadens the economic base and lets the market work out the details. Progress so far has been slow.

Two other recent developments that will affect Hong Kong in the long run should be noted. One is the opening of the Shenzhen Special Economic Zone in China, just across the border from Hong Kong. By providing cheap land and labor, it has started to attract foreign investment in manufacturing, a substantial portion of which is from Hong Kong. This poses no immediate problem to Hong Kong, since the zone is still in its infancy. Even in the long run, it may be advantageous if some kind of complementary relationship can be developed. Hong Kong's land and labor-intensive industries can be relocated in Shenzhen while it concentrates its efforts in the development of skill- and capital-intensive industries. From Hong Kong's point of view, this actually would facilitate the restructuring of its manufacturing sector.

But the other development is less than favorable. From 1977 to 1981, more than half a million immigrants flocked into Hong Kong, legally and illegally, across the border from China. Even though illegal immigration has been effectively halted, Hong Kong is left with a greatly increased population. This has depressed the rise of real wages, and the rate of unemployment had gone up from around 3 percent in 1978 to 4 percent in 1981. From the standpoint of factor endowment and prices, this may well

---

9. See *Estimates of Gross Domestic Product, 1966 to 1980*, Census and Statistics Department, Hong Kong (1982).

10. See *Report of the Advisory Committee on Diversification 1979*, pp. 326–35.

have adverse effects on Hong Kong's current attempt to replace its labor-intensive industries.

For Hong Kong's long-run future—trade and development and all—there is the so-called Problem of 1997. That is the year a large part of Hong Kong will be returned to China by treaty. This problem has been perceived ever since 1949, but it did not hinder economic growth. But the fact that the crucial date is not much more than a decade away has more than a psychological effect. This is especially true for the kind of industrial investment Hong Kong now needs, for which long-term planning and heavy capital commitment are required. Even though China has indicated that investors need not worry, it takes more than verbal assurances to facilitate rational investment decisions.

Negotiations are underway between London and Peking, and it is generally felt that, somehow, an acceptable solution will be found. Until that time, Hong Kong will have to muddle through. While many people are waiting, this might well be the best time for the bold to go ahead. Judging from history, Hong Kong does not have a shortage of this kind of entrepreneur.

References

Chenery, H. B. 1960. "Patterns of Industrial Growth." *American Economic Review* (September): 624–54.

Hung, C. L. 1980. "Foreign Investments." Chapter 6 in David G. Lethbridge, ed., *The Business Environment in Hong Kong*, 200–233. Hong Kong: Oxford University Press.

Kojima, Kiyoshi. 1977. *Japan and a New World Economic Order*. London: Croom Helm.

Lin, Tzong-biau, and Yin-ping Ho. 1979. "Export Instabilities and Employment Fluctuations in Hong Kong's Manufacturing Industries." *The Developing Economies* (June).

Lin, Tzong-biau, Yin-ping Ho. 1981. "Export-Oriented Growth and Industrial Diversification in Hong Kong." In Wontack Hong and Lawrence B. Krause, eds., *Trade and Growth of the Advanced Developing Countries in the Pacific Basin*, 69–123. Seoul: Korea Development Institute.

Lin, Tzong-biau, Victor Mok, and Yin-ping Ho. 1980. *Manufactured Exports and Employment in Hong Kong*. Hong Kong: The Chinese University Press.

Leontief, W. W. 1953. "Domestic Production and Foreign Trade: The American Capital Position Re-examined." *Proceedings of The American Philosophical Society* (September): 331–49.

Mok, Victor. 1980. "Factor Proportion and Technology in Hong Kong's Exports." *Hong Kong Economic Papers*, 1–16.

Mun, Kin-chok, and Ho Suk-ching. 1979. "Foreign Investment in Hong Kong." In T. B. Lin, Rance P. L. Lee, and Udo-Ernst Simonis, eds., *Hong Kong: Eco-*

nomic, Social and Political Studies in Development, 275–96. White Plains, N.Y.: M.E. Sharpe; Folkstone, Kent, England: Wm. Dawson & Sons, Ltd.

Tyszynski, H. 1951. "World Trade in Manufactured Commodities, 1899–1950." *Manchester School of Economic and Social Studies*, 19.3 (September): 272–304.

Hong Kong Government Publications

Census and Statistics Department. 1969. *Hong Kong Statistics 1947–1967*.

Census and Statistics Department. *Hong Kong Trade Statistics*. Various issues.

Census and Statistics Department. *Hong Kong Monthly Digest of Statistics*. Various issues.

Census and Statistics Department. *Economic Prospects*. Various issues.

Census and Statistics Department. *Employment Statistics*. Various issues.

Census and Statistics Department. *Estimates of Gross Domestic Products*. Various issues.

Census and Statistics Department. 1976. *1973 Census of Industrial Production*.

Census and Statistics Department. 1981. *1978 Survey of Industrial Production*.

Commerce and Industry Department. 1975. *Overseas Investments in Hong Kong Manufacturing Industries: Industrial Survey Report*. (August).

Government Secretariat. 1979. *Report of the Advisory Committee on Diversification 1979*.

IV   Singapore

6 The Role of Foreign Trade and Investment in the Development of Singapore
Chia Siow Yue

Development Strategy and Performance Since 1960

Historically, entrepôt trade and the British military base formed the twin pillars of the Singapore economy. Singapore's entrepôt dominance of Southeast Asia can be attributed partly to geographical factors—its strategic location at the southern entrance of the Straits of Malacca astride the shipping routes between the Indian and Pacific Oceans, and its deep-water harbor with a sheltered anchorage—and partly to the existence of a British colonial policy that fostered political stability, free trade, and private enterprise. Singapore's position was consolidated over time by the growth of a complex and efficient network of commercial, financial, and transport and communications services and institutions. With the growth of competing ports in Southeast Asia, the economic hinterland shrank and the Malay Peninsula became the major trading partner. In the post–World War II period entrepôt growth was inhibited by the rise of economic nationalism in Southeast Asia; to an increasing extent Singapore's neighbors developed direct trading and domestic processing of raw materials, and restricted imports of manufactures to promote industrialization. After the commodities boom during the Korean War, Singapore's trade entered a period of slow growth and stagnation. The ensuing economic difficulties were compounded by rapid population and labor-force growth, turbulent political developments, and industrial unrest.

The achievement of self-government in 1959 was followed by the adoption of industrialization as the major development strategy of Singapore. Manufacturing replaced entrepôt trade as the leading sector of the economy and the main source of employment growth. The manufacturing sector was underdeveloped in relation to Singapore's per capita income level, mainly because of the lack of natural resources, which prevented the natural evolution of resource-processing industries; the existence of a small domestic market and free imports, which precluded the development of industries with scale economies; and high wages in the entrepôt sector, which inhibited the development of labor-intensive industries such as garments and textiles that normally characterize the initial phase of industrialization. The industrialization strategy emphasized direct foreign investment, since the policy makers felt that the process of transforming domestic commercial entrepreneurs into industrial entrepreneurs would be too slow and uncertain. The government played the supportive role of ensuring a favorable investment climate through the provision of a physical infrastructure, fiscal incentives, and manpower development, and it also enforced labor discipline and encouraged peaceful industrial relations.

As in other countries, the initial emphasis of industrialization was on import substitution, in the belief that the proposed Malaysian common market would materialize.[1] Following political separation from Malaysia in August 1965, the abortion of the common market proposal, continuing high unemployment, and fears of a recession with the impending withdrawal of the British military base, the industrialization strategy switched toward accelerated encouragement of foreign investment to produce for export. Draconian political, economic, and social measures were introduced in 1967–68, including new investment incentives, restrictive labor legislation, and restructuring of the educational system to provide more technically trained workers. The upshot of these measures was a rapid rise in foreign investment, manufacturing production, and export. Favorable external conditions were contributory factors, as world trade and international investment expanded. The Vietnam War provided additional export demand, and political problems in Hong Kong and Taiwan led to further investment inflows. Income expanded rapidly, unemployment diminished, and pressures for wage increases emerged.

The changing factor endowment led to the introduction in the early seventies of a new development strategy stressing skill-intensive and higher-technology industries and high value-added services for the export market. The scarcity of natural resources, including land, water, and fuel, precluded any extensive development of basic heavy industry and the chemical industry. The growing tendency of producing countries to undertake their own resource processing and the concern over pollution offset the advantages arising from geographical proximity and easy access to the region's raw materials. The obvious development alternative was to rely increasingly on Singapore's human resources. Unfavorable world economic conditions in 1974–75, however, led to a temporary postponement

---

1. Political merger among the states of Malaya, Sabah, Sarawak, and Singapore took place in September 1963. Singapore's main economic rationale for merger was that the proposed common market would provide a large enough market for the city-state's nascent industries.

of economic restructuring, and policy makers continued to encourage labor-intensive investments and to exercise wage restraints.

Economic restructuring was resumed in 1979 in the face of growing domestic and external pressures. The pressures emanated from increasing domestic labor shortages and growing dependence on foreign workers; increased external competition from labor-abundant, low-wage countries embarking on labor-intensive export manufacturing; growing protectionism of OECD countries directed increasingly at labor-intensive imports from the Newly Industrializing Countries (NICs); and anticipated reclassification of Singapore's development status and a consequent loss of trade preferences. The economic restructuring entails the shift away from low-wage, low-skilled, and low value-added manufacturing and service activities toward those paying higher wages, requiring more skill, and with more value added. Three parallel policies were implemented to promote restructuring: allowing wages to find their market levels, reducing the inflow of foreign workers, and developing manpower further. A three-year wage-correction policy, covering the period 1979–82, was adopted; the non-mandatory annual guidelines of the tripartite National Wages Council recommended annual wage increases of 14–20 percent, representing a sharp departure from past practices. The government also announced its intention to phase out guest workers completely by 1990. Manpower development, automation and mechanization, research and development, and improvements in management practices and labor productivity were being fostered through a wide variety of measures.

By 1981 Singapore's per capita GNP stood at S$10,801 (US$5,122), one of the highest in the developing world.[2] Per capita GNP grew at an average annual rate of 7.1 percent in real terms in the 1960–81 period, resulting in a quadrupling of incomes in two decades. The rapid growth was achieved through a sharp reduction in population growth, from over 4 percent in the early fifties to only 1.2 percent in recent years, and as a result of sustained high GDP growth for most of the period. Growth in the 1960–72 period was achieved with remarkable price stability, as the Consumer Price Index increased at an annual average rate of only 1.2 percent. Contributory factors were the free-trade policy, which made possible low-cost imports, the existence of excess capacity and unused resources, and prudent government fiscal and monetary policies. Prices escalated, however, in the 1972–81 period, with an average annual increase of 8.0 percent in the Consumer Price Index, because of rising import prices (especially of

2. Fear of reclassification as a developed country led Singapore's government statisticians to devise the concept of indigenous GNP, which excludes the share of GNP of all foreigners resident in the country. The indigenous per capita GNP in 1981 was 85 percent of the per capita GNP.

petroleum), upward pressures under conditions of full employment, and the overheating of some nontraded sectors of the economy as a result of rapid growth. Budgetary restraint continued to be pursued, the upward movement of the Singapore dollar following the 1973 float offset to some extent the rising import prices in terms of foreign currency, and the increasing provision of public low-cost housing offset some of the inflationary trends in the construction and home-ownership sectors.

Economic growth was made possible by rapidly rising levels of investment and saving. The investment/GNP ratio rose from 11.6 percent in 1960 to 43.8 percent in 1981. Starting from a situation of dissaving in 1960, gross national savings rose rapidly to 29.8 percent of GNP by 1981, partly because of the steady rise in compulsory personal savings under the Central Provident Fund.[3] Although national savings financed a growing share of capital formation, Singapore continued to depend heavily on capital inflows, mainly in the form of private direct foreign investment. There was only limited dependence on private foreign borrowing and even less on official development assistance.

Labor-intensive development during the years of rapid economic growth transformed a labor-surplus economy, in which the unemployed made up over 10 percent of the labor force in the early sixties, into a labor-scarce economy, in which foreign workers made up 11 percent of the labor force in 1980. The unemployment rate is currently less than 3 percent. Labor-intensive development, however, contributed to poor productivity performance. For the 1970–80 period, growth in labor productivity slowed down to an average annual rate of 3.7 percent, as compared with 7.1 percent in the 1966–70 period.

Fragmentary wage data indicate that average real wages showed little improvement in the sixties. However, real wages increased after 1972, particularly in the 1979–82 period. Thus, while real wage increases in the sixties and early seventies lagged behind productivity growth, there has been a catching up process since the late seventies. But the Singapore development experience has not resulted in the growth and equity conflict so evident in many developing countries. Economic policies stressed growth, but social policies helped to distribute the fruits of economic progress. A 1976 income-distribution study showed a small decline in the Gini ratio between 1966 and 1973 (Pang 1976), mainly because of the sharp

---

3. The Central Provident Fund scheme was introduced in 1955 as a compulsory savings plan for workers. The rates of contribution from employers and employees have been increased over the years and as of 1982 stood at 22 percent of salary contributed by employee and 23 percent of salary contributed by employer, subject to an employee maximum contribution of S$690 per month.

decline in unemployment and the increase in formal wage jobs. In addition, the real incomes of workers have been substantially augmented by the sharp increase in the rates of Central Provident Fund contributions from employers, and by the government provision of low-cost housing, education, and medical and other social amenities. The official emphasis on meritocracy rather than elitism based on inherited privileges served to ensure social mobility. In this compact city-state, the trickle-down effect has been faster, facilitated by sustained high growth.

Several general factors contributed to Singapore's economic success in the last two decades. First has been the quality of the political leadership and government bureaucracy. Their development orientation, economic pragmatism, honesty, and efficiency contributed to political stability, an efficient public sector, a sound investment climate, and the ability to mobilize the population in support of consensus measures for economic and social development. The second important factor has been the quality of Singapore's human resources, with a value system that emphasizes hard work and thrift. Third, Singapore's geographical location has been a crucial economic resource. Historically it was the reason for the development of the entrepôt trade and the establishment of the British military base. In recent decades it provided the rationale for the location of processing industries, shipyards, the Asian dollar market, and tourism, transport, and communications services. The fourth factor is an outward-oriented development philosophy and strategy as manifested by the absence of restrictions on trade in goods and services and movement of capital, and the open door to foreign investment, managerial and professional resources, and even foreign unskilled labor. There is an absence of economic nationalism in the generally accepted sense, and little evidence of xenophobia. The Singapore economy is one of the most open in the world. Finally, an accommodating external environment during the transition from entrepôt to manufacturing enabled Singapore to benefit from the open approach.

The Role of Foreign Trade

Trade Dependence

Singapore's city-state economy is characterized by a high dependence on foreign trade for both the importation of essential foodstuffs, raw materials for industry, fuels, and capital goods, and for the exportation of goods and services to finance such imports. A large entrepôt trade and the growing volume of nonentrepôt trade have made Singapore a leading seaport. Its share of global trade is much higher than its share of global income. The trade/GNP ratio has increased since the early sixties, reflecting that industrialization has been even more trade-oriented than traditional entrepôt trading. In 1981 total trade was 417 percent of GNP; imports of goods and services were 242 percent and exports of goods and services were 229 percent of GNP.[4]

Singapore's trade relations with the rest of the world are characterized more by dependence than interdependence. Whereas imports and exports are crucial for the survival and material well-being of Singapore, its exports of goods and services are not really crucial to the economic well-being of its major trading partners; it conforms well to the small country assumption in international trade. The high degree of trade dependence renders it highly vulnerable to changes in world trade and trading conditions. Domestic economic policies play a relatively passive and responsive role, taking advantage of the opportunities offered by international trade and international investment, and offsetting some of the adverse effects. In spite of the highly open economy, instability has not been a serious problem in recent years, as the economy's production and trade structures have become increasingly diversified. Only the Indonesian confrontation in 1964–65[5] and the world recessions in 1974–75 and 1982 have had sufficiently strong adverse impacts to cause serious downturns in economic performance.

The extent of the import and export dependence of the Singapore economy is obvious from the Singapore input-output tables available for the year 1973.[6] Direct imported inputs accounted for 32.3 percent of gross output. Import dependence, however, is more accurately reflected in total direct and indirect imported inputs. As table 6.1 shows, total import content for all sectors averaged 38.3 percent. Even the traditional nontraded sectors have a significant import content. The import content was extremely high in the processing activities, exceeding 90 percent in rubber processing, and more than 75 percent in oil and fat processing, sawmilling, and petroleum refining, as well as in the manufacture of animal feeds and the manufacture of jewelry. Sectors in which the import content was less than 10 percent of gross output were wholesale and retail trade, water utility, financial services, real estate, ownership of dwellings, and domestic services and private nonprofit organizations. Within the manufacturing sector, over half the industries had an import content exceeding 50 percent.

In 1973, of total retained imports, 71.8 percent went into intermediate demand, with only 28.2 percent into final demand; of the latter, 10.2

---

4. The import/GNP and export/GNP ratios still exceed 100 percent even if entrepôt trade were to be excluded.

5. Indonesia, in protest against the formation of Malaysia in September 1963, embarked on a policy of economic confrontation with Singapore and the other Malaysian states. As Indonesia was then the second largest trading partner after Peninsular Malaya, the cessation of Singapore-Indonesia trade resulted in a sharp drop in entrepôt trade.

6. Unfortunately, there is, as of end 1982, only one set of official input-output tables for Singapore, covering the year 1973.

Table 6.1. Import and Export Dependence, 1973 (%)

Total direct and indirect import requirement per unit of output	
Total, all sectors	38.3
Agriculture, fishing, & quarrying	30.2
Manufacturing	64.8
Utilities	13.0
Construction	38.2
Services	16.7
Import content of final demand	
Total, final demand	48.0
Private consumption expenditure	35.3
Government consumption expenditure	32.2
Gross domestic fixed capital formation	58.5
Export of goods and services	53.9
Export share of output	
Total, all sectors	20.1
Agriculture, fishing, & quarrying	9.0
Manufacturing	65.0
Utilities	3.7
Construction	0.0
Services	22.9

Source: Singapore, Department of Statistics (1978).

percent was for consumption and 17.9 percent for investment. Thus, an overwhelming share of imports served to meet production and investment requirements.

The Singapore economy is also highly dependent on exports of goods and services. In 1973, the manufacturing sector accounted for 71.7 percent of total exports, followed by services with 27.6 percent, agriculture, fishing, and quarrying, 0.5 percent, and utilities, 0.1 percent. The dominance of manufactured exports followed upon the successful implementation of export-oriented industrialization. The export/output ratio for total gross output was 20.1 percent, but it showed wide sectoral variations. The ratio was 65.0 percent in the manufacturing sector, 22.9 percent in the services sector, and only 9.0 percent in agriculture.

Trade Policies

Singapore has largely adhered to the traditional free-trade principle. There are no export restrictions or taxes and no foreign exchange controls. Import restrictions are minimal and consist of a limited number of tariffs, a legacy of the import-substitution period. The free-trade regime and outward-looking development strategy have been influenced by the small economic size, the geographical location, the traditional entrepôt role of the city, and by the attitude of people who migrated there in response to the opportunities created by free trade. The emergence of nationalism in the fifties and of industrialization in the sixties did not diminish the free-trade outlook, as the small domestic market necessitated exporting and the high import content of production meant that import restrictions would severely hinder export competitiveness.

Apart from the infant industry argument, there were few economic pressures for the imposition of import restrictions. The balance of payments did not pose a problem, because of the nature of Singapore's currency and exchange-rate system and because of the large net earnings on services, as well as large-scale capital inflows. The government budget was not critically dependent on revenue from import duties, thanks to a fairly wide tax base, an efficient tax administration, a prudent expenditures policy, and the rapid growth of incomes. The first protective import tariffs, excluding the traditional revenue import tariffs on liquor, tobacco products, and petroleum products, were imposed in September 1960 to offset dumping of soaps and detergents. Tariffs were imposed with increasing frequency in the 1962–65 period in anticipation of the formation of the Malaysian common market and the consequent need to harmonize tariff structures. The collapse of the common market proposal in 1965, consequent upon Singapore's political separation from the Malaysian Federation, led to an immediate increase in protective tariffs to protect domestic industries faced with increased barriers to exporting to Malaysia, and with excess capacity. Domestic producers, however, were allowed duty exemptions on imported inputs. During 1966–67, few new tariffs were imposed. In 1968 a new round of tariff impositions took place to offset the anticipated recession arising from the planned withdrawal of the British military base. Although quota restrictions on imports were introduced in 1963, they were seldom used after 1966 because they usually triggered speculative imports prior to the quota imposition.[7] After 1969, as fears of a recession proved unfounded and the economy showed accelerating growth, tariffs were either abolished or scaled downward. Two official reasons were given for tariff liberalization—that industrialists had been afforded an adequate period of infant industry protection and should have become internationally competitive, and that the removal of import tariffs would lower the cost of imported goods and thus reduce the impact of imported inflation on consumer prices. By 1973 all quota restrictions were removed, and by 1975

7. In the early and mid-sixties, when the number of new industries being established was relatively small, speculators were able to anticipate the imposition of quotas, with the result that they imported large stocks before the quotas were imposed, causing a glut on the local market.

import licensing restrictions were largely discontinued. Tariff reduction and abolition were escalated in 1973 as imported inflation became serious. Since then there has been only a gradual dismantling of existing import tariffs, probably because of the need to maintain some tariffs for purposes of negotiating tariff reductions under the ASEAN Preferential Trading Arrangement. Among the ASEAN countries, Singapore has the lowest level and smallest number of import tariffs; product-by-product negotiations under the arrangement presupposes that Singapore could offer some reciprocal tariff preferences to its ASEAN partners.[8]

A study by Tan and Ow (1978) shows that in 1967, the system of nominal protection in Singapore was simple and moderate—tariff rates were low, there were few quota restrictions, and there were no other forms of protection, while duty exemptions were granted on imported inputs which had no close domestic substitutes. Tariff rates were generally no higher than 25 percent, with only 14 commodity items having tariff rates exceeding 50 percent. The overall nominal protection for the manufacturing sector was 4.3 percent on domestic sales and 3.0 percent on total sales. The normal pattern of escalation of protection into durable consumer goods industries was absent in the case of Singapore. The average effective protection rate for the manufacturing sector as a whole was low—6.0 percent (Balassa method) and 5.2 percent (Corden method) on total sales and 8.6 percent (Balassa method) and 7.5 percent (Corden method) on domestic sales.[9] For the individual industries there was a wide variation of effective protection rates, although the majority of the industries clustered around protection rates of 10 to 20 percent.

Policies toward exports in Singapore form an integral part of its industrial development strategy. Measures were aimed at both the expansion of export production capacity as well as increasing the ability and willingness of manufacturers to export. Various measures were introduced in the sixties and the first half of the seventies to promote industrial investment. Most of these measures affected both the import-substituting as well as

---

8. The five ASEAN countries of Indonesia, Malaysia, the Philippines, Singapore, and Thailand could not reach agreement on the formation of a customs union or a free-trade area. Instead, the ASEAN Preferential Arrangement came into force in January 1978, providing for tariff preferences to promote intra-ASEAN trade; such tariff preferences were negotiated on a product-by-product basis, with each country making an equal number of offers.

9. The Balassa and Corden methods of computing effective protection rates differ in the treatment of nontraded goods. In the Balassa method, nontradable inputs are treated as tradable inputs with zero protection. In the Corden method, the value added part of the nontradable inputs is included in the value added of the protected industry and the inputs of the non-tradable inputs are treated in the same way as other tradable inputs with the relevant tariffs. For a discussion of the Balassa and Corden methods, see Balassa and Associates (1971).

export industries, and were applicable to both foreign and domestic investors.

The 1959 Pioneer Industries Ordinance granted designated enterprises a five-year exemption from the standard 40 percent corporate income tax. Pioneer status was given on a discretionary basis to firms producing products which were considered "essential" to the economy, or whose further development was considered desirable. The parallel 1959 Industrial Expansion Ordinance provided tax concessions to established enterprises with approved expansion plans.

After political independence in 1965, the need to develop exports necessitated further incentives. The first tentative steps were taken in late 1965 to allow double tax deductions for expenses incurred in export promotion. In addition, selected industries were allowed accelerated depreciation allowances. Under the 1967 Economic Expansion Incentives Act, the 1959 tax concessions were streamlined: the pioneer tax-exempt period was made variable from two to five years, depending on the size of capital investment, and the investment allowances for expanding firms were made more stringent.

New incentives were introduced under the 1967 act. To promote export expansion and market diversification, the tax rate on profits from new exports was reduced from 40 percent to 4 percent for a period of 15 years. To facilitate foreign borrowing by local firms for capital equipment purchases, interest earnings on approved foreign loans were made tax exempt, provided that the minimum size of the loan was at least S$200,000 and that the tax exemption benefited the foreign lender and was not appropriated by his government in the form of higher taxes payable. To encourage the inflow of foreign technology, a concessionary tax rate of 20 percent (rather than the standard 40 percent) was granted on payments to foreigners of royalties, technical assistance fees, and research and development contributions.

The 1967 legislation was intended to meet the situation prevailing in the immediate postindependence years, when the economic future was fraught with uncertainty. By 1970 there was improvement in the political and economic climate, so that tax incentives began to be viewed as overly generous to the investors. Amendments were introduced in 1970 to tighten the 1967 incentives. For pioneer enterprises, the tax-exempt period reverted to a standard five years, but the qualifying level of investment was raised. Investment allowances for enterprises engaged in expansion of productive capacity were restricted to new capital outlays of at least S$10 million, while accelerated depreciation allowances were restricted to larger investments. The export tax concession was reduced from 15 years to 8 years for pioneer enterprises and to 5 years only for nonpioneer enterprises; the 15-year export tax concession was reserved only for enterprises with large fixed investments.

Apart from the fiscal incentives, direct measures to encourage export development remained limited as the government continued to rely on foreign investments to effect exports. In the mid-sixties, an Export Promotion Centre was established within the Economic Development Board. This unit was later absorbed into the International Trading Company (INTRACO), formed as a joint venture between the government and the private sector to promote the development of Singapore's manufactured exports. The resources of the organization were limited and it never played a major role in export development.

Export recession in 1974–75 prompted the government to assist exporters further. In October 1974 the government allocated funds to the Development Bank of Singapore for financing export bills at a fraction below the prime rate and for financing manufacturers who wished to expand their capital equipment. The Monetary Authority of Singapore opened its rediscount facility to banks for eligible export and pre-export issuance bills. The Export Credit Insurance Corporation of Singapore (ECICS) was formed in mid-1976 as a joint venture between government and private enterprise to provide insurance coverage against political and commercial risks in exporting. Special financing terms were provided to the shipbuilding and ship-repairing industry, which faced global recession and intense competition from foreign shipyards.

The Department of Trade embarked on extensive export promotion programs. Concern over poor export performance in 1981–82 led to the formation of a Trade Development Board in early 1983 to replace the Department of Trade in order to secure greater operational flexibility and concentration on export promotion.

The study by Tan and Ow (1978) attempted to measure the effective subsidy rate in Singapore, as well. The study confined the incentives to corporate income tax concessions and loans at preferential interest rates. For the manufacturing sector as a whole, the average effective subsidy rates on total sales in 1967 were 6.0 percent (Balassa method) and 5.2 percent (Corden method), and on export sales they were 0.6 percent (Balassa and Corden methods). Domestic sales had effective subsidy rates of 8.3 percent (Balassa method) and 7.2 percent (Corden method). The petroleum industry had the highest positive subsidies, with the effective subsidy reaching 14.3 percent of value added at world prices.

Trade Growth and Changing Structure

Trade in services is sizable and in the seventies it showed rapid expansion. In fact, by 1981 trade in services exceeded the entrepôt trade in value and accounted for 23 percent of total trade. Singapore achieved a continuous surplus in trade in services, with net service earnings outpacing net capital inflows throughout the seventies. Rising service-export earnings resulted from the development-planning emphasis on Singapore as a regional center for transportation and communications, finance, and tourism, as well as reflecting the city's strategic geographical location. The largest component in the trade in services consists of port disbursements by ships and aircraft, payments and receipts of passenger fares, and miscellaneous services such as management, professional, and consultant services. The large net earnings in this category shows the contributions of Singapore Airlines, Port of Singapore Authority, and the airport, among others.

Singapore also has a surplus in travel expeditures. Efforts to boost tourism in the last decade brought in 2.8 million tourists in 1981, while increasingly affluent Singaporeans travel abroad on holidays. In the past, earnings from the stationing of foreign armed forces formed an important source of foreign exchange, but this declined sharply following the withdrawal of the British military base at the beginning of the seventies.

In spite of the establishment of a national shipping line, payments for freight and insurance represented the largest net drain of foreign exchange in the services. Investment income made a sizable contribution to service foreign exchange earnings in earlier years because of Singapore's large overseas assets, including those held by the country's monetary authorities. Growing direct foreign investment has led to increasingly large payments of profits, dividends, and interest and has resulted in net outflows of investment income in recent years. This trend can be expected to continue as the stock of direct foreign investment in the country continues to expand rapidly.

Singapore, like the other Asian NICs of Hong Kong, the Republic of Korea, and the Republic of China, has experienced export-led growth, especially since the late sixties. Merchandise exports rose in real terms at 12.0 percent a year in the seventies, as compared to only 4.2 percent in the sixties. Merchandise imports showed a parallel growth trend, accelerating from 5.9 percent in the sixties to 9.9 percent in the seventies. Official trade statistics, however, underrecorded the growth in merchandise trade. The published data include trade with Indonesia up to 1963 and exclude such trade since then, and it is generally believed that the Singapore-Indonesia bilateral trade has been buoyant, especially in the seventies, when Indonesia's import capacity increased rapidly with its oil boom.

The rapid growth of merchandise trade has been characterized by wide annual fluctuations, with somewhat dampened effects on other sectors of the economy, and by the growing merchandise trade gap. The persistent and growing deficit in merchandise trade contrasts sharply with the trade in services, and is due primarily to the excess of retained imports over nonentrepôt exports. The gap so far has not presented a problem to the country's policy makers, since service net earnings and capital inflows have been more than adequate to cover the merchandise deficit, so that the city-state's official foreign reserves have shown an uninterrupted upward trend since the mid-sixties.

Rapid growth in merchandise trade has been due more to the growth in the nonentrepôt than the entrepôt component. In 1960, entrepôt trade still accounted for 85.8 percent of Singapore's merchandise trade, but by 1981 the share had dropped to only 25 percent. Part of the decline is purely statistical, due to the omission of data on trade with Indonesia; such trade is largely of an entrepôt character. The real factors in the relative decline of entrepôt trade, which continued to grow in absolute value in the sixties and seventies, are the growing practice of direct trading by neighboring countries, depressed prices for major primary commodities, the rapid development of manufactured exports and the consequent sharp increase in import requirements, and the escalating value of oil imports and exports, due to both price and quantity increases, which form an increasing share of nonentrepôt trade. On the export side, the share of entrepôt in total merchandise exports declined from 93.8 percent in 1960 to only 33.5 percent by 1981; no comparable data are available for entrepôt imports and retained imports.

Table 6.2 summarizes the changing composition of Singapore's merchandise imports and exports. The composition of imports reflects increasing domestic demand and decreasing entrepôt demand. The overall pattern of merchandise imports shows the growing dominance of manufactures, in particular machinery and equipment, in response to both the changing pattern of entrepôt imports away from primary commodities toward manufactures required by neighboring countries, and to the growing domestic demand for capital formation and industrial inputs. The share of food and crude materials imports declined sharply from 56.6 percent in 1960 to only 12.1 percent by 1981. Nonetheless, the city-state remains extremely dependent on imported food supplies. In contrast to the trend in food and crude raw materials, the share of mineral fuel imports rose from 14.5 percent to 34.0 percent in the same period, as a result of the twin effects of increased import demand consequent upon the rapid expansion in petroleum refining capacity in Singapore in the last two decades and the increases in oil prices in world markets in the seventies. In recent years, however, import demand for crude petroleum has abated, since the refining industry can no longer expand, because of the global shift toward relocation of refining activities in the producing countries and the depressed demand for the Singapore industry's output. Imports of manufac-

Table 6.2. Composition of Imports and Exports, 1960, 1965, and 1981

	Percentage Distribution			
	Imports	Exports	Entrepôt Exports	Nonentrepôt Exports
1960 value (S$ million)	4,078	3,477	3,260	217
SITC 0,1	18.3	15.3	14.2	31.9
2,4	38.3	46.3	48.4	13.5
3	14.5	11.3	12.0	0.0
5,6,8	19.9	14.4	12.2	46.9
7	7.0	6.8	6.7	7.7
9	2.0	6.0	6.4	0.0
1965 value (S$ million)	3,807	3,004	2,264	740
SITC 0,1	21.4	16.0	16.8	13.7
2,4	20.0	29.3	37.4	4.6
3	13.4	14.4	8.7	31.5
5,6,8	28.8	20.6	19.3	24.7
7	14.5	10.5	12.8	3.3
9	2.0	9.2	4.9	22.2
1981 value (S$ million)	58,248	44,291	14,839	29,452
SITC 0,1	6.1	5.2	11.1	2.2
2,4	6.0	10.1	26.1	2.1
3	34.0	32.0	2.3	47.0
5,6,8	24.5	18.4	27.6	13.8
7	28.3	26.6	30.0	24.9
9	1.1	7.7	2.9	10.0

Source: Singapore, Ministry of Trade and Industry, *Economic Survey of Singapore 1981*.
Note: SITC 0,1—Food & live animals; beverages & tobacco.
  2,4—Crude materials inedible; animal & vegetable oils & fats.
  3—Mineral fuels.
  5,6,8—Chemicals; manufactured goods by material; miscellaneous manufactured articles.
  7—Machinery and transport equipment.
  9—Miscellaneous transactions.

tures (SITC 5 to 8) grew rapidly in the sixties and seventies so that its import share rose from 26.9 percent in 1960 to 52.8 percent in 1981. Within this group, machinery and transport equipment showed the fastest expansion.

The composition of exports also demonstrates the increasing share of manufactures. Entrepôt exports have been exerting a diminishing influence on the overall structure of exports. Traditionally, the bulk of the entrepôt trade consisted of transshipment, sorting, and processing of raw materials from the surrounding region for re-export to industrial countries. The most important commodities were rubber, tin, coconuts, palm oil, and timber. Such trade has grown in absolute value but declined in relative

Table 6.3. Major Nonentrepôt Exports, 1981

SITC categories	Value in S$ million	Percentage of total
Petroleum products	13,830	47.0
Oil bunkers	2,948	10.0
Television and radio	2,053	7.0
Electronics components	1,977	6.7
Ships, boats, & oil rigs	966	3.3
Clothing	800	2.7
Electrical motors & resistors	509	1.7
Office machines	283	1.0
Veneer & plywood	276	0.9
Medicinal products	237	0.8
Textile yarn & fabrics	216	0.7
Industrial machines	184	0.6
Watches & clocks	175	0.6
Optical & photographic equipment	141	0.5
Iron & steel	120	0.4
Musical instruments	115	0.4
Subtotal, above	24,831	84.3
Total nonentrepôt exports	29,452	100.0

Source: Singapore, Ministry of Trade and Development, *Economic Survey of Singapore 1981*.

importance, while re-exports of manufactures have grown faster in response to both the demands of the region for capital formation and the consumption demand resulting from improved living standards. The traditional British agency houses engaged in commodity trade in Singapore have been gradually replaced by international companies using Singapore as their regional headquarters and as a storage and distribution center for manufactures and parts and components destined for the regional market.

The development of export manufacturing has been the single most important factor determining the growth and changing structure of nonentrepôt exports since 1960. As noted earlier, the petroleum refining industry has emerged as the largest contributor to nonentrepôt exports. As table 6.3 shows, petroleum product exports, including oil bunkers, accounted for over half of total nonentrepôt exports by 1981. The refineries in Singapore supply markets in Japan, Hong Kong, and Malaysia, while flags-of-convenience countries feature prominently in the oil-bunkering trade. The refining industry is completely dependent on imported crude, mainly from the Middle East, although in recent years there has been some sourcing from Indonesia and Malaysia, with the refineries undertaking contract processing from the latter two countries to increase capacity utilization.

Geographical location and a favorable investment climate, including generous fiscal incentives, have turned Singapore into one of the largest refining centers in the world. The industry in Singapore, however, now faces uncertain prospects, as world demand slows and competitive refining capacity is expanding rapidly in oil-producing countries. Owing to the low value added content—a value added/output ratio of about 13 percent—and high capital intensity, exports of petroleum products contributed much less to income and employment growth than its export dominance would suggest. It is estimated that in 1981 the value added contribution amounted to 7 percent of GDP as compared with 3 percent in 1973. The industry employed fewer than 4,000 workers. Of course the total impact of the refining industry is much greater, in terms of the linkage effects and the income multiplier effects.

The second largest group of nonentrepôt exports is machinery and transport equipment. Major exports within this group consisted of telecommunications apparatus, other electrical machinery (mainly electronic valves), and ships, boats, and oil rigs. Together these commodities accounted for export sales of 22.0 percent of total nonentrepôt exports in 1981. The major markets for electrical-electronic products and components are the United States and the European Economic Community, while for oil rigs China also provides a major market. Other important nonentrepôt exports are veneer and plywood, textiles and clothing, and photographic apparatus.

Data from the annual industrial censuses show that direct exports from the manufacturing sector rose from a mere S$164 million in 1960 to S$19.2 billion by 1980 (table 6.4). The emphasis on export-oriented industrialization is reflected not only in the growing value of manufactured exports but also in the rising share of exports in the sales of manufacturing establishments. The export/total sales ratio stood at 36.0 percent in 1960 but declined for most of the decade. Contributory factors were the import-substitution emphasis of the early and middle sixties and the growing restrictions faced in the Malaysian market, the traditional export outlet for Singapore's manufacturers. After 1968, the switch to export-oriented manufacturing and the accompanying large-scale inflows of export-oriented foreign investments led to the rapid rise of export values and of the export/total sales ratio. That the growth of the manufacturing sector in Singapore has been export-led is borne out not only by the rapid growth of such exports but by the increasing export orientation of most industries. The overall ratio reached a high of 64.6 percent in 1978 before declining somewhat to 62.0 percent in 1980 as external demand conditions worsened.

At the start of the industrialization program in 1960, the major export

Foreign Trade and Investment in Singapore

Table 6.4. Direct Exports of the Manufacturing Sector, 1960 and 1980

		Percentage distribution		Export/total sales ratio (%)	
ISIC	Industry Group	1960	1980	1960	1980
311–2	Food manufacturing	14.2	4.5	31.3	52.0
313	Beverages	11.0	0.3	44.7	22.6
314	Tobacco products	0.2	0.1	0.9	10.4
321	Textiles & textile manufactures		1.2		71.0
322	Wearing apparel except footwear	2.5	3.1	29.3	71.0
324	Footwear		0.1		38.1
323	Leather & leather products		0.1		40.7
331	Sawn timber & wood products	10.5	2.1	48.4	54.6
332	Furniture & fixtures	0.7	0.5	29.0	44.2
341	Paper & paper products	0.9	0.1	27.3	9.1
342	Printing & publishing	4.4	0.5	21.5	18.1
351	Industrial chemicals & gases		0.9		52.2
352	Other chemical products	17.7	1.8	45.9	61.9
353–4	Petroleum refineries & petroleum products		39.7		67.3
355	Processing of gums	7.8	0.1	70.6	63.4
356	Rubber products		0.2		48.2
361–9	Nonmetallic mineral products	9.1	0.7	60.2	20.4
371	Iron & steel	1.8	0.4	57.4	22.0
372	Nonferrous metals		0.8		76.7
381	Fabricated metal products	7.9	1.9	42.4	29.4
382	Nonelectrical machinery	2.4	5.7	24.0	68.9
383	Electrical machinery & electronics	8.3	26.6	79.4	83.1
384	Transport equipment & oil rigs	0.4	5.1	2.2	51.2
385	Precision equipment & photographic goods		1.8		91.7
357	Plastic products	0.2	0.6	3.7	21.9
390	Other manufacturing		1.1		46.3
Total		100.0	100.0	36.0	62.0
Value of exports (S$ million)		164	19,173		

Source: Singapore, Department of Statistics, *Report on the Census of Industrial Production* (1960 and 1980).

industries of Singapore were, in descending order, chemical products, food manufactures, beverages, and sawn timber and wood products; together they accounted for over half the exports of the manufacturing sector. By 1980 the leading export industries had become petroleum refineries, electrical machinery and electronics, nonelectrical machinery, and transport equipment and oil rigs; these four accounted for over three-fourths of the manufacturing sector's exports. Of the dominant export industries in 1960, only food manufacturing remained relatively important, but its share of total manufacturing exports slipped from 14.2 to only 4.5 percent.

The new leading export industries have been fostered under the system of industrial incentives. Apart from being a major oil-refining center, Singapore has emerged as a major center for oil-rig construction and ship repairing. It has also a sizable off-shore production of electronics products and components and other precision instruments. Unlike the situation in many other developing countries, or even the other Asian NICs, the textile and garment industries remained relatively small in their contribution to manufacturing production and export; there was little indigenous evolution of the industry, and its growth took place in the sixties and early seventies under the impetus of third world foreign investments.

Singapore's leading export industries show a multiplicity of factor intensities, so that it is not easy to identify the city-state's comparative advantage. The leading export industries in 1960 showed a mixture of labor/capital intensity; geographical proximity to the Malaysian market enabled the Singapore industries to enjoy a competitive edge over imports from faraway countries. The leading export industries in 1980 again showed mixed factor intensity, as measured by value added per worker, remuneration per worker, and the share of worker remuneration in output and value added. Petroleum refining is highly capital-intensive, with very high value added per worker and very low labor share in value added. The competitive advantage of Singapore as a refining center, dependent as it was on imported crude, lay mainly in its location astride major shipping lanes and consumer markets, and its large oil-bunkering trade. This competitive edge is being eroded by the policies of oil-producing countries to encourage the location of refineries within their own territorial boundaries.

The electronic components and products industry has medium labor productivity, but pays low wages so that the labor share of value added remains low; investment incentives coupled with the ready availability of low-cost labor in the late sixties and early seventies led to the development and growth of this industry in Singapore. The textile and garment industries pay low wages, but their low labor productivity has meant a high labor share in value added and output. These industries seem the least able to face the challenge of rising wages and growing labor scarcity in Singapore and face an uncertain future, aggravated by protectionist quotas imposed by several OECD countries.

Trade Relations

Singapore's rapidly changing composition of trade since the early sixties has been paralleled by changes in the country direction of trade. The most significant factors have been the growth of the petroleum trade and the rise of Japan and the NICs as suppliers of manufactures. Trade with Pacific Basin countries, covering the ASEAN countries, the East Asian NICs, and the industrialized countries of Japan, Australia, New Zealand, the United States, and Canada,[10] has advanced more rapidly than trade with non-Pacific countries, and accounts for well over half of Singapore's global trade. Trade with ASEAN countries continued to increase in value but declined in relative share to only 17.3 percent in 1981 (excluding trade with Indonesia). The relative decline of Singapore-ASEAN trade reflects the reduced role of Singapore as the entrepôt of the region and the adoption by Singapore of the practice of export-manufacturing for a global market. The formation of ASEAN and regional economic cooperation, in particular the implementation of the ASEAN Preferential Trading Arrangement, has had little impact on the declining trend.

Among the ASEAN countries, Malaysia remains Singapore's leading trading partner, although in its traditional preeminent share of Singapore trade it has been superseded by Japan and the United States. These two countries accounted respectively for 15.1 percent and 12.9 percent of total trade in 1981, as compared with a combined share of 11.3 percent in 1960. Similarly, the East Asian NICs expanded their trade share rapidly to 7.9 percent in 1981. Outside the Pacific Basin countries, the main trends are the relative declines in Singapore-EEC trade and the growing share of Singapore–West Asia trade. Trade with the European Economic Community has been adversely affected by the severance of colonial ties with the United Kingdom and the latter's preoccupation with the Community since 1970. With the growth of the petroleum trade, trade with West Asia boomed. Singapore suffers a chronic and growing deficit in its merchandise trade, and the largest deficit is in the trade with West Asia, as a result of the phenomenal growth in petroleum imports and the slow growth of entrepôt and manufactured exports to and from the region. Large deficits are also recorded in the trade with Japan and the United States.

Singapore imports from a wide variety of sources, as shown in table 6.5. Generally, imports from the advanced industrial countries consisted largely of manufactures, particularly of machinery and equipment. The United States, Australia, and New Zealand however, are also important suppliers of food and the European Economic Community is a supplier of

---

10. The proponents of the Pacific Basin Community usually include the industrialized countries of Japan, the United States, Canada, Australia, and New Zealand, the five ASEAN countries of Indonesia, Malaysia, the Philippines, Singapore, and Thailand, and the East Asian NICs of Hong Kong, Republic of Korea, and Taiwan. Some argue that the countries bordering the Pacific are far larger in number and should include Latin American states on the Pacific Ocean, and some of the other Asia-Pacific countries.

Table 6.5. Major Sources of Merchandise Imports, 1960, 1970, and 1981

	Percentage distribution		
	1960	1970	1981
Southeast Asia	56.5	22.0	16.0
Malaysia	26.4	18.6	12.4
Thailand	3.6	2.0	1.7
Philippines	0.05	0.4	0.4
Northeast Asia	13.5	29.3	26.8
Japan	7.3	19.4	18.8
Hong Kong	2.2	2.5	1.9
Taiwan	0.5	1.7	2.0
Republic of Korea	—	0.5	1.1
South Asia	1.4	1.8	0.9
West Asia	4.3	9.3	26.9
Saudi Arabia	0.3	1.1	18.5
Kuwait	—	4.8	3.4
EEC	14.1	15.6	9.8
United Kingdom	8.9	7.6	3.0
Federal Republic of Germany	1.8	3.4	2.8
France	0.7	1.1	1.7
Other Western Europe	1.7	2.2	2.0
Socialist Eastern Europe	0.4	0.9	0.4
North America	4.2	11.4	13.1
U.S.A.	3.8	10.8	12.6
Canada	0.3	0.5	0.5
Oceania	2.9	5.1	2.6
Australia	2.6	4.5	2.1
New Zealand	0.2	0.5	0.4
Rest of world	1.0	2.5	1.6
Total	100.0	100.0	100.0
Value of imports (S$ million)	4,078	7,534	58,248

Source: Singapore, Ministry of Trade and Industry, *Economic Survey of Singapore 1981*.

alcoholic beverages and tobacco manufactures. Imports from the East Asian NICs consisted largely of manufactures, mainly textiles and electronics, but also food from Taiwan; watches, clocks, toys, and games from Hong Kong; and iron and steel from the Republic of Korea. The main imports from Malaysia are crude rubber, crude petroleum, and, to a lesser extent, vegetable oils and electronic valves.

Foreign Trade and Investment in Singapore

Table 6.6. Major Destinations of Merchandise Exports, 1960, 1970, and 1981

	Percentage distribution		
	1960	1970	1981
Southeast Asia	39.6	34.9	23.5
Malaysia	28.8	21.9	15.6
Thailand	3.1	3.3	4.2
Philippines	1.7	0.3	1.3
Northeast Asia	9.7	14.9	22.7
Japan	4.5	7.6	10.1
Hong Kong	1.7	4.1	8.8
Taiwan	0.2	0.8	1.4
Republic of Korea	—	0.7	1.4
South Asia	2.6	1.7	5.9
West Asia	1.3	2.2	6.5
Saudi Arabia	0.1	0.3	2.4
EEC	18.4	16.3	10.5
United Kingdom	8.2	6.8	2.4
Federal Republic of Germany	2.3	2.9	2.5
France	2.6	2.0	1.8
Other Western Europe	3.5	2.8	1.5
Socialist Eastern Europe	4.7	4.9	1.2
North America	8.4	12.3	14.1
U.S.A.	7.0	11.1	13.2
Canada	1.4	1.2	0.9
Oceania	5.8	4.8	7.3
Australia	3.9	3.4	4.0
New Zealand	1.5	0.4	1.3
Rest of world	5.9	5.3	6.8
Total	100.0	100.0	100.0
Value of exports (S$ million)	3,477	4,756	44,291

Source: Singapore, Ministry of Trade and Industry, *Economic Survey of Singapore 1981*.

As with imports, Singapore's exports show a shift toward Northeast Asia and North America and away from Southeast Asia and Western Europe (see table 6.6). Entrepôt exports to Southeast Asia are dominated by manufactures, while those to Western Europe and Northeast Asia consist largely of nonmanufactures.

For nonentrepôt exports, the major destinations in 1981 were the United States, Japan, the European Economic Community, Hong Kong, and Malaysia, which together accounted for three-fifths of the total nonentrepôt exports. The main markets for petroleum products are in the Asia-Pacific region, particularly Japan, Hong Kong, Malaysia, Australia, New Zealand, and Thailand. By contrast, exports of manufactures are more dependent on markets in North America and Western Europe. The principal markets for clothing, radio and television receivers and other telecommunications apparatus, office and data machines, and photographic apparatus are the United States and the European Economic Community. Plywood and veneer are exported mainly to the European Economic Community and the Middle East, while oil rigs go to the United States and the People's Republic of China. The large exports of electronic valves are destined largely for the United States and the European Economic Community, with lesser markets in Hong Kong, Malaysia, Thailand, and Japan.

Singapore's nonentrepôt exports of petroleum products and manufactures are highly dependent on the multinational corporations which have invested in Singapore. There is thus a close link between foreign investment and the composition and direction of exports. Singapore is also a major beneficiary under the Generalized System of Preferences (GSP) of the United States and the European Economic Community. As a Newly Industrializing Country, Singapore faces the major problems of increasing protectionism by advanced industrial countries and possible graduation to a higher economic status, with the consequent loss of GSP benefits. In the international forums, in ASEAN dialogues with the European Economic Community, the United States, Japan, Canada, Australia, and New Zealand, and in bilateral negotiations, Singapore has lobbied for improved market access for its exports. In exports to the United States, Singapore faces quantitative restrictions on textiles and garments, and the removal of GSP treatment on radios, electric irons, and radio telegraphic equipment. The city-state is particularly concerned about any U.S. move toward country graduation.

The Role Of Direct Foreign Investment

Foreign Investment Policy

Although Singapore's balance of payments on current account has been in chronic deficit, despite the healthy balance in the trade in services, its external reserves continue to rise and its external public debt remains small. Official external reserves in 1980 was over half the size of the GNP and nearly 15 times the size of the external public debt. Debt service in that year accounted for only 2.5 percent of GNP and 1.1 percent of exports of goods and services. The major part of Singapore's external capital requirement has been met by private direct foreign investment, which considerably outweighs private and public external borrowing. In 1980, net inflows of public and publicly guaranteed medium- and long-term loans amounted to only US$30 million, while net foreign direct private investment amounted to US$1.5 billion.

Singapore's official policy toward foreign investment is characterized by three features—the presence of liberal incentives, the absence of restrictions, and a pattern of consistency over the last two decades—which, together with general conditions in the economy, have made this city-state one of the most attractive investment centers in the world. Although there is no specific foreign investment law as such, a wide range of policies and measures have been adopted to attract foreign investment. These include promotion of political stability and social discipline, development of the physical and institutional infrastructure, efficient administrative support, wage restraint and orderly wage increases, enforcement of peaceful industrial relations, manpower development and training, and provision of fiscal incentives. More important than the fiscal incentives has been the general absence of restrictions concerning either the entry or the operation of foreign enterprises. There are no exchange controls, no rules and restrictions governing equity participation, repatriation of capital and remittance of profits, dividends, and interest, and no enforcement of domestic value added content and employment of nationals. There are also no restrictions on the importation of goods and services, and the low level and limited scope of import tariffs facilitate production for export. All the official policies and measures aim at minimizing investment risk, reducing production and marketing costs, and raising the rate of return after tax for the foreign investor.

Singapore's liberal foreign investment policy is part of its overall outward-looking development strategy and philosophy. The enthusiastic encouragement of, and dependence on, private foreign investment for economic development and industrialization since 1960 is perhaps somewhat unusual among developing countries. The main rationale is not lack of domestic financial capital as such, but the officially perceived dearth of industrial entrepreneurs in the absence of any manufacturing tradition, even at the cottage industry level, as well as the urgency of industrialization. In 1978 the Prime Minister succintly explained the official rationale for the open policy toward foreign investment and foreign expertise:

> ... the rate of development necessary if we were to generate the jobs to mop up unemployment, running at 10 percent of the workforce in 1960, could never be achieved at the pace at which Chinese and Indian Singaporean enterprises was slowly moving from traditional retail and entrepôt trade into new manufacturing or servicing industries. [There is] a far greater potential in the expanding subsidiaries of American, European and Japanese corporations. What made Singa-

> pore different in the 1960s from most other countries of Southeast
> Asia was that she had no xenophobic hangover from colonialism. . . .
> We have never suffered from any inhibitions in borrowing capital,
> knowhow, managers, engineers, and marketing capabilities. Far
> from limiting the entry of foreign managers, engineers, and bankers,
> we encourage them to come. . . . Had we tried to go into industry on
> our own, working from first principles, we would never have made it.
> . . . The capital we could have raised from domestic savings and
> foreign loans. However, to acquire the knowhow, to develop the
> management and the markets would have cost us dearly. . . .[11]

Singapore's foreign investment policy is thus entirely pragmatic and devoid of ideological or nationalistic overtones. As an illustration that learning from scratch is a costly business, the Singaporean Prime Minister went on to cite the results of a study by the Economic Development Board (EDB) which showed the different survival rates of local and foreign export-oriented industrial enterprises established since 1960. The failure rate for wholly locally owned enterprises was 38 percent, but that for wholly foreign-owned U.S., European, and Japanese enterprises was only 6 percent; of the latter, there was not a single casualty among the large multinational corporations. The failure rate of wholly foreign-owned enterprises from Hong Kong and Taiwan was 13 percent. Singapore entrepreneurs improved their survival rates when they entered into joint ventures with foreign enterprises. The failure rate for joint ventures with U.S., European, and Japanese enterprises dropped to 7 percent, while that for joint ventures with partners from Hong Kong and Taiwan dropped to 17 percent. Thus, the most successful enterprises, in descending order, were U.S., European, and Japanese wholly foreign-owned enterprises, joint ventures between Singapore and these developed country entrepreneurs, wholly foreign-owned enterprises from Hong Kong and Taiwan, joint ventures between Singapore and other NIC entrepreneurs, and lastly wholly Singapore-owned ventures.

Compared to the turbulent fifties, Singapore in the eighties appears politically stable and socially cohesive and disciplined. Through policy measures, campaigns, and speeches, the political leadership of the People's Action Party (PAP), in power since 1959, has exhorted, molded, and mobilized the population toward the attainment of rapid economic development. The government is effective, if somewhat authoritarian, although it is accused in some quarters of being unnecessarily repressive. It is difficult to quantify the relationship between political stability, and

---

11. Speech delivered by Mr. Lee Kuan Yew to a conference of international business at Orlando, Florida, and reprinted in the *Economic Bulletin*, November 1978.

more particularly social discipline, and the inflow of foreign investment. It can only be inferred that in so far as stability contributes to the continuation of favorable policies toward foreign investment, to the smooth and profitable functioning of business, and to increasing profitability, minimizing investment risks, it provides an important condition for investment inflows. Countries which have experienced political turmoil have witnessed a sharp deceleration in investment inflows. More recently, the uncertainties surrounding Hong Kong's political future have not only somewhat discouraged investment inflows but have led to capital flight on the part of its own entrepreneurial class.

Singapore has established a comprehensive and continually expanding network of physical infrastructures to service the foreign community and the increasingly affluent domestic population. Imports and exports are enhanced by the expansion and modernization of port, airport, and other transportation facilities. Heavy investment in telecommunications facilitates business transactions with the rest of the world. In manufacturing, the provision of estates equipped with industrial amenities and ready-built factory sites contributes to optimal use of land in land-scarce Singapore, and reduces the capital investment requirements of investors, as well as the preproduction planning and implementation period. In addition, various institutions have been established to facilitate the consideration of investment proposals and to develop and manage the various services and facilities required by trade, industry, and financial investors. These include the Economic Development Board, Development Bank of Singapore, Jurong Town Corporation, National Productivity Board, and the like. The public provision of industrial facilities without significant and overt public subsidy is one of the better economic policies aimed at attracting the foreign investor, since there are substantial social as well as private net benefits.

The policies of enforcing industrial peace and wage restraint and orderly wage increases are among the more controversial measures adopted in the last two decades. Because militant trade unionism was seen to be a serious deterrent to both foreign and domestic investment in the late fifties and early sixties, labor laws were enacted to curb the power of trade unions and to provide for a subsequent "symbiotic relationship" between the trade union movement and the ruling political party. Industrial disputes dropped markedly in the latter part of the sixties and industrial peace was maintained throughout the seventies. In more recent years, the trade union movement has not only played a positive role in contributing to industrial peace, but has also been in the forefront in improving worker productivity through promotion of better worker attitudes, constructive rather than confrontational labor-management relations, quality control circles, and programs for upgrading the educational and skill level of the workforce.

Restrictive labor legislation and high unemployment kept the lid on wage increases in the sixties. As the economy moved toward full employment at the turn of the seventies, upward pressures on wages became more evident. Labor scarcity was to some extent relieved by relaxing restrictions on the inflow of foreign workers and encouraging more women to enter the labor force. In 1972 the National Wages Council was formed, with tripartite representation from government, employers, and labor to provide for orderly wage increases through annual nonmandatory wage guidelines. Annual wage guidelines were determined by factors such as productivity growth, inflation rates domestically and abroad, relative wage levels of Singapore and its competitors in world markets, export competitiveness of Singapore's goods and services, and the general profitability of companies. Overall, the NWC guideline recommendations in the 1972–78 period were considered modest, after discounting for the sharp increases in the Consumer Price Index in 1973–74. Although nonmandatory, the NWC guidelines were the main factor in actual wage determination, covering almost all employees in the public sector, and more than 80 percent of employees in the private sector by 1978. Actual wage increases, however, show variations, being above, below, or actually in line with the NWC guidelines.

The slow wage movements in the economy led subsequently to distortions in the labor market. Workers resorted to job hopping to secure higher wages. Employers, helped by the large inflow of foreign workers, continued to adopt labor-intensive practices which became increasingly incompatible with the decelerating growth of the domestic labor force and had adverse effects on productivity performance. In 1979, the NWC departed from earlier policy and instituted a three-year accelerated wage increase to bring wage levels more in line with market forces. The guidelines provided for increases in national wage costs of some 20 percent in 1979/80, 19 percent in 1980/81 and 14–20 percent in 1981/82. During this period the increase in the Consumer Price Index ranged from 4.0 to 8.5 percent. The wage guidelines for 1982/83 returned to a moderate level, and the government announced its intention of playing a lesser role in NWC deliberations and allowing greater labor and management discretion to avoid labor-market distortions.

After the implementation of the wage-correction policy in 1979, the Economic Development Board reported that there had been no let-up in the number of investment inquiries and the inflow of foreign investments. Although rising wage costs have reduced the competitiveness of Singapore as a manufacturing base for labor-intensive industries, the investment promotion strategy in recent years, and particularly after 1978, emphasizes attracting foreign investments with higher technology, skills, and value added content.

Manpower development is also an important aspect of forming an industrially competitive workforce. Until the late sixties, Singapore's educational system was heavily biased toward nontechnical education, with more than 90 percent of all students enrolled in nontechnical schools. The acute shortage of technically trained youths and the high unemployment rate among those who had nontechnical backgrounds led to the revamping of the educational system in 1968. The system began to emphasize technical education in schools and engineering education in tertiary institutions, supplemented by accelerated vocational and industrial training provided by the government Vocational and Industrial Training Board, Economic Development Board, and National Productivity Board. In 1979 the government established the Skills Development Fund from levies on employers, which were increased to 4 percent of employee earnings in 1980. The fund furnishes financial grants to companies with approved training schemes.

When we consider the sort of fiscal incentives which Singapore provides to encourage foreign investment, we find that there has been only a limited use of the tariff instrument because of the obvious limitation of the small domestic market and the emphasis on exports, and a more liberal use of tax concessions and exemptions. The efficacy of tax incentives in attracting foreign investment continues to be debated. Critics point to questionnaire surveys which show that the tax incentive is only marginal in investment decision making.[12] In so far as some countries offer tax holidays and others do not, however, in the eyes of the investor, the latter would appear to be less favorably inclined toward foreign investment. Moreover, while investment in resource development and processing as well as in industries and activities catering to the domestic market may be location-specific, export-oriented industries and services are generally footloose. For such industries as electronics, textiles, and clothing, which are commonly found in export-processing zones in developing countries, the tax holiday may be a marginal but nonetheless important factor in choosing between alternative off-shore production locations; the tax holiday, it is argued, is initially intended to compensate the investor for the disadvantages of establishing a business in a particular foreign location. The major tax incentives which Singapore has offered investors have been outlined in an earlier section of this chapter.

As other aspects of the investment climate in Singapore improve, less

---

12. See, for example, Helen Hughes' summary (Hughes and You 1969).

reliance will need to be placed on tax incentives. The incentives can also become increasingly selective; instead of an overall instrument to promote foreign investment inflows, they can be designed to attract certain types of foreign investors and can be tied, for example, to export performance and the development of local research and development facilities. In fact, with the current emphasis on economic restructuring in Singapore, tax incentives have been directed at encouraging technological upgrading, including mechanization and automation and the establishment of local research and development facilities.

Direct foreign investments are welcomed in almost all areas of economic activity in Singapore, with the notable exceptions of defense industries and the mass media. Emphasis, however, has been on industrial investment, so that foreign investment has become highly dominant in the manufacturing sector. In the other sectors of the economy, although there has been a longer tradition of foreign investment, there is less foreign dominance. In trade, the British agency houses have phased out or restructured their operations in the Singapore-Malaysia region. In 1978, foreign equity participation in wholesale trade amounted to 34.1 percent.

Some trading concerns have been established in Singapore as a service to industrial clients that moved to Singapore earlier. Tax incentives have also been offered in recent years to entice international trading companies to establish regional headquarters, warehousing, and distribution centers in Singapore.

Foreign paid-up capital accounted for a third of equity capital in the financial sector, being highest among merchant banks. Since the late sixties, foreign financial institutions have been actively encouraged, in an effort to promote Singapore as an off-shore financial center, which has necessitated the development of a wide range of financial institutions and services and the upgrading of local financial expertise. In recent years various fiscal incentives have been introduced to further promote Singapore as a financial center.

Lately, attention of policy makers has been directed to encouraging greater inflow of foreign expertise in professional services, as well as in the construction and retail trade sectors. Foreign participation is increasingly welcomed in all sectors of the economy, not only to augment domestic resources, but also to provide competition in the local market and to impel local entrepreneurs to restructure, modernize, and upgrade their production and service activities.

Trends and Patterns in Foreign Investment in Manufacturing

A study by Hughes and You (1969) found that up to the outbreak of World War II, there were only 11 foreign manufacturers in Singapore. These were the subsidiaries of British, U.S., and Australian enterprises. The slow growth of foreign manufacturing enterprises in the prewar and immediate postwar years may be attributed to the relative attraction of investment in the booming rubber and tin industries in neighboring Malaya, and in rubber processing, tin smelting, trading, and financial activities in Singapore. Manufacturing investment was not attractive because of the small domestic market, the free-trade policy which further segmented this market, the high prevailing wages in trade and service activities which rendered labor-intensive manufacturing uncompetitive, and the widespread industrial unrest prevalent in the fifties.

It is difficult to establish the extent to which foreign investment inflows into manufacturing activities in Singapore after 1960 can be ascribed to Singapore's policies toward such investments. The difficulty is that these investments took place in response to both home-country push factors and host-country pull factors, as well as to industry-specific and firm-specific factors. Hymer, Kindleberger, Vernon, and others have explained foreign investment by Western-type multinational corporations largely in terms of oligopolistic market structures, technological leads, and the product cycle.[13] Kojima (1978) and Ozawa (1977) explained Japanese direct overseas investments in terms of push factors arising from the rapid development of the Japanese economy in the postwar years. Wells (1977) has identified other motivations for investment from developing countries.

During the import-substitution phase of industrialization in the first half of the sixties, the volume of investment inflows was not large, amounting to only S$157 million by 1965 (see table 6.7). Among the reasons for this are the small size of the domestic market, uncertainties concerning the implementation of the Malaysian common market proposal, the low level of tariff and quota protection, and the generally unfavorable political and industrial relations climate. When the common market proposal collapsed there was some shelving of investment commitments and scaling down of plant sizes. Import-substituting investments were concentrated in food processing and manufacture, metal products, and to a lesser extent in chemicals, rubber products, wood, and paper products.

Export-oriented foreign investments in manufacturing prior to 1968 were undertaken mainly in petroleum refining and in textile and garment manufacture. The first petroleum refinery was installed by Shell in the early sixties as a logical extension of its oil-bunkering installation and in response to the pioneer tax holiday. Given the oligopolistic structure of the industry, the Shell move was followed in quick succession by the other oil majors with distribution facilities in Singapore. In spite of liberal tax

---

13. For a summary, see Agarwal (1980).

Table 6.7. Foreign Investment in the Manufacturing Sector, 1965 and 1980

	Percentage Distribution of Cumulative Foreign Gross Fixed Assets in Manufacturing	
Industry Group	1965	1980
Food, beverages, & tobacco products	5.7	3.2
Textiles		2.9
Wearing apparel, made-up textiles, & footwear	4.5	2.0
Leather & rubber products	5.1	0.8
Wood & cork products	1.9	3.3
Paper & paper products		1.4
Industrial chemicals	3.2	1.6
Other chemical products		2.3
Petroleum products	63.1	42.0
Plastic products	1.9	1.3
Nonmetallic mineral products	1.9	1.7
Basic metal industries		0.8
Fabricated metal products	12.1	3.5
Nonelectrical machinery		7.5
Electrical machinery & electronics	0.6	16.1
Transport equipment & oil rigs	0.0	4.5
Precision equipment & photographic goods	0.0	4.2
Other manufacturing industries		1.0
Total	100.0	100.0
Value (S$ millions)	157	7,520

Source: Singapore, Economic Development Board, Annual Report.

holidays, the main factor determining location in Singapore was geographical. In the sixties the oil majors were locating refinery capacities near market centers, and Singapore was suitably sited along the main tanker route between the Middle East on the one hand, and Japan and Australia on the other. It was the hub of Southeast Asia, with a deep water harbor and relatively stable political and economic situation. The refineries in Singapore were essentially balancing refineries and the products, besides servicing the domestic market and providing bunkering for ships and aircraft stopping at Singapore, were exported largely to Asian markets.

Foreign investment in textiles and garments was differently motivated and came from other sources. The chief investors were from Hong Kong and Taiwan. Investments were undertaken largely by family-type enterprises rather than by large multinational corporations, and came about in response to two main factors. The first was the need to circumvent quota restrictions imposed by major OECD importers on Hong Kong and Taiwan textiles and garments. Locating in Singapore allowed these suppliers to continue to expand their operations and export to these markets, and they could enjoy the additional advantages of geographical proximity to their homelands, cultural familiarity, and the availability of generous investment incentives. The second factor was that unsettled political conditions in Hong Kong and in the late sixties in Taiwan led to further inflows of investment into Singapore in search of risk diversification. The fact that Singapore offered permanent residence to investors made it even more attractive.

The main upsurge of foreign investment into export manufacturing in Singapore took place from 1968 on and has been concentrated in the electrical-electronics and precision-instrument group of industries. The first investments were undertaken by U.S. multinational corporations, followed later by the Europeans, the Japanese, and then firms from Hong Kong. Oligopolistic market structures, and widening wage differentials motivated U.S. multinational corporations to move into off-shore production. In Asia, the first locations were in Japan and then in Hong Kong, the Republic of Korea, and Taiwan. For the major part of the sixties such investments were not attracted to Singapore because of high wages, political uncertainties, and the poor industrial relations climate. It was only after 1967, when various measures were implemented to promote export manufacturing and to stabilize the labor market, that Singapore was able to attract Western multinational corporations in search of global sourcing.

During this period there were also substantial inflows of foreign capital to establish shipyards. The nucleus of the shipbuilding and ship-repairing industry was established by two government-owned shipyards converted to commercial use from the British naval dockyard. Increased shipping traffic, particularly of tankers, and oil exploration activities in surrounding waters, provided the demand pull for this highly location-specific industry, and Singapore became a major ship repair center and builder of oil rigs.

The dominance of foreign investment in manufacturing is evident from table 6.8. Foreign investors have dramatically increased production, exports, and employment contributions in both absolute and relative terms, reflecting the success of Singapore's efforts to attract foreign investment as well as the absence of restrictions on 100 percent foreign equity holdings. Although wholly foreign-owned enterprises were not disallowed or restricted, the government through the Economic Development Board sought to encourage joint ventures between local and foreign enterprises to maximize the domestic-linkage and learning effects. Thus, the number of joint ventures between 1963 and 1980 grew from 69 to 686, with corre-

Table 6.8. Relative Shares of Foreign and Local Investments in the Manufacturing Sector, 1963 and 1980

Capital Structure of Establishments	Number of Establishments	Output	Value Added	Export Sales	Employment
1963					
Total manufacturing	858	100.0	100.0	100.0	100.0
Wholly foreign-owned	40	30.9	28.5	33.1	12.4
Joint ventures	69	22.7	29.0	24.3	20.3
Wholly locally-owned	749	46.4	42.5	42.6	67.3
1980					
Total manufacturing	3,355	100.0	100.0	100.0	100.0
Wholly foreign-owned	516	58.7	54.1	71.5	39.9
Joint ventures	686	25.7	26.8	21.4	31.9
Wholly locally-owned	2,153	15.6	19.1	7.1	28.2

Columns 3–6 show Percentage distribution.

Source: Singapore, Department of Statistics, *Report on the Census of Industrial Production* (1980) and unpublished data for 1963.

spondingly increased shares of manufacturing output and employment. However, the joint venture contribution to export sales showed a relative decline. Although wholly locally owned manufacturing enterprises grew rapidly from 749 in 1963 to 2,153 by 1980, the majority of them remained small and their relative contribution to production, export sales, and employment slipped dramatically.

Foreign-owned and locally owned establishments show widely different performance characteristics (table 6.9). On the average, wholly foreign-owned establishments are much larger in size than locally owned establishments, and the differential has widened since 1963. Labor productivity, as measured by value added per worker, is much higher in the wholly foreign-owned establishments than in the joint ventures, and in turn, higher in the joint ventures than in the wholly locally owned establishments. However, the productivity differentials among the three categories of establishment narrowed between 1963 and 1980. This is also evident in the average remuneration paid to workers. While a substantial gap existed between foreign-owned and locally owned establishments in 1963, by 1980 the differential was reduced to less than 10 percent.

Labor cost per unit of output or value added, that is, the labor content, continues to show wide differentials between foreign-owned and locally owned establishments. The high ratios for wholly locally owned establishments reflect the high labor intensity of these enterprises, both in terms of industry-product mix and the process mix. As such, the wage-correction

Table 6.9. Selected Characteristics of Foreign and Local Establishments in the Manufacturing Sector, 1963 and 1980

	Wholly Foreign-owned Establishments	Joint Venture Establishments	Wholly Locally-owned Establishments	Total Manufacturing Establishments
1963				
Employment per establishment (number)	114	108	33	43
Output per worker (S$ thousands)	57	26	16	23
Value added per worker (S$ thousands)	16	10	4	7
Remuneration per worker (S$ thousands)	4.2	3.2	2.2	2.7
Remuneration/output ratio (%)	7.3	12.5	14.0	11.6
Remuneration/value added ratio (%)	26.2	32.6	51.1	38.6
Export/total sales ratio (%)	28.4	28.3	24.8	26.7
1980				
Employment per establishment (number)	221	133	37	85
Output per worker (S$ thousands)	163	89	62	111
Value added per worker (S$ thousands)	40	25	20	30
Remuneration per worker (S$ thousands)	9.1	9.1	8.3	8.9
Remuneration/output ratio (%)	5.6	10.2	13.4	8.0
Remuneration/value added ratio (%)	22.4	36.2	40.9	29.6
Export/total sales ratio (%)	74.8	52.8	28.0	62.0

Source: Singapore, Department of Statistics, *Report on the Census of Industrial Production* (1980) and unpublished data for 1963.

policy of the 1979–82 period impinged most heavily on locally owned enterprises, forcing them either to restructure to escape the burden of rising labor costs and increasing labor scarcity, or to cease operations altogether.

The most glaring performance differential between foreign-owned and locally owned establishments lies in the area of exporting. In 1963, low export orientation, as measured by the export/total sales ratio, characterized both foreign-owned and locally owned establishments. The attraction of foreign investment catering largely to the export market raised the export/total sales ratio of wholly foreign-owned establishments to 75 percent, and of joint ventures to more than 50 percent. Wholly locally owned establishments, however, showed only a very marginal improvement in overall export orientation. Why locally owned enterprises on their own have been unable to respond to the export-oriented manufacturing objective of the government requires further analysis.

Singapore's foreign investment policy is to encourage investment from diverse sources and to provide no preferential treatment from any particular source, in order to minimize the negative effects of a high dependence on such investment. Inevitably, however, the sourcing pattern of foreign investment reflects the relative importance of various countries as capital exporters. Data on gross fixed assets show that as of 1979, the European Economic Community was the largest foreign investor group in Singapore, accounting for 36.1 percent of total foreign gross fixed assets in manufacturing, followed by the United States (28.6 percent), Japan (16.5 percent), Hong Kong (5.1 percent), and Taiwan (4.4 percent).[14]

Investments from the European Economic Community were dominated by the Shell Group, which represented the largest single foreign investment in Singapore. Secondary concentrations of British and Dutch investment were in food, beverages, and tobacco, transport equipment, chemicals, electronics and electrical machinery, and supplies. The largest investment from West Germany was in the photographic-equipment industry. However, in 1981 the Singapore subsidiary of Rollei Werke went into receivership as a result of financial difficulties in the parent company. United States investments also were dominated by the petroleum refineries, but the United States had the additional role of being a leading investor in the electronics industry and in nonelectrical machinery.

Unlike European and U.S. investors, the Japanese have not invested in petroleum refineries in Singapore. One of the earliest Japanese investments in Singapore was in such a refinery, but it was soon sold to a major British oil firm. Since then, Japanese investments have shown a more even spread across industries. Japanese investments in Singapore tend to be undertaken by large Japanese corportions; unlike the pattern of Japanese investment in many East Asian and ASEAN countries, small and medium-sized Japanese enterprises are not prominent investors in Singapore. Investments from Hong Kong and Taiwan have an industrial distribution which differs from that of investments from advanced countries; they are concentrated mainly in food, textiles and garments, transport equipment, and wood products.

The contributions of investments from major investor countries to production, export sales, and employment in the manufacturing sector are shown in table 6.10. Investors from the European Economic Community and other European countries combined accounted for less than 5 percent of manufacturing establishments in 1980, but contributed 34.0 percent to output, 44.6 percent to export sales, and 12.5 percent to employment in that sector. Of these countries, the Netherlands clearly leads with its huge investments in petroleum refining. The United Kingdom made a surprisingly small contribution to manufacturing development in Singapore in

---

14. Data from the Economic Development Board.

Table 6.10. Investments in the Manufacturing Sector by Major Source of Capital, 1980

	Percentage distribution				
Major Source of Capital	Establishments	Output	Value Added	Export Sales	Employment
Total manufacturing	100.0	100.0	100.0	100.0	100.0
Local establishments	75.6	31.0	33.4	18.0	42.5
Foreign establishments	24.4	69.0	66.6	82.0	57.5
Europe	4.9	34.0	24.5	44.6	12.5
U.S.A.	2.9	17.1	21.2	19.0	12.8
Japan	5.2	9.5	10.8	10.4	15.6
Hong Kong	2.5	3.0	3.6	3.6	6.0
Taiwan	0.4	0.6	0.5	0.6	1.1
Others	8.4	4.9	6.0	3.8	9.7

Source: Singapore, Department of Statistics, *Report on the Census of Industrial Production, 1980*.

view of its long colonial tradition there. Since European investments are dominated by petroleum refining, their contributions to employment creation have been much smaller than their contributions to output and export sales.

United States investors made the second largest contribution to manufacturing output and exports and the third in terms of employment; the U.S. employment contribution has also been affected by its petroleum investment. By way of contrast, Japanese investors led in contribution to manufacturing employment, reflecting the greater labor intensity of Japanese operations. Investments from Hong Kong and Taiwan contributed more to employment than to output and export sales; they are relatively labor-intensive and more domestic-market-oriented.

Development Prospects And Issues

In the late fifties, when Singapore was preparing for self-government after nearly one and a half centuries of British colonial rule, doubts were raised about the economic viability of the colony as an independent political entity because of its physical size—581 square kilometers—its lack of an economic hinterland and natural resources, the poor growth prospects for entrepôt trade, and the small domestic market. There was thus an economic rationale for the political merger with Malaya and the British Borneo territories, forming the Federation of Malaysia in September 1963. The merger proved to be short-lived and Singapore became an unplanned and an unwilling independent republic in August 1965. Singapore remained an essentially free-trade but no longer laissez-faire economy as the government embarked on development planning and took bold measures to guide the economy. The years since political independence have seen the Singapore economy not only surviving, but reaching the ranks of the Newly Industrializing Countries in the seventies, and somewhat fearfully awaiting the inevitable graduation into developed country status in the eighties.

The economic future of Singapore seems much more secure in the eighties than it did in the turbulent late fifties or the traumatic mid-sixties. Growth, however, remains the primary preoccupation of policy makers, who continually exhort the work force to shun complacency and the welfare state, lest the growth momentum dissipate. For a city-state highly dependent on foreign trade, and with a development strategy which focuses on foreign investment, prospects for growth must necessarily be tied to a large extent on the condition of the world economy. At the present time and in the near future, Singapore has three major concerns. One is with OECD protectionism which impinges on the city-state's ability to export and thus to attract export-oriented foreign investment. The second is Singapore's need to restructure rapidly to meet external pressures of competition from lesser developed countries. The third is the internal constraint of rising wages and a growing labor shortage. For the longer term, there is concern over the aging population and labor force and the implications of this demographic change for the social service burden and the city-state's ability to respond continuously to changing external circumstances.

Of increasing interest, apart from growth prospects, are the related issues of the pattern and quality of development, not in the traditional sense of rural-urban, agricultural-industrial, inward-outward-looking, and growth-equity dichotomies, but rather in terms of the appropriate role for the government, the relative development of the industrial and service sectors, and the relative reliance on foreign investment and domestic enterprise.

Regarding the government's role, there is debate whether the government should continue to maintain its dominant economic role and at the same time play a reduced social role. The government, especially in the economic sphere, is generally credited with being a strong positive factor in Singapore's development performance. However, critics point to Hong Kong with its laissez-faire economy to refute the claim that government intervention and participation in the development process is necessary. Advocates of a return to laissez-faire emphasize the efficiency of the market, and argue that even though the Singapore government has performed more efficiently than most, largely by adhering closely to the price mechanism, it has also been guilty of lack of foresight and has made some wrong decisions. Specific examples which are cited are government promotion of a petrochemical industry, which took more than a decade to reach the production stage, and the government's undue influence in the tripartite National Wages Council negotiations, which contributed to the distortion of the labor market and the delay in economic restructuring. Advocates of government intervention, however, point to the weakness of domestic industrial entrepreneurship and the need for the government both to play a catalytic role and to act as a counterpoise to the dominant foreign enterprises. This group maintains even more strongly that the government should not attempt to play a reduced role in the provision of such social services as medical and welfare benefits by placing a greater responsibility for such care on the individual, the family, and the private sector employer. It argues that reduced government responsibility in these areas will affect the poor, the handicapped, and the aged more severely than other segments of society.

For many countries, the development-strategy debate centers on the relative merits of domestic-oriented, self-reliant development and export-led industrialization, especially when the latter takes on the form of enclave development in export-processing zones. In the city-state of Singapore there is common agreement that industrialization must be export-led. What remains to be done is the creation of more effective domestic linkages. More debatable, however, is the question whether government incentives should be directed at manufacturing more than at other sectors of the economy, in particular the services. Traditionally Singapore has prospered as a service economy, while industrialization has been fostered through a high degree of government intervention and is increasingly dependent on foreign capital, enterprise, technology, and marketing expertise. To a large extent, the industry-service sector debate represents a false dichotomy. In the final analysis, the economic activities to be fostered must be those which show the greatest competitive edge and export potential. Such activities straddle both the manufacturing and service sectors of the economy.

Perhaps the most controversial aspect of Singapore's development strategy is the heavy and growing dependence on foreign investment, expertise, and labor. Of the four Asian NICs (Singapore, Hong Kong, Republic of Korea, and Taiwan) Singapore is the most heavily dependent on direct foreign investment and expertise. After two decades of industrialization, the dependence on direct foreign investment has increased rather than lessened. The most serious aspect of the problem is the inability of local entrepreneurs to export and to move into the more dynamic sectors of manufacturing. With economic restructuring in the eighties, local entrepreneurs appear even less competitive. Unlike the situation in many Newly Industrializing Countries, local entrepreneurs in

Singapore have not been nurtured by infant industry protection, and existing investment incentives tend to discriminate against them, since foreign enterprises qualify more easily under the various criteria that govern the award of those incentives. Although local entrepreneurs may be blamed for their inertia during the period of rapid economic growth, increased government efforts can be directed at promoting joint ventures with foreign enterprises, upgrading the technical, managerial, and marketing skills of local enterprises, offering financial assistance for the adoption of modern machinery and technology, and providing export market information. Fortunately, in recent years, there has been increased government recognition of the plight of local entrepreneurs, with greater efforts, as a result, to help them upgrade. But support for local enterprise should not be taken to imply a denigration of direct foreign investment, which has played a significant and generally beneficial role in Singapore's rapid development.

References

Agarwal, J. P. 1980. "Determinants of Foreign Direct Investment: A Survey." *Weltwirtschaftliches Archiv* 116.

Balassa, Bela, and Associates. 1971. *The Structure of Protection in Developing Countries*. Baltimore, Md.: Johns Hopkins Press.

Chia Siow Yue. 1980. "Singapore's Trade and Development Strategy and ASEAN Economic Cooperation, with special reference to the ASEAN Common Approach to Foreign Economic Relations." In Ross Garnaut, ed., *ASEAN in a Changing Pacific and World Economy*. Canberra: Australian National University Press.

Chia Siow Yue. 1982. *Export Processing and Industrialization: The Case of Singapore*. Bangkok: ILO-ARTEP (April). Monograph.

Chia Siow Yue. 1982. *Direct Foreign Investment in Manufacturing and the Impact on Employment and Export Performance in Singapore*. CAMS Funded Project. Singapore: National University of Singapore (May). Monograph.

Hughes, Helen, and You Poh Seng, eds., 1969. *Foreign Investment and Industrialisation in Singapore*. Canberra: Australian National University Press.

Kojima, Kiyoshi. 1978. *Direct Foreign Investment: A Japanese Model of Multinational Business Operations*. London: Croom Helm.

Ozawa, Terutomo. 1979. "International Investment and Industrial Structure: New Theoretical Implications from the Japanese Experience." *Oxford Economic Papers* 31.

Pang Eng Fong. 1976. "Growth, Equity and Race." In Riaz Hassan, ed., *Singapore: Society in Transition*. Kuala Lumpur: Oxford University Press.

Tan, Augustine, and Ow Chin Hock. 1978. *A Study of Industrial Protection in Singapore*. Singapore: University of Singapore. Monograph.

Wells, Louis T., Jr. 1977. "The Internationalisation of Firms from Developing Countries." In T. Agmon and Charles Kindleberger, eds., *Multinationals from Small Countries.* Cambridge, Mass.: MIT Press.

World Bank. 1982. *World Development Report, 1982.* Washington, D.C.

Singapore Government Documents

Department of Statistics. *Report on the Census of Industrial Production.* Various years.

Department of Statistics. 1978. *Singapore Input-Output Tables 1973* (July).

Department of Statistics. *Singapore Trade Statistics—Imports and Exports.* Various issues.

Department of Statistics. *Singapore Yearbook of Statistics.* Various issues.

Ministry of Trade & Industry. *Economic Survey of Singapore.* Various issues.

National Wages Council. 1978. *Information Booklet.*

V Comparative Aspects of Development in the Four Nations

7   Foreign Trade and Investment as Boosters for Take-off: The Experiences of the Four Asian Newly Industrializing Countries
S. C. Tsiang and Rong-I Wu

Introduction

The process through which a poor, underdeveloped country gradually breaks loose from stagnation at a low per capita income level and develops the capability for continuous growth in the living standard of its people has been described by W. W. Rostow (1961) as the economic take-off. This term aptly conveys the idea that what used to be a strenuous and often futile, self-defeating struggle for a developing country can, after a certain stage of preparation is attained, become a facile self-sustaining process. The recent experience of the four Asian Newly Industrializing Countries (NICs)—the Republic of China in Taiwan, South Korea, Hong Kong, and Singapore—provides a good illustration of this kind of transformation process.

The mechanism of growth in the real per capita income of a country is essentially the gradual increase in its productive capacity. Assuming that the natural resources of the country are more or less fixed, the ways to increase per capita productivity are principally (1) to increase the productive capital per head, and (2) to increase productivity by improved techniques and other means. The introduction of improved techniques, however, is often connected with the increase in capital, since the improved technique is often incorporated in, or has to be applied together with, new capital equipment. Consequently, the increase in productive capital is commonly regarded as the most essential condition for real economic growth.

Such an increase must be financed by savings, which in the early stage of development may be borrowed or secured as grants and aid from abroad. For the country to advance into continuous self-sustained growth, however, the necessary funds must eventually come from domestic savings. W. A. Lewis once remarked that "the central problem in the theory of economic growth is to understand the process by which a community is converted from being a 5 percent to 12 percent saver (investor)—with all the changes in attitudes, in institutions and in techniques which accompany this conversion" (1955, pp. 225–26).

The figure of 12 percent for the ratio of savings to national income as a rough dividing line between a post-take-off and pre-take-off economy was not pulled out of thin air. The implicit assumption behind this rough estimate is that the annual rate of population growth can be expected to be about 3 percent, and that the appropriate capital/output ratio in most cases is roughly between 3 and 4 percent. Thus with a domestic savings ratio of 12 percent or more, the economy should be able to increase its capital/labor ratio continuously through its own domestic savings.

An underdeveloped country is by definition a country with a low per capita income, so low that it is not far above the bare subsistence level. It is extremely hard for such a country to save any significant percentage of its national income. Even the low 5 percent mentioned by Lewis might be an optimistic estimate. Yet with modern improved medical services, the population often increases in spite of a low standard of living. The rate of population growth would thus offset any increase in capital that the country might manage to finance with domestic savings and foreign assistance, and cause real per capita income (or standard of living) to stagnate at a low level. Such stagnation is sometimes called the poverty trap, and the attempts of a poor, underdeveloped country to break loose from it by its own efforts has frequently been compared with lifting oneself up by one's own bootstraps.

Four Asian countries, all of which are heavily overpopulated and none of which is by any standard richly endowed with natural resources, have managed during the past 20 years or so to get out of the poverty trap, apparently without much difficulty, and have successfully launched themselves into continuous self-sustained growth with spectacular increases in real per capita income.

The Theoretical Framework

How this process can come about can be shown by a diagram that one of the authors developed in a previous article (Tsiang 1964).[1] Since the growth of the real per capita income of a country, given its natural resources, depends essentially upon the productive capital per capita, we measure capital per unit of labor, $r = K/L$, along the horizontal axis as the all-important explanatory variable, and draw first the real income per head $\bar{Y}$ of the country as a function of r (taking as givens the natural resources and the state of technology). Assuming a usual well-behaved production func-

1. For a condensed version of the model, see the appendix.

tion of positive but diminishing marginal productivity of capital per unit of labor, this will be a rising curve with a diminishing upward slope. The savings per unit of labor $\overline{S}$ may be drawn as a curve some distance below the output-per-capita curve, as savings is generally a fractional function of income. We shall not, however, adopt the stylized assumption of R. M. Solow (1958) that savings is a constant proportion of the national income, as it does not accord with the cases of developing countries. Instead, we shall assume more realistically that at very low income per capita savings will be negative, and that when real per capita income approaches the subsistence level, savings will gradually rise to a positive level and then rise even faster than income per head, thus becoming an increasing proportion of the latter. That is, the supply of savings per capita, (the $\overline{S}$ curve), will take the shape shown in figure 7.1.

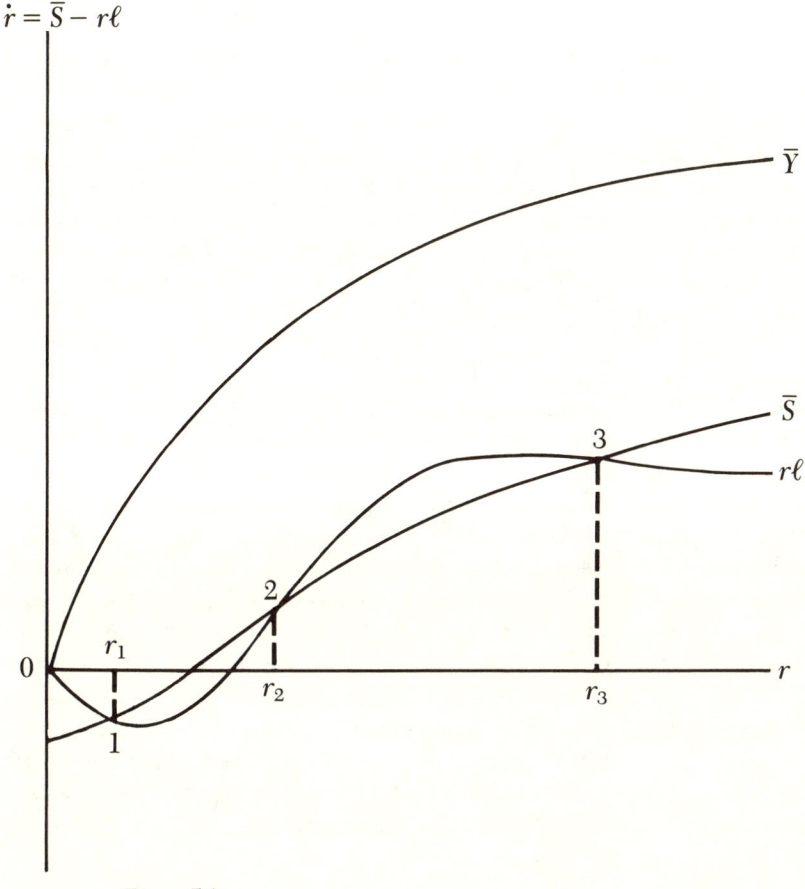

$\dot{r} = \overline{S} - r\ell$

Figure 7.1.

Next we shall draw a curve, the vertical coordinate of which measures the requirement of capital on a per capita basis to maintain the increase in the working population with the same amount of capital per head as has already been attained, i.e., $K/L \cdot \dot{L}/L = r\ell$, where $\ell = \dot{L}/L$, is the rate of growth of population. This quantity obviously rises with the increases in r, but it will also vary with ℓ. We shall assume, in accordance with the neo-Malthusian population theory, that population growth is a function of real income per head such that below the subsistence level of income per head, ℓ will be negative, and that it will increase with real income per head, mainly because of the falling off of the death rate, until it reaches a certain maximum. After that, the theory continues, ℓ will gradually decline because higher real per capita income brings the awareness of the possibility of family planning to an increasing proportion of the population. Thus, the curve representing $r\ell$ would first dip to the negative side because ℓ would be negative for a very low level of real income per head, and hence for a very low level of r, and then rise rather rapidly as r increases, because ℓ would also rise toward its maximum. After ℓ reaches its maximum, the rising slope of the $r\ell$ curve would gradually decline as ℓ declines. The $r\ell$ curve, therefore, will be S-shaped as shown in figure 7.1.

It is likely that $\bar{S}$ and $r\ell$ curves will intersect at several points as shown in figure 7.1, creating stable as well as unstable equilibrium points for economic growth. For instance, points of intersection like 1 and 3 are unstable equilibria, whereas 2 is a stable one. An excess of $\bar{S}$ over $r\ell$ (i.e., when the $\bar{S}$ curve lies above the $r\ell$ curve) implies that r, the capital per unit of labor, will increase (i.e., $\dot{r} > 0$), whereas an excess of $r\ell$ over $\bar{S}$ (i.e., when the $r\ell$ curve lies above the S curve) implies that r will decrease (i.e., $\dot{r} < 0$).[2] A slight deviation of r from either r_1 or r_3, corresponding to the intersection 1 or 3, respectively, in either direction would bring about movement of r (i.e., $\dot{r}$), as measured by the vertical distance between $\bar{S}$ and $r\ell$ curves, pushing it further and further away from r_1 or r_3, as the case may be. On the other hand, any deviation of r from r_2 corresponding to intersection point 2 in either direction would bring about changes in r (as measured by the vertical distance between $\bar{S}$ and $r\ell$ curves) and bring it back to r_2.

An underdeveloped economy, before achieving take-off, may be characterized as one that is bogged down at a low-income stable equilibrium point such as 2, where the corresponding capital/labor ratio r_2 yields a real income per head close to the bare subsistence level (i.e., the real income per head that corresponds to the point of intersection of the $r\ell$ curve with the horizontal axis). The fundamental problem of economic development is how to raise the capital/labor ratio in the economy from such a low yet

---

2. $\dot{r} = dr/dt = d(K/L)/dt = \dot{K}/L - (K/L)(\dot{L}/L) = \bar{S} - r\ell$, when $\bar{S} = \dot{K}/L$.

stubbornly stable level as r_2, against the forces tending always to push it back to where it started, to a level beyond r_3, from which it will be able to take off into self-sustained growth—until perhaps some possible high-level equilibrium point is reached again (not shown in our diagram).

Thus it has been suggested that the hurdle for take-off might be cleared if the current capital/labor ratio r could be pushed beyond the hump of the $r\ell$ curve between interesections 2 and 3 by an injection of a giant additional dose of capital either coming from outside or created through forced extra exertion of the domestic population as attempted in some totalitarian countries (i.e., the Big Push Theory, or the Great Leap Forward).[3] This is certainly theoretically possible, provided the push is carried through to a genuine take-off point like r_3. If the push stops short of reaching a point like r_3, the economy will retrogress toward a low-income stable equilibrium point such as r_2 and remain bogged down there.

External assistance such as foreign economic aid and capital imports can be powerful boosters for domestic preparation for the take-off, and would undoubtedly shorten the process even if they were not massive enough in themselves to propel a country into a successful take-off. Domestic measures which an underdeveloped country may adopt on its own to prepare for take-off are (1) to lower the $r\ell$ curve by reducing the net reproduction rate of the domestic population at each level of per capita income (hence at each level of r); (2) by raising the $\bar{S}$ curve through increasing the willingness of the domestic population to save at each level of per capita income and hence at each level of r; (3) by introducing improved technology that would increase the real capita productivity at each level of the capital/labor ratio to overcome the possible adverse effect of the increasing population pressure on fixed natural resources. This would have the effect of shifting the $\bar{S}$ curve upward and to the left relative to the $r\ell$ curve (Tsiang 1964, pp. 327–37). When the $\bar{S}$ curve is sufficiently shifted upward and/or leftward relative to the $r\ell$, the two points of intersection 2 and 3 converge so that the $\bar{S}$ and $r\ell$ curves would become tangent to each other at a single point, as is shown in figure 7.2.

Once such a situation is reached, the economy would take off easily into continuous self-sustained growth. For the point of tangency (2' and 3') is stable in the leftward (backward) direction but unstable in the rightward (forward) direction. A slight deviation of r to the left would set up changes

---

3. Since $(\bar{S} - r\ell)$ in the diagram measures only the domestic supply of savings available for increasing the capital equipment per unit of labor, therefore, the $\dot{r}$ as defined in our diagram represents only the domestically financed increases in r. If foreign capital inflows and foreign aids are available to finance domestic investment in addition to domestic savings, they are to be regarded as an exogenous push that would propel forward the capital/labor ratio of the country concerned, independently of domestic saving.

$$\dot{r} = \bar{S} - r\ell$$

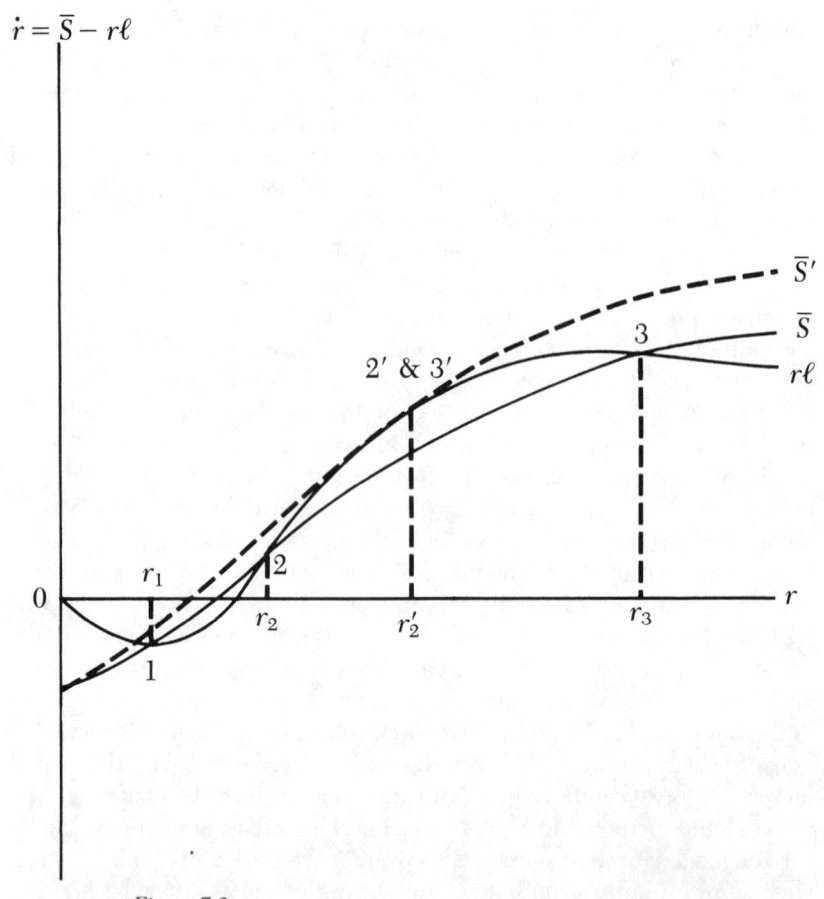

Figure 7.2.

in r, moving it back to the point of tangency, whereas a deviation to the right would bring about changes in r that would move it further and further to the right (the direction of positive increase). Thus the excess of savings per capita over the requirement of capital investment (also on a per capita basis) to maintain the existing capital/labor ratio in the face of population growth may be regarded as the basic condition for the take-off into continuous self-sustained growth. It signifies that the supply of domestic savings must be more than sufficient to maintain a constant capital/labor ratio in spite of the continuous population increase and thus must be capable of increasing that ratio steadily. This would in turn yield a steadily increasing output per capita, provided that the adverse effect upon it exerted by the increasing population pressure on land is sufficiently offset by technical progress, which may be regarded as a supplementary condition for take-off (see appendix at the end of this chapter).

The condition that $\bar{S} > r\ell$, or $S/L > (K/L)\ell$, can be transformed into a more familiar form by multiplying both sides of it with the inverse of the average income (output) per head (L/Y), which is always a positive magnitude. Then we would get the alternative formulation of the basic condition for take-off,

$$S/Y > (K/Y)\ell,$$

which means that the average propensity to save should be greater than the average capital/output ratio times the rate of population growth.

The Role of Trade Liberalization in the Preparation for Take-off

Economic policy for promoting development should include the following measures: (1) campaigns to reduce the birth rate; (2) efforts to raise the propensity to save; (3) monetary and taxation policies that provide incentives to save as well as to invest in productive enterprises; (4) the introduction of appropriate improved technology in all fields of production; (5) allocation of the available resources of the country to achieve the highest possible real per capita income with the given natural resources, capital, and the known state of technology.

Here is where foreign trade comes significantly into the picture. Fully utilizing the opportunity to trade has the same effect on income as an enormous improvement in the technology of production because it enables a country to specialize in those industries in which it has the highest comparative advantages, and then to exchange its products on the world market for products in which it has a comparative disadvantage. As a result, the country can enjoy more of both its own products and imported products than it could if it tried to produce both at home without trading. Conversely, if a country that originally had the opportunity to trade decides to cut itself off from trading relations with other parts of the world, or to put up barriers in order to develop industries in which it has a comparative disadvantage, it will set back its own progress toward take-off just as if there had been a catastrophic decline in its aggregate productive capacity. It would cause the $\bar{S}$ curve to shift downward and to the right more than the $r\ell$ curve, and would thus increase the hump to be crossed on the way to takeoff.

In preparing for take-off, the East Asian group behaved more wisely than many other developing countries. During the early postwar years, most underdeveloped countries were influenced by then-prevalent misguided theories that the surest way to speed up industrial development was to provide a safe, sheltered market for import-substituting industries. These theories also promoted the policy of keeping domestic currency overvalued in the face of inflation at home, because it was believed that devaluation would greatly worsen the terms of trade and exacerbate domestic inflation by imparting a strong cost-push to the price level.

Taiwan was probably the first among the underdeveloped countries to deliberately steer a course against the mainstream of contemporary economic thinking in drastically devaluing its own currency to an exchange rate that was calculated to ensure a more or less balanced trade without strict import controls, export subsidies, or discriminatory exchange rates for different industries. The basic official exchange rate of NT$15.55 to US$1 that had been in force from 1953 until 1958 was gradually devalued to NT$40.00 in 1960. This was accomplished through an intermediate stage during which the government issued exchange surrender certificates. Exporters could trade the certificates freely on the market and importers were required to obtain them in order to secure foreign exchange from the monetary authorities at the official exchange rate. Thus the official rate of NT$15.55 plus the market price of the exchange surrender certificates provided a fair indicator of the equilibrium exchange rate. The effective rate of NT$40.00 to US$1.00 thus established by market forces was then fixed as the new official rate at the exhortation by the International Monetary Fund in 1960.[4]

In taking this bold measure of devaluation, the economic authorities of the Republic of China in Taiwan had implicitly opted for an export-oriented development policy instead of an import-substitution policy supported with strict exchange and trade controls. Exporters began to receive the full worth of their foreign exchange proceeds in terms of importable goods, and importers were thenceforth permitted to bring in goods in proportion to the much-expanded foreign exchange earnings. This policy of devaluation combined with trade liberalization was carried out in successive steps over the period from 1955 to 1961. The effects upon the foreign trade of Taiwan were truly remarkable.

The de facto devaluations and the tax rebate on exports which started in 1955 were already showing their effects in the late fifties in reviving export trade from its low point of 1954 and setting it on an upward trend. But it was only in the sixties, after the exchange devaluation was linked with further liberalization of imports, that the expansion of exports really took off. In 1960, the total value of exports was US$164 million, which was already 71 percent higher than that of 1954, the year before the series of exchange reforms started. Three years later, in 1963, the total value of exports rose

---

4. See Tsiang (1980), especially pp. 329–31.

by more than another 100 percent to US$333.7 million. By 1970, the end of the decade, total exports had already reached US$1,468.6 million, which was nearly nine times that of 1960. A decade later, in 1980, total exports attained the level of US$19,575 million, more than 13 times that of 1970 and more than 200 times that of 1954.

The success of devaluation coupled with trade liberalization in Taiwan was quickly noticed in Korea. As in most underdeveloped countries of the day, Korea had the full paraphernalia of quantitative import restrictions and exchange controls, and a complex structure of multiple exchange rates that were biased against the more viable exports and favored the less competitive ones.

Exports simply had no chance to grow. In 1961, partly through the persuasion of American academics who had been invited to be advisors and partly out of a desire to emulate the successful reforms in Taiwan, the Korean government unified the exchange rate system and devalued the won from 65 per US$1.00 to 130 per US$1.00 in order to correct the overvaluation of the inflated domestic currency. Since no effective measures were taken to stop inflation, however, the won had to be devalued repeatedly, first to 255 per US$1.00 in May 1964 and then to 272 per US$1.00 in June 1965.

At the same time, the Korean government adopted many trade-promotion measures, such as the exemption of imported materials used in export industries from tariffs and domestic commodity taxes, the provision of wastage allowances on imported raw materials used for export production for tax purposes, preferential treatment in corporate income tax (50 percent exemption) for profits arising from export activities, low preferential interest rates on bank loans related to export activities, and the establishment of the government-financed Korea Trade Promotion Corporation to promote exports and develop marketing networks abroad.

As a result, Korea's exports, which had stagnated in the fifties, began to rise sharply after 1961 and attained an amazing average annual rate of growth of 38 percent for the decade 1961–70 and an average annual rate of 36 percent for 1971–80. In 1980, Korea's exports reached US$17.5 billion, some 534 times its exports in 1960. Despite this truly spectacular performance, some of Korea's export-promotion measures might reasonably suggest that the country discriminated excessively in favor of export industries as against domestic industries and thus enabled some nonviable export industries without a comparative advantage to export their products at a real loss to the nation.

Hong Kong and Singapore differed from Taiwan and Korea in that they each had a history of serving as an entrepôt for neighboring regions. Entrepôt trade and the accompanying services of transport, insurance, and banking had been the mainstays of their national incomes. Certain postwar developments, however, had forced them to diversify their activities toward manufacturing for export.

In the case of Hong Kong, the United Nations' embargo on trade with Mainland China after the latter joined the North Koreans in the Korean War dealt a lethal blow to its traditional entrepôt trade. In spite of its political independence, Hong Kong had always relied upon Mainland China as its hinterland and had served as the funnel for China's foreign trade. With its traditional means of making a living severely restricted, and with the population sharply increased by refugees, Hong Kong had to find a new way to survive. Fortunately, among the refugees from China were some entrepreneurs with previous industrial and manufacturing experience. Thus, in the face of Hong Kong's total lack of natural resources, it was quickly realized that the best solution was to utilize the abundant and cheap local labor supply to manufacture labor-intensive products with imported raw materials from wherever they could be obtained most cheaply, and to export the products to labor-scarce countries. Since Hong Kong had always been an open entrepôt, its entrepreneurs were also fairly well informed about the tastes and preferences of foreign markets and the practices of foreign trade. At first the trade statistics provided no clear evidence of the eventual success of the industrialization strategy of developing labor-intensive industries mainly for export purposes, because before 1959 no distinction was made between domestic exports and re-exports in Hong Kong's trade statistics. What was observable from the raw data was a sharp dip in total exports in 1952 after a peak reached in the preceding year during the short-lived trade boom following the outbreak of the Korean War. It took Hong Kong fully 11 years to reach that peak level again. This figure is misleading, however, for in the beginning of the fifties the bulk of Hong Kong's exports were re-exports. By the end of that decade more than two-thirds of Hong Kong's total exports were domestically produced goods, and from then on, re-exports never accounted for more than one-third of Hong Kong's total exports. By the end of the fifties, Hong Kong was transformed from a pure entrepôt into an industrial city. The annual growth rates of exports in the sixties and seventies, 14.5 percent and 17.1 percent respectively, though not as spectacular as those of Taiwan and Korea, were nonetheless remarkable. They fully reflect the expansion of domestically produced exports.

Singapore was also an entrepôt for the neighboring regions. After World War II, its entrepôt activities were seriously circumscribed by the rising economic nationalism of the newly independent nations of the region, each with its own aspirations for direct trading with foreign markets and for processing its own raw materials prior to export, eager to promote domestic industrialization by restrictions on manufactured imports. After a brief commodity boom in 1950–51 following the outbreak of the Korean War, the entrepôt trade of Singapore went into a period of sluggish growth and stagnation. In the meantime, the rapid growth of population resulted in a much-expanded labor force, which could not all be absorbed by the stagnant trade. The People's Action Party, which attained power in 1959, advocated industrialization as the solution to Singapore's growing unemployment.

At first, federation with Malaysia obliged Singapore to go along with a common import-substitution policy for the Malaysian common market. This strategy made little headway. It was only after Singapore seceded from the Malaysian Federation in August 1965 that it began to embark upon an export-oriented industrialization policy like that of the three other Asian NICs. To make up for the scarcity of experienced local entrepreneurs, Singapore undertook to open up its excellent location to foreign investors by creating a favorable investment climate with an excellent physical and financial infrastructure, good labor discipline, total freedom from exchange controls on capital movements, and no tariff barriers against imports of materials and equipment.

This strategy had two advantages. First, it built up the new export-manufacturing industries that were best suited for Singapore's factor endowment and location. Second, it brought in the capital needed to finance them. In terms of our diagrammatic explanation of the take-off process, it not only directed domestic resources into highly productive export industries, thus shifting the $\bar{S}$ curve upward, but at the same time also elicited a big exogenous push by foreign capital inflows to propel the country with great speed along the horizontal axis toward the take-off point.

Thus, although Singapore experienced little export growth during the decade before its independence, 1955–65, in the five years after independence, exports were already increasing at an average annual rate of 9.2 percent. In the seventies the average annual growth rate accelerated to 28.8 percent, so that in 1980, Singapore's exports were US$19 billion a year, as compared with US$915 million in 1964, the year before independence, an increase of more than 20 times in 16 years.

Structural Changes in the Economies Brought about by the Expansion of Exports

The rapid development of new export industries in the four Asian NICs naturally brought about changes in the composition of their exports as well as in the structures of their economies. In 1952, Taiwan's natural and processed agricultural products constituted 91.9 percent of the total value of its exports. By 1960, the combined share of these two items had dropped

Table 7.1. Relative Shares of Agricultural and Industrial Products in Exports (%)

	1951	1955	1960	1965	1970	1975	1980
Taiwan							
Agricultural[a]	91.9	89.6	67.7	54.0	21.4	16.4	9.2
Industrial & mineral	8.1	10.4	32.3	46.0	78.6	83.6	90.8
Korea							
Agricultural[b]	n.a.	n.a.	47.7	24.5	14.9	13.7	8.0
Industrial & mineral	n.a.	n.a.	52.3	75.5	85.1	86.3	92.0
Hong Kong							
Agricultural[b]	n.a.	n.a.	7.6	3.6	2.0	4.8	4.1
Industrial & mineral	n.a.	n.a.	92.4	96.4	98.0	95.2	95.9
Singapore							
Agricultural[b]	—	—	17.7	19.9	18.3	11.1	9.5
Industrial & mineral[c]	—	—	82.3	80.1	81.7	88.9	90.5

Sources: For Taiwan, Council for Economic Planning and Development (1981), *Data Book.*
For Korea, Bank of Korea (1971 and 1981).
For Hong Kong, Census and Statistics Department (1979), *Hong Kong Statistics 1947–67.* Census and Statistics Department (1971, 1974, and 1977), *Hong Kong Review of Overseas Trade in 1970, 1973 and 1976.*
For Singapore, *Yearbook of Statistics,* various years.
[a]Includes processed agricultural products, but not tobacco.
[b]Includes SITC 0, 22, 24, 26, 29, 4.
[c]Total minus agricultural products.

to 67.7 percent; by 1970, to 21.4 percent; and by 1980 to a mere 9.2 percent. Conversely, the share of industrial products in exports rose sharply, from a mere 8.1 percent in 1952 to 90.8 percent in 1980 (see table 7.1).

Korea's exports exhibited almost the same pattern of change in the relative shares of agricultural and industrial products. In 1960, industrial products (including mineral products) accounted for 52.3 percent of her exports. Their share rose rapidly to 92.0 percent by 1980. Due to the negligible size of the agricultural sector and the scarcity of natural resources in Hong Kong and Singapore, exports, apart from mere re-exports, were perforce composed mainly of industrial products. Nevertheless, for both these city-states, we can also observe a marked increase in the percentage share of exports of more processed products at the expense of less processed products, indicating increasing values added locally for exports as a whole.

The changes in the composition of exports brought about corresponding changes in the structure of the economies. In 1951, the share of agricultural output in the gross domestic product of Taiwan was 32.5 percent, while

Table 7.2. Relative Shares of Agricultural and Industrial Products in Gross Domestic Product (%)

	1951	1955	1960	1965	1970	1975	1980
Taiwan							
Agricultural	32.5	29.2	28.7	23.7	15.5	12.8	7.7
Industrial[a]	23.9	26.4	29.6	33.9	41.3	45.9	52.2
Service	43.6	44.4	41.7	42.4	43.2	41.3	40.1
Korea							
Agricultural	n.a.	46.9	40.0	41.3	29.7	27.0	17.8
Industrial	n.a.	14.6	18.5	23.9	27.2	31.3	37.9
Service	n.a.	38.5	41.5	34.8	43.1	41.7	44.3
Hong Kong							
Agricultural	n.a.	n.a.	3.4	n.a.	2.0	1.3	—
Industrial	n.a.	n.a.	32.5	n.a.	37.1	31.4	—
Service	n.a.	n.a.	64.1	n.a.	60.9	67.3	—
Singapore							
Agricultural	n.a.	n.a.	3.5	2.9	2.3	1.9	1.3
Industrial	n.a.	n.a.	17.3	23.4	30.0	34.5	37.7
Service	n.a.	n.a.	72.9	73.7	67.7	63.6	61.0

Sources: For Taiwan, Directorate-General of Budget, Accounting, and Statistics (1980), *National Income of the Republic of China*.
For Korea, Bank of Korea (1974 and 1980).
For Hong Kong, for 1970–74, Census and Statistics Department, Hong Kong (1977), *Estimates of Gross Domestic Product, 1961–75*. For 1960–61 and 1976, Chen (1980).
For Singapore, for 1960–69, *Singapore National Accounts 1960–73*. For 1970–80, *Yearbook of Statistics, Singapore, 1980/81*.
[a]Includes food- and other agricultural-produce-processing industries.

that of industrial output (including mining, manufacturing, utilities, and construction) was 23.9 percent. By 1980, the agricultural share was down to 7.7 percent and the industrial share up to 52.2 percent (see table 7.2). In Korea, we can also find an increasing trend in the relative share of industrial products in the GDP, from 14.6 percent in 1955 to 37.9 percent in 1980, while the share of the agricultural sector in the gross domestic product dropped rapidly from 46.9 percent in 1955 to only 17.8 percent in 1980.

In Hong Kong and Singapore, although the agricultural sector was always small, the structure of the gross domestic product still showed discernible change. The share of agricultural production in the GDP, small to begin with, shrank further in both cases. In Hong Kong, the share of industrial output increased from 32.5 percent in 1960 to 37.1 percent in 1970, but then declined in the seventies because of the rapid expansion of the service sector, particularly banking, although the agricultural sector continued its decline in importance. In Singapore the rapid increase in the relative share of industrial products apparently took place at the expense of both agriculture and service industries.

This shift of weights in the gross domestic product away from agriculture to industry in Taiwan and Korea, which had depended so heavily on agriculture, was of importance to the preparation of those countries for their economic take-off. As we pointed out above, one of the two sufficient conditions for take-off was that the net favorable effect of technical progress on aggregate output should be greater than the adverse effect of increasing population pressure on land, i.e., $g^* > \gamma \ell$. The rapid development of foreign trade, which enabled both Taiwan and Korea to shift the major weight of their domestic production to industry, and which required land as a factor of production to a much lesser extent than agriculture had, was equivalent to a great change in technology that greatly reduced the importance of land in the aggregate production function.[5]

Furthermore, the development of foreign trade on the basis of trade liberalization meant that the respective economies would be able to concentrate more on those industries in which they had comparative advantages, and to exchange their exported products for commodities with higher production costs. This specialization in production, by itself, meant a tremendous improvement in technology. On top of this basic change in the structure of the economy, the expansion of export industries, with much of their new machinery imported from abroad, also meant that new technology was imported with the new equipment. In the case of Taiwan, the Sino-American Joint Commission for Rural Reconstruction was effective in improving agricultural techniques, developing new high-yield varieties or new crops, and improving irrigation; in addition there was the increased incentive for farmers provided by the land-to-the-tillers reform successfully carried out in 1953.

All this combined to bring about a substantial increase in overall per capita productivity that could counteract the adverse effects of increasing population pressure on land.[6] That problem, moreover, was substantially lightened not only by the lesser importance of land in the aggregate production function, but also by the decreased rate of population growth brought about by the successful spread of family planning.

The Importance of Promoting the Propensity to Save

With the increase in real per capita income brought about by foreign trade, the domestic population had to be induced to save larger amounts in order to achieve an economic take-off; a basic condition for take-off into con-

---

5. In terms of our Cobb-Douglas aggregate production function, it signifies a great reduction in the exponent γ for land or natural resources N (see appendix).
6. That is, this should ensure that $g^* > \gamma l$, which we treated above as the supplementary condition for take-off.

tinuous self-sustained growth is that savings per capita must exceed the per capita investment required just to maintain the existing capital/labor ratio in the face of domestic population growth, i.e., $\bar{S} > r\ell$. This condition may also be formulated as $S/Y > (K/Y) \cdot \ell$, meaning that the average propensity to save must be greater than the average capital/labor ratio times the rate of domestic population growth.

In this respect, the four Asian NICs again seemed to have acted more sensibly than many other developing countries. During the early postwar years most other developing countries, under the prevailing influence of Keynesian economics, adopted the misguided policy of maintaining the interest rates of their domestic banking systems at the low conventional level of developed countries with more stable prices. The justification for this policy was the mistaken view that it would check cost-push inflation and stimulate real investment and growth. Actually, enforced low interest rates in the face of great scarcity of capital and inflationary conditions, tend to add fuel to domestic inflation by creating an excess demand for bank credits as well as by slowing down real capital formation by discouraging depositors from investing savings in organized financial intermediaries. Instead, savings typically are used to hoard precious metals and foreign exchange and to purchase real estate, or are diverted to other nonproductive channels.[7]

In 1950, Taiwan boldly abandoned the low interest rate policy and raised the rates for savings deposits to approximately the prevailing rate of inflation, which was well above 100 percent in the beginning of that year. It may have been the first developing country to do so. The results were dramatic. The three-digit inflation rate was brought to a halt within three months, and the banking system, which had completely failed to attract any significant amount of savings, began to function again as an intermediary between the suppliers of savings and the demanders of investable funds. From 1951 to 1960, the rate of annual price inflation was successfully kept down to moderate levels, below 15 percent. After 1961 the rate of price inflation was further reduced and kept well within the one-digit limit (mostly under 4 percent per annum) until 1973. Two successive years of large trade surpluses, amounting to US$647 million and US$766 million in 1972 and 1973 caused the money supply (M_1) to increase by 34.6 percent and 47.0 percent respectively, and the price level to rise first by 7.3 percent in 1972 and then by a further 40.3 percent in 1973 (Tsiang 1979, pp. 595–97).

---

7. The harm done by a government-enforced low interest policy in the face of inflation and the benefits to be expected from the reversal of such a policy have been discussed in some detail in Tsiang (1979) and Tsiang (1980).

The relative stability of prices and the fairly attractive interest rates revived and stimulated the traditional thrifty habits of the Chinese people. Other tax measures were also adopted to encourage savings and investment, for example, exempting from personal income tax the interest income from savings and time deposits with maturity terms of two years or more, and exempting from corporate income tax those profits that were plowed back for investment. As incomes rose, these inducements were further reinforced by the natural tendency for consumption to lag behind rising income. In this way, Taiwan was rapidly turned from a country with a very low propensity to save into a country with a remarkable high savings propensity.

In 1952 only 5.2 percent of Taiwan's national income was saved. In 1963 the percentage had risen to 13.4, surpassing the corresponding figures for both the United Kingdom (9.8 percent) and the United States (9.1 percent) in the same year. By 1973, it had climbed to the level of 35 percent, exceeding Japan's 28.4 percent for that year (see table 7.3).

During the Korean War (1950–53), Korea suffered from severe inflation, with consumer prices increasing an average of 165 percent annually. After the fighting had ceased, the rate of inflation was gradually brought down to 10 percent or less in the period from 1958 to 1962. After 1963, however, inflation again rose into double digits.

The Korean monetary authorities had maintained a low interest policy in the face of the rampant domestic inflation up to September 1965. Nominal interest rates, even on long-term deposits, ranged from only 10 to 15 percent per annum. Real rates of interest were frequently negative after allowing for expected price inflation. As a result the average propensity to save in Korea was naturally very low and, indeed, had been negative for many years; it was negative from 1956 to 1962, and ranged no higher than from 1.9 percent to 4.0 percent from 1963 to 1965 (see table 7.3).

Finally on September 30, 1965, the Monetary Board of the Republic of Korea took a lesson from Taiwan's success with its high interest rates policy and sharply raised the nominal interest rate on 18-month time deposits to 34.5 percent per annum, 2.5 percent per month compounded monthly (Brown 1973, pp. 179–211). In 1963–64, the annual rate of inflation, as measured by the GNP deflator, had been about 30 percent. The new nominal rate of interest was expected to ensure a substantial positive real rate of interest for depositors, and after it was instituted the ratio of savings to national income rose abruptly from 1.9 percent in 1965 to 7 percent in 1966. It continued to rise steadily, so that by 1969 it reached almost 15 percent of the national income (see table 7.3).

In the seventies, although nominal interest rates were gradually reduced as the inflation rate slowed down, the propensity to save in Korea con-

Table 7.3. Savings as Percentage of National Income or Gross Domestic Product in Taiwan, Korea, Hong Kong, and Singapore compared with Selected Developed Countries

Year	Taiwan[a]	Korea[a]	Hong Kong[b]	Singapore[b]	Japan[a]	U.K.[a]	U.S.A.[a]
1952	5.2	—	—	—	24.1	6.4	10.4
1953	5.0	4.4	—	—	17.3	8.0	10.0
1954	3.3	1.4	—	—	18.2	8.0	8.9
1955	4.9	0.5	—	—	20.4	9.8	12.2
1956	4.8	−7.4	—	—	25.5	10.4	12.8
1957	5.9	0.9	—	—	27.4	10.5	11.1
1958	5.0	−0.1	—	—	24.2	9.9	8.2
1959	5.0	−1.3	—	—	26.5	10.2	10.4
1960	7.6	−4.8	—	−2.6	27.7	10.9	8.6
1961	8.0	−2.3	5.3	−3.5	29.9	11.0	8.4
1962	7.6	−2.4	7.7	4.6	28.4	9.4	9.0
1963	13.4	3.9	12.3	2.2	26.6	9.8	9.1
1964	16.3	4.0	12.6	8.2	25.2	11.2	9.8
1965	16.5	1.9	16.5	9.9	23.3	12.4	11.5
1966	19.0	7.0	15.1	13.7	24.7	11.5	10.3
1967	20.1	6.2	19.0	13.8	27.5	10.4	9.7
1968	19.8	10.3	17.1	18.4	29.4	11.2	9.8
1969	22.1	14.8	21.5	18.0	29.8	13.8	9.8
1970	23.8	13.2	23.9	18.4	30.5	13.6	7.6
1971	27.6	10.8	23.0	18.5	27.4	11.3	7.6
1972	31.6	10.1	26.3	24.2	26.8	9.8	8.2
1973	35.0	18.3	24.3	29.0	28.4	9.5	9.5
1974	31.5	14.0	23.5	27.6	25.1	5.7	6.7
1975	25.3	13.0	23.4	26.4	21.4	5.3	3.8
1976	32.2	19.0	32.8	29.6	20.9	7.1	4.9
1977	32.3	21.6	28.0	30.4	20.3	8.4	5.7
1978	35.2	—	23.1	29.6	20.0	8.3	6.5
1979	34.9	—	—	30.7	—	—	—
1980	32.9	—	—	29.6	—	—	—

Sources: For Taiwan, Council for Economic Planning and Development (1981).
For Korea, The Bank of Korea (1978).
For Hong Kong, Census and Statistics Department, Hong Kong (1977); and Census and Statistics Department, Hong Kong (1980).
For Singapore, *Yearbook of Statistics, Singapore 1980/81*; and *Singapore National Accounts 1960–73*.
For other countries, United Nations (1979), *Yearbook of National Accounts Statistics*.
[a]Net domestic savings/NI.
[b]Gross domestic savings/GDP.

tinued to increase with the rapid rise in real per capita income because of the tendency for consumption to lag behind the rise of real income. Thus the percentages of income saved in Korea rose until it attained 22 percent of the national income in 1977. The dire predictions of bankruptcies, reduced growth, accelerated inflation, and other negative results projected as inevitable consequences by the opponents of this new interest rate policy were not borne out. On the contrary, just as in Taiwan, Korea actually experienced accelerated growth following the interest rate reform, as the increased rate of saving enabled the country to finance a higher rate of productive capital formation, and the rate of inflation subsided.[8]

The monetary experiences of Hong Kong and Singapore were different because of the status of each as an open entrepôt, which did not permit fully independent monetary policies, and because of the ability of each to rely upon inflows of foreign capital in addition to domestic savings. In both cases, prices were more stable and interest rates lower due to the openness of the economies and the greater accessibility to international markets. Supplies of domestic savings were less important to them than to Korea and Taiwan, and for each of them economic growth was more of a mixture of the exogenous-push type and the self-generated type, with a very heavy component of the former.

Because of their close links with the international market, neither Hong Kong nor Singapore had ever subscribed to such an unwise policy as a government-enforced low interest rate. Nor could either of them arbitrarily raise interest rates to stimulate saving and to encourage capital inflow. Nevertheless, the Singapore government adopted a measure that was seemingly very successful in significantly raising the propensity to save. It established the Central Provident Fund, a sort of combined pension and social insurance fund to which both employees and employers were legally required to contribute. Currently (as of 1982) the employee contributes as much as 22 percent of his or her wages or salary and the employer contributes 20.5 percent.

The effectiveness of this measure in raising the aggregate propensity to save in Singapore can be observed from Table 7.3. Singapore's gross propensity to save was very low indeed before 1964. It was either negative or at a very low percentage from 1960, the year statistics on savings became available, to 1963. In 1964, however, the gross savings ratio jumped 6 percentage points from a mere 2.2 percent in 1963 to a respectable 8.2

8. In the late seventies, Korean monetary authorities tended to lapse into the old misguided policy of enforcing low interest rates on banks with the result that inflation was showing signs of getting out of control again. Fortunately, in 1982 the new Korean government under President Chun renounced the excessively expansionist policy of the previous administration and reverted to a more conservative monetary policy.

percent of the GDP. From then on, the gross savings ratio increased steadily. By the end of the seventies it stood at 30 percent of the GDP.

Reliable statistics on savings in Hong Kong have been available only since 1961, when gross domestic savings was put at 5.3 percent of the GDP. It climbed steadily to well above 20 percent in the seventies.

Certainly, in none of these four countries did the high propensities to save result in high rates of unemployment, proneness to recession, sluggish growth due to the lack of effective demand, or the other calamities feared by Keynesian economists. Rather, as classical economists have always claimed, high domestic savings supplemented by capital inflows have enabled these NICs to carry out very high rates of domestic capital formation without creating undue inflationary pressures. The concurrent expansion of the export industries opened up great investment opportunities that could easily absorb any available supply of domestic savings.

Thus gross capital formation as a percentage of gross national expenditure in Taiwan increased from 14.5 percent in 1952 to 17.7 percent in 1963, at which point it was already abreast with that of the United States. After 1967 this percentage climbed into the twenties, and after 1972 it further increased into the thirties, becoming comparable with the rate in Japan.

In Korea, the percentage of gross capital formation first fluctuated between 11 and 18 percent from 1953 to 1965 without any definite upward trend. Between 1965 and 1966, however, the propensity to save jumped from 1.9 percent to 7 percent and the percentage of gross capital formation rose from 15 to 21.6 percent. And as the propensity to save continued to grow, the percentage of gross capital formation also continued to rise so that during the five years 1966–70 it averaged 25 percent. The growth continued in the seventies and in 1979 reached 35.4 percent.

Capital Inflows as Additional Boosters of Domestic Capital Formation

As we have pointed out, in the two city-states of Hong Kong and Singapore, capital inflows played an important role in financing investments, accounting for very high ratios of gross capital formation even while domestic savings ratios were still low or negative. In Hong Kong, the percentage of gross domestic capital formation was already 21.4 percent in 1961 when the ratio of gross domestic savings to gross domestic income was only 5.3 percent, and in Singapore when the ratio of gross domestic savings to GDP was still negative, the percentage of gross capital formation was already over 11 percent. In the case of Hong Kong, however, when the domestic savings propensity picked up strength, it largely replaced the inflows of foreign capital and turned the country from a heavy capital importer into a net capital exporter in the late sixties and the seventies. Consequently, the percentage of gross capital formation in Hong Kong seldom increased much above 25 percent of the GDP. By contrast, in Singapore the rapidly increasing percentage of domestic savings simply reinforced the unabated inflows of foreign capital in the financing of domestic capital formation; the percentage of the latter to the GDP rose so rapidly that for the decade 1971–80 it averaged 39.2 percent. In 1980 it stood at 43.2 percent, which was the highest in the world, surpassing even that of Japan.

Estimating the Approximate Take-off Years of the Four Asian NICs

The basic condition for take-off presented in the introduction to this chapter was that savings per capita needed to be more than sufficient to maintain the capital/labor ratio, or rather its transformation

$$S/Y > (K/Y)\ell.$$

Applying this criterion, we can claim that the four Asian NICs achieved successful take-off into self-sustained growth within a few years of each other. Let us look first at Taiwan. The average propensity to save in Taiwan jumped from between 7.6 and 8.0 percent during 1960–62 to the level of 13.4 percent in 1963 and started a steep climb from there which carried it to more than 20 percent after 1967. The rate of population growth was still very high in the early sixties, though it had already shown a decreasing trend, from 3.5 percent in 1960 to 3.0 percent in 1965. The average capital/output ratio for the same period has been estimated at between 3.7 and 2.7. Multiplying the K/Y ratio by the population growth rate, and comparing it with the average propensity to save, we may observe that the average savings ratio began to exceed $(K/Y) \times (L/L)$ in 1963 (see table 7.4). Indeed, the excess for that year was quite small, only approximately 3 percentage points. As we pointed out in our theoretical model above, however, such a take-off point is likely to be unstable in the right-hand direction (see figure 7.2). Indeed, the gap grew progressively to 7.3 percentage points in 1964, 8.4 in 1965, and 11.5 in 1966. In the seventies, the ratio of savings to national income continued to rise rapidly and climbed well above 20 percent, eventually reaching 35 percent. The gap between S/Y and $(K/Y) \times (L/L)$ had continued to widen. Thus, our theoretical expectation that capital per capita, and hence real per capita income, would grow cumulatively after take-off was apparently borne out (see table 7.8).

We can similarly claim that the take-off point for Korea occurred around 1966–67. Even though the initial gap between S/Y and $(K/Y \times (L/L)$ was only around 2 percentage points in 1966–67, it soon began to grow (see table 7.5).

Comparative Foreign Trade and Investment 321

Table 7.4. Estimates of the Approximate Year of Take-off in Taiwan

Year	K/Y	$\dot{L}/L$	(K/Y) × ($\dot{L}/L$)	S/Y	S/Y − (K/Y) × ($\dot{L}/L$)
1952	6.0	3.3	19.8	5.2	−14.6
1953	5.5	3.8	20.9	5.0	−15.9
1954	5.1	3.7	18.9	3.3	−15.6
1955	4.8	3.8	18.2	4.9	−13.3
1956	4.6	3.4	15.6	4.8	−10.8
1957	4.3	3.2	13.8	5.9	−7.9
1958	4.1	3.6	14.8	5.0	−9.8
1959	3.9	3.9	15.2	5.0	−10.2
1960	3.7	3.5	13.0	7.6	−5.4
1961	3.6	3.3	11.9	8.0	−3.9
1962	3.4	3.3	11.2	7.6	−3.6
1963	3.2	3.2	10.2	13.4	3.2
1964	2.9	3.1	9.0	16.3	7.3
1965	2.7	3.0	8.1	16.5	8.4
1966	2.6	2.9	7.5	19.0	11.5
1967	2.5	2.3	5.8	20.1	14.3
1968	2.4	2.7	6.5	19.8	13.3
1969	2.3	2.5	5.8	22.1	16.3
1970	2.2	2.4	5.3	23.8	18.5
1971	2.1	2.2	4.6	27.6	23.0
1972	2.0	2.0	4.0	31.6	27.6
1973	2.0	1.8	3.6	35.0	31.4
1974	2.1	1.8	3.8	31.5	27.7
1975	2.3	1.9	4.4	25.3	20.9
1976	2.2	2.2	4.8	32.2	27.4
1977	2.1	1.8	3.8	32.3	28.5
1978	2.0	1.9	3.8	35.2	31.4
1979	2.1	2.0	4.2	34.9	30.7

Sources: K/Y: Our own estimates.
$\dot{L}/L$ and S/Y: Council for Economic Planning and Development (1981).

Applying the same criterion to Hong Kong and Singapore, we must bear in mind that it merely indicates that following the take-off point the economy should be capable of self-sustained growth in real per capita income, however slowly it begins. In these two city-states, growth had always been propelled by massive capital imports. Our criterion might, therefore, appear to be insignificant or even irrelevant. Nevertheless, it would still indicate when their economies would be ready to grow through the internal forces, if the exogenous push should let up. Their take-off points should thus surely be considered significant even if the exogenous push continues to propel the economy forward and upward.

Table 7.5. Estimation of the Approximate Year of Take-off in Korea

Year	K/Y	$\dot{L}/L$	(K/Y) × ($\dot{L}/L$)	S/Y	S/Y − (K/Y) × ($\dot{L}/L$)
1953	2.8	0.9	2.5	4.4	1.9
1954	2.7	1.3	3.5	1.4	−2.1
1955	2.6	1.7	4.4	0.5	−3.9
1956	2.6	2.9	7.5	−7.4	−14.9
1957	2.5	2.9	7.3	0.9	−6.4
1958	2.4	2.9	7.0	−0.1	−7.1
1959	2.4	2.9	7.0	−1.3	−8.3
1960	2.4	2.9	7.0	−4.8	−11.8
1961	2.3	2.9	6.7	−2.3	−9.0
1962	2.3	2.9	6.7	−2.4	−9.1
1963	2.2	2.8	6.2	3.9	−2.3
1964	2.1	2.6	5.5	4.0	−1.5
1965	2.0	2.6	5.2	1.9	−3.3
1966	1.9	2.5	4.8	7.0	2.2
1967	1.9	2.3	4.4	6.2	1.8
1968	1.9	2.3	4.4	10.3	5.9
1969	1.9	2.3	4.4	14.8	10.4
1970	1.9	2.2	4.2	13.2	9.0
1971	1.9	2.0	3.8	10.8	7.0
1972	1.9	1.9	3.6	10.1	6.5
1973	1.8	1.8	3.2	18.3	15.1
1974	n.a.	1.7	n.a.	14.0	n.a.
1975	n.a.	1.7	n.a.	13.0	n.a.
1976	n.a.	1.6	n.a.	19.0	n.a.
1977	n.a.	1.6	n.a.	21.6	n.a.

Sources: K/Y: Hong (1976), p. 49.
$\dot{L}/L$: 1962–77, *Indicators of Major Statistics*. 1953–61, International Monetary Fund, (1980b).
S/Y: The Bank of Korea (1978).

With this in mind, we will examine the approximate years of take-off for Hong Kong and Singapore. There are statistical difficulties to overcome. First, there are no statistics for these countries on net savings as percentages of respective national income or net national product. We have only the ratios of gross savings to gross national product. Yet our theory requires that we should compare the net savings ratio with the product of the capital/output ratio and the population growth rate. Second, no official or authoritative estimates of capital/output ratios are available for these two countries. The only estimates we have found are those made by Edward K. Y. Chen (1979). His estimates for the capital/output ratios of these two city-states are extraordinarily low as compared with our own estimates for

Table 7.6. Estimation of the Approximate Year of Take-off in Hong Kong

Year	K/Y	$\dot{L}/L$	$(K/Y) \times (\dot{L}/L)$	S/Y	S/Y − $(K/Y) \times (\dot{L}/L)$
1961	1.4	3.0	4.2	−5.2	−9.4
1962	1.4	4.3	6.0	−2.5	−8.5
1963	1.4	3.5	4.9	2.5	−2.4
1964	1.4	2.5	3.5	2.9	−0.6
1965	1.4	2.7	3.8	7.2	3.4
1966	1.5	0.9	1.4	5.7	4.3
1967	1.5	2.6	3.9	10.0	6.1
1968	1.4	2.2	3.1	7.9	4.8
1969	1.3	1.6	2.1	12.8	10.7
1970	1.3	2.5	3.3	15.4	12.1
1971	1.3	2.2	2.9	14.4	11.5
1972	1.3	0.8	1.0	18.1	17.1
1973	1.2	2.0	2.4	15.9	13.5
1974	1.3	3.8	4.9	15.0	10.1
1975	—	1.8	—	14.9	—
1976	—	1.1	—	25.3	—
1977	—	1.6	—	20.0	—

Sources: K/Y: Chen (1979).
$\dot{L}/L$: Hong Kong Annual Report, various years; Lethbridge (1980).
S/Y: Converted from the gross domestic savings/GDP as given in table 7.3 by a method of adjustment described in the text.

Taiwan and Wontack Hong's (1976) estimates for Korea, indeed, so low as to raise questions about their credibility.

We attempt to solve the first problem by making adjustments to the available gross savings ratios to turn them into rough estimates of the ratios of net savings to net domestic product. We assume that capital depreciation constitutes roughly 10 percent of the gross domestic product for both countries. By subtracting 10 percentage points from the gross savings percentage and then dividing it by 0.9, we can turn it into a rough estimate of the net savings ratio. Applying this method of adjustment to the gross domestic savings ratios of Hong Kong and Singapore, we arrive at the estimated net domestic savings ratios S/Y for these countries, as shown in tables 7.6 and 7.7.

If we simply used Chen's estimates for capital/output ratios in testing the basic condition for economic take-off, then the take-off years for Hong Kong and for Singapore might be placed at about 1965 and 1966 respectively. In these years, the net savings ratio minus the product of the capital/output ratio times the rate of population growth began to rise from negative to positive. In view of the crudeness of our estimates of net savings

Table 7.7. Estimation of the Approximate Year of Take-off in Singapore

Year	K/Y	$\dot{L}/L$	(K/Y) × ($\dot{L}/L$)	S/Y	S/Y − (K/Y) × ($\dot{L}/L$)
1960	1.7	3.2	5.4	−14.0	−19.4
1961	1.5	3.7	5.6	−15.0	−20.6
1962	1.5	3.6	5.4	−6.0	−13.4
1963	1.3	2.9	3.8	−8.6	−12.4
1964	1.4	2.2	3.1	−2.0	−5.1
1965	1.4	2.7	3.8	−0.1	−3.9
1966	1.3	2.1	2.7	4.1	1.4
1967	1.3	2.6	3.4	4.2	0.8
1968	1.3	1.5	2.0	9.3	7.3
1969	1.3	1.5	2.0	9.0	7.0
1970	1.2	1.5	1.8	9.3	7.5
1971	1.3	1.9	2.5	9.4	6.9
1972	1.3	1.9	2.5	15.8	13.3
1973	1.3	1.9	2.5	21.1	18.6
1974	1.5	1.4	2.1	19.6	17.5
1975	n.a.	1.4	n.a.	18.2	n.a.
1976	n.a.	1.3	n.a.	21.8	n.a.
1977	n.a.	1.3	n.a.	22.7	n.a.
1978	n.a.	0.9	n.a.	21.8	n.a.
1979	n.a.	1.3	n.a.	23.0	n.a.

Sources: K/Y: Chen (1979).
$\dot{L}/L$: International Monetary Fund (1980b).
S/Y: Converted from the gross domestic savings/GDP as given in table 7.3 by a method of adjustment described in the text.

ratios and the doubt we entertain about the validity of Chen's estimates of the capital/output ratios of these two countries, however, we shall see how robust our estimates of the take-off years are when the capital/output ratio is raised, say, first to a level comparable to that of Korea (2.0), and then to a level comparable to that of Taiwan (2.5).

In the case of Hong Kong, it seems that regardless of whether the capital/output ratio of Hong Kong is taken to be 1.4, as Chen estimated, or assumed to be 2.0, or even 2.5, the year of take-off can be fixed at 1965. In the case of Singapore, however, the net savings ratio began to exceed the product of the capital/output ratio and the population growth rate in 1966 by only a slim margin even with Chen's low estimate of the capital/output ratio—1.3—so that if we raise the capital/output ratio to 2, the year of take-off is postponed to 1968. When the capital/output ratio is further raised hypothetically to 2.5, the take-off year for Singapore can still be said to be 1968. Thus, to be on the safe side, we shall say that 1968 is the year

Singapore became capable of self-sustained growth even without relying upon foreign capital inflow, whereas Hong Kong might be said to have acquired this capability in 1965.

The growth rates of national income (or GDP), both in the aggregate and on a per capita basis, of these four countries before and after their respective take-off years are given in table 7.8. For Taiwan and Korea, there was a notable speed-up in the rate of growth after take-off. In Hong Kong and Singapore, the potential differences in the rates of growth were presumably blurred by the influence of capital inflows, which these two city-states, even before their take-offs, enjoyed to a much greater extent than Taiwan and Korea. Especially in the case of Hong Kong, which shifted from being a heavy capital importer to being a net capital exporter soon after the presumptive year of take-off, there was hardly any significant increase in the average rate of growth after take-off.

Foreign Investments as Transmitters of Technological Improvements

We have defined the supplementary condition for take-off as the requirement that the aggregate effects of technical improvements be more than enough to offset the adverse effects of the increasing population pressure on natural resources, (i.e., $g^* > \gamma \ell$). There is no question that this criterion could be satisfied by the rapid development of export industries on the basis of comparative advantages, thus enabling an economy to shift away from agriculture, which is particularly subject to the limitations of land resources. It also could be satisfied by a steady inflow of new technological improvements.

In this connection the import of foreign capital is of particular help. We have already seen that the import of foreign capital can supplement domestic savings in financing domestic capital formation and thus help to push the domestic capital/labor ratio over the hump to the take-off point. Direct foreign investments frequently, though not always, carry with them new technological advances that are not yet widely known or adopted in the receiving countries. They can thus serve as a medium for the transmission of new technology. Furthermore, foreign-operated firms and plants often use more efficient management techniques, and can have a positive effect by stimulating domestic firms to emulate them. All this could also help the process of take-off through raising g^* relative to $\gamma\ell$ as well as shifting the $\bar{S}$ curve upward and to the left relatively more than the $r\ell$ curve.

The utilization of foreign capital can be very important as a booster in the pre-take-off period to facilitate and speed up the take-off. Once take-off has been achieved, the reliance on foreign capital would, theoretically speaking, no longer be necessary, but it could still play a significant role in

Table 7.8. Annual Growth Rate of Real National Income or Gross Domestic Product in Taiwan, Korea, Hong Kong, and Singapore (%)

	Taiwan[a]		Korea[b]		Hong Kong[c]		Singapore[d]	
Year	Real National Income	Per Capita Real Income	Real GDP	Per Capita Real GDP	Real GDp	Per Capita Real GDP	Real GDP	Per Capita Real GDP
1952	13.1	9.3	n.a.	n.a.	n.a.	n.a.	n.a.	n.a.
1953	9.1	5.7	n.a.	n.a.	n.a.	n.a.	n.a.	n.a.
1954	8.7	5.0	5.6	4.2	n.a.	n.a.	n.a.	n.a.
1955	8.8	4.9	4.2	2.4	n.a.	n.a.	n.a.	n.a.
1956	4.6	0.9	−1.7	−4.4	n.a.	n.a.	n.a.	n.a.
1957	7.3	4.0	7.6	4.5	n.a.	n.a.	n.a.	n.a.
1958	7.1	3.7	5.5	2.5	n.a.	n.a.	n.a.	n.a.
1959	6.6	3.2	3.6	0.7	n.a.	n.a.	n.a.	n.a.
1960	5.0	1.7	0.9	−4.7	n.a.	n.a.	n.a.	n.a.
1961	6.8	3.5	6.2	0.3	n.a.	n.a.	8.4	4.8
1962	8.7	5.5	1.7	3.2	10.1	5.5	7.0	4.0
1963	9.2	8.2	9.1	6.1	11.9	8.1	10.0	7.2
1964	16.1	10.5	9.9	7.0	7.7	5.2	−3.5	−5.9
1965	7.6	4.6	5.3	2.6	18.2	15.2	7.5	4.9
1966	9.4	6.5	12.1	9.3	8.9	7.9	11.1	8.4
1967	10.5	7.8	5.2	2.8	7.8	5.1	11.8	9.4
1968	9.0	6.4	10.7	8.2	4.7	2.5	13.9	11.9
1969	10.1	7.7	13.6	11.1	14.8	13.0	13.7	12.0
1970	11.1	8.8	7.9	5.5	6.2	3.7	13.7	12.0
1971	12.3	10.1	8.8	6.6	5.0	2.8	12.5	10.6
1972	13.2	11.1	5.7	3.7	9.7	7.8	13.4	11.5
1973	12.0	10.0	14.4	12.4	15.8	12.8	11.5	9.5
1974	−1.9	−3.7	7.5	5.6	1.8	−0.7	6.3	4.6
1975	3.3	1.4	7.8	6.0	2.2	0.5	4.1	2.6
1976	15.4	13.1	12.4	10.6	18.8	17.6	7.5	6.0
1977	9.0	6.8	10.0	8.2	9.8	8.1	7.9	6.4
1978	11.9	9.8	n.a.	n.a.	10.0	7.8	8.6	7.3
1979	7.7	5.7	n.a.	n.a.	n.a.	n.a.	9.4	8.0
1980	4.4	2.4	n.a.	n.a.	n.a.	n.a.	10.2	8.8

Sources: For Taiwan, Council for Economic Planning and Development (1981).
For Korea, GDP: The Bank of Korea (1978). Population after 1962: *Indicators of Major Statistics*; and Population before 1961: International Monetary Fund (1980).
For Hong Kong, 1962–66: Census and Statistics Department, Hong Kong (1977); 1967–75: Census and Statistics Department, Hong Kong (1980).
For Singapore: *Yearbook of Statistics* (1981), pp. 2 and 27; and *Singapore National Accounts 1960–73*.
[a] At constant 1976 prices adjusted for gains or losses due to changes in the terms of trade.
[b] At constant 1975 prices.
[c] At constant 1973 prices
[d] At constant 1968 prices.

Table 7.9. Sources of Funds for Gross Domestic Capital Formation (average %)

Period	Gross Domestic Capital Formation	Gross Domestic Savings	Foreign Capital Inflow Total	Direct Foreign Investment % of total	Statistical Discrepancies
		Taiwan			
1952–55	100.0	59.3	40.7	1.2	—
1956–60	100.0	60.0	40.0	1.4	—
1961–65	100.0	85.1	14.9	4.1	—
1966–70	100.0	95.0	5.0	7.5	—
1971–75	100.0	97.4	2.6	5.9	—
1976–80	100.0	106.0	−6.0	2.9	—
		Korea			
1953–55	100.0	51.7	48.3	—	—
1956–60	100.0	19.5	77.8	—	2.7
1961–65	100.0	41.3	59.5	—	−0.8
1966–70	100.0	59.1	38.8	—	2.1
1971–75	100.0	70.9	31.4	2.3[a]	−2.3
1976–77	100.0	91.0	5.9	1.1	3.1
		Hong Kong			
1961–65	100.0	39.9	60.1	—	—
1966–79	100.0	113.6	−13.6	—	—
1971–75	100.0	113.8	−13.8	—	—
1976–78	100.0	120.2	−20.2	—	—
		Singapore			
1961–65	100.0	19.5	80.5	—	—
1966–70	100.0	61.7	38.3	—	—
1971–75	100.0	62.1	37.9	—	—
1976–80	100.0	79.8	20.2	—	—

Sources: For Taiwan, Council for Economic Planning and Development (1980); and Wu et al. (1980).
For Korea, Bank of Korea (1978), pp. 272–73; and International Monetary Fund (1980a).
For Hong Kong, Census and Statistics Department, Hong Kong (1977 and 1980).
[a] For 1972–75 only.

accelerating post-take-off growth, as in the cases of Singapore and Korea, and in the transmission of new techniques in production and management.

In the case of Taiwan, it can be seen from table 7.9 that foreign capital inflows and transfers (consisting chiefly of U.S. aid before its termination in 1965) constituted between 30 and 50 percent of the sources of funds for gross capital formation until 1962. After 1963, however, there was a sharp decline in foreign capital inflows and transfers as U.S. aid was rapidly switched off in anticipation of its termination date in 1965. Apparently in

1963 the economy took off under its own steam, and thereafter domestic savings not only successfully filled the gap left by the loss of foreign aid, but also increasingly supported domestic capital formation. After 1970, Taiwan began to become a capital-exporting country.

For Hong Kong, foreign capital inflows accounted for as much as 75 percent of gross domestic capital formation in 1961. In the following years, the proportion of domestic capital formation financed by foreign capital declined rapidly and dropped to only 33 percent in 1966. After 1967, Hong Kong was self-sufficient in the domestic supply of capital and thereafter became a net exporter of capital. This is perhaps due less to the relative decline of the supply of foreign capital in Hong Kong than to the fact that the political uncertainty of Hong Kong's future presumably has inhibited the long-term commitment of investment in capital-intensive industries and has thus dampened the demand for investible funds in Hong Kong.

In the cases of Korea and Singapore, particularly the latter, the reliance upon foreign capital after take-off continued to be important, though the share of gross domestic capital formation financed by foreign capital inflows gradually decreased.

Direct foreign investment was not a very important component of total gross domestic capital formation in any of the four Asian NICs except Singapore. In Taiwan, it averaged only 3.3 percent of the total gross capital formation for the whole period from 1951 to 1980. The corresponding figure in Korea was only 2 percent for 1972–77.

There is reason to believe, however, that direct foreign investments may have played a significant role in the transmission of new methods of production and management. As we may observe from table 7.10, foreign investment tends to concentrate chiefly in the electronics and electrical, chemical, and petroleum industries, which are relatively more technology-intensive. Other fields of concentration are machinery and technical instruments, basic metal, and nonferrous metal, which are also relatively technology-intensive. Foreign-operated plants, as well as plants operated jointly by domestic and foreign capital, are apt to adopt more up-to-date methods of production and management, and to produce newer types of products. Their techniques tend to spread to other domestic firms through emulation, movement of trained personnel, and technical assistance to local suppliers. Thus, although direct foreign investments may not have been very important in terms of the total amount of funds invested, they may have been significant vehicles for transmission of technology. Furthermore, direct foreign investment usually brings with it guaranteed foreign markets for its own products, and thus helps expand the exports of the host countries and increases their foreign exchange earnings. Because these

Table 7.10. Structure of Direct Foreign Investment in Manufacturing Sector (%)

Major Industries	Taiwan (1952–79)	Korea (1962–80)	Hong Kong (at end of 1980)	Singapore (1965–80)
Electrical & electronics	43.8	17.5	32.2	16.1
Chemical & petroleum	14.9	37.5	12.0	45.9
Metal & machinery	17.5	21.3	13.5	20.5
Textile & clothing	6.9	16.1	16.3	4.9
Others	16.9	7.6	26.0	12.6
Total	100.0	100.0	100.0	100.0

Sources: For Taiwan, *Statistics on Overseas Chinese and Foreign Investment, the Republic of China* (December 31, 1979).
For Korea, supplied by Economic Planning Board, Korea.
For Hong Kong, supplied by Trade, Industry, and Customs Department, Hong Kong.
For Singapore, Economic Development Board (various issues).

four NICs have an ample supply of their own domestic savings and because the dominant proportion of their capital formation is financed by their own domestic savings, they do not harbor obsessive fears of domination by foreign capital or multinational corporations, the sort of fears which one finds in developing countries that are unable to generate adequate supplies of domestic savings.

Concluding Remarks

In sum, the experience of rapid economic growth in Taiwan, Korea, Hong Kong, and Singapore during the past two or three decades was achieved not by economic tricks, but by sensible policies based on sound neoclassical economic principles. It should provide useful lessons for other developing countries on how to achieve an economic take-off without tears or bloodshed.

Appendix

The mathematical model of Tsiang (1964), upon which the diagrammatical representation of the theory of economic take-off in the introductory section of this paper is based, is a simple one-commodity model with an aggregate production function of the Cobb-Douglas type, such as

$$Y = AK^{\alpha(t)}L^{\beta(t)}N^{\gamma(t)} \exp\left(\int_0^t g(\tau)d\tau\right), \tag{7.1}$$

where K, L, and N stand for the total amount of capital, labor and natural resources (land), respectively, and A is a constant. The parameters α, β, and γ are supposed to be variable over time according to the biased nature of technical progress, but always subject to the restriction that

$$\alpha(t) + \beta(t) + \gamma(t) = 1. \tag{7.2}$$

Assuming that N, the amount of natural resources, is an inaugmentable constant, the rate of growth of output in general, or real GDP, is then

$$y = \dot{Y}/Y = \alpha k + \beta \ell + g^*, \tag{7.3}$$

where
$$k = \dot{K}/K, \ \ell = \dot{L}/L,$$
and
$$g^* = g + \dot{\alpha}\ln K + \dot{\beta}\ln L + \dot{\gamma}\ln N. \tag{7.4}$$

Therefore, g^* is the net effect upon the rate of growth of output of technical progress, which might be biased towards different factors of production at different times. When technical progress is strictly neutral, g^* would be identical with g, which then represents the rate of neutral technical progress (in the Hicksian sense).

The rate of growth of population, and hence labor supply, is assumed to be a function of current real wage rate, so that

$$L_t = L_0 \exp(\int_0^t \ell(Y_L)d\tau), \tag{7.5}$$

where Y_L, the marginal productivity of labor, is equal to $\beta(Y/L)$ or $\beta\bar{Y}$, $\bar{Y}$ being defined as Y/L.

Write $\bar{y}$ for the rate of growth of $\bar{Y}$. Then

$$\bar{y} = (1/\bar{Y})\,d\bar{Y}/dt = \alpha\hat{r} + g^* - \gamma\ell \tag{7.6}$$

where $\hat{r}$ is the rate of growth of $r = K/L$.

Assuming that domestic savings always results in equal increase in domestic capital and for the time being that there is no investment financed by foreign capital inflows or aids, then

$$\bar{S} = \dot{K}/L$$

and

$$\hat{r} = (1/r)(dr/dt) = (1/r)[\dot{K}/L - (K/L)\dot{L}/L] = (1/r)(\bar{S} - r\ell).$$

Thus, we may conclude that provided that the two conditions

(i) $\bar{S} - r\ell > 0$,

and

(ii) $g^* - \gamma\ell > 0$,

are satisfied, then the real per capita income of the economy will be capable of continuous self-sustained growth. These two are what we called in the text the basic condition and the supplementary condition for take-off respectively.

References

Bank of Korea. 1971, 1974, 1978, 1980. *Economic Statistics Yearbook*.
Bank of Korea. 1978. *National Income in Korea*.
Brown, Gilbert T. 1973. *Korean Pricing Policies and Economic Development in the 1960s*. Baltimore, Md.: The Johns Hopkins University Press.
Chen, Edward K. Y. 1980. "The Economic Setting." In David G. Lethbridge, ed., *The Business Environment in Hong Kong*. London: Oxford University Press.
Chen, Edward K. Y. 1979. *Hyper-Growth in Asian Economies*. London: Macmillan.
Chia Siow Yue. 1979. "Singapore's Trade Strategy and Industrial Development, with Special Reference to the ASEAN Common Approach to Foreign Economic Policy." Mimeo.
Geiger, T., and F. M. Geiger. 1973. *Tales of Two City-States: The Development Progress of Hong Kong and Singapore*. Washington, D.C.: National Planning Association.
Hong, Wontack. 1976. *Factor Supply and Factor Intensity of Trade in Korea*. Seoul: Korea Development Institute.
Hsueh, Tien-tung. 1979. "Hong Kong Model of Economic Development." In T. B. Lin, Rance P. L. Lee, and Udo-Ernst Simonis, ed., *Hong Kong: Economic, Social and Political Studies in Development*. White Plains, N.Y.: M.E. Sharpe; Folkstone, Kent, England: Wm. Dawson & Sons, Ltd.
International Monetary Fund. 1980a. *Balance of Payments Yearbook*.
International Monetary Fund. 1980b. *International Financial Statistics*.
Lethbridge, David G. 1980. *The Business Environment in Hong Kong*. London: Oxford University Press.
Lewis, W. A. 1955. *The Theory of Economic Growth*. Homewood, Ill.: Richard D. Irwin.
Mun Kin-chok and Ho Suk-ching. 1979. "Foreign Investment in Hong Kong." In T. B. Lin, Rance P. L. Lee, and Udo-Ernst Simonis, eds., *Hong Kong: Economic, Social and Political Studies in Development*, 275–96. White Plains, N.Y.: M.E. Sharpe.
Rostow, W. W. 1961. *The Stages of Economic Growth: A Non-Communist Manifesto*. London: Cambridge University Press.
Solow, R. M. 1958. "A Contribution to the Theory of Economic Growth." *Quarterly Journal of Economics* 62 (November): 65–94.
Tsiang, S. C. 1964. "A Model of Economic Growth in Rostovian Stages." *Econometrica* 32: 619–48.
Tsiang, S. C. 1979. "Fashions and Misconceptions in Monetary Theory and Their Influences on Financial and Banking Policies." *Zeitschrift für die gesamte Staatswissenschaft* 135 (December): 584–604.
Tsiang, S. C. 1980. "Exchange Rate, Interset Rate, and Economic Development, The Experience of Taiwan." In L. Klein, M. Nerlove, and S. C. Tsiang, eds., *Quantitative Economics and Development*, 309–46 New York: Academic Press.
Wu, R. I., C. F. Wang-Lien, T. C. Chou, and C. K. Li 1980. *American Investments and Their Effects on Our Country*. Taipei: Institute of American Culture, Academia Sinica.

Government Publications

Taiwan
- Council for Economic Planning and Development. 1981. *Taiwan Statistical Data Book.*
- Directorate-General of Budget, Accounting and Statistics. 1980. *National Income of the Republic of China.*

Korea
- *Indicators of Major Statistics.*

Hong Kong
- Census and Statistics Department. 1980. *The 1980–1981 Budget: Estimates of Gross Domestic Product 1966–78.*
- Census and Statistics Department. 1979. *Hong Kong Statistics 1947–67.* Hong Kong: Government Printer.
- Census and Statistics Department. 1971, 1974, 1977. *Hong Kong Review of Overseas Trade in 1970, 1973 and 1976.* Hong Kong: Government Printer.
- *Hong Kong Annual Report.* Various years.

Singapore
- *Singapore National Accounts 1960–73.*
- *Yearbook of Statistics, Singapore, 1980/81.* 1981.
- Economic Development Board. *Annual Report.* Various issues.

United Nations. 1979. *Yearbook of National Accounts Statistics.*

8   Industrialization and Employment in
    Hong Kong, Korea, Singapore,
    and Taiwan
    Gary S. Fields

What are the links between macroeconomic growth and microeconomic development objectives? The initial view held by many economists, especially Latin America specialists, was that the goals of growth, employment, and income distribution are mutually incompatible and that the pursuit of all these objectives at once is bound to be futile. But in the last few years, studies of the economies of the Asian Newly Industrializing Countries (NICs), Hong Kong, Korea, Singapore, and Taiwan—the so-called "Group of Four"—have emerged, and they point to very rapid aggregate growth and marked improvements in labor market conditions and in income distribution.[1] This chapter assembles the latest available information and

For helpful discussions and suggestions, I wish to thank Walter Galenson, Shirley Kuo, Paul Liu, Pang Eng Fong, M. K. Ramakrishnan, Chia Siow Yue, Edward Chen, Tzong-biau Lin, Victor Mok, Se-Il Park, Vivian Fields, Jorge Ducci, Olivia Mitchell, Lawrence Krause, and the participants in seminars at the University of Hong Kong, the Korea Development Institute, the Brookings Institution, and Harvard University. None of these persons or institutions should be held responsible for the contents of this paper. It is a pleasure to acknowledge the invaluable research assistance of Jorge Ducci and the able typing of Debbie Nivison.

1. Among the useful sources are:
Hong Kong: Ronald Hsia and Laurence Chau, *Industrialization, Employment and Income Distribution* (London: Croom Helm, 1978), and Steven Chow and Gustav Papanek, "Laissez Faire, Growth, and Equity—Hong Kong," *The Economic Journal* (June 1981).
Korea: Irma Adelman and Sherman Robinson, *Income Distribution Policy in Developing Countries* (New York: Oxford University Press, 1979) and Hakchung Choo, "Economic Growth and Income Distribution," in *Human Resources and Social Development in Korea*, edited by Chong Kee Park (Seoul: Korea Development Institute, 1980).
Singapore: V. V. Bhanoji Rao and M. K. Ramakrishnan, *Income Inequality in Singapore* (Singapore: Singapore University Press, 1980), and Pang Eng Fong, "Economic Development and the Labor Market in a Newly Industrializing Country: The Experience of Singapore," *The Developing Economies* (March 1981).
Taiwan: John C. H. Fei, Gustav Ranis, and Shirley W. Y. Kuo, *Growth with Equity: The Taiwan Case* (New York: Oxford University Press, 1979), and Walter Galenson, ed., *Eco-*

examines the interrelationships between the macroeconomy and the labor market, with special reference to foreign trade and foreign investment.

The impressive macroeconomic improvements that have taken place in Hong Kong, Korea, Singapore, and Taiwan are well known and include:

1. Extremely high rates of GDP growth. Economic growth rates averaged 8 percent and more in real terms throughout the sixties and seventies. Growth of this magnitude would be expected to shift the derived demand for labor curve outward, raising employment.
2. High rates of growth of exports. Each country achieved high GNP growth through export-led growth in which foreign investment played an important role. In the seventies, the rates of export growth ranged from 4.8 percent per year in Hong Kong to 28.8 percent in Korea. Because the export industries are labor-intensive, export growth would imply improvements in labor market conditions.
3. Structural shifts in the locus of economic activity. Over the last two decades, important sectoral changes have taken place. Most notable are the decline of agriculture and the rising importance of manufacturing in Korea, Singapore, and Taiwan, and the growth of finance relative to other economic sectors in Hong Kong. The labor market implications of these structural shifts are examined below.

As impressive as the macroeconomic improvements, though a subject of less attention, are the gains that have taken place with respect to labor market conditions and income distribution. Unemployment rates have fallen below 4 percent while labor force participation rates have been rising. The industrial composition of employment has improved, in that workers have left agriculture, self-employment, and unpaid family work—all relatively low paying activities—and moved into modern-sector jobs, where earnings are higher. The occupational structure of modern-sector employment has improved. Real wages have increased by as much as a factor of four.[2] Relative income inequality has fallen in three of the economies (Hong Kong, Singapore, and Taiwan). Absolute poverty has sharply

---

nomic Growth and Structural Change in Taiwan (Ithaca, N.Y.: Cornell University Press, 1979).

For an overall comparison of Hong Kong, Japan, Korea, Singapore and Taiwan: Edward K. Y. Chen, *Hyper-Growth in Asian Economies* (New York: Holmes and Meier, 1979).

2. Throughout this chapter, I use the terms "earnings" or "wages" to refer to pay per week or month.

diminished in all four. Real wages and incomes are a great deal higher throughout the four Asian NICs than they were two decades ago.

But not everything is entirely rosy. Korea suffered a serious recession in 1980, and there is some worry that the structural problems leading up to that recession have not been dealt with satisfactorily. Income inequality appears to be on the rise in Hong Kong and Korea. Wage growth in Singapore has lagged seriously behind the growth of national income. All four economies are vulnerable to world recession, to changing trade opportunities and conditions, and to possible squeezes from above by the Organization for Economic Cooperation and Development (OECD) countries and Japan and from below by emerging less developed economies such as Malaysia and the Philippines. Political uncertainties also loom on the horizon.

Improvements in Labor Market Conditions and Income Distribution

Rates of Employment and Unemployment

The most commonly used indicator of labor market conditions is the unemployment rate. Unemployment rates at the beginning of the eighties were: Hong Kong, 4.3 percent; Korea, 4.1 percent; Singapore, 3.1 percent; and Taiwan, 1.3 percent. Compared to the unemployment rates in many Western nations, this is a very favorable performance.

Table 8.1 presents time series data on changes in unemployment over time. In two of the countries—Korea and Taiwan—data have been available on an annual basis since the fifties and sixties. They indicate quite steady declines in unemployment rates. In Hong Kong and Singapore, the data until the mid-seventies are more fragmentary. In each case, the earliest source is a population census. I am hesitant to compare these unemployment rates with later ones, because of major methodological differences between the earlier sources and subsequent ones.[3] If, then, we use only later data, we find that the unemployment rate in Hong Kong rose in the early seventies and then fell to about 4 percent of the labor force, whereas in Singapore unemployment hovered around 10 percent throughout the late sixties, then fell sharply to the neighborhood of 3 percent in the early eighties.

---

3. For instance, in Hong Kong, the *Population Census 1961*, Table 215, categorizes the entire population, including infants and children, into various groups of employees, unemployed, retirees, independent workers, students, housewives, etc. Later censuses, much more sensibly, tabulate only persons in the economically active population over the age of 14; these persons are broken down into "working persons" and "unemployed persons," omitting entirely students, housewives, retirees, and other economically inactive people. Thus, the groupings in the 1961 figures do not conform to those in later censuses, so intercensus comparisons of unemployment rates should probably not be made.

Table 8.1. Unemployment Rates (%)

	Hong Kong			Singapore		Taiwan[a]		
	Censuses & Household Surveys	Labor Force Surveys[b]	Korea	Censuses & Household Surveys	Labor Force Surveys	Labor Force Surveys	Shirley W. Y. Kuo	Census of Population
1953							6.3	
1954							6.0	
1955							6.0	
1956							5.6	6.3
1957				5.2[c]			5.7	
1958							5.9	
1959							6.0	
1960							6.1	
1961	1.7[c]						6.2	
1962							6.3	
1963			8.2				6.4	
1964			7.7			4.3	6.4	
1965			7.4			3.3	5.2	
1966			7.1	9.1[d]		3.1	4.2	6.1
1967			6.2			2.3	3.4	
1968			5.1			1.7	2.8	
1969			4.8			1.9	3.4	
1970			4.5	10.4[c]		1.7	3.0	4.6
1971	4.4[d]		4.5			1.7	3.0	
1972			4.5	7.0[d]		1.5	2.8	
1973			4.0		4.0[d]	1.3	2.2	
1974			4.1		3.9	1.5	2.7	
1975		Sept. 9.1	4.1		4.5	2.4	3.7	
1976	4.3[e]	Mar. 5.6	3.9		4.4	1.5		
1977		Mar. 4.5; Sept. 4.1	3.8	4.8[d]	3.9	1.3		
1978		Mar. 3.8; Sept. 2.7	3.2		3.6	1.7		
1979		Mar. 2.3; Sept. 3.4	3.8		3.3	1.3		
1980		Mar. 3.2; Sept. 4.3	5.2	3.5[d]	3.1	1.2		
1981			4.1[f]			1.3		

Sources: For Hong Kong, computed from official census publications and Census and Statistics Department, *Report on Labor Force Survey* (various issues).

For Korea, Bank of Korea, *Economic Statistics Yearbook* (1981), table 145, pp. 270–71; and *Monthly Economic Statistics* (December 1981), table 96, p. 125.

For Singapore, Census and Household Surveys, computed from the respective official publications; *Report on the Labor Force Survey of Singapore* (various issues).

For Taiwan, Walter Galenson, "The Labor Force, Wages and Living Standards," in Galenson, ed., *Economic Growth and Structural Change in Taiwan* (Ithaca, N.Y.: Cornell University Press, 1979), table 6.13; *Taiwan Statistical Data Book 1981*, table 2.9; Directorate-General of Budget, Accounting and Statistics, *Statistical Yearbook of the Republic of China* (1981), supplementary table 4, p. 60.

[a] Age not specified.
[b] As proportion of labor force, ages 15 through 64.
[c] As proportion of economically active population, all ages.
[d] As proportion of economically active population, ages 10 and over.
[e] As proportion of economically active population, ages 14 and over.
[f] Third quarter, 1981.

All four economies achieved low rates of unemployment despite two demographic factors that made the attainment of full employment more than ordinarily difficult—population growth and rising labor force participation.

Table 8.2 displays population growth figures for each country. These growth rates, though moderate by international standards, nonetheless obligated the economies of these countries to create more jobs to attain a given employment rate. Population growth rates declined in all four countries as a result of falling birth rates and/or reduced immigration. Birth rates fell for a variety of reasons: the desire for smaller families, a decline in birth rates catching up with an earlier decline in child mortality, improved access to birth control information and technology, and government encouragement of small families. Immigration declines reflected restrictive government policies. Table 8.2 also shows that Korea, Singapore, and Taiwan clearly were able to expand employment at a rate faster than that at which the population was growing. Not so for Hong Kong. There, employment growth did not keep up with population growth, in part because of spurts of massive immigration; in 1980, immigration was severely restricted.

The other important demographic factor at work was rising labor force participation. Economic development frequently causes labor force participation rates to change. The reasons differ for men and women. For women, economic development commonly creates new job opportunities

Table 8.2. Population Growth and Employment Growth (% per annum)

Hong Kong[a]	Korea	Singapore	Taiwan
Employment Growth	*Employment Growth*	*Employment Growth*	*Employment Growth*
1961–76 = 3.1	1963–77 = 3.8	1957–79 = 3.7	1950–79 = 3.5
	1963–70 = 3.0		
	1970–78 = 4.1		
Population Growth	*Population Growth*	*Population Growth*	*Population Growth*
1961–76 = 3.4	1960–80 = 2.1	1960–79 = 1.9	1950–79 = 2.9

Sources: For Hong Kong, *Hong Kong Annual Report*, various issues.
For Korea, Population growth: Economic Planning Board, *Korea Statistical Yearbook* (1981), table II.1, p. 37. Employment growth: Bank of Korea, *Economic Statistics Yearbook* (1979), table 136, pp. 256–57.
For Singapore, Population growth: *Singapore Yearbook*, various issues. Employment growth: Computed from 1957 Census and 1979 Labor Force Survey.
For Taiwan, Directorate-General of Budget, Accounting, and Statistics, *Statistical Yearbook of the Republic of China* (1980), supplementary table 1, p. 4.
[a] For population ages 15 and over.

and raises the return on work in the labor market relative to work in the home, inducing larger numbers of women to participate in the labor force. For men, higher standards of living raise life expectancy, increase the likelihood that an older worker will live long enough and be able to afford to retire before he dies, and permit young males to remain in school longer—all of which lower male labor force participation rates.

Table 8.3 shows changing labor force participation rates in the four countries. In each, labor force participation rates rose for women and, except in Singapore, fell for men. The aggregate participation rate for both sexes went up in Korea, Singapore, and Taiwan and was effectively unchanged in Hong Kong. With labor force participation rates on the rise, the fall in unemployment rates is all the more impressive, since enough new jobs were created to employ those who were attracted into the labor force by improved job opportunities as well as those who previously were unemployed.

Note too the range in labor force participation rates across the four economies. Taiwan's is the highest. Although to the best of my knowledge, the reasons for these differences have not been explored rigorously in any empirical study, one contributing factor appears to be the four economies' respective rates of unemployment. Observe that the rank ordering of labor force participation rates is: Taiwan highest, then Singapore, Korea, and Hong Kong, whereas the rank ordering of unemployment rates is just the opposite—Hong Kong highest, then Korea, Singapore, and Taiwan. This is consistent with an "encouraged worker effect," that is, the availability of jobs encourages additional persons to enter the labor force and fill those jobs.

Employment Composition

Besides improvements in the rate of employment, employment composition also improved during the sustained period of growth in the four Asian NICs. These improvements are revealed in the following data on the mix of jobs by industry, activity status, occupation, and education.

Employment by Industry. The industrial mix of employment has shifted in favor of relatively high-paying activities. To establish this, we must first identify the well-paying industries. Table 8.4 presents the current structure of earnings by one-digit industry. In each country, two industries—agriculture and manufacturing—exhibit wage levels below their economy-wide averages. The below-average wage position of agriculture is not surprising; the same is generally true around the world. But the position of manufacturing as a relatively low-wage industry is unusual by international standards. In other developing regions, manufacturing wages are above

Table 8.3. Labor Force Participation Rates (as % of population ages 15 and over)

	Hong Kong			Korea			Singapore			Taiwan		
	1961	1971	1963	1970	1980	1957	1970	1979	1960	1970	1979
Males	76.5	70.9	76.4	75.1	73.6	76.6	67.6	80.7	87.2	80.4	82.4
Females	32.3	37.1	36.3	38.5	41.6	19.3	24.6	41.9	25.0	30.2	46.7
Both sexes	55.0	54.2	55.3	55.9	57.6	49.0	46.6	61.4	56.8	57.1	65.5

Sources: For Hong Kong, Census and Statistics Department, *Hong Kong Social & Economic Trends, 1964–1974*, table 2.1, p. 5.
For Korea, Economic Planning Board, *Annual Report on the Economically Active Population, 1974*, tables 5.2 and 5.3, p. 31; and *Korea Statistical Yearbook, 1981*, table III.1, p. 69.
For Singapore, *Population Census 1970*, table 10.1; and *Report on Labor Force Survey, 1979*, table 1.
For Taiwan, *Statistical Yearbook of the Republic of China, 1980*, supplementary tables 1 and 8.

Table 8.4. Current Structure of Earnings (wages) by Industry

	Earnings (wages)						Percentage of Average Earnings					
	Hong Kong[a]	Korea[b]	Singapore		Taiwan		Hong Kong	Korea	Singapore		Taiwan	
Industry	1980	1980	1977[c]	1979[d]	1979[e]		1980	1980	1977	1979	1979	
Agriculture	⎰1,000	n.a.	282	118	63		⎰0.72	1.15	0.71	0.83	0.60	
Mining	⎱	203		215	110		⎱			1.50	1.05	
Manufacturing	1,070	147	359	119	96		0.78	0.83	0.90	0.83	0.91	
Utilities	1,750	283	430	165	138		1.27	1.61	1.08	1.15	1.31	
Construction	1,770	258	434	139	106		1.28	1.46	1.09	0.97	1.01	
Commerce	1,790	211	400	135	135		1.30	1.20	1.00	0.94	1.29	
Transport	1,850	203	417	162	143		1.34	1.16	1.05	1.13	1.36	
Finance	1,850	282	687	194	145		1.34	1.60	1.72	1.36	1.38	
Services	1,480	275	366	164	125		1.07	1.56	0.92	1.15	1.19	
Unclassified					76						0.72	
All industries	1,380	176	399	143	105		1.00	1.00	1.00	1.00	1.00	

Sources: For Hong Kong, Report on Labor Force Survey (September 1980), table I.49.
For Korea, Economic Planning Board, Korea Statistical Yearbook, 1981, table 3.8, p. 83.
For Singapore, Survey of Households 1977, table 10; Yearbook of Labor Statistics, 1979, table 28.
For Taiwan, Survey of Personal Income 1979, table 7.

[a] Median earnings per month (HK$).
[b] Mean monthly earnings of regular employees by industry (thousands of won).
[c] Mean earnings per month (S$), based on survey of households.
[d] Weekly earnings of employees, based on survey of establishments.
[e] Annual primary income per working recipient (NT$ thousands).

average. The premium of manufacturing wages over agricultural wages is about 20 percent in the four Asian NICs, compared to about 100 percent elsewhere.[4] Reasons for these differences are examined below.

Data on changes in employment structure over time are given in table 8.5. The four countries started the sixties with varying employment structures. Hong Kong was the most industrialized of the four; there, manufacturing was the largest sector of employment, engaging 43 percent of the labor force in 1961. In Taiwan as well, manufacturing was the largest employer, accounting for 32 percent of nonagricultural employment in 1964. In contrast, Korea and Singapore were notably less industrialized 20 years ago, the shares of manufacturing in total employment having been 22 percent and 18 percent respectively.

These initial conditions partly explain how the industrial structure of employment evolved in the last 20 years. Hong Kong, having the most advanced manufacturing sector around 1960, had the least scope for growth of manufacturing employment. Indeed, Hong Kong's industrial structure of employment has been the most stable of the four, the growth of employment in manufacturing in the sixties and seventies being only slightly above the average for nonagricultural employment as a whole (4.1 percent per year versus 3.6 percent). By contrast, commerce and finance expanded employment by 8 percent and 9 percent per year respectively in Hong Kong. Thus, while the share of manufacturing in nonagricultural employment virtually held constant, the share of commerce and finance more than doubled (from 12 percent to 26 percent).

In the other three countries, the percentage of the work force employed in manufacturing was initially smaller. Manufacturing employment was able to grow quickly, because of the growth of manufacturing output oriented primarily toward the export market. In Korea and Taiwan, the only other industries to achieve comparable rates of employment growth were the construction sectors, while in Singapore only the finance sector grew faster than did manufacturing. By 1979, the share of manufacturing employment in total employment in Taiwan (41 percent) was nearly as large as in Hong Kong (42 percent).

On the other end of the industrial distribution, agricultural employment has diminished in relative importance in each country. As recently as the early sixties, half or more of Taiwan's and Korea's labor forces were employed in agriculture; those shares were about halved by the late seventies. In absolute terms, agricultural employment remained un-

---

4. In Mexico, for example, average weekly wages among manufacturing workers were 127 percent of the economy-wide average and the agricultural wage 64 percent, producing a manufacturing/agriculture wage differential of 2:1. (David Turnham, *The Employment Problem in Less Developed Countries* [Paris: OECD: 1971], p. 75).

Table 8.5. Changes in the Structure of Employment by Industry

Percentage Distribution of Employment

Industry	Hong Kong 1961	Hong Kong 1971	Hong Kong 1976	Hong Kong 1980	Korea 1963	Korea 1970	Korea 1980	Singapore 1957	Singapore 1970	Singapore 1979	Taiwan 1964	Taiwan 1970	Taiwan 1979
Mining	0.8	3.3	0.1	0.0	2.0	2.3	1.4				3.0	3.3	1.2
Manufacturing	43.1	43.8	46.1		21.6	26.6	32.8	17.4	22.8	29.2	31.7	32.3	41.3
Construction	9.1	11.0	5.9	7.7	6.8	5.9	9.3	5.0	6.9	5.4	5.9	7.9	10.2
Utilities	1.7	0.6	0.5	0.5	0.9			0.9	1.2	1.0	1.6	1.2	0.6
Commerce	10.4	⎱ 13.5	19.7	26.8	26.8	⎱ 65.2	⎱ 56.5	⎱ 30.8	24.3	23.6	⎱ 20.3	23.2	19.5
Finance	1.5	⎰	3.4	4.9		⎰	⎰	⎰	3.7	7.2	⎰		
Transport	6.9	7.6	7.6	7.6	4.0			11.2	12.6	11.8	8.4	8.5	7.5
Services	24.0	20.3	15.4	16.3	37.9			33.7	28.2	21.6	25.7	23.3	19.7
Unclassified	1.5	n.a.	1.3		n.a.			0.8	0.4	0.2	3.3	0.3	n.a.
Percentage of nonagricultural employment	100.0	100.0	100.0	100.0	100.0	100.0	100.0	100.0	100.0	100.0	100.0	100.0	100.0
Agriculture as a percentage of total employment	7.4	4.0	2.5	1.4	63.2	50.4	34.0	6.9	3.5	1.5	50.0	36.8	21.5

Annual Rates of Growth of Employment by Industry

Industry	Hong Kong 1961-76	Hong Kong 1961-71	Hong Kong 1971-76	Korea 1963-78	Korea 1963-70	Korea 1970-78	Singapore 1957-79	Singapore 1957-70	Singapore 1970-79	Taiwan 1964-79	Taiwan 1964-70	Taiwan 1970-79
Mining	-13.0	19.2	-53.6	4.0	9.4	-0.5	n.a.	n.a.	n.a.	0.3	9.1	-5.1
Manufacturing	4.1	3.7	4.8	11.0	10.7	11.3	6.3	4.9	8.3	8.5	7.2	9.4
Construction	0.6	5.5	-8.5	9.9	5.1	14.2	4.2	5.3	2.6	10.6	12.2	9.5
Utilities	-4.3	-7.3	1.9				4.2	5.1	2.9	-0.4	1.6	-1.8
Commerce	8.1	4.9	15.4	5.2	6.4	4.2	2.6	1.0	5.0	6.4	9.3	4.4
Finance	9.2								13.5			
Transport	3.3	3.2	3.5				4.1	3.7	4.7	5.9	7.2	4.9
Services	0.6	1.8	-1.8				1.7	1.4	2.2	4.8	5.2	4.5
Unclassified	n.a.	n.a.	n.a.	n.a.	n.a.	n.a.	n.a.	n.a.	n.a.	n.a.	n.a.	n.a.
Percentage of nonagricultural employment	3.6	3.6	3.7	7.2	7.4	7.0	3.8	2.8	5.3	6.6	6.9	6.4
Agriculture as a percentage of total employment	-3.8	-3.0	-5.4	0.2	-0.3	0.7	-3.4	-2.8	-4.3	-2.2	-2.3	-2.1

Sources: For Hong Kong, *Census 1961*, table 238; *Census 1971*, table 11; *Census 1976*, table 13; *Report on Labor Force Survey, Sept. 1980*, table I.49.

For Korea, Bank of Korea, *Economic Statistics Yearbook* (1965 and 1979) and Economic Planning Board, *Economic Statistics Yearbook*, 1981, table III.8, p. 83.

For Singapore, *Census 1970*, table 10.48; *Report on LF Survey 1979*, table 44.

For Taiwan, Directorate-General of Budget, Accounting, and Statistics, *Statistical Yearbook of the Republic of China* (1980), Manpower, supplementary table 1.

Table 8.6. Employment by Activity Status (%)

	Hong Kong 1961	1971	1980
Employers	4.8	2.7	4.0
Own account	10.4	8.6	5.8
Employees	83.8	87.3	89.4
On commission	0.8	0.4	
Permanent	66.2	78.0	85.4
Casual	11.5	6.3	
Unpaid family workers	4.4	2.3	1.8
Out worker	0.9	0.3	2.2
Trainees & learners, miscellaneous		0.9	1.4	0.7
Total	100.0	100.0	100.0

	Korea 1963	1971	1980
Self-employed	37.2	34.2	33.9
Unpaid family workers	31.3	26.5	18.8
Employees	31.5	39.3	47.3
Regular	12.3	23.1	30.4
Temporary	6.5	5.7	7.4
Daily	12.7	10.5	9.5
Total	100.0	100.0	100.0

	Singapore 1957	1970	1979
Employers	3.7	2.8	4.0
Own account	17.5	17.1	9.3
Unpaid family workers	5.1	3.6	3.2
Employees	73.7	76.5	83.5
Total	100.0	100.0	100.0

	Taiwan 1956	1964	1970	1979
Employers	3.2	2.4	2.8	4.1
Own account	35.5	29.9	26.0	21.0
Unpaid family workers	24.4	28.5	20.3	11.2
Private employees	21.3	25.5	38.2	51.8
Government employees	15.5	13.7	12.5	11.9
Total	100.0	100.0	100.0	100.0

Sources: For Hong Kong, *Census 1961*, table 215, *Census 1971*, table 8. *Report on Labor Force Survey* (September 1980), table I.3.

(source notes continued on facing page)

changed in Korea and declined in the other three countries. "Pull" rather than "push" forces were responsible for these changes; that is, rather than being forced from the land, labor willingly left agriculture to take jobs in expanding sectors, especially manufacturing.

At present, the shares of agriculture in total employment are, not surprisingly, a great deal lower in the city-states than in the two larger countries: 1.4 percent in Hong Kong, 1.5 percent in Singapore, 21.5 percent in Taiwan, and 34.0 percent in Korea. In fact, agriculture is still by far the largest employment sector in Korea. As for the industrial distribution of nonagricultural employment, manufacturing is now the single largest sector in each country, ranging from 29 percent in Singapore to 42 percent in Hong Kong. In each case, commerce and services also constitute a large share of employment. Other sectors are of relatively minor importance.

Combining the information in tables 8.4 and 8.5, we find evidence that the composition of employment has shifted systematically in favor of higher-paying sectors. One such shift is the movement from agriculture into manufacturing which took place in each country. In as much as manufacturing wages are higher than agricultural wages, the rising share of manufacturing in total employment combined with the falling share of agriculture provides one piece of evidence of job upgrading. Other important shifts are: the rising importance of employment in commerce and finance (high-wage industries) in Hong Kong; the diminishing importance of service employment (mixed evidence on whether service is a high-wage or low-wage industry) in Singapore; and the increasing share (as a proportion of total employment) of employment in Taiwan's service sector (a high-wage industry).

Employment by Activity Status. When economic development is successfully taking place, another dimension of structural change is to be found in the mix of jobs by activity status, i.e., a rising proportion of a country's labor force working as employees and smaller proportions engaged as own-account workers, unpaid family workers, and casual employees such as day workers. The data presented in table 8.6 indicate that such improvements have occurred in the four Asian NICs.

For Korea, Se-Il Park: *Wages in Korea*, table 5, p. 29. Economic Planning Board, *Korea Statistical Yearbook, 1981*, table III.2, p. 73.

For Singapore, *Population Census 1970*, table 10.10; *Report on Labor Force Survey, 1979*, table 11.

For Taiwan, Directorate-General of Budget, Accounting, and Statistics, *Statistical Yearbook of the Republic of China, 1980*, supplementary table 9, p. 24, and supplementary table 3, p. 48.

Employees constitute a considerably higher proportion of total employment in Hong Kong and Singapore than in Korea and Taiwan. By contrast, Korea and Taiwan have much larger proportions of their labor forces in own-account employment and unpaid family work than do Hong Kong and Singapore. These differences reflect the city-states' higher levels of national income and the consequent expansion of wage employment relative to the other activity status categories.

Employment by Occupation. A third indicator of employment upgrading is the occupational structure of employment. Data on the current structure of earnings by occupation and on changes in the occupational distribution of employment are presented in tables 8.7 and 8.8 respectively.

As in other developing economies, the occupations that earn the highest wages are administrative and managerial, and professional and technical. Those occupying intermediate pay positions are clerical, sales, and service occupations.[5] Production workers are next lowest. Agricultural workers are at the bottom.

The occupational structure of employment has shifted somewhat in favor of better-paying occupations. Agriculture is the lowest-paying sector, and the fraction of the labor force employed in that sector has diminished with economic development in each country. Many of the persons who left agriculture found jobs as production workers; the figure for production workers increased as a proportion of total nonagricultural employment in Korea and Taiwan and held steady in Hong Kong and Singapore, reflecting the fact that economic growth in Korea and Taiwan was based to a large degree on the production of manufactured goods for export. Professional and technical occupations, relatively high-income categories, expanded their shares of total employment, as is typical in the course of economic development. The rapid expansion of employment in professional, technical, and production employment caused service employment to expand less rapidly in the four Asian NICs than in many other developing economies.

Employment by Education. A fourth indicator of employment upgrading is an improving educational level of the labor force. The evidence presented

---

5. Service occupations and service industries occupy different earnings rankings. Service occupations are moderate to low-paying (table 8.7), whereas service industries pay relatively well (table 8.4). The difference is that service industries include government, medicine, law, and other high-paying activities, but government workers are in administrative and clerical occupation and doctors and lawyers are in professional occupations, not service occupations.

Table 8.7. Structure of Earnings by Occupation

| | Earnings in National Currency ||||| Earnings Index (Average = 1.00) |||||
Occupation	Hong Kong 1980[a]	Korea 1980[b]	Singapore 1977[c]	Singapore 1979[d]	Taiwan 1979[e]	Hong Kong 1980	Korea 1980	Singapore 1977	Singapore 1979	Taiwan 1979
Professional & technical	2,960	266	846	}342	163	2.14	1.76	2.12	}2.39	1.55
Administrative & managerial	4,380	438	1,563		244	3.17	2.91	3.93		2.32
Clerical	1,490	177	412	}117	122	1.08	1.17	1.03	}0.82	1.16
Sales	1,470	109	408		134	1.07	0.72	1.02		1.28
Services	1,270	115	266		111	0.92	0.76	0.67		1.06
Agricultural	1,070	131	266	}97	63	0.78	0.87	0.67	}0.68	0.60
Production	1,540	118	289		90	1.12	0.78	0.72		0.86
Not classified	1,350				95	0.98				0.90
Total	1,380	151	399	143	105	1.00	1.00	1.00	1.00	1.00

Sources: For Hong Kong, *Report on Labor Force Survey* (September 1980), table I.42.
For Korea, Department of Labor Affairs, *Report on Occupational Wage Survey, 1980.*
For Singapore, *Report on the Survey of Households 1977*, table 11; *Yearbook of Labor Statistics, 1979*, table 28.
For Taiwan, *Report on the Survey of Personal Income, 1979*, table 7.

[a]Median monthly earnings (HK$).
[b]Mean monthly earnings (thousands of won); data based on survey of establishments.
[c]Mean monthly earnings (S$).
[d]Mean weekly wages (S$); data based on survey of establishments.
[e]Primary income per year per working income recipient (NT$ thousands).

Table 8.8. Shares of Employment in Various Occupations (%)

Occupation	Hong Kong 1961	Hong Kong 1971	Hong Kong 1976	Hong Kong 1980	Korea 1963	Korea 1970	Korea 1980	Singapore 1957	Singapore 1970	Singapore 1979	Taiwan 1964	Taiwan 1970	Taiwan 1979
Professional & technical	4.7	5.0	5.4	6.1	2.5	4.7	5.4	4.8	8.6	8.6	4.2	4.1	5.2
Administrative & managerial	3.1	4.6	2.1	2.5	0.8	}		1.9	1.7	2.8	2.7	3.1	0.9
Clerical	6.0	} 16.2	9.5	13.1	3.5	5.9	9.4	11.9	12.9	15.8	5.2	6.6	11.8
Sales	13.7		11.3	10.8	10.1	12.3	14.7	18.2	16.2	15.3	10.3	13.1	12.1
Services	15.1	14.9	14.8	17.5	5.4	6.5	8.1	15.6	13.6	11.1	5.6	5.9	6.9
Production	48.6	51.7	52.4	50.0	15.0	20.3	29.6	39.6	39.3	38.6	23.0	30.7	41.9
Agriculture	7.7	3.6	2.6	1.4	63.0	50.3	32.9	7.8	4.1	1.8	49.1	36.5	21.2
Not classified	1.1	4.0	1.9					0.2	3.6	6.0			
Total	100.0	100.0	100.0	100.0	100.0	100.0	100.0	100.0	100.0	100.0	100.0	100.0	100.0

Sources: For Hong Kong, *Census 1961,* table 234; *Census 1971,* table 11; *Census 1976,* table 13; *Report on Labor Force Survey, September 1980,* table I.4.

For Korea, Bank of Korea, *Economic Statistics Yearbook, 1965 & 1979* and Economic Planning Board, *Korea Statistical Yearbook, 1981,* table III.2, pp. 72–73.

For Singapore, *Census 1970,* table 10.56, *Report on the Labor Force Survey, 1979,* table 47.

For Taiwan, Directorate-General of Budget, Accounting, and Statistics, *Statistical Yearbook of the Republic of China, 1975, 1980,* Manpower, Supplementary table 2.

in table 8.9 indicates large increases in the proportion of the work force that has secondary and higher levels of education and similar reductions in the proportion without education. It is difficult to decide how to interpret these changes, since educational upgrading is both a cause of economic growth and a consequence of it. Nonetheless, the fact that better-educated persons earn more than less-educated persons and are employed in higher occupational categories suggests that workers are now better off as a result of improved education.

One anomaly emerging from table 8.9 is that the proportions of workers with university education are higher in Taiwan and Korea, the two poorer economies, than in Hong Kong and Singapore. Why did Taiwan and Korea invest more in human capital, and did they grow faster as a result? To answer these questions would be a study in itself.

Real Wage Growth (Expressed in Terms of Real Monthly Earnings)

We have seen that higher proportions of the populations are employed and the mix of jobs is improved. Are average real wages higher? Table 8.10 speaks to this issue, and the answer is a definite yes. In Korea and Taiwan, real wages per worker doubled every 10 years. Real wages in Hong Kong grew by 150 percent in 20 years. These improvements are the envy of the rest of the world. In Singapore, however, wages grew less rapidly because of a deliberate government policy, until 1978, of restraining wages.[6] The wage restraint policy was intended to maintain international competitiveness. Average real monthly earnings per *worker* failed to grow between 1966 and 1975 in Singapore;[7] but due to a doubling of the female labor force participation rate, and the falling unemployment rate, real wages per *family* increased by about 40 percent over the same time period.[8] Beginning in 1978, however, wage growth was encouraged by means of a "wage correction policy," and indeed real wages grew between 1978 and 1980 at rates comparable to those of the other three economies. The Singapore government allowed the wage correction policy to lapse in 1981. Singapore's future wage policy is still under debate.

In sum, Singapore's uneven experience notwithstanding, the overall record is one of rising real wages. Those who were employed earned more

---

6. Essentially, the National Wages Council knowingly recommended that wages rise at below market rates. For further discussion of wage policy, see chapter 6 by Chia Siow Yue in this volume and the articles by Pang Eng Fong and Linda Lim and Pang Eng Fong cited in the notes to table 8.10.

7. It is possible that natives' real wages rose while their places at the bottom were being taken by guest workers, but no statistics are available to test this proposition.

8. The available wage figures for Singapore exclude employers' contributions to the Central Provident Fund. This is a substantial omission, inasmuch as the employer's rate of contribution has risen over time and now amounts to 22 percent of salary.

Table 8.9. Employment by Educational Attainment of Worker (%)

	Hong Kong			
	1961	1971	1976	1980
No schooling	20.2	16.2	13.9	10.4
Private tutor	6.4	5.5	45.4	38.1
Primary	46.3	46.1		
Junior middle or lower secondary	13.6	12.2	15.8	16.9
Senior middle or higher secondary	9.4	15.2	19.1	24.5
Postsecondary	1.4	1.9	2.2	5.0
University	2.9	3.0	3.6	4.4
Total	100.0	100.0	100.0	100.0

	Korea		
	1960	1970	1980
No schooling	44.7	23.8	16.0
Elementary school	39.5	43.6	35.5
Middle school	7.3	26.4	20.1
High school	6.2		21.8
University & college	2.4	6.1	6.7
Total	100.0	100.0	100.0

	Singapore			
	1966	1972	1977	1980[a]
None	54.1	20.6	13.8	22.5
Primary	29.2	36.9	35.2	50.0
Secondary	13.3	36.2	40.5	16.2
Upper secondary		4.4	7.7	7.7
Tertiary	3.4	2.0	2.7	3.6
Total	100.0	100.0	100.0	100.0

	Taiwan			
	1965	1970	1975	1980
Illiterate	26.0	20.7	15.9	9.0
Primary	54.3	52.7	47.9	39.6
Junior high & vocational	9.0	12.1	15.4	19.8
Senior high & vocational	7.5	10.5	14.7	20.8
University	3.1	3.9	6.1	10.9
Total	100.0	100.0	100.0	100.0

(Source notes on following page)

Comparative Industrialization and Employment 351

for their labor than workers a generation ago did. In Korea, Taiwan, and Hong Kong, the rates of real-wage increase were substantially similar to the rates of increase of the GNP—an impressive record.

Income Inequality

The high and rising levels of inequality that characterize most other rapidly growing economies have been avoided for the most part in Hong Kong, Singapore, and Taiwan. Some of the relevant data are presented in table 8.11.

The Gini coefficient of inequality in developing countries ranges from below .3 (low inequality) to above .6 (high inequality). By comparison, inequality is at low-to-moderate levels in the four Asian NICs. In fact, Taiwan has the most nearly equal income distribution of any developing country except Yugoslavia.[9] In Hong Kong, Korea, and Singapore, inequality levels are not high by international standards.

Over time, since data first became available, inequality has fallen overall in Hong Kong, Singapore, and Taiwan. These reductions in income inequality are impressive both when regarded in their own right and when matched against other countries' experiences. In the majority of other developing countries for which information is available, income inequality rose over time.[10] Inequality in Singapore and Taiwan, however, has about leveled off; it is apparently rising in Hong Kong. This may portend a new era of less equitable growth, but it is too early to tell. As for Korea, inequality appears to have increased if the data are to be believed; but I am inclined to dismiss the Korea figures as too unreliable to be useful.[11]

9. World Bank, *World Development Report 1980*, table 24.
10. See Gary S. Fields, "Poverty, Inequality, and Development: A Distributional Approach," *Journal of Policy Modeling* 3.3 (1981), table 2.
11. Whether the data are to be believed is debatable. According to Chen, *Hyper-Growth in Asian Economies*, p. 156: "There are many estimates of personal distribution of income in

---

Sources: For Hong Kong, *Census 1961*, table 236; *Census 1970*, table 10; *By-Census 1976*, table 17; *Report on Labor Force Survey, September 1980*, table I2.
For Korea, Economic Planning Board, *Population Census* (1960 and 1970); and *Survey on Economically Active Population*.
For Singapore, *Census of Population 1980, Release No. 4*, table 14, p. xxiv; and *Reports on the Household Surveys, 1966, 1972, 1977*.
For Taiwan, Directorate-General of Budget, Accounting, and Statistics, *Monthly Bulletin of Labor Statistics, Republic of China* (October 1981), table 1.5; and Walter Galenson, "The Labor Force, Wages, and Living Standards," in Galenson, ed., *Economic Growth and Structural Change in Taiwan* (Ithaca, N.Y.: Cornell University Press, 1979), table 6.9, p. 396.
[a]The 1980 census reports a much higher proportion of employees with less than secondary education than is reported from the earlier household surveys for 1966, 1972, and 1977, on which the figures for those years are based.

Absolute Poverty

If relative income inequality is changing by only small amounts, and if inequality levels are low to moderate, it follows that the poor must have participated more or less proportionately in the fruits of development. And indeed, table 8.12 shows that poverty was reduced in all four economies. While poverty fell in most other developing economies it did not fall in all.[12] Undoubtedly, the main reason for the reduction of poverty in the four Asian NICs is that more people were employed in better-paying jobs.[13] Still, we must be careful to remember that these benefits are insufficient; much poverty remains.

Industrialization and Employment

A country's economic growth experience is related to its labor market in two important ways: product demand affects conditions in the labor market, by way of the elementary relationship that the demand for labor is derived from the demand for product; and labor market conditions affect the product market, by way of the ability of firms to produce competitively in the world market.

In this section, I offer empirical evidence in support of three propositions:

> 1. In interindustry analysis in the four Asian NICs, employment growth is related *directly* to the growth of output and of exports.

Korea. But they are mostly based on small samples and contain considerable biases, and since they are based on different methodology their degree of comparability is rather low." And Adelman and Robinson, *Income Distribution Policy in Developing Countries*, p. 48, state: "There are no acceptable data for the size distribution of income in Korea . . ." before the mid-seventies. On the other hand, in private correspondence, Robinson has expressed his confidence in the data since 1970, and a Korean economist, Hakchung Choo, has written extensively on income distribution change, at least through 1976. Although the estimates of relative inequality in Korea are based on the best available evidence, after reading all the qualifiers I conclude that we lack a firm enough statistical basis for inferring how income inequality has changed there. See Hakchung Choo, "Economic Growth and Income Distribution," in Chong Kee Park, ed., *Human Resources and Social Development in Korea* (Korea Development Institute, 1980), pp. 284–88.

12. See Fields, "Poverty, Inequality, and Development, table 3.

13. This claim follows from two facts. The first is that most families get most if not all of their incomes from the work they do. Second, decomposition studies from a number of countries including Taiwan indicate that labor-income inequality is the primary factor accounting for overall income inequality. The Taiwan evidence is presented by John C. H. Fei, Gustav Ranis, and Shirley W. Y. Kuo, "Growth and the Family Distribution of Income by Factor Components," *Quarterly Journal of Economics* (February 1978), pp. 17–53. This and other evidence is reviewed in Gary S. Fields, *Poverty, Inequality, and Development* (New York and London: Cambridge University Press, 1980), especially pp. 111–14.

Table 8.10. Growth of Real Monthly Earnings

Hong Kong
Index of Average Real Monthly Manufacturing Wage, 1948 = 100

1960	105
1965	157
1970	167
1975	194
1980	253

Korea
Index of Real Monthly Earnings, 1975 = 100

1966	52
1972	88
1978	154
1980	159

Singapore
Index of Real Monthly Earnings per Worker, 1970 = 100

1960	90
1970	100
1980	120

Taiwan[a]
Index of Real Monthly Earnings in Manufacturing, 1954 = 100

1954	100
1960	102
1970	183
1979	400

Sources: For Hong Kong, Steven Chow and Gustav Papanek, "Laissez Faire, Growth, and Equity—Hong Kong," *The Economic Journal* (June 1981), p. 475; and *Commissioner for Labour Annual Department Report*, various issues.

For Korea, Wontack Hong, "Export Promotion . . . ," pp. 377–78; and Economic Planning Board, *Korea Statistical Yearbook* (1981), tables XIV.1, p. 407, and XIV.12, pp. 436–37.

For Singapore, V. V. Bhanoji Rao and M. K. Ramakrishnan, *Income Inequality in Singapore* (Singapore: Singapore University Press, 1980); and *1980 Singapore Yearbook of Labor Statistics*, tables 27 and 196; Pang Eng Fong, "Economic Development and the Labor Market in a Newly-Industrializing Country: The Experience of Singapore," *The Developing Economies* (March 1981); and Linda Lim and Pang Eng Fong, *Trade, Employment and Industrialization in Singapore* (International Labor Organization, 1982).

For Taiwan, Directorate-General of Budget, Accounting, and Statistics, *Statistical Yearbook of the Republic of China, 1980*, table 18, p. 448; *Taiwan Statistical Data Book, 1980*, table 9–1, p. 165.

[a] Data available for manufacturing only.

Table 8.11. Changes in Relative Income Inequality in the Four Asian Newly Industrialized Countries

Hong Kong

Gini Coefficient among Households			Ratio of Income Share of Richest 20% of Households to Poorest 20%[a]	
	I[b]	II[a]		
1966	.487	.50	1966	10.9
1971	.411	.45	1971	9.9
1976	.435	.44	1976	9.8
1981	.447			

Korea

Gini Coefficient among Households		Ratio of Income Share of Richest 20% of Households to Poorest 20%	
1965	.34	1965	7.3
1970	.33	1970	5.7
1976	.38	1976	7.6

Singapore

Gini Coefficient among Individuals	
1966	.499
1975	.452
1980	.455

Taiwan

Gini Coefficient among Households		Ratio of Income Share of Richest 20% of Households to Poorest 20%	
Early 1950s	.5	1964	5.3
1968–72	.3	1972	4.5
1976–78	.27	1979	4.3

Sources: For Hong Kong:
[a]Steven Chow and Gustav Papanek, "Laissez Faire, Growth, and Equity—Hong Kong," *The Economic Journal* (June 1981), table 4.
[b]Ronald Hsia and Laurence Chau, *Industrialization, Employment and Income* (London: Croom Helm, 1978), 1976 and 1981 Censuses.

For Korea, Hakchung Choo, "Economic Growth and Income Distribution," in Chong Kee Park, ed., *Human Resources and Social Development in Korea* (Korea Development Institute, 1980), table 3, p. 289.

For Singapore, Unpublished materials provided by Economic Research Centre, National University of Singapore.

For Taiwan, Directorate-General of Budget, Accounting, and Statistics, *Report on the Survey of Family Income Distribution in Taiwan Area*, cited in Paul Liu, "Determinants of Income Inequality Over Family Development Cycle," *Academia Economic Papers* (March 1981), p. 100; and Council for Economic Planning and Development, *Economic Development, Taiwan, Republic of China*, p. 46.

Note: The Gini coefficient measures income inequality. A higher Gini coefficient signifies greater inequality. The Gini coefficient has the value zero when income is distributed perfectly equally. It has the value 1 when one income recipient has all the income and the rest have none.

Table 8.12. Changes in Absolute Poverty in the Four Asian Newly Industrializing Countries (%)

Hong Kong
Proportion of Households with Annual Incomes Less than HK$3,000
(in constant 1966 HK$)

1966	18
1971	11
1976	7

Korea
Proportion of Households with Incomes below a Constant Real Poverty Line[a]

1965	41
1970	23
1976	15

Singapore
Proportion of Persons with Incomes below S$200 per Month
(in 1975 prices)

1966	37
1975	29
1980	18

Taiwan
Proportion of Households with Incomes below Specified Amount in Specified Year

NT$20,000 (constant)	
1964	35
1972	10
NT$30,000 (constant)	
1964	55
1972	20
NT$40,000 (constant)	
1964	80
1972	35

Sources: For Korea, Sang Mok Suh, "The Patterns of Poverty," in Chong Kee Park, ed., *Human Resources and Social Development in Korea* (Korea Development Institute, 1980), p. 350.

For Hong Kong, Singapore, Taiwan, computed from sources cited in table 8.11.

[a] Poverty lines are defined separately for rural and urban households. These figures, based on dietary requirements and Engel curves, amounted to 12,930 won per person per month for urban households and 10,853 won for rural households.

2. Also in interindustry analysis in the four Asian NICs, employment growth, output growth, and export growth are related *inversely* to wage growth, apparently for market reasons.
3. In comparative analysis, high rates of wage growth, apparently for institutional reasons, *cause* low or even negative rates of growth of employment, output, and exports.

Growth of Output, Exports, and Employment by Manufacturing Sector

There can be no doubt that the improvements in employment, wages, and income distribution in the four Asian NICs were due to economic growth. In particular, if we wish to relate employment expansion to growth of output and growth of exports, the natural starting point is to identify those industries that are major employers and/or those that have experienced major changes in employment. The three industries that stand out in this regard, based on the data in table 8.13, are:

Metal Products.[14] This sector is noteworthy because it is the largest employment sector in Singapore and Taiwan and the second largest in Hong Kong and Korea and because it is the fastest-growing sector of employment. Metal products increased in importance in all four economies, its share of manufacturing employment rising from 13 percent to 27 percent in Hong Kong, from 12 percent to 28 percent in Korea, from 20 percent to 55 percent in Singapore, and from 20 percent to 33 percent in Taiwan.

Textiles and Garments. This sector is noteworthy because of its large size. It is the single most important employment sector in Hong Kong and Korea, and the second most important in Singapore and Taiwan. In Singapore, textiles employment increased at an annual rate of 20 percent during the sixties and seventies, resulting in a quadrupling of textiles' employment share. The textiles sector held its own in the other three countries, keeping pace with employment growth in the rest of manufacturing.

Food, Beverages, and Tobacco. This sector is noteworthy because of its declining importance. Its shares of manufacturing employment fell from 14 percent to 3 percent in Hong Kong, from 16 percent to 9 percent in Korea, from 19 percent to 5 percent in Singapore, and from 13 percent to 7 percent in Taiwan.

14. The metal products industry includes such items as metallic products, machinery, parts, appliances, electronics, electrical machinery, shipbuilding, motor vehicles, and precision instruments.

In sum, relative employment shares are large and growing in metal products, large and steady in textiles and garments, and small and declining in food, beverages, and tobacco. And as I shall now show, these employment patterns accord with the growth of output and of exports in each sector in the four economies.

Take the case of the metal products industry first. Metal products was a growth industry in employment terms in every country. As shown in table 8.14, the structure of manufacturing production also shifted in favor of metal products in each case. When these increases in the metal product share of manufacturing production are combined with the rising importance of manufacturing production in total national product, the growth of production in that sector is all the greater.

To a large extent, the metal products sector expanded output for export purposes. Direct evidence on this is available for two of the countries. In Hong Kong, the share of metal product output that was exported nearly doubled, rising from 37 percent to 66 percent. In Singapore, the situation was nearly identical: machinery and transport (the closest category to metal products) exported 33 percent of its production in 1960, 69 percent in 1979.[15]

The same is true of the volume and composition of exports. In all four countries, the value of machinery and transport exports increased enormously from 1960 to the late seventies: from US$77 million to $9,314 million in Hong Kong, from US$0.9 million to $2,587 million in Korea, from US$15.5 million to $5,068 million in Singapore, and from US$2 million to $4,500 in Taiwan. As a result of these increases, the shares of machinery and transport exports in total exports grew rapidly: from 3 percent of the total to 17 percent in Hong Kong, from 2 percent to 20 percent in Korea, from 8 percent to 28 percent in Singapore, and from 1 percent to 28 percent in Taiwan.

It is apparent that foreign trade was a driving force underlying the expansion of employment in the metal products sector in each country. All took advantage of export opportunities and increased the value of metal products exports enormously. As firms increased output for the export market, they also expanded employment. The result was a trade-induced increase in metal products employment, offering hundreds of thousands of new modern-sector jobs that did not exist previously.

The situation was similar in textiles, though the precise figures are different. In brief, textile employment grew at rapid rates as did textile production and exports. In Taiwan, for example, in the sixties and seventies, textile employment grew at an annual rate of 8.3 percent, textile

15. These percentages are for domestic exports, excluding entrepôt.

Table 8.13. Changes in the Structure of Employment by Manufacturing Sector

Percentage Distribution of Employment

Sector	Hong Kong[a] 1961	Hong Kong[a] 1977	Korea 1961	Korea 1970	Korea 1979	Singapore[b] 1960	Singapore[b] 1970	Singapore[b] 1979	Taiwan[c] 1966	Taiwan[c] 1975	Taiwan[c] 1981
Food, beverages, & tobacco	14.2	2.6	15.7	13.6	8.8	19.1	10.0	5.2	12.7	10.1	6.7
Textile, garments, leather & footwear	45.2	47.8	35.4	31.1	30.4	4.0	15.8	15.6	21.5	25.2	21.9
Wood & furniture	6.3	2.2	6.0	5.2	3.6	8.8	8.8	6.3	6.0	5.4	6.7
Paper & printing	5.4	4.2	7.4	5.7	4.4	13.7	7.7	5.7	5.6	4.5	4.8
Chemicals, petroleum, rubber, & plastics	12.0	11.9	12.1	11.8	12.1	23.7	11.8	7.8	13.1	16.2	13.2
Nonmetallic minerals	1.9	0.5	6.0	5.9	4.8	7.3	3.8	1.6	14.9	8.3	4.3
Basic metals	1.7	0.5	2.5	3.7	4.3	1.5	1.2	0.8			3.0
Metal products	13.4	27.1	12.5	17.4	28.2	20.4	34.5	54.7	20.1	26.0	33.4
Miscellaneous		3.1	2.2	5.6	3.5	1.5	6.5	2.2	6.1	4.3	5.9
Total	100.0	100.0	100.0	100.0	100.0	100.0	100.0	100.0	100.0	100.0	100.0

Annual Rate of Growth of Employment by Manufacturing Sector

Sector	Hong Kong 1961–77	Korea 1961–79	Korea 1970–79	Korea 1961–70	Singapore 1960–79	Singapore 1970–79	Singapore 1960–70	Taiwan[c] 1966–75	Taiwan[c] 1975–81
Food, beverages, & tobacco	−7.5	8.4	5.3	11.7	4.4	1.4	7.1	3.7	4.7
Textile, garments, leather & footwear	3.3	11.0	10.2	11.9	20.1	8.8	31.3	8.3	9.5
Wood & furniture	−3.7	8.8	5.9	11.8	9.8	5.0	14.3	5.1	16.1
Paper & printing	1.4	8.8	7.3	10.4	6.7	5.4	7.9	3.8	13.4
Chemicals, petroleum, rubber & plastics	2.9	12.0	10.9	13.2	5.4	4.2	6.5	8.9	8.3
Nonmetallic minerals	−4.7	10.5	8.0	13.1	3.2	−1.0	7.2	−0.3	9.7
Basic metals	−4.0	15.2	12.3	18.2	8.1	4.3	11.6		
Metal products	8.3	17.2	16.6	17.7	17.7	14.7	20.5	9.5	16.9
Miscellaneous		19.9	5.0	25.6	14.1	−3.1	32.1	2.2	18.4
All products	2.9	12.0	10.5	13.5	11.7	9.0	14.3	6.4	12.1

Sources: For Hong Kong, *Census 1961*, table 231, *The Commissioner for Labor 1977 Departmental Report*, table 1B. For Korea, Bank of Korea, *Economic Statistics Yearbook, 1972*, table 111; *1963*, table 182 and Economic Planning Board, *Korea Statistical Yearbook 1981*, table V.2, pp. 162–63. For Singapore, *Report on the Census of Industrial Production, 1979*, table 13; *1960*, table 2.1. For Taiwan, Walter Galenson, "The Labor Force, Wages and Living Standards," in Galenson, ed. *Economic Growth and Structural Change in Taiwan* (Ithaca, N.Y.: Cornell University Press, 1979), table 6.4; and Directorate-General of Budget, Accounting, and Statistics, *Monthly Bulletin of Labor Statistics, Republic of China* (October 1981), table 1.6.

[a] Data for 1977 covers only registered establishments (about 90% of all employment in manufacturing); data for 1961 is from Population Census.

[b] Rubber processing is included in chemicals, petroleum, rubber, and plastics; this activity accounted for 16.7% of manufacturing employment in 1960, 3.7% in 1970, and 0.7% in 1979.

[c] 1975 and 1981 figures are derived from different sources and so may not be directly comparable.

359

Table 8.14. Changing Structure of Manufacturing Production

Hong Kong[a]

	Output (HK$ millions)	Sales (HK$ millions)			% Distribution			Exports/ Output (%)[b]	
	1960/61	1971	1978	1960/61	1971	1978	1960/61	1971
Food, beverages, & tobacco	486.1	1,058.0	2,837	10.9	5.9	4.5	37.0	25.1
Textiles & clothing	1,910.0	8,726.4	27,883	42.9	48.3	43.8	81.0	71.6
Wood & furniture	162.4	379.4	1,031	3.6	2.1	1.6	22.6	45.4
Paper & printing	202.3	676.2	2,585	4.5	3.7	4.1	19.9	12.0
Leather & rubber	70.9	239.7	534	1.6	1.3	0.8	83.1	75.1
Chemicals & plastics	203.3	2,016.9	5,726	4.6	11.2	9.0	26.0	76.6
Nonmetallic minerals	66.4	118.7	898	1.5	0.7	1.4	29.0	24.4
Basic metals	26.3	337.0	1,042	0.6	1.9	1.6	80.0	16.9
Metal products	877.9	3,356.5	18,882	19.7	18.6	29.6	36.7	65.9
Miscellaneous	721.1	1,140.1	2,312	16.2	6.3	3.6	67.0	82.1
Total	4,452.5	18,048.9	63,729	100.0	100.0	100.0	62.0	65.0

Korea

	Value Added (billion won)			% Distribution		
	1961	1970	1979	1961	1970	1979
Food, beverages, & tobacco	4.2	141	1,523	19.3	25.6	16.5
Textiles & leather	6.4	94	1,807	29.4	17.1	19.6
Wood & furniture	1.4	19	218	6.4	3.5	2.4
Paper & printing	1.7	28	399	7.8	5.1	4.3
Chemicals, oil, coal, rubber, & plastics	2.9	121	1,607	13.3	22.0	17.5
Nonmetallic minerals	2.0	33	530	9.2	6.0	5.8
Basic metals	0.5	22	731	2.3	4.0	7.9
Metal products, machinery, & equipment	2.3	76	2,225	10.6	13.8	24.2
Others	0.4	16	169	1.8	2.9	1.8
Total	21.8	550	9,208	100.0	100.0	100.0

Table continues on the following pages, notes to table are on page 363.

Table 8.14. Changing Structure of Manufacturing Production (Continued)

Singapore

	Value Added[c] (US$ millions)			% Distribution			Direct Exports as Proportion of Value of Production		
	1960	1970	1977	1960	1970	1979	1960	1970	1979
Food, beverages, & tobacco	44.1	136.0	369.9	31.0	12.4	5.5	28.1	28.3	44.9
Textiles, leather, & footwear	4.4	56.3	397.8	3.1	5.1	5.9	29.8	53.5	62.3
Wood products & furniture	11.4	71.1	278.2	8.0	6.5	4.2	46.4	41.5	55.2
Paper & printing	26.4	63.5	288.2	18.6	5.8	4.3	22.2	14.0	14.7
Chemicals, petroleum, & plastics	13.0	292.0	1,692.1	9.1	26.7	25.2	51.4	45.2	71.1
Nonmetallic mineral products	5.5	33.3	167.8	3.9	3.0	2.4	60.2	28.1	23.3
Basic metals	1.9	22.2	128.3	1.3	2.0	1.9	57.4	21.1	41.6
Machinery & electrical products	33.6	390.4	3,274.3	23.6	35.7	48.8	32.6	41.9	68.5
Miscellaneous	1.8	28.9	106.8	1.3	2.6	1.6	3.7	30.5	42.1
Total	142.1	1,093.7	6,703.4	100.0	100.0	100.0	35.0	39.1	64.1
Rubber-processing	42.9	35.0	87.7	23.2	3.1	1.3	73.6	72.1	59.9
Total	185.0	1,128.8	6,791.0	100.0	100.0	100.0	63.2	44.3	63.4

Taiwan

Manufacturing GDP
(NT$ millions)

	1951	1960	1970	1979	1951	1960	1970	1979
Food, beverages, & tobacco	505	3,016	8,685	30,252	33.4	31.8	16.5	8.5
Textile & apparel	288	1,530	9,489	55,332	19.0	16.1	18.1	15.5
Wood & furniture	64	495	2,494	16,103	4.2	5.2	4.7	4.5
Paper & printing	114	811	2,600	18,445	7.5	8.5	4.9	5.2
Leather & rubber	37	145	649	10,745	2.4	1.5	1.2	3.0
Chemicals	236	629	6,419	40,841	15.6	6.6	12.2	11.4
Petroleum & coal	56	512	4,760	16,038	3.7	5.4	9.1	4.5
Nonmetallic mineral	64	760	2,737	14,382	4.2	8.0	5.2	4.0
Basic metal	6	387	1,301	26,754	0.4	4.1	2.5	7.5
Metal products & machinery, electrical products	79	1,073	11,251	93,421	5.2	11.3	21.4	26.1
Miscellaneous	63	138	2,162	34,952	4.2	1.5	4.1	9.8
Total	1,512	9,496	52,547	357,265	100.0	100.0	100.0	100.0

Percentage Distribution

Sources: For Hong Kong, 1960/61: Laurence C. Chau, "Estimates of Hong Kong Domestic Product, 1959–1969," *Hong Kong Economic Papers* 7 (1972), p. 18; 1971: Census and Statistics Department, *1971 Census of Manufacturing Establishments.* 1978: *Hong Kong Monthly Digest of Statistics* (January 1981), p. 88.

For Korea, Bank of Korea: *Economic Statistics Yearbook* (1963), table 183, pp. 300–01, and *Economic Statistics Yearbook* (1972), table 111, pp. 216–16.

For Singapore, *Census of Industrial Production*, various issues; *Economic Development Board Report* (1972).

For Taiwan, Directorate-General of Budget, Accounting, and Statistics, *National Income of the Republic of China* (December 1980), ch. 4, table 2.

[a] Data based on Mining & Manufacturing Census, which excludes establishments with fewer than 5 workers.
[b] Data for 1978 are not available.
[c] Establishments with ten or more employees.

output grew from NT$1,530 million to $55,332 million, and textile exports grew from US$28 million to $5,226 million in value and from 17 percent to 33 percent in share.

On the other hand, in food, beverages, and tobacco, the growth rates of employment, output, and exports were all much lower. In three of the countries (Korea, Singapore, and Taiwan), employment in that sector grew but at below-average rates; in the fourth (Hong Kong), absolute employment actually fell. In all four, production in food, beverages, and tobacco increased absolutely but fell in relative terms. The situation is similar with respect to exports: the absolute value of food, beverage, and tobacco exports increased but relative shares declined in all four countries.

We may conclude from this evidence that economic growth of the rate and character realized in the four Asian NICs had large direct effects on employment. By tapping export markets, these NICs succeeded in raising output in key sectors of the economy at rapid rates. Because this export-led growth was of a labor-intensive character, employment also grew rapidly. Employment growth rates varied directly with the growth rates of output and exports in these three industries.

Wage Growth and Employment Growth: Market Forces

In contrast to the positive relationship between employment growth, output growth, and export growth, if we look at wage change in the same three industries (see table 8.15), we find a clear inverse relationship between the rates of employment growth and real wage growth:

Metal products: Employment growth in each country has been at above-average rates compared to manufacturing as a whole. Wage growth, however, has been at a rate less than or equal to the rate of wage increase overall.

Textiles, garments, leather, and footwear: The story here is similar to metal products but the numbers are slightly different. Employment growth in textiles has been at average or above-average rates: equal to employment growth in Korean manufacturing as a whole, twice as high as the average in Singapore, and one-third higher than the average in Taiwan. Wage growth in each country has been at a rate below the rate of wage increases in manufacturing as a whole.

Food, beverages, and tobacco: This sector presents the opposite picture from metal products and textiles. Employment growth has been at average or below-average rates. In each country, however, wage growth has been at average or above-average rates.

Table 8.15. Changes in Employment and Wages by Manufacturing Sector, Three Countries (excluding Hong Kong because of noncomparability)

Manufacturing	Korea[a] Employment Structure 1977	Korea[a] Employment Growth 1961–79	Korea[a] Wages Structure 1978	Korea[a] Wages Growth 1960–78	Singapore[b] Employment Structure 1979	Singapore[b] Employment Growth 1960–79	Singapore[b] Wages Structure 1978	Singapore[b] Wages Growth 1960–78	Taiwan[c] Employment Structure 1975	Taiwan[c] Employment Growth 1966–75	Taiwan[c] Wages Structure 1979	Taiwan[c] Wages Growth 1960–79
Food, beverages, & tobacco	8.8	8.4	1.15	10.2	5.2	4.4	1.11	3.7	10.1	3.7	1.05	8.0
Textiles, garments, leather, & footwear	34.3	11.0	0.75	7.5	15.6	20.1	0.64	1.3	25.2	8.3	0.82	7.5
Wood & furniture	3.7	8.8	1.02	8.2	6.3	9.8	0.88	1.1	5.4	5.1	0.90	8.5
Paper & printing	4.4	8.8	1.34	9.7	5.7	6.7	1.05	2.1	4.5	3.8	1.13	6.5
Chemicals, petroleum, rubber, & plastics	12.4	12.0	1.14	9.6	7.8	5.4	1.36[d]	5.1[d]	16.2	8.9	1.15	8.1
Nonmetallic minerals	4.0	10.5	1.27	10.5	1.6	3.2	1.26	4.1	8.3	−0.3	1.02	6.1
Basic metals	3.7	15.2	1.51	9.9	0.8	8.1	1.51	5.0			1.34	9.0
Metal products	24.4	17.2	1.09	9.1	54.7	17.7	1.05	1.8	26.0	9.5	1.05	7.0
Miscellaneous	4.2	14.9	0.76	8.3	2.2	14.1	0.77	3.0	4.3	2.2	0.83	7.0
Total	100.0	12.0	1.00	9.0	100.0	11.7	1.00	2.5	100.0	6.4	1.00	8.0

Note: Employment structure: percentage distribution.
Employment growth: annual rate of growth.
Wage structure: ratio of wages to average.
Wage growth: annual rate of growth of real earnings.

[a] Monthly earnings of regular employees; Bank of Korea: *Economic Statistics Yearbook* (1972), table 159; (1979) table 138. Employment: see table 8.5.
[b] Annual employee renumerations: *Report on the Census of Industrial Production* (1960), table 5.1; (1970) tables 1 and 12; (1978) tables 22 and 26. Employment: see table 8.5.
[c] Earnings Data: Computed from *Statistical Yearbook 1980*, table 181. Earnings within each sector are an unweighted average of subsectors. Employment: See table 8.5.
[d] Includes rubber-processing.

How is the inverse relationship between employment growth and wage growth to be explained? Take first the metal products and textile industries: I infer that relatively low wage growth in those industries permitted high employment growth in each country. Relatively low wage growth, however, still meant that wage increases ranged from 1.3 percent per annum in Singapore textiles to 9.1 percent in Korean metal products. And remember that these are real wage increases. That is, growing demand for labor pulled up real wages; workers already in those industries benefited, plus large numbers of additional workers were employed at higher wages.

On the other side of the coin, how can the high rates of wage increase in food, beverages, and tobacco be reconciled with the below-average growth of employment in that industrial group in each country (and, for that matter, with the below-average growth of output and exports of food, beverages, and tobacco products)? One is tempted to look for some sort of institutional force that pushed wages up prematurely, leading firms to reduce their rates of employment, export, and output expansion, if not actually to cut them all back. But the actual cause appears to be quite different: capital-labor substitution.

The success of the four Asian NICs with labor-intensive, export-led growth has led to full employment and even labor shortages. The tight labor market situation has generated stiff competition for labor. In metal products and textiles as in most industries, firms responded by raising wages in order to hold their existing labor forces and attract new workers. But some firms, especially in food, beverages, and tobacco industry, responded to rising wages by shifting to more capital-intensive production methods (e.g., automated bottling plants), the technology for which could readily be obtained in the United States, Japan, and elsewhere. This capital-intensive growth was accompanied by a shift in the skill mix of employment in food, beverages, and tobacco, as skilled labor was hired and unskilled workers trained to man the machines. This claim is based on case studies. No figures are available on educational qualifications of various industry work forces. In support of this claim of a higher skill mix in food, beverages, and tobacco than in textiles or metal products, however, figures on production and employment may be combined to give indices of "productivity" (see table 8.16). Workers in food, beverages, and tobacco exhibit higher productivity, in part because they are thought to be better skilled. Since firms have to pay skilled workers more than unskilled workers, wages are even higher. As physical and human capital replaced unskilled labor in production, total costs increased. This provides a consistent market explanation for the relatively rapid growth of wages and the relatively slow growth of employment, exports, and output in food, beverages, and tobacco.

Table 8.16. Index of Productivity in Selected Industries Around 1979

(Food, Beverages, and Tobacco in Each Country = 100)

Industry	Hong Kong[a]	Korea[b]	Singapore[b]	Taiwan[c]
Food, beverages, and tobacco	100	100	100	100
Textiles	53	34	35	60
Metal products	64	40	85	18

Source: Computed from tables 8.13 and 8.14.
[a]Sales per worker.
[b]Value added per worker.
[c]GNP per worker.

We may conclude that wage growth was inversely related to growth of employment, output, and exports because of market forces. Where substitution of capital for labor could take place, it did. Labor was redeployed to areas of greatest need. And because other sectors of the economy needed workers in order to grow, full employment of labor in the economy was maintained.

The Importance of the Wage-Setting Process

Wage and employment growth are high in the four Asian NICs, higher than elsewhere. How can these differences be explained? One possible explanation—that the differences in their labor market experience are due to their respective macroeconomic experience—is far too superficial. Although it is accurate in an accounting sense, it is not an explanation. It only pushes the question one step further back and leads us to ask: why were their growth experiences different?

Some analysts explain the four Asian NICs' successes in terms of cultural differences (i.e., the Confucian ethic). Clearly, cultural factors do have a role to play, but can they be *that* important? Political economists would point elsewhere: to the willingness of the major capitalist powers to permit and even aid the development of other capitalist economies. Others would focus on the character of foreign trade and foreign investment. The Asian NICs have relied on exports for a major part of their economic growth and their exports have two key attributes: they are produced using labor-intensive methods, and the export industries have strong linkages with the rest of the economy. Contrast this with countries which rely on land-based or mineral-based export industries. Often, these industries are highly intensive in capital and energy and have few intersectoral linkages. Another factor that bears mention is the relatively equal distribution of assets, both physical and human, that characterized these economies at the beginning of their take-offs into rapid economic growth.

While all these factors undoubtedly contribute to explaining why the four Asian NICs have been more successful than other countries, I would like to call attention to one other difference that has been largely overlooked: differences in the wage-setting process between these NICs and the rest of the world. The key sector to focus on is manufacturing, since growth of manufacturing exports is the driving force behind the four Asian NICs' economic growth. The manufacturing wage in those four countries is about 20 percent higher than the agricultural wage. By contrast, throughout Latin America, the Caribbean, and Africa, wages are more than twice as high in manufacturing as in agriculture.

The difference has to do with the wage-setting mechanisms at work. Four institutional forces, singly or in combination, have potent influences on manufacturing wages outside of East Asia.[16] Minimum wage laws are commonplace and when enforced cause wages to be higher than they otherwise would be. Labor unions often are very strong. At times, this is because of the close association between organized labor and the political party in power. At other times, it is because labor unions are encouraged as a means of achieving higher wages for workers. Government pay policy often sets the pattern of wages for the rest of the economy, and those in charge have a propensity to pay high wages to all government workers (including themselves). Lastly, multinationals often pay high wages, partly to maintain parity between expatriate and local employees, and partly (in some instances) to appear to be good corporate citizens and thereby to avoid expropriation or expulsion.

The striking feature about wage-setting in Hong Kong, Korea, Singapore, and Taiwan is the absence of such institutional forces. Economic development in the four Asian NICs has been based on low labor costs.

16. Among the relevant studies of wage structure and institutional aspects of wage setting in less developed countries are Elliot Berg, "Major Issues of Wage Policies in Africa," in A. M. Ross, ed., *Industrial Relations and Economic Development* (New York: Macmillan, 1966); Elliot Berg, "Wage Structure in Less Developed Countries," in A. D. Smith, ed., *Wage Policy Issues in Economic Development* (London: Macmillan, 1969); Lloyd G. Reynolds, "Wages and Employment in a Labor Surplus Economy," *American Economic Review* (March 1965); Lloyd G. Reynolds, "Relative Earnings and Manpower Allocation in Developing Economies," *The Pakistan Development Review* (Spring, 1969); Michael P. Todaro, "Income Expectations, Rural-Urban Migration and Employment in Africa," *International Labour Review* (November 1971); Michael P. Todaro, *International Migration in Developing Countries* (Geneva: International Labour Office, 1976); David Turnham, *The Employment Problem in Less Developed Countries* (Paris: Development Centre of the Organization for Economic Cooperation and Development, 1971); Gene M. Tidrick, "Wage Spillover and Unemployment in a Wage-Gap Economy: The Jamaican Case," *Economic Development and Cultural Change*, 1975; John B. Knight and Richard H. Sabot, *Why Wages Differ* (Washington: World Bank, 1980); and Gary S. Fields, *Analyzing Income Inequality in Colombia: A Micro Perspective*, mimeo, 1981.

These countries recognized that if they were first to penetrate and then to hold their positions in the world markets, they would have to do so on the basis of price, taking advantage of their abundant supplies of labor. Accordingly, they pursued a variety of policies which had the effect of restraining wage growth. The four institutional forces causing higher-than-market-clearing wages elsewhere—trade unions, minimum wage laws, government pay policy, and multinational corporations—do *not* interfere with market wage setting in the four Asian NICs. Although trade unions bargain over wages, only in Hong Kong do they do so free of government restraint. Minimum wage laws are on the books in some of the countries, but the minimum wage is below the market wage and is therefore irrelevant. Government pay policy in each country is to follow the private sector, not to lead it as it does in other developing regions, especially Africa. And multinationals, too, follow market forces.[17] The result is that wages increase in the four Asian NICs if, and only if, firms find it in their profit-maximizing interest to raise them, after taking full account of the need to hold costs down to internationally competitive levels.

I see these differences in wage-setting processes—supply and demand in the four Asian NICs, institutional wage determination elsewhere—as a major reason for the differential rates of economic success between the four Asian NICs on the one hand and the rest of the developing world on the other. For obvious reasons, higher wages raise input costs, and this is likely to result in reduced exports and hence lower output, unless either (1) higher wages cause higher productivity, and/or (2) the wage bill increases so much that domestic demand increases faster than foreign demand falls off.

Consider next the employment effects of the different wage-setting mechanisms. Simple supply-and-demand analysis suffices to show that a higher-than-market-clearing wage causes employment to be less than it might otherwise be if wages were set at market-clearing levels, because employers hire fewer workers when wages are greater. The wage elasticity of demand for labor would be especially high in an open economy because higher costs (unless accompanied by higher productivity) may result in large losses of export sales.

Next, consider inequality. Quite simply, if everyone in the labor force is employed at a market-clearing wage, inequality is less than if some are employed at higher-than-market-clearing wages and others are unemployed and earn nothing. So unless this is offset by losses of profits among those at the top of the income distribution, inequality will rise.

Finally, what about poverty? Clearly, some people are poorer than

---

17. In Taiwan, for example, multinationals pay the same wages as indigenous firms.

before: those who would have been employed when the wage is at the market-clearing level but are not employed when the wage is higher. But those who remain employed are less poor than before, and may even escape from poverty altogether. The income gap between the poorest of the poor and everyone else has increased. Most poverty indices would give heavy weight to the increasing number of zero-income people, and so would register an increase in poverty resulting from a higher-than-market-clearing wage, but this is not an unambiguous result.

I conclude that the functioning of labor markets, especially the wage-setting mechanism, is a *cause* of a country's macroeconomic growth rate and export experience as well as an *effect* of its macroeconomic conditions. The macroeconomic success of the four Asian NICs is caused in part by the reliance on market-wage determination in each of their economies.

Development economists and planners who hold out the export-oriented development strategy of the four Asian NICs as a model perceive that a policy package is needed for successful export-led growth. The measures usually mentioned are realistic exchange and interest rates, lowering of tariff barriers and other trade restrictions, and the pursuit of comparative advantage. Less frequently mentioned, but equally important to sound policy formulation, is reliance on supply and demand in labor markets to determine wages. Whether success is gauged in terms of output growth, export growth, or employment, an outward orientation in a regime of artificially high (or low) wages must be given very little chance of succeeding.

Lest any misunderstanding arise from my calling attention to the advantages of market-wage determination, I should make three important points. The first is that the goal of any economic system is to provide more real purchasing power to more people, and higher employment at higher rates of pay is the primary way income gains are realized. Too often, in the pursuit of macroeconomic objectives, this fundamental truth is overlooked. Second, market-wage determination need not lead to wage stagnation or to a shift in the functional distribution of income against labor. Quite to the contrary, market-wage determination has led to increases in wages and employment in the four Asian NICs, even in Singapore, where wage growth was repressed for most of the seventies. And this leads to the third observation: that it is one thing to discourage wages from rising above market-clearing levels and it is quite another to hold wages below market-clearing levels. The first has many attractive features; the second does not.

The record of the four Asian NICs in the last 20 years is clear. Production for world markets through labor-intensive methods financed in part by foreign investment resulted in full employment and wage increases at high rates for the bulk of the labor force. If these gains are to take place elsewhere, premature and excessive wage increases must be avoided. Other pertinent conditions are discussed in the conclusion.

Conclusions and Discussion

For the last two decades, Hong Kong, Korea, Singapore, and Taiwan have pursued policies of export-led growth financed by high rates of domestic savings and with active participation of foreign investors. The labor market and income distribution experiences during this growth phase have been overwhelmingly favorable. Six measures register clear improvement:

1. Increases in total employment, reductions in unemployment rates, and increased employment-to-population ratios.
2. Shift of employment out of agriculture and into manufacturing, a relatively higher-paying activity.
3. Upgrading of employment composition by activity status, occupation, and education.
4. Rising real earnings.
5. Constant or falling relative income inequality.
6. Diminishing absolute poverty.

Unemployment rates fell from 8 to 10 percent to less than 4 percent in all four countries. Real wages rose by as much as a factor of four. Inequality levels have fallen to low to moderate levels. In Taiwan, for example, it is estimated that the Gini coefficient fell from .5 to .3 over a 20-year period. The employment mix also has been upgraded. The share of employment in agriculture, the lowest-paying economic sector in each country, fell by more than half in Korea and Taiwan. In those two economies, the share of manufacturing to total employment increased several-fold. The composition of employment by activity status improved, so that the proportion of unpaid family workers was cut by at least 50 percent in all four countries, while the proportion of workers engaged as employees as much as doubled. The occupational mix improved, reflecting in part the higher levels of education attained by the labor forces; in Hong Kong, for example, the proportion of workers with post-secondary or university education more than doubled. That such large increases could have taken place within a single generation is an enviable achievement.

An important force contributing to improvement in labor market conditions and income distribution is the expansion of foreign trade and foreign investment. It has been estimated in Korea, for example, that the fraction of employment linked directly or indirectly to the export sector increased from 3 percent to 30 percent. The need for more workers in the export sectors was a major factor responsible for increases in aggregate employment in each of the four countries. In part, these workers were drawn into the export sectors from other sectors of the economy; in the process, their incomes rose. In addition, the expanded employment opportunities attracted new workers into the labor force—this might be called an "encouraged worker effect." Employment-to-population ratios rose as a consequence, raising family incomes and lowering dependency ratios. Also, when coupled with the end of the labor-surplus phase, the need to attract new workers to the export sectors bid up wages and permitted further improvements in standards of living.

The shift of employment into manufacturing reflects, of course, the shift of production into manufacturing as a result of foreign investment in manufacturing industries and the export of manufactured goods. What is impressive is the sheer volume of these increases. Take the case of Taiwan. In the sixties and seventies, while real national income per capita increased by a factor of four, the contribution of manufacturing to national income nearly tripled, and the value of manufacturing exports increased more than a hundredfold! What employment consequences resulted? Manufacturing employment tripled and its share of total employment doubled, reflecting the choice of labor-intensive production methods for export goods. Similar patterns, though on a lesser scale, are recorded in Hong Kong, Singapore, and Korea.

The labor intensity of exports is central to "modern-sector enlargement," that is, the process whereby the creation of more jobs with relatively good pay attracts workers from other, lower-paying sectors of the economy. Modern-sector enlargement results in enhanced economic status of workers, as reflected in the statistics presented above on upgrading of employment by industry, occupation, activity status, and education.

Labor-intensive development has been made possible by market-wage determination in the export sectors. Products of the four Asian NICs have remained competitive in world markets because wages have risen only when competitiveness would not be undermined. And indeed, real wages have risen: by 300 percent in Taiwan from 1954 to 1979; by 190 percent in Korea from 1966 to 1980; and by 150 percent in Hong Kong from 1960 to 1980. Singapore is different. There, real wages per *worker* stagnated between 1966 and 1975; but because full employment was achieved and many more jobs were created, real earnings per *household* increased by about 40 percent over the same period. Since 1975, real wages per worker have risen by about 20 percent. Thus, in each of these countries, in addition to "modern-sector enlargement" referred to earlier, we have ample evidence of "modern-sector enrichment," (increases in real incomes for those already employed in the modern sector).

When high rates of modern-sector enlargement and high rates of modern-sector enrichment both take place, as in the four Asian NICs, the result is that the benefits of growth are widespread. Income inequalities in these four countries are low to moderate by world standards. Inequality has fallen in Taiwan in Singapore and is largely unchanged in Hong Kong.[18] This, combined with rising real incomes, implies rapidly declining absolute poverty, as indeed was the case in all four economies.

Can export-led growth have similarly favorable effects on labor market conditions and income distribution in other Less Developed Countries (LDCs) in other parts of the world? The answer, I suggest, depends on five factors:

1. The ability of other LDCs to penetrate world markets under current conditions.
2. The asset distribution and infrastructure in those LDCs.
3. The role of private enterprise and the free market.
4. The labor intensity of their export goods.
5. Wage-setting behavior.

Protectionism: It is common these days to hear fears expressed about the future of world trade. Protectionist sentiments are growing as developed countries react to domestic economic difficulties. Many fear that LDCs may be unable to penetrate world markets to the same degree in the future as the four Asian NICs were able to in the past. This prospect is a worrisome one, and only time will tell whether these fears prove to be well founded.

Asset Distribution and Infrastructure: For a variety of reasons, each country of the four Asian NICs started on its recent development epoch with a well-developed infrastructure, with a relatively (by LDC standards) well-educated population, and without great inequalities in the distribution of land or other assets. These initial conditions made it more likely that economic growth would have widespread effects throughout the economy, improving labor market conditions and income distribution. Absent these initial conditions, might it not be expected that the primary gainers from free-market growth would be large landowners and industrialists?

The Private Sector and the Free Market: The governments of Hong Kong, Korea, Singapore, and Taiwan regard private enterprise and multinationals as partners in development. These countries are widely thought to have created an environment that allows the private sector to flourish. But private-sector development does not always enhance social welfare.

---

18. Excluding Korea because of an unreliable data base.

One of the most chilling demonstrations that free market systems may be unjust under some circumstances is Amartya Sen's recent book, *Poverty and Famines*.[19] Most of us believe that famines are the result of lack of food production owing to an excess or a deficit of rainfall, a pest infestation, or some other natural cause. But Sen shows that in a number of recent famines the case was otherwise. Production of food in the famine regions actually increased, yet people starved to death by the tens or even hundreds of thousands. This tragic circumstance came about because food was being exported out of the famine areas, where people had lost their purchasing power and food prices were relatively low, and sent into other regions of the country or even abroad, where food prices were higher. Sen's thesis is that it was a breakdown in the system of market entitlements to food, and not a breakdown in the production of foodstuffs, that was responsible for mass hunger and starvation. The private sector did what it was supposed to do, at least at one level—sell its products for the greatest return—but at another, more human level, in these instances, reliance on market forces failed the people miserably. We must recognize that whether the effects of private-sector development of the mass of the population are beneficial or not depends on other structural conditions of an economy. The desirable features of market systems must be preserved without the system's being allowed to run to excess.

Labor Intensity: One structural feature on which the desirability of a free market system depends, and one that is particularly characteristic of the Asian NICs, is the labor intensity of exports. These countries were successful in achieving full employment, rising real wages, and favorable income distribution outcomes, because their current export phases were preceded by the development of export industries intensive in unskilled labor, in which they had a comparative advantage. The more typical experience in Latin America, the Caribbean, and Africa is to try to export land-based or capital-intensive products, even under conditions of labor abundance. Labor market conditions and income distribution would be expected to improve little, if at all, from an expansion of such export activities. Export growth cannot be relied upon to raise employment, improve wages, and satisfy income distribution goals if the export sector employs relatively few people, if the export sector has few linkages with the rest of the economy, or if both situations obtain, as is often the case elsewhere. Only when labor is a productive resource—a resource that is employed with both technological and economic efficiency—can export expansion in a private economy be counted on to raise employment and wages for large numbers of

19. Oxford: Clarendon Press, 1981.

workers. But when conditions are suitable, as they were in the four Asian NICs, the ability of the mass of the labor force to benefit from further economic expansion through export-led growth is very large indeed.

Wage Setting Behavior: Full employment was achieved and wage rose substantially in real terms in the four Asian NICs. This happened, I argue, because wages were pulled up by supply and demand rather than being pushed up above market-clearing levels by a variety of institutional forces. In most other parts of the world, the situation is just the reverse; that is, what is common elsewhere is that wages are set at higher-than-market-clearing levels. Such wage-setting behavior hampers employment and output growth wherever it occurs. But if it takes place in export sectors, which must be competitive in world markets if the goods are to be sold, the adverse effect is even greater. The economies of South Asia, Africa, and Latin America and the Caribbean cannot be successful exporters unless wage growth is restrained and wages are allowed to reach market-clearing levels. Otherwise, whatever policies these countries might follow to promote economic development, the pursuit of export-led growth ought not to be among them. The interrelationships between industrialization and trade strategies on the one hand and the functioning of labor markets on the other is a largely unexplored area, but one that holds much promise for future analysis.

Index

Index

Agriculture and agricultural exports, 312–13
  Hong Kong, 225, 312–13
  Singapore, 265, 312–13
  Taiwan, 47–49, 53–55, 60, 81, 87–89, 312–13
Animal and vegetable oils, 146, 225
Argentina
  balance-of-payments, 162
  exhange rates, 161
  import-export controls, 163
  incentives offered, 151–52
Australia
  Hong Kong trade and investments, 228, 243–44
  Singapore trade, 277–80
Automation (robotics), 3

Balance-of-trade
  Hong Kong, 229, 238, 251
  Korea, 161–63, 176–77, 179–80, 186, 193, 195–200
  Singapore, 266, 280
  Taiwan, 306
Balassa, Bela, 19
Beverages, 356–66
  Hong Kong, 225
  Korea, 146
  Singapore, 275, 292
  Taiwan, 88, 102, 105, 106–16, 118, 123, 132
Brazil
  balance-of-payments, 162
  export growth, 152–53
  import-export controls, 161, 163

Building and construction materials, 242, 245, 248–49

Caltex, 208, 209
Canada
  Hong Kong trade, 228
  Singapore trade, 277–80
Capital and labor promotion of economic growth, 302–5
Cave, Richard, 183
Cement
  Hong Kong, 142, 147
  Taiwan, 88
Central Provident Fund, Singapore, 13, 262–63, 318
Chemicals, 358–63, 365
  Hong Kong, 27, 225, 229, 241–42, 245–49
  Korea, 25, 146–47, 169, 179, 184–86, 189, 197, 203
  Singapore, 275
  Taiwan, 88, 101–2, 105–16, 118–19, 122–23, 132
Chen, Edward K. Y., 323–34
Chenery, H. B., 229
Chile
  balance-of-payments, 162
  export growth, 152–53
  import-export controls, 161
China
  Hong Kong import trade, 228
  Shenzhen Special Economic Zone, 254
Clocks and watches. *See* Horological instruments

Clothing, 356, 357–65
  Hong Kong, 16, 19–20, 26–27, 226–27, 229–30, 234–36, 240, 246, 250
  Korea, 145–46, 169
  Singapore, 17, 28, 273–76, 280, 285, 287–89
  Taiwan, 14, 101–2, 105, 106–18, 121–23, 132
Coconuts, 272
Cohen, B., 213
Colombia
  balance-of-payments, 162
  import-export controls, 161
  incentives offered, 151–52
Commerce, employment in, 340–43
Communications, 270
Construction and services, employment in, 340, 342–43
  Korea, 144, 184, 185, 210–12
  Singapore, 265
  Taiwan, 103–5
Control date, 205
Currency control, 307
  Korea, 8–9, 31, 147–48, 150, 170–71, 309
  Taiwan, 46–61, 92

Dai Nong Petrochemical, 211
Data processing, computers, 183
Domestic capital formation and economic growth, 319–20
Dow Chemical-Korea, 211

Economic development and export performance, 17–21
Economic disturbances, effect of, 4
Economic growth and foreign investment, 176–215
  self-sustained growth, 320–25
Economic nationalism, Singapore, 11–12
Education and employment, 346–49
Electrical products
  Hong Kong, 226–27, 231, 234, 236, 240–42, 245–49
  Korea, 146, 183–86, 197, 203
  Singapore, 273–75
  Taiwan, 14, 60, 70, 82, 102, 105–19, 121, 123, 132
Electronics
  Hong Kong, 16, 26–27, 227, 235, 240, 242–43, 245–49, 252

  Korea, 145, 147, 169, 183–86, 197, 203
  Singapore, 28, 273–76, 280, 285, 288–89, 292
  Taiwan, 14, 60, 93, 101–2, 105–19, 121, 123, 132
Employment and industrialization, 333–75
  educational factors, 344–50
  Hong Kong, 335–39, 341–46
  Korea, 335–39, 341–46
  Singapore, 335–39, 341–46
  Taiwan, 335–39, 341–46
  and wage growth, 349–54, 364–67
Entrepreneurship and export expansion, 47, 51, 55, 58, 89
European investments, 181–82, 185, 187, 189, 193, 212
Exchange rates and trade balance
  Korea, 165–69
  Taiwan, 78–80
Export-processing zones
  Hong Kong, 10
  Kaohsiung Export Processing Zone, 51
  Singapore, 11, 16–17
  Taiwan, 7, 22–23, 51, 94, 96–98, 105, 119, 129
Exports
  Hong Kong, 219–24, 229, 236
  Korea, 200
  manufactured products, 4–5
  —, expansion of, 311–14
  Hong Kong, 312–13
  Korea, 312–14
  Singapore, 312–13
  Taiwan, 45–84, 311–14
  —, promotion of
  Korea, 9, 148, 150–54, 163
  Singapore, 12–13
  Taiwan, 48–55
    foreign trade and payments, 6–7
Export trade performance
  Hong Kong, 15–16
  Korea, 15, 166
  Singapore, 16–17
  Taiwan, 13–14

Fairchild Semiconductor, 205
Fertilizers, 183–85, 190, 193
Fields, Gary, 31–32
Financial services
  employment in, 340–42
  Hong Kong, 224, 236–39

Index

Korea, 184, 185
Taiwan, 53–57
Fiscal incentives, Singapore, 260, 269, 276, 281
Fish and fisheries
   Korea, 142–43, 184, 185
   Singapore, 265
Food processing, 356–66
   Hong Kong, 224, 229–30, 241–42, 245, 249
   Korea, 146, 184, 185
   Singapore, 271, 275, 288, 292
   Taiwan, 52–53, 60, 70, 82, 88–89, 97, 101–2, 105–10, 112–15, 118–19, 123, 132
Footwear, 358–59, 362
   Hong Kong, 16, 19–20, 226–27, 229–31, 233–35
   Korea, 145–46
   Singapore, 275
   Taiwan, 101–2, 105, 107–15, 118–19, 121–23, 132
Foreign capital and development, 21–29, 85–137
   Singapore, 260, 267–73, 281–86
   Taiwan, 21–24, 47–48, 53–55
Foreign trade and economic growth, 307–11
   Korea, 141–75
   Taiwan, 45–87
Foreign trade and payments, 6–7
   Hong Kong, 10–11
   Korea, 8–10
   Singapore, 11–13
   Taiwan, 6–7
Forest products, Korea, 143, 184, 185
France, Hong Kong investments, 243
Free Export Zones
   Korea, 178, 181, 187, 214–15
   Shenzhen Special Economic Zone, China, 254
Free trade, 6
   Hong Kong, 6, 10, 12, 219, 252–53
   Korea, 149
   Singapore, 6, 17, 259, 265, 267, 293–94
Furniture, 358–59, 360–63, 365
   Hong Kong, 19–20, 229–30
   Singapore, 275

Garments. *See* Clothing
Ginseng, 145

Government role in development, 35–36, 40
Gulf Oil, 208

Honam Petrochemical, 211
Hong, Wontack, 155, 233
Hong Kong
   Advisory Committee on Diversification, 236–39, 254
   agricultural exports, 312–13
   agriculture, employment in, 340–43, 345–46
   animal and vegetable oils, 225
   balance-of-trade, 229, 238, 251
   beverages, 225, 257–59
   buildings and construction materials, 242, 245, 248–49
   chemicals, 27, 225, 228, 241–42, 245–49, 358–59, 365
   clothing, 16, 19–20, 26–27, 226–27, 229–31, 234–36, 240, 246, 250, 356, 358–59, 360
   construction, employment in, 340–43
   development, trade and foreign investment, 219–56
   domestic capital formation, 319–20
   electrical products, 226–27, 231, 234, 236, 240–42, 245–49
   electronics and electrical machinery, 16, 26–27, 227, 235, 240, 242–43, 245–49, 252
   employment and industrialization, 335–76
   educational factors, 347–50
   exports, 165, 219–24, 228, 236
   distribution center, 10
   export performance, 15–16, 166
   financial services, 224, 238–39, 340–43
   food processing, 225, 229–30, 241–42, 245, 249, 356, 358–59, 360
   footwear, 16, 226–27, 229–31, 233–35, 356, 358–59
   foreign trade and payments, 10–11
   free trade, 6, 219, 252–53, 229–30, 358–59, 360
   furniture, 19–20, 229–30, 358–59, 360
   horological products, 227, 229, 236, 240, 242, 244–46, 248–49, 252
   illegal immigration, 254–55
   imports and exports, 228
   industrial exports, 312–13

Hong Kong (continued)
  industrialization, 10–11, 15–16, 26–27, 219–20, 224, 226, 235–36, 239–55, 310
  labor market, 11–13, 20, 33
  leather products, 356, 358–59, 360
  machinery and transport equipment, 225–26
  manufacturing, 219–32, 234–36, 239–55, 340–43
  meat products, 356
  metal products, 226, 231, 234–36, 240, 242, 245–49, 358–59, 360
  minerals, 225, 358–59, 360
  mining, 340–43
  Multi-Fibre Agreement, 226
  Overseas Chinese investment, 26
  paper and printing, 358–59, 360
  petroleum products, 358–59
  plastic products, 20, 227, 235–36, 240, 358–59, 360
  precision instruments, 19, 229–30
  printing and publishing, 27, 241–42, 245, 248–49
  protectionism, 221
  rubber products, 358–59, 360
  savings, promotion of, 317–19
  self-sustaining growth, 30, 321–25
  services, employment in, 340–43
  Singapore, trade, 278–80
  technological improvements and foreign investments, 326–29
  textiles, 220, 226–27, 231, 234–36, 240, 242–43, 245–49, 356, 358–59, 360
  tobacco products, 225, 356, 358–59, 360
  tourism, 224
  toys, 20, 227, 240, 242–43, 245–49
  trade promotion, 309–10
  transportation, employment in, 340–43
  travel goods, 226
  utilities, 241–44
  wage growth, 349, 350–54
  wood products, 358–59, 360
Horological instruments
  Hong Kong, 20, 227, 229, 236, 240, 242, 244–46, 248–49, 252
  Singapore, 273
Hyosung BASF, 211

Illegal aliens, 254–55

Import-export controls
  duty-free imports, 9
  Korea, 142–43, 147–52, 154–73
  liberalization of, 6
  Taiwan, 48, 89–90, 92–94, 98–101, 129, 131–32, 308
India
  balance-of-payments, 162
  export growth, 152–53
Industrial exports
  Hong Kong, 312–13
  Korea, 312–13
  Singapore, 273, 312–13
  Taiwan, 47–49, 53–55, 60, 81, 312–13
Industrialization
  expansion of exports, 312–13
  Hong Kong, 10–11, 15–16, 26–27, 219–20, 224, 226, 235–36, 239–55, 310
  investment and foreign trade, 301–32
  Korea, 142, 147, 179, 183–85, 195, 212–13
  Singapore, 11, 259–60, 267, 287, 310–11
  Taiwan, 14, 18, 45–46, 48, 54, 66–73, 81, 87–88, 90, 97, 101–32
Inflation, national experience
  Korea, 147–48, 150
  Singapore, 5
  Taiwan, 5, 45–49, 76–78, 90, 99
International Business Machines, 205
Investment allocation, Korea, 165–69
Investment Committee in Taipei, 22
Iron and steel, 142, 146–47
  Singapore, 273
Israel
  balance-of-payments, 162
  incentives offered, 151–52
  protectionism, 161

Japan
  Hong Kong import and export trade, 228
  investments in, 240, 243–45
  Korea, investments in, 177, 181–83, 186–89, 193, 205, 206–8, 210, 212
  Singapore trade, 277–80
  Taiwan, investments in, 88–89, 111, 115–16, 133–35
Job training, 204, 260, 281, 285

Index

Keohane, Robert, and Joseph Nye, 40
Kim, Chungsoo, 157
Kim, Kwang Suk, 155
Kojima, Kiyoshi, 23, 287
Kolon Petrochemical, 211
Komy Corporation, 205
Koo, Bohn Young, 24–26
Korea
  agriculture, 142–44, 155, 171, 184, 185
    employment in, 340–45, 346
    exports, 312–13
  animal and vegetable oils, 146
  balance-of-payments, 161–63, 176–77, 179–80, 186, 193–94, 197–200
  banking and finance, 184, 185, 340–43
  beverages, 146, 356, 358–59, 361, 365
  cement, 142, 147
  chemicals, 25, 146–47, 169, 179, 184–86, 189, 197, 203, 358–59, 361, 365
  clothing, 145–46, 169, 356, 358–59, 361, 365
  commerce, employment in, 340–43
  construction and services, 144, 184, 185, 210–12, 340–43
  currency control, 8–9, 31, 147–48, 150, 170–71, 309
  data processing, computers, 183
  duty-free imports, 9
  economics and growth, 4, 176–215
    characteristics of foreign investment, 179–89
  electrical machinery and appliances, 146, 183–86, 197, 203
  electronics, 145, 147, 169, 183–86, 197, 203
  employment and education, 347–49, 350
  European investments, 182–83, 185–86, 187, 189, 193, 212
  exchange rates, 165–69
  export promotion program, 9, 148, 150–54, 163, 312–14
  exports, 200
    trade performance, 15, 166
  fertilizer, 184–85, 190, 193
  15-Year Social and Economic Development Plan, 167
  Fifth Five-Year Economic and Social Plan, 172
  First Five-Year Economic Plan, 177
  fish and fisheries, 142–43, 184, 185
  food processing, 146, 184, 185, 357–59, 361, 365
  footwear, 145–46, 357–59
  Foreign Capital Inducement Promotion Act, 177
  foreign trade and economic development, 141–75
    trade payments, 8–10
  forest products, 143, 184, 185
  Fourth Five-Year Plan, 160
  Free Export Zones, 178, 181, 187, 214–15
  free trade, 149
  furniture, 358–59, 361, 365
  ginseng, 145
  government policies, 177–81, 183, 186–89, 193, 208–10
  gross domestic product, 143–45, 160, 167, 171
  import and export controls, 142–43, 147–52, 154–73
    liberalization of, 6
  industrial exports, 312–13
  industrialization, 142, 147, 149, 183–85, 195, 212–13
    and employment, 335–75
  inflation, 147–48, 150
  investment allocations, 165–69
  iron and steel, 142, 146–47
  Japanese investments, 24–25, 177, 181–83, 185–89, 193, 205–8, 210, 212
  labor market, 19, 25–26, 167
    and economic growth, 176, 179, 181, 183, 188
    employment effects of foreign investments, 196–97
    job training, 204
    productivity, 155–59
  land reform, 34–35
  leather products, 356, 358–59, 361, 365
  machinery and transport equipment, 146–47, 167, 169–70, 183–86, 190, 197, 203, 212–13
  manufacturing, 25, 144–45, 151–52, 155–60, 165, 167, 183–86
    employment in, 340–43
  meat products, 356

Korea (continued)
  metal products, 143, 145, 183, 186, 197, 358–59, 361, 365, 366
  minerals, 142–43, 146, 155, 358–59, 361, 365
  mining, 340–43
  monetary reforms, 147–48
  overseas construction work, 5
  paper and printing, 142, 358–59, 361, 365
  petrochemicals, 183, 210–12
  petroleum products, 25, 183–86, 190, 193, 197, 208–10, 358–59, 365
  pharmaceuticals, 184, 185, 210
  plastic products, 258–59, 361, 365
  plywood and veneer, 145, 186
  policy changes and world economy, 159–71
  price stabilization, 8
  protectionism, 9, 148, 150–51, 161
  Rhee, Syngman, 148
  rice, 142
  rubber products, 358–59, 361, 365
  saving, promotion of, 316–19
  self-sustained economic growth, 30, 320, 322, 324–25
  services, employment in, 340–43
  shipbuilding, 169, 186
  silk, 142, 145
  steel, 142, 146–47, 186
  tariffs, 147
  tax incentives, 148–50, 161, 167, 177, 309
  technological improvements and foreign investments, 326–29
  textiles, 145–46, 169, 184, 186, 197, 206, 208, 209, 356, 358–59, 360, 365
  tobacco products, 146, 356, 358–59, 361, 365
  tourism, 183, 184, 186
  trade promotion, 309
  transport equipment, 184, 185, 340–43
  tungsten ores, 145
  United States investments, 177, 182–83, 185–89, 193, 205, 212
  utilities, employment with, 340–43
Korea Development Institute, 160
Korea Economic Planning Bureau, 160
Korea Oil Co., 208–10
Korea Pacific, 211
Korea Petrochemical, 211
Korea Polyol, 211
Korea Synthetic Rubber, 211
Korea Trade Promotion Corporation, 309

Labor, 31–34, 36–37
  and capital promotion economic growth, 302–5
  costs of labor, 3, 167
  educational system for, 12–13
  Hong Kong, 11–13, 20, 33
  job training and education, 33
  Korea, 19, 25–26, 155–59, 176, 179, 181, 182, 196–97, 204
  manpower development
    Singapore, 260–61, 281, 283–84, 289–90, 291, 294
    Taiwan, 57–58
  Singapore, 33
  Taiwan, 7, 18–19, 22–23, 45, 48, 61–66, 69–76, 82–83, 86, 97, 108–19
  trade promotion, 310–11
  wage growth, 349–54, 364
  wage policy, Singapore, 28
  wage setting policy, 367–71
  wage stabilization, 12
Lall, Sanjaya, 195
Land reform, 34–35, 88
Leather products, 356, 358–63, 364, 365
  Singapore, 275, 288
  Taiwan, 102, 105, 107–10, 112–14, 118, 123, 132
Lee, Chung H., 188
Lee, Park Chung, 148, 169–70
Leontief, W. W., 231
Lewis, W. A., 301–2
Lucky Continental Carbon, 211
Lumber and bamboo products, 102, 105, 107–10, 112–14, 118, 123, 132

Machinery and transport equipment
  Hong Kong, 225–26
  Korea, 146–47, 167, 169–70, 183–86, 190, 197, 203, 212–13
  Singapore, 275, 288
  Taiwan, 102, 105, 107–10, 112–14, 117–18, 123, 132
Malaysia, Singapore trade, 277–80
Malaysian common market, 311
Manufacturing
  employment in, 340–45

Index

Hong Kong, 11, 219–32, 234–36, 239–55
Korea, 25, 183–86
Singapore, 28, 259, 265, 267, 271–74, 286–93
Taiwan, 7, 46–48, 52–53, 55, 58, 60, 67–70, 72–73, 88, 91–94, 97–98, 104
Mason, Edward S., 9
Mason, R. Hal, 188
Meat products, 356
Medicinal products, 273
Metal products, 357–66
Hong Kong, 226, 231, 234–36, 240, 242, 254–49
Korea, 143, 145, 183, 186, 197
Singapore, 275, 288
Taiwan, 88, 102, 105, 107–10, 112–14, 118, 121, 123, 132
Mexico
balance-of-payments, 162
exchange rates, 161
export growth, 152–53
Minerals, 358–59, 360–63, 365
Hong Kong, 225
Korea, 142–43, 146, 155
Singapore, 271, 275, 288
Taiwan, 102, 105, 107–11, 112–14, 118, 123, 132
Mining, 340–43
Monetary reform, 147–48
Taiwan, 48–61
Motorola, 205
Multi-Fibre Agreement, 6, 226

National Iranian Oil Co., 209, 210
Natural resources, 39, 46, 86, 89–90
Netherlands, Hong Kong investments, 243
New Zealand, Singapore trade, 277–80
Non-Chinese investments, Taiwan, 103–6, 110–11, 113, 120, 122–23, 129–32

Office machines, 273, 280
Oil bunkers, 273, 276, 287–88
Oil rigs, 270, 273–76, 280, 288–89
Optical and photographic equipment, 273–75, 280, 292
Overseas Chinese investments
Hong Kong, 22, 26
Taiwan, 22, 38, 86, 103–6, 109–10, 113, 120, 122–23, 238, 244
Ow Chin Hock, 267, 269
Ozawa, Terutomo, 287

Pacific Basin Connection, 37–38
Palm oil, 272
Paper, printing and paper products, 358–63, 365
Hong Kong, 27, 241–42, 245, 248–49
Korea, 142
Singapore, 275
Petroleum products, 358–59
Korea, 25, 183–86, 190, 193, 197, 208–10
Singapore, 17, 35, 271, 273–77, 280, 287–88, 292
Taiwan, 76–78, 88, 99
Pharmaceuticals, 184, 185, 210
Taiwan, 117
Philippines, Hong Kong investments, 243
Plastic products, 262–64, 266–67
Hong Kong, 20, 227, 235–36, 240
Korea, 258–59, 361, 365
Singapore, 275, 288
Taiwan, 101–2, 105, 107–18, 121, 123, 132
Plywood and veneer
Korea, 145, 186
Singapore, 273–74, 280
Policy change and world economy, 159–71
Population growth and economic development, 30–31, 34, 302–5, 307
Precision instruments
Hong Kong, 19, 229–30
Singapore, 28, 275, 288–89
Price stabilization, 7, 45, 47
Protectionism, 5–6, 308
Hong Kong, 221
Korea, 9, 148, 150–51, 161
Singapore, 266–67, 280, 285, 294
Taiwan, 51–53, 90, 92, 99
Pulp and paper products, 88, 102, 105, 107–14, 118, 123, 132. *See also* Paper, printing and paper products

Quarrying, 265

Ranis, Gustav, 7, 21–24
Recession of 70's and Asian economy, 4
Rhee, Syngman, 8, 148
Rice, export of, 47–49, 54, 81, 88–89, 142
Rostow, W. W., 301
Royal Dutch Shell Company, 28
Rubber products, 272, 275, 358–59, 360–61, 363, 365

Samsung Petrochemicals, 211
Savings, promotion of, 307, 314–19
Schive, Chi, 21–24
Services, employment in, 340, 342–43
Shenzhen Special Economic Zone, China, 254
Shipbuilding
　Korea, 169, 186
　Singapore, 269, 276, 289
Shoes. *See* Footwear
Signetics, 205
Silk, export of, 142, 145
Singapore
　agricultural exports, 312–13
　agriculture, employment in, 265, 340–43, 345–46
　ASEAN Preferential Trading Agreement, 267, 277, 280
　balance-of-payments, 162, 266, 280
　beverages, 275, 292, 356, 358–59, 362, 365
　Central Provident Fund, 13, 262–63, 318
　chemicals, 275, 358–59, 362, 365
　clothing, 17, 28, 273–76, 280, 285, 287–89, 356, 358–59, 365
　coconuts, 272
　commerce, employment in, 340–43
　communications, 270
　construction and services, 265
　　employment in, 340–43
　development, foreign trade and investment, 259–96
　Development Bank of Singapore, 269, 283
　domestic capital formation, 319–20
　Economic Development Board, 283–85, 289–90
　Economic Expansion Incentive Act, 268
　economic nationalism, 11–12
　electrical motors and resistors, 273–75
　electronics, 28, 273–76, 280, 285, 288–89, 292
　employment and education, 248–49
　Export Credit Insurance Corporation of Singapore, 269
　exporting distribution center, 11, 16–17
　export promotion, 12–13
　exports, 165
　　expansion of, 312–13
　　trade performance, 16–17, 166
　finance, 270
　　employment in, 340–42
　fiscal incentives, 260, 269, 276, 281
　fishing, 265
　food processing, 271, 275, 288, 292, 356, 358–59, 362, 365
　footwear, 275, 356, 358–59, 362, 365
　foreign investments, 260, 267–73, 280–86
　foreign trade and payments, 11–13
　free trade, 6, 17, 259, 265, 267, 293–94
　furniture, 275, 358–59, 362, 365
　Hong Kong import and export trade, 228
　horological products, 273
　import-export controls, 161, 163
　Industrial Expansion Ordinance, 268
　industrial exports, 312–13
　industrialization, 11, 259–60, 267, 287, 310–11
　　and employment, 335–75
　industrial machines, 273
　inflation affecting, 5
　International Trading Company, 269
　iron and steel, 273
　job training and education, 12–13, 204, 260, 281, 285
　Jurong Town Corporation, 283
　labor market and workers, 33
　leather and leather products, 275, 288, 356, 358–59, 362, 365
　machinery, 275, 288
　Malaysian common market, 260, 266
　manpower development, 260–61, 281, 283–84, 289–90, 294
　manufacturing, 28, 259, 265, 267, 271–74, 286–93, 340–43
　meat products, 356
　medicinal products, 273
　metal products, 275, 288, 358–59, 362, 365
　minerals, 271, 275, 288, 358–59, 362, 365
　mining, 340–43
　Monetary Authority of Singapore, 269
　National Productivity Board, 283, 285
　National Wages Council, 286, 295
　office machines, 273, 280
　oil bunkers, 273, 276, 287–88
　optical and photographic equipment, 273–75, 280, 292

Index

palm oil, 272
paper and paper products, 275, 358–59, 362, 365
petroleum products, 17, 35, 271, 273–77, 280, 287–88, 292, 358–59, 362, 365
Pioneer Industries Ordinance, 268
plastic products, 275, 288, 358–59, 362, 365
plywood and veneer, 273–74, 280
political stability, 263, 266, 281–83
population growth and development, 30–31, 34
precision instruments, 28, 275, 288–89
printing and publishing, 275
protectionism, 266–67, 280, 285, 294
quarrying, 265
rubber products, 272, 275, 358–59, 365
savings, promotion of, 317–18
self-sustained economic growth, 30, 321–25
services, employment in, 340–43
shipbuilding, 269, 276, 289
Skills Development Fund, 13, 285
tariffs, 12, 266–67, 281, 285, 287
tax incentives, 28, 151, 268–69, 285–88
technological improvements and foreign investments, 326–29
television and radio, 273, 280
textiles, 273–76, 285, 287–89, 356, 357–59, 362, 364–67
timber and wood products, 272, 275
tin, 272, 287
tobacco products, 275, 292, 356, 358–59, 362, 365
tourism, 270
trade dependence, 263–65, 295
Trade Development Board, 269
trade growth and structure changes, 269–76
trade policies, 265–69
trade promotion, 309–11
trade relations, 276–80
transportation and oil rigs, 268, 272, 274–75, 288–89, 292, 340–43
utilities, 265, 340–43
Vocational and Industrial Training Board, 285
wages
  growth, 349–54
  policy, 28

stabilization, 12
wood products, 272, 273–74, 275, 287–88, 358–59, 362, 365
Singer Sewing Machine Company, 24, 124, 126–29
Skills Development Fund, Singapore, 13
Sperry Rand, 205
Steel, 142, 146–47, 186
Sugar, export of, 47–49, 53–55, 56, 60, 81, 87–88
Switzerland, Hong Kong investments, 243–45

Taesung Methanol, 211
Taiwan
  agriculture and agricultural exports, 47–49, 53–55, 60, 81, 87–89, 312–13, 340–43, 345–48
  balance-of-payments, 162, 306
  cement, 88
  chemicals, 88, 101–2, 105, 106, 107–10, 112–14, 116, 118–19, 122–23, 132, 358–59, 363, 365
  clothing, 14, 101–2, 105, 106–18, 121–23, 132, 356–59, 363, 365
  colonial period and capital inflows, 87–89
  commerce, employment in, 340–43
  commodity content of exports and imports, 60–62
  construction and services, 103–5, 340–43
  currency control, 48–61, 92, 308
  electrical appliances, 102, 105–19, 121, 123, 132
  electrical machinery, 14, 60, 70, 82, 121
  electronics, 14, 60, 93, 101–2, 105–19, 121, 123, 132
  employment and education, 346–50
  entrepreneurship and export expansion, 47, 51, 55, 58, 89
  exchange rates and trade balance, 78–80
  export performance, 166
  export-processing zone, 22–23, 94, 96–98, 105, 119, 129
  exports, 165
    expansion and foreign trade, 45–84, 311–14
    promotion of, 48–55
  financing, 53–57, 340–43
  food processing, 52–53, 60, 70, 82, 88–89, 97, 101–2, 105–10, 112–15,

Taiwan (continued)
  118–19, 123, 132, 356, 358–59, 363, 365
  footwear, 101–2, 105, 107–15, 118–19, 121–23, 132, 356, 358–59, 365
  foreign capital and development, 21–24, 47–48, 53–55, 85–137
  foreign trade and export expansion, 45–84
    and trade payments, 6–7
  furniture, 358–59, 363, 365
  garments. *See* Taiwan, clothing
  Hong Kong import trade, 228
  investments, 243
  import and export controls, 48, 89–90, 92–94, 98–101, 129, 131–32, 161, 163, 308
    liberalization of, 6
  industrial exports, 312–13
  industrialization, 45–46, 48, 54, 66–73, 81, 87–88, 90, 97, 101–32
    employment resulting, 335–59, 363–75
    trade performance, 14
  industrial products, 47–49, 53–55, 60, 81
  inflation affecting, 5, 90, 99
    and export expansion, 45–49
    terms of trade, 76–78
  Investment Committee in Taipei, 22
  Japanese investments, 88–89, 111, 115–16, 133–35
  Kaohsiung Export Processing Zone, 51
  labor, 7, 18–19, 22–23
    and economic growth, 62–66, 70–76
    export processing zones, 86, 97, 108–19
    foreign trade and export expansion, 45, 48, 61–62, 69–76, 83
    manpower utilization, 57–58
  land reform, 34–35, 88
  leather and fur products, 102, 105, 107–10, 112–14, 118, 123, 132, 358–59, 363, 365
  lumber and bamboo products, 102, 105, 107–10, 112–14, 117–18, 123, 132
  machinery equipment, 102, 105, 107–10, 112–14, 117–18, 123, 132
  manufacturing, 88, 91–94, 97–98, 104
    employment in, 340–44

export expansion, 46–48, 52–53, 55, 58, 60, 67–70, 72–73
growth, 7
meat products, 356
metals and metal products, 88, 102, 105, 107–10, 112–14, 118, 121, 123, 132, 358–59, 363, 365
minerals, 102, 105, 107–10, 112–14, 118, 123, 132, 358–59, 363, 365
mining, 340–43
monetary reform, 48–61
natural resources, 46, 86, 90
"Nineteen-point Supporting Measures," 50, 81, 92
non-Chinese investments, 103–6, 110–11, 113, 120, 122–23, 129–32
Overseas Chinese investment, 22, 86, 103–6, 109–10, 111, 113, 120, 122–23
paper and printing, 358–59, 363, 365
petroleum products, 76–78, 88, 99
pharmaceuticals, 117
plastic products, 101–2, 105, 107–18, 121, 123, 132, 358–59, 363, 365
post-independence policies, 89–92
price stabilization, 45, 47
protectionism, 51–53, 90, 92, 99, 358–59
pulp and paper, 88, 102, 105, 107–14, 118, 123, 132
rice exports, 47–49, 54, 81, 88–89
rubber products, 101–2, 105, 107–14, 121, 123, 132, 358–59, 363, 365
savings, promotion of, 315–18
self-sustained economic growth, 30–31, 320–21, 325
services, employment in, 340–43
Singer Sewing Machine Co., 24, 124, 126–29
Sino-American Joint Commission for Rural Reconstruction, 314
Statute for Encouragement of Investment, 50–51, 81
sugar exports, 47–49, 53–55, 60, 81, 87–88
tariff rebate system, 51–53
tax incentives, 50–53, 55–57, 81, 92, 151, 307–8, 316
tea exports, 87
technical progress, 58, 99–132

Index

technological improvements and foreign investments, 325–29
textiles, 49–53, 60, 69–70, 82, 88, 93, 97, 101–2, 105, 107–16, 118, 121, 123, 132, 356, 358–61, 363, 364–65, 366–67
tobacco products, 356, 358–59, 363, 365
trade balance and exchange rates, 78–80
trade performance and exports, 13–14
trading partners, 59–60
transition growth, 87–101
transportation, employment in, 340–43
unemployment, 45
United States investments, 103, 111–12, 114, 115–16
utilities, employment in, 340–43
wage growth, 349–54
wood products, 358–59, 363, 365
Taiwan Production Board, 50
Taiwan Sugar Corporation, 49
Tan, Augustine, 267, 269
Tariffs
 Korea, 147–48, 150–52, 161
 Singapore, 12, 266–67, 281, 285, 287
 Taiwan, 51–53, 87
Tax incentives
 Korea, 148–51, 161, 167, 177, 309
 Singapore, 28, 151, 268–69, 285–88
 Taiwan, 50–53, 55, 81, 92, 151, 307–8, 316
Technological improvements, 119, 121, 301, 307, 325–29
 Taiwan, 58, 99–132
Television and radio, 273, 280
Textiles, 356, 357–67. *See also* Clothing
 Hong Kong, 220, 226–27, 231, 234–36, 240, 242–43, 245–49, 356, 358–60, 367
 Korea, 145–46, 169, 184, 186, 197, 206, 208, 209
 Singapore, 273–76, 285, 287–89
 Taiwan, 49–53, 60, 69–70, 82, 88, 93, 97, 101–2, 105, 107–16, 118, 121, 123, 132
Thailand
 Hong Kong investments, 243, 245
 Singapore trade, 278, 279, 280
Tin, 272, 287
Tobacco products, 356–67
 Hong Kong, 225
 Korea, 146
 Singapore, 275, 292
Tong Suh Petrochemical, 211
Tourism
 Hong Kong, 224
 Korea, 183, 184, 186
 Singapore, 270
Toys, 20, 227, 240–41, 242–43, 244–46, 247–49
Trade
 liberalization of policies, 30–31
 Singapore, 263–80, 309–11
Trade balance and exchange rates, 78–80
Trade promotion, 308–9
Trading partners, 59–60
Transportation equipment
 employment with, 340, 342–43
 Korea, 184, 185
 Singapore, 270, 273–76, 280, 288–89, 292
Travel goods, 226
Tungsten ores, 145
Tyszynski, H., 233

Union Oil, 208–9
United Kingdom
 Hong Kong import and export trade and investments, 228, 237, 243–45
 Singapore trade, 277–80
United States
 Hong Kong import and export trade and investments, 228, 240, 243–46
 Korean investments, 177, 182–83, 185–89, 193, 205, 212
 Singapore trade, 277–80
 Taiwan, investments in, 103, 111–12, 114, 115–16
Univac, 205
Uruguay
 balance-of-payments, 161–63
 import-export controls, 161–63
Utilities
 employment in, 340–43
 Singapore, 265

Vernon, Ray, 183, 287

Watches and clocks. *See* Horological instruments
Wells, Louis T., Jr., 287

West Germany, Hong Kong trade and investments, 228–29, 243–44
Westphal, L. E., 155
Wigs, 145, 186
Wood products, 358–63, 365
  Korea, 145–46, 287
  Singapore, 272, 273–74, 275, 287–88

Yin, K. Y., 50

Yue, Chia Siow, 11, 21, 29
Yue, Lee Kwan, 11
Yugoslavia
  balance-of-payments, 162
  export growth, 152–53
  import-export controls, 163–64
  protectionism, 161

COMPOSED BY MODERN TYPOGRAPHERS, DUNEDIN, FLORIDA
MANUFACTURED BY EDWARDS BROTHERS, INC.
ANN ARBOR, MICHIGAN
TEXT AND DISPLAY LINES ARE SET IN CALEDONIA

Library of Congress Cataloging in Publication Data
Main entry under title:
Foreign trade and investment.
Includes bibliographies and index.
1. Asia—Economic conditions—1945—   —Addresses,
essays, lectures. 2. Investments, Foreign—Asia—
Addresses, essays, lectures. 3. Asia—Commerce—
Addresses, essays, lectures. 4. Economic development—
Addresses, essays, lectures. I. Galenson, Walter,
1914–
HC412.F64   1985   338.95   84-40495
ISBN 0-299-10100-2